TOURISM POLICY AND INTERNATIONAL TOURISM

IN OECD MEMBER COUNTRIES

ORGANISATION FOR ECONOMIC CO-OPERATION AND DEVELOPMENT

ORGANISATION FOR ECONOMIC CO-OPERATION AND DEVELOPMENT

Pursuant to Article 1 of the Convention signed in Paris on 14th December 1960, and which came into force on 30th September 1961, the Organisation for Economic Co-operation and Development (OECD) shall promote policies designed·

— to achieve the highest sustainable economic growth and employment and a rising standard of living in Member countries, while maintaining financial stability, and thus to contribute to the development of the world economy;
— to contribute to sound economic expansion in Member as well as non-member countries in the process of economic development; and
— to contribute to the expansion of world trade on a multilateral, non-discriminatory basis in accordance with international obligations.

The original Member countries of the OECD are Austria, Belgium, Canada, Denmark, France, Germany, Greece, Iceland, Ireland, Italy, Luxembourg, the Netherlands, Norway, Portugal, Spain, Sweden, Switzerland, Turkey, the United Kingdom and the United States. The following countries became Members subsequently through accession at the dates indicated hereafter: Japan (28th April 1964), Finland (28th January 1969), Australia (7th June 1971) and New Zealand (29th May 1973). The Commission of the European Communities takes part in the work of the OECD (Article 13 of the OECD Convention). Yugoslavia has a special status at OECD (agreement of 28th October 1961).

Publié en français sous le titre :

POLITIQUE DU TOURISME
ET TOURISME INTERNATIONAL
DANS LES PAYS MEMBRES DE L'OCDE

Foreword

The Tourism Committee has, for more than thirty years, published information on government policies in the field of tourism. This has been accompanied by statistics on recent trends observed in the development of international tourism in the OECD area.

Chapter I of this year's report examines each Member country'policy and action in the field of tourism for the years 1989 and 1990. It presents the importance of tourism as an economic activity in the given country and the prospects for its development, it lays out the government policy in terms of objectives, priorities, plans and programmes, and it describes the specific actions and measures undertaken in implementing those policies, with particular reference to the development of supply, marketing, protection of the tourist as a consumer, staggering of holidays and international co-operation.

Every two or three years, this Chapter alternates, in the Report, with the presentation of issues of common interest and Member countries'concern; this was the case in the 1990 edition of the discussion on the future of tourism in the context of the development of transport policies.

Chapters II and III and the Statistical Annex study the evolution of international tourism supply and demand in the OECD Member countries, bringing out the trends observed in 1989 and 1990.

This work has been carried out using information provided by national delegations and by the delegates to both the Tourism Committee and its Statistical Working Party.

This Report was adopted by the Tourism Committee which recommended its derestriction by the Council. The OECD Council agreed on 9th June 1992 to make it publicly available.

TABLE OF CONTENTS

INTRODUCTION

INTERNATIONAL TOURISM IN 1990: A BETTER YEAR THAN EXPECTED

Despite the Middle East crisis and the economic downturn in a number of the world's major travel markets, international tourism in the OECD are registered another year of growth in 1990. Growth slowed as a result of the political and economic uncertainties during the second half of the year, but the full impact of the negative developments was not felt until after the Gulf war started in early-1991. For the OECD area overall, the following results were recorded in 1990:

-- Arrivals at frontiers: +4 per cent (compared with +11 per cent in 1989);

-- Nights spent in various forms of accommodation: +4 per cent (+1 per cent); and

-- International tourist receipts in real terms: +5 per cent (+6 per cent).

Nevertheless, these favourable trends did mask some fairly wide variations from region to region and more especially, from country to country.

Tourism flows region by region

In Europe, the arrivals' growth rate was 3 per cent, compared with close to 9 per cent in 1989. The increase in international tourist receipts in real terms was slightly below the OECD average, at +3 per cent, - the same rate of growth as in 1989. The number of nights also showed a much healthier growth overall (+4 per cent) than
in the previous year (+1 per cent).

North America performed better than the OECD average, thanks partly to a comparative weakness of the US dollar, although its 5 per cent increase in arrivals at frontiers was well below the 21 per cent growth recorded in 1989. International tourist receipts rose by 7 per cent in real terms - and by 13 per centin US$ - a four point decline over the 1989 level.

International tourism was most buoyant in the Australasia-Japan region in 1990. In the three Member countries of the Pacific region, arrivals at frontiers increased by close to 11 per cent, compared with +6 per cent in 1989. The number of bednights recorded was up by more than 13 per cent (+1 per cent) and international tourist receipts rose by 11 per cent in real terms after a decline of 2 per cent the previous year.

Frontier arrivals' data are only available for 15 OECD Member countries and not all Members compile bednight statistics, so results are not strictly comparable and need to be interpreted with caution. But they do provide an overview of general trends and confirm certain changes in market behaviour and travel patterns that have been developing over the past few years.

Europe still accounts for a major share of OECD tourism in terms of international tourist receipts, although its share has been declining steadily since the 1970s and fell by a further three points to 62 per cent in 1990. As can be seen from the detailed results, this decline has not been due to an absolute decline in European arrivals or bednights, but rather to a relative slowdown in the growth of intra-regional travel and to a greater percentage rise in travel by Europeans to other regions.

European travellers themselves are becoming more and more travel experienced and, therefore, more sophisticated in their travel demands, looking increasingly to new exotic destinations outside their region. But competition from other regions has also increased and new emerging markets, notably in the Pacific Asia region, are registering very strong intra-regional growth.

As far as arrivals at frontiers were concerned, Europe's two leading destinations, France and Spain, both performed less well than in 1989. France maintained its position as favourite European destination for international travellers - and second favourite in the world behind the United States - but its arrivals' growth slowed to 7 per cent after a 29 per cent rise in arrivals in 1989. This record performance in 1989 was, of course, largely attributable to the attractions of the Bicentenary of the French Revolution. France's increase in bednights in hotels and similar establishments was also well down on the 1989 level, although the operating results of other forms of commercial accommodation improved during the twelve-month period.

Spain recorded a drop in its number of arrivals for the second consecutive year. While the American market was down by some 12 per cent, the decline was largely due to a weaker performance from other European markets, which account for over 90 per cent of all arrivals. The United Kingdom, which suffered the most, fell more than 14 per cent. The downturn, which was heavily concentrated in the inclusive tour sun and beach holiday sector of the market, reflects signs of a general trend away from sun and beach destinations in the Mediterranean by the traditional package holiday markets of Northern Europe.

This trend, which has been intensifying since the late-1980s, seems to have been caused by a number of factors. These include a rise in relative prices coupled with the economic downturn in some major source countries, and the increasing pollution in some traditionally popular Mediterranean beach resorts. As a result of this, the public authorities concerned have gone into action to improve the situation. The policy of the Spanish Minister of Public Works and Transport has been, since 1983, to get the beaches cleaned up, involving an investment of Ptas 34 billion on the part of the ten autonomous coastal authorities concerned over the period 1983-91. In line with the increasing travel experience and sophistication of the Northern European travel market, leisure travellers have become much more conscious of their environment and are increasingly in search of unspoilt and unpolluted destinations. They appear to be less and less willing to trade quality for cheap prices, even at the lower end of the package holiday market.

After a 1 per cent fall in 1989, tourist arrivals to Italy recorded a positive growth of 3 per cent, but bednights continued to fall. This was partly attributed to an increased demand for shorter stays, but also to a growth in the number of excursionists - or visitors staying less than 24 hours in the country.

Four other European destinations also registered negative trends in bednights: Sweden, Finland, Austria and Belgium. In the case of Sweden, changes in local taxation affecting the competitiveness of its hotel and restaurants seem to have been the major contributing reason.

In terms of percentage growth in arrivals at frontiers, the best performing destinations in Europe in 1990 were Turkey, up 21 per cent over 1989, Portugal (+13 per cent) and Ireland (+12 per cent). In all cases, the respective growth in bednights registered from abroad was lower, again reflecting the trend towards shorter stays.

A boom in travel from Central and Eastern Europe as a result of the easing of restrictions on outbound travel from that region was the major contributor to Turkey's record performance. There was also a sharp rise in short break travel to the Netherlands from neighbouring Western European markets, generating more than a 13 per cent rise in overnights, thanks partly to the impact of its Van Gogh exhibition.

An increasing fragmentation of holiday travel, with Europeans travelling more frequently throughout the year but for shorter trips, is particularly marked in the Northern European source countries, in many of which the overall level of trip-taking appears to be approaching its ceiling. The increase in travel volume is not so much due to a rise in the proportion of the population taking at least one trip abroad every year, but rather to an increase in secondary trips in preference to one long annual holiday.

Short breaks of one to three nights in length now account for an estimated 20 per cent of the total volume of trips taken by Europeans abroad and the share is rising faster than for other sectors of the leisure market.

Nevertheless, the level of foreign trip-taking can be expected to rise from Southern European countries for some years to come. Italy is now one of the largest growth markets in Europe. This is partly the result of increased purchasing power and the easing of exchange controls during the 1980s, but it is also due to a change in thinking about holidays among the predominantly Latin Mediterranean bordering markets of Europe. Although a major share of Italians, Spaniards and French still spend their main annual holidays in their own countries, foreign travel is fast gaining in popularity.

Inbound travel to Europe from inter-continental markets also continued to register healthy growth in 1990, despite a slowdown in the growth rate in the last three months of the year. This seems to have been due both to the increasing perception of terrorism threats in the period before the outbreak of the Gulf war, but also to the worsening economic situation in its major long-haul market, the United States, coupled with a rise in the cost of air travel as a result of soaring fuel prices.

Cumulative arrivals from the United States to individual European destinations increased by 4 per cent and actual departures from the United States to Europe rose by an even higher 9 per cent, according to the European Travel Commission (ETC). This can be explained by the growing trend for Americans to visit just one or two countries per trip rather than cover several destinations in one and the same trip. However, the 5 per cent growth in bednights from the US market was lower than in 1989. Europe also attracted a 7 per cent increase from Canada and +21 per cent from Japan, its second and third biggest long-haul markets respectively. Japanese visitors topped the one million mark for the first time ever, generating a 15 per cent rise in bednights.

International tourism to North America was favourably influenced by a sharp rise in European travel to the United States, stimulated by the low US dollar, competitive air fares and a continued high quality/price ratio of the North American tourism product. Traditional markets all performed well, but there was also very strong percentage growth from new markets like Spain and Belgium, albeit from a small base.

The continued rise in long-haul travel from Europe - that is, to destinations outside Europe and the Mediterranean region - also contributed to the Australasia-Japan region's double digit growth in tourist arrivals and bednights. But the shares of both Europe and North America have declined further as their growth levels have been increasingly outpaced by that of intra-regional tourism. Japan also registered a 49 per cent increase in arrivals from Latin America in 1990, although this was obviously from a small base.

The economic contribution of tourism

International tourist receipts and expenditure in the OECD area both rose by 21 per cent in 1990, in dollar terms, compared with +5 per cent and +4 per cent respectively the previous year. The sharp improvement is largely due to the fact that virtually all the national currencies of OECD Member countries appreciated against the dollar in which tourism's foreign exchange contribution is generally expressed. The data, therefore, need to be interpreted with caution.

In real terms - that is, allowing for inflation and exchange rate fluctuations - international tourist receipts increased by an estimated 5 per cent as against +6 per cent in 1989.

The deficit on the OECD balance of tourism account was nearly US$1 billion higher in 1990, at close to US$17 billion. This was due to a faster rise in expenditure on tourism abroad than in tourist receipts. The sharpest rise was from the Australasia-Japan region, up 30 per cent, generating a 38 per cent increase in the deficit of the region's tourism account. North America's deficit was largely unchanged at -US$2 billion and Europe slightly improved its position, ending the year with a positive balance of US$6 billion.

After several years of research, the Tourism Committee, through its Statistical Working Party, has now developed an integrated statistical system, entitled Manual on Tourism Economic Accounts, to evaluate the economic

Trend of international tourism in the OECD area

Per cent change over previous year

	Arrivals at frontiers[1]		Nights spent in means of accommodation[2]		Receipts in national currency		Receipts in real terms[3]	
	% 89/88	% 90/89	% 89/88	% 90/89	% 89/88	% 90/89	% 89/88	% 90/89
Austria			8.4	–0.2	13.8	–5.7	10.9	–8.7
Belgium[4]			14.8	6.1	–3.8	1.8	–6.7	–1.6
Denmark			5.6	8.9	3.6	21.6	–1.0	18.3
Finland			9.5	–2.0	5.8	1.9	–0.7	–4.0
France	29.4	7.3	–6.4	4.4	26.2	6.1	22.0	2.6
Germany			11.5	3.8	10.6	4.9	7.6	2.2
Greece	3.9	9.8	–1.8	6.3	–6.0	25.6	–17.4	4.3
Iceland	–0.4	8.2	1.8		31.3	15.9	8.7	0.3
Ireland	16.5	12.3	19.9	7.2	15.3	15.9	10.8	12.2
Italy	–0.8	2.9	–5.9	–2.9	1.9	43.9	–4.4	35.6
Luxembourg[4]			5.0	5.8	–3.8	1.8	–6.7	–1.6
Netherlands			12.1	15.6	12.8	2.7	11.6	0.2
Norway			2.8	5.4	–3.6	3.0	–7.8	–1.1
Portugal	7.4	12.7	2.5	6.1	21.7	18.3	8.0	4.3
Spain	–0.2	–3.7	–11.4		–1.0	–2.4	–7.3	–8.5
Sweden			6.6	–13.3	14.0	4.5	7.1	–5.4
Switzerland	7.7	4.8	4.4	2.6	9.1	4.2	5.7	–1.1
Turkey	6.9	20.9	1.8	11.8	60.8	58.2	–5.2	–1.3
United Kingdom	9.7	3.9	8.4	4.8	11.3	12.1	3.2	2.4
EUROPE[5]	8.9	3.6	1.0	3.6			3.5	3.2
Canada	–2.7	1.0	–2.0		4.8	3.4	–0.2	–1.3
United States[6]	33.5	6.7			17.9	14.0	12.5	8.2
NORTH AMERICA[5]	20.5	5.0					10.9	7.1
Australia	–7.5	6.5	–1.3	13.6	–5.7	17.4	–12.4	9.4
New Zealand	4.2	8.3	1.8	9.5	0.5	12.0	–5.1	6.5
Japan	20.4	14.2			17.4	19.1	14.8	15.5
AUSTRALASIA-JAPAN[5]	6.3	10.5	–0.6	12.6			–2.3	11.2
OECD[5]	11.1	4.1	0.9	4.4			5.6	4.8
Yugoslavia	15.1	16.0	–6.1	–11.8	1155.7	332.6	327.2	–68.0

1. Arrivals of tourists except in Australia, Ireland, Japan, Spain, Turkey , United kingdom and Yugoslavia where arrivals concern visitors.
2. Nights spent in all means of accommodation except in Finland, Iceland, Luxembourg and Spain where nights spent concern hotels and similar establishments.
3. After correcting for the effects of inflation. For the regional and OECD totals, the receipts of the individual countries are weighted in proportion to their share in the total expressed in dollars.
4. Receipts apply to both Belgium and Luxembourg.
5. Overall trends for countries with data available from 1988 to 1990.
6. New series for receipts and expenditure from 1985 affecting regional as well as overall OECD volumes and trends.

importance of tourism in Member countries using, inter alia, the National Accounts' concepts and definitions.

This Manual will enable Member countries to identify more clearly and precisely the economic contribution of tourism in terms of production, value added, consumption, gross fixed capital formation and employment. In 1992, the Tourism Committee will begin the implementation of the Manual (collection of data, creation of a data base, etc.).

Major developments affecting tourism in 1990

Two major developments impacted on world travel and tourism in 1990: the political changes in Central and Eastern Europe that started in late-1989, and the Middle East crisis.

Changes in central and eastern europe

The early euphoria over the abandonment of communism in Central and Eastern Europe, and over the move from planned towards market based economies, has now given way to a more realistic assessment of the problems facing these countries. Nevertheless, the opening up of the region and the easing of restrictions on visas and foreign exchange resulted in a huge boom in travel both into and out of the region in 1990.

The changes have also led to increasing interest on the part of OECD Member countries in establishing concrete projects to stimulate tourism flows, both for international trade and cultural exchanges, and to assist in the development and improvement of the tourism infrastructure in Central and Eastern Europe and in vocational training. There have been a number of exchanges of experts and promotional and marketing materials, and several tourism co-operation and technical assistance programmes have been launched.

Within the context of the work programme of the Centre for Co-operation with European Economies in Transition (CCEET), the Tourism Committee organised a Seminar in November 1991 on the Prospects of Tourism in those countries. The Agenda for the meeting focused on three main topics:

-- the current situation of the tourism industry in Central and Eastern European countries;

-- market opportunities and prospects;

-- the transition process towards a market-based economy in the tourism industry.

The proceedings of the Seminar will be published in 1992.

The impact of the Gulf war

It is extremely difficult to disentangle the effects of the Gulf war and the economic recession with any reliable precision.

While there is no firm concensus as to the evidence of a threat of recession hanging over the world's leading economies before the invasion of Kuwait by Iraq in August 1990, there was a clear slowdown in several of the leading national economies before the second half of 1990, notably in the United States, Canada, the United Kingdom, Sweden and Australia. Rising inflation resulted in a slackening demand for labour and a subsequent rise in unemployment. The trend in interest rates was unequivocally upwards, producing a steady tightening of the international economy. Of more relevance than nominal interest rates were real rates - representing the margin by which nominal rates exceeded the rate of inflation. Here again, the trend was upwards, from around 5 per cent at the beginning of 1988 to over 6 per cent by mid-1990, slowing the underlying capacity of individual countries to sustain the cost of shorter term discretionary borrowing.

Consumer confidence had already fallen, but the political and economic uncertainties caused by the Middle East crisis exacerbated the situation. Eight leading source markets together accounted for some 77 per cent of all OECD Member countries' expenditure on travel abroad in 1990 (in dollar terms) - the United States, Germany, Japan, the United Kingdom, Italy, France, Canada and the Netherlands.

Although there were reports of a sharp fall in discretionary travel overall from October 1990, not all sectors of the market were affected. Air travel declined as a result of the perceived threat of terrorist incidents but there was an increase in private car and coach travel abroad. The market seemed determined to maintain vacation travel even as the economy dimmed future prospects.

Consequently, there was also a shift in destinations. Those that suffered the most from cancellations were the Middle East, North Africa and parts of the Eastern Mediterranean. Cancellations for Turkey from Western Europe were compensated by an increase in tourism from Eastern Europe and Greece was much less affected than might have been expected.

By and large, people preferred to travel to destinations closer to home and countries traditionally regarded as safe and secure havens, such as Switzerland, benefited from the trend. In addition, abundant snow in Europe's mountain resorts, after three years of poor skiing conditions, resulted in the cancellation of winter sun holidays in favour of winter sports.

In some markets, business travel was actually stimulated in the last few months of 1990 as companies looked for alternative trading partners. But there were early signs of a tightening in overall corporate budgets, with corporations increasingly trying to gain better travel deals from suppliers and agents.

The transport sector

The airline industry was the sector hardest hit by the Middle East crisis. For many airlines, there was already evidence of a strong decline in financial performance early in 1990 before the Gulf crisis broke out. Two months after the start of the Gulf crisis, fuel prices in most areas had more than doubled - from 66 cents per US gallon in July to 140 cents in October.

The impact of the rising jet fuel prices was exacerbated by soaring labour costs, user charges and insurance. So it was extremely difficult for airlines to offset increasing costs through traffic driven revenue increases. In the last months of 1990, for example, the war risk insurance market introduced high premiums which cost the industry an extra US$200 million by year end.

Despite a 7 per cent increase in passengers carried to 262 million and a small operating profit of US$0.5 billion, the member carriers of the International Air Transport Association (IATA) recorded a US$2.7 billion loss on international scheduled services in 1990 after interest - compared with an overall profit of US$0.3 billion in 1989. This result was the worst ever recorded in the 46 year history of the association.

Financial prospects for 1991 are even worse, with a US$3.7 billion loss after interest projected by IATA. The airlines are only now beginning to assess the full impact of rising operating costs and falling traffic at least into the fourth quarter of 1991. Capacity adjustments have been made, but over-capacity on some routes has encouraged heavier discounting of fares which has added to the existing problems of the financially weaker carriers.

Another major concern for the airline industry is how carriers will be able to replace assets and finance future growth. Despite the downturn in traffic in 1991, the longer term growth prospects for the industry have not changed.

However, growth is threatened by an inadequate infrastructure - principally in terms of airport and airway capacity - the symptoms of which are delays, cancelled flights and congestion.

Congestion is also a growing problem for road transportation. The heavy demands placed on the infrastructure and on passenger transportation by travel and tourism growth have created problems that, in the long run, risk having an adverse effect on tourism growth itself. The impact is compounded by the safety and security risks associated with it.

As a result of the increasing pressures on roads, at airports and in the air, there has been growing interest from both the public and private sector in rail transportation. After a decline in market share throughout much of this decade, rail transportation is beginning to show healthy growth in some regions, notably Europe. This is mainly because of the improvements in rail services and particularly, the expansion of high-speed rail networks like the Train-à-Grande-Vitesse (TGV) and Inter-City Express (ICE), which offer competitive alternative transportation for inter-city travellers, whether time-sensitive business travellers or urban tourists.

Improved pricing policies and higher standards of comfort and service are proving an alternative attraction to crowded roads and airports for journeys of up to three to four hours at least. The Eurotunnel project, which is due to be completed in 1992, is still beset by numerous problems, but it can also be expected to stimulate increased demand from both the leisure and business travel markets.

Elsewhere in the OECD area, there are a number of new projects, either under development or on the drawing board, for high-speed rail networks. In some countries, notably Japan and the east coast of the United States between New York and Washington, rail transportation already accounts for an important share of overall passenger traffic.

Member countries' tourism policy and actions

Few industries have such a pervasive impact on the local community as travel and tourism. There has been a growing recognition on the part of OECD Member countries as to the economic contribution of the industry on economic growth, whether measured in terms of total sales, value added, capital investment, tax contributions, or employment.

The results of a study commissioned by the World Travel and Tourism Council (WTTC) early in 1991 suggest that travel and tourism is the world's largest industry, accounting for between 5 per cent-6 per cent of world GNP in 1989. It employs more than 112 million people around the world, or close to 7 per cent of the world's workforce and invests more than US$350 billion a year in new facilities and capital equipment, or over 7 per cent of worldwide capital investment.

OECD Member states have intensified their efforts over the past year to accord the priority to tourism that the industry deserves. Facilitation to stimulate tourism flows, the easing of visa requirements and foreign exchange controls, and the liberalisation of conditions for foreign investment have also contributed to ensuring increased private sector interest in tourism development.

Social tourism - for low income groups of all ages - has been earmarked as a high priority by a number of Member governments, such as France and Greece. In France, construction aid has been redefined to take account of changes in the economic and social environment and more financial assistance is being provided for individuals through the form of holiday vouchers (the "chèque-vacances") and other incentives. In Greece, social tourism programmes are combined with efforts to encourage off-season travel.

Elsewhere in Europe, international co-operation on the staggering of school holidays has increased in a concerted attempt to improve seasonal tourism flows and ease congestion. A study into ways of improving the seasonal spread of tourism was commissioned by the Dutch Ministry of Economic Affairs as a prelude to an international conference on the subject in September 1991.

Key action and policy areas in the last twelve months have also included congestion at airports, in the airways and on the roads, as well as the safety and security risks resulting from pressures on the infrastructure. OECD Members are in general agreement that transportation deficiencies should not hinder market access.

Problems due to the seasonality of holidays have encouraged the main transport companies in Spain to take measures to ease transport congestion during holiday periods. Iberia has adopted a policy of launching specific products during low season periods of the year, offering new or alternative destinations to those traditionally visited, such as South America in the winter. Lower fares have also been introduced for travel outside periods of peak demand.

The Middle East conflict brought home the vulnerability of travel and tourism to factors beyond the direct control of the industry and governments. Terrorism has fortunately been less frequent over the last few years. But it remains the primary threat to civil aviation, and one incident - or even threat of an incident - can have a profound effect on air travel. Airports around the world have increasingly stepped up and tightened security. But this has also served to make air travel more tedious and time-consuming.

Consumer protection continues to be a major issue. The World Tourism Organisation (WTO) organised a seminar on the subject of "Security in Tourism" in September 1990 in Madrid with the support of Spain's Secretary General for Tourism. Spain is also a member of the Group of Experts formed within the WTO which is currently drawing up two documents, the first concerning "Security in Tourism" and the second, "A Deontological Code for Handicapped Tourists".

A proposal from the Universal Federation of Travel Agents Associations (UFTAA) in 1990 for the establishment of a new tourism industry compensation plan to be funded by consumers through a ticket tax - developed at the initiative of the Australian Federation of Travel Agents (AFTA) - has in principle received support from the Australian Ministers for Tourism and Aviation. Other OECD Member countries are also seriously considering the merits of the scheme, which would cover consumers not only against failure by travel agents but also against default by airlines and other transport operators.

The harnessing of technology is seen by many Member countries as a means of improving the competitiveness of their tourism products and providing greater accessibility of these products through "on-line" international travel networks and distribution systems.

Environmental protection is now recognised as a major factor in economic growth. The Tourism Stream of Globe '90, the first in a series of bi-annual conferences on environment and the economy organised by the Government of Canada, addressed the issue of integrated resource planning and demonstrated through practical case studies how competing industrial sectors can successfully coexist. The Stream examined the environmental impact of other resource users on the tourism industry and suggested ways for the tourism sector to cope with the changes.

A document entitled "An Action Strategy for Sustainable Tourism Development" was produced from Globe '90, incorporating broad guiding principles, measurable objectives and outlines for specific actions and recommendations to be undertaken on a global basis by governments, businesses, industries and individual tourists to achieve sustainable tourism development goals.

Careful and sensitive planning and management of tourism growth will be required to ensure that the fragile resources which form the basis of the industry are not compromised. One of the main priorities of Members from developed countries is to ensure the mistakes of the past are not repeated and that coastal areas are protected from further uncontrolled buildings and other development. With the increased interest in tourism in rural areas, management schemes have also been drawn up for sensitive inland areas, such as lakes, waterways and mountains.

A study on "Integrated Alpine Protection" was compiled for the Austrian government and Austria, as well as other Member countries concerned, has actively participated in the preparation of the "Alpine Convention".

Efforts have also been intensified to identify and understand labour force needs for the tourism industry so that future labour force planning can incorporate the necessary education and training possibilities to meet these needs. Australia is currently preparing a tourism industry labour force plan to the year 2000. A report is being drawn up to identify and recommend solutions to critical education and training supply issues facing the industry. This will also identify the remaining information gaps needed to refine the labour force model of the tourism industry.

A Canadian Tourism Industry Standards and Certification Committee, chaired by Tourism Canada, has been established to coordinate the development of occupational standards and nationally recognised industry based certification programmes. To date, occupational standards and certification programmes have been established for more than 20 occupations and another 20 are under development. A Federal-Provincial Territorial Working group on Tourism Industry Human Resource Issues has also been set up to provide a forum for governments to share information on and coordinate their human resource policies and programmes.

The importance of research and the monitoring of quantitative market trends is increasingly being recognised by OECD Member countries. From the beginning of 1991, the holiday survey conducted in Finland was upgraded to a ontinuous monitor. This will enable changes in demand and travel patterns to be observed more rapidly, which is vital for marketing planning.

France's Ministry of Tourism has established a tourism observatory involving government departments, local authorities, representatives of the industry, universities and researchers who are well placed to follow developments in travel in France. The objective of the observatory will be to collect all available tourism related data, analyse them and circulate the findings to interested parties.

International tourism in the 1990's

The beginning of the 1990's was probably the most difficult period the travel and tourism industry has ever faced. The last recession in the United States, for example - from 1981-82 - precipitated a prolonged slump in travel that continued until the middle of the decade.

A part of the reason was that Americans postponed more than just travel. They also postponed buying new homes, cars and other major consumer durables.

After the recession ended, it was these items that experienced a boom, and not travel. As a result, travel had to wait until these other consumer needs were satisfied before beginning to register a recovery in 1985.

Several factors argue for a quicker turnaround this time than was experienced in the early 1980s. The latest recession has been shorter; the travel industry has been much more united and proactive in response to the current crisis; and some of the latest economic indicators also justify projections of an upturn in travel in 1992. In some markets, there have already been clear signs of a revival.

Nevertheless, the indications are that the Gulf crisis and economic recession have accelerated changes in market demand for travel and tourism that were beginning to emerge at the end of the 1980s.

Changing markets

Destination popularity in the 1990s is likely to be directly linked to factors such as pollution and the environment. The Pacific Asia region is expected to be the fastest growing destination in percentage terms. But continuing sharp growth to the United States is predicted from major OECD markets over the next few years - especially if the US dollar remains attractive.

The advent of the Single European Market and the sweeping changes taking place across Central and Eastern Europe are also focusing increased attention on Europe.

As far as outbound markets are concerned, a boom in travel is also likely from the Pacific Asia region. Some 11 million Japanese travelled abroad in 1991 and the volume could well double by the end of the century, or even before, if current projections are proved accurate. The Japanese government is continuing to encourage travel abroad, as well as shorter working hours and greater participation in leisure pursuits. In percentage terms, Japan's annual rise in outbound travel could be exceeded by growth from two other newly emerging markets in the region over the next few years, namely Korea and Taiwan.

In Eastern Europe, Germany will continue to dominate overall travel volume and spending - but the economies of some of the newer EC member states like Spain, Portugal and Greece are likely to benefit from rising standards of living. So this should generate a more rapid percentage growth in travel from Southern European markets.

In the developed world, there will perhaps be less concern about geographic sources of business than with the implications of demographic shifts across all populations. There has also been a major impact on travel from the rise in numbers of working wives and DINKS - couples with "double income and no kids". Single person households are also on the increase. And these young people can not only better afford to travel, they are also better educated than they were 20 years ago - the number of students attending institutions of higher education has tripled since the 1970s.

Even more significant is the ageing of the population in developed countries. Between now and the year 2000 in Europe, for example, while the number of young people aged 15-24 will fall by an estimated 20 per cent, there will be a 10 per cent rise in the share of people over the age of 60. Many of these "senior citizens", as they are known by the travel trade, are well travelled already. They also have more time to spend on travel and greater financial resources to spend on leisure pursuits.

In addition, all those born in the baby-boom years after the Second World War are now approaching their 50s. Although hardly "senior citizens", it will not be long before they retire and they will be much more enthusiastic and more adventurous travellers when this time comes than their parents are. So this group of "empty nesters", who have paid off their mortgages and whose children have left home, offer tremendous potential for the industry.

Alongside the demographic changes, there are psychological changes in the market that will also be critical in determining travel trends for the future. Personal values, such as relaxation, having fun and self-fulfilment, have become increasingly important. Leisure travel is no longer considered a luxury, but has become a major priority in a household's expenditure. It is often more important than material goods like new televisions, washing machines, or cars.

This increasing priority accorded to travel and tourism also means that people are travelling more frequently. So even in major source markets, where the level of trip-taking appears to be approaching a ceiling, the overall volume of travel will grow because of the increased number of trips per trip-taker. A significant share of these trips will be short breaks.

Along with the continued growth in environmental consciousness, tourists will also become less and less willing to trade quality for cheap prices, even at the lower end of the market. This desire for improved quality, which is becoming more evident in all sectors of the leisure travel market, will affects not only the tourism product, but also customer service, and can be expected lead to even greater pressure on the travel and tourism workforce and more intense competition within the industry in coming years.

Trends of international tourism in Europe
(Indices 1982 = 100)

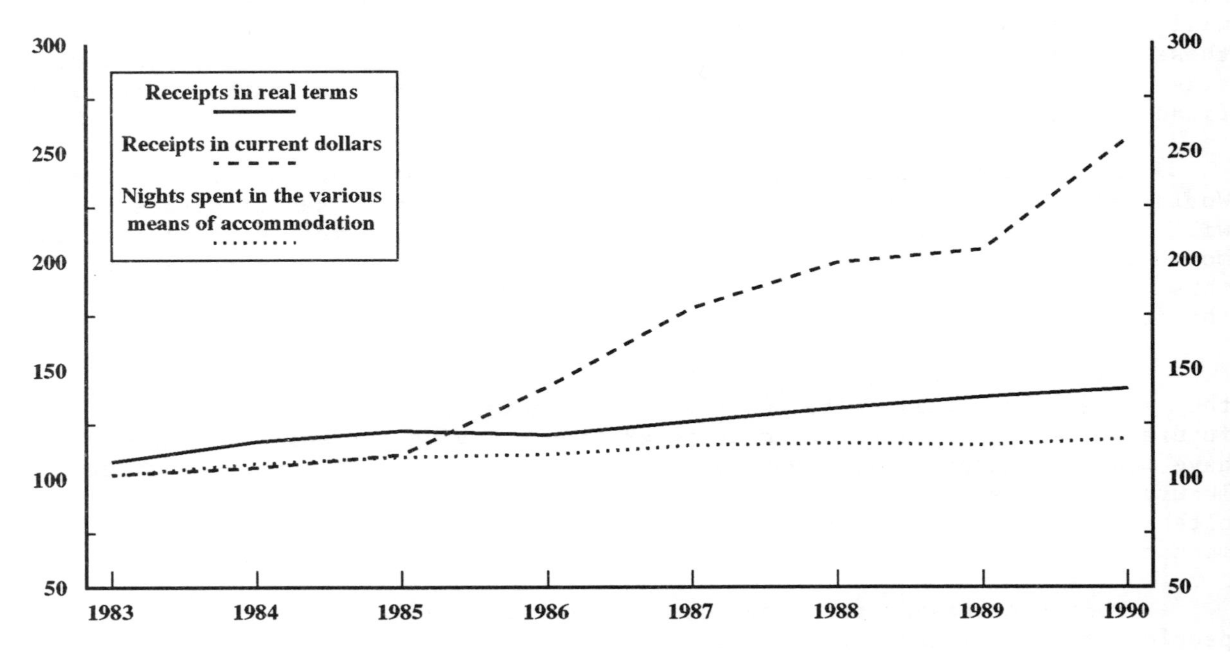

Source: OECD

Trends of international tourism in North America
(Indices 1984 = 100)

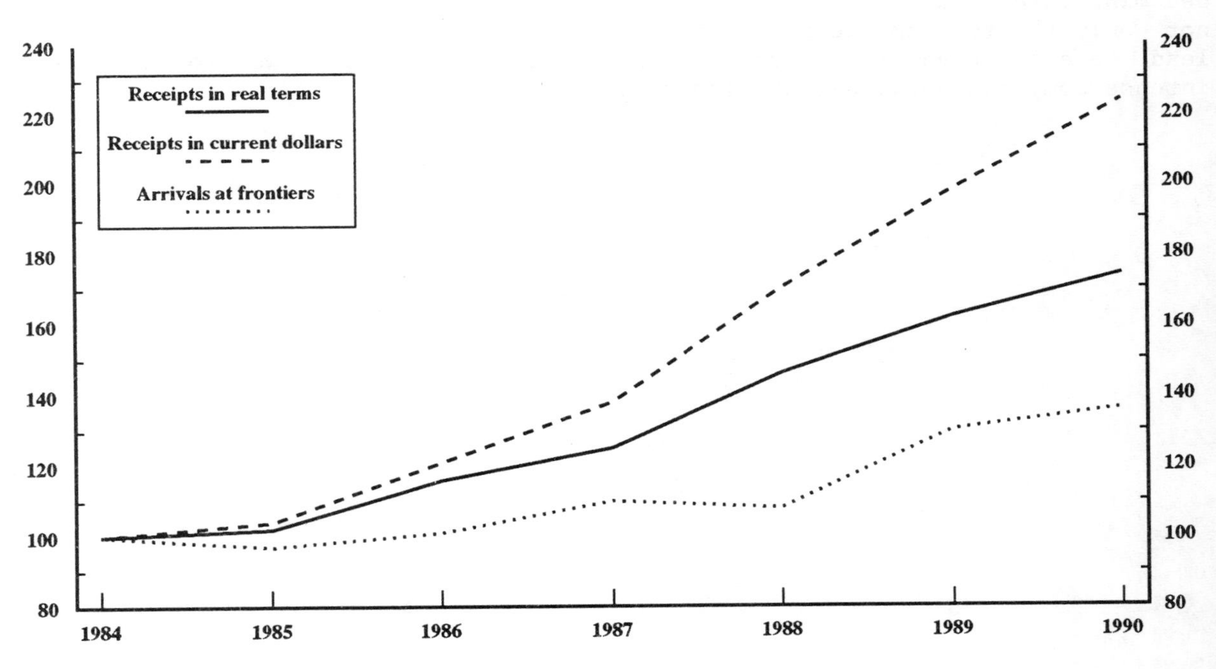

Source: OECD

Trends of international tourism
in Australasia-Japan
(Indices 1982 = 100)

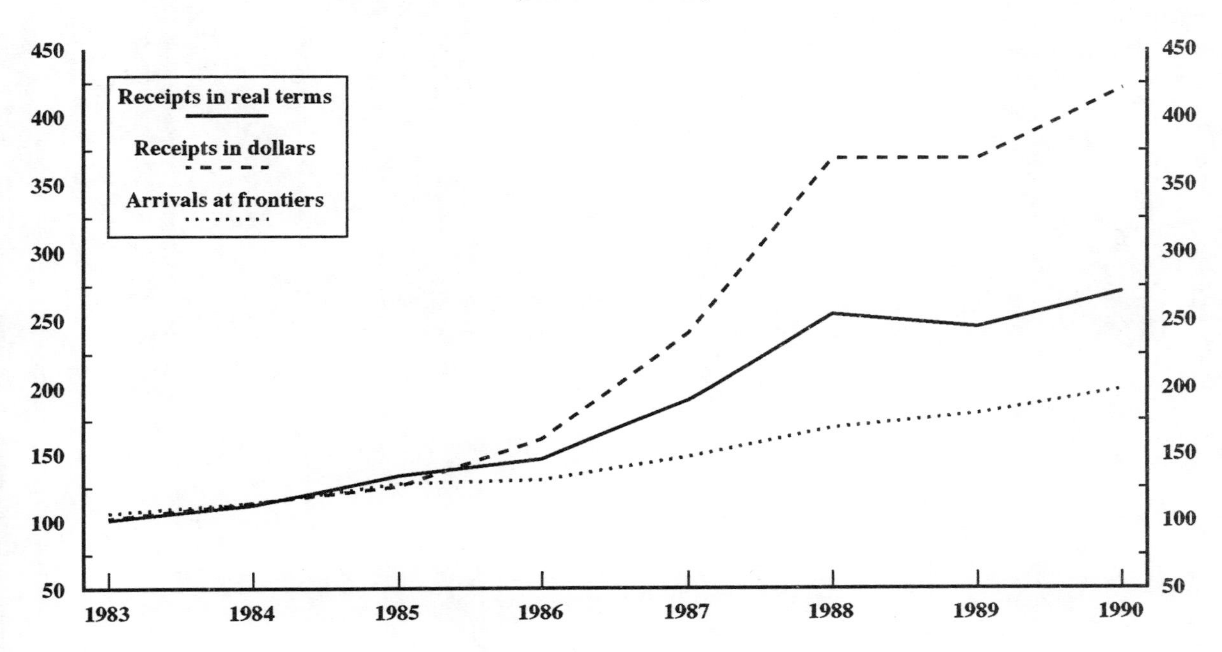

Source: OECD

CHAPTER I

GOVERNMENT POLICY AND ACTION IN 1989 AND 1990

As from the 1987 edition, material concerning each Member country and Yugoslavia has been modified from that of earlier editions and arranged by country. This development is in response to the request by the Tourism Committee that the publication should set out the policies for tourism in a clearer manner, with the aim of making analysis of its importance easier and of assisting the decision-making process.

The information on government policy and action in the OECD area, assembled by means of an questionnaire is therefore set out as follows:

-- An introductory section covering the importance of tourism as an economic activity in the country and the prospects for its development; followed by

-- Governement policy: objectives, priorities, plans and programmes together with the institutional framework; and

-- Actions and measures undertaken during 1989 and 1990 in implementation of the tourism policies, including the development of supply (accommodation, transport, vocational training, etc.), marketing (research, strategies, etc.), the protection of the tourist as a consumer, the staggering of holidays and international co-operation.

Since this information gathered by the Secretariat intends only to update former information, the reader who is looking for more detailed information on the government policy of a particular country should consult the 1983, 1986 and 1989 editions (covering the years 1982, 1985, 1987 and 1988) in which consolidated summaries are set out.

AUSTRALIA

Tourism as an economic activity

Following the strong and sustained growth of Australia's tourism industry during the mid 1980s, which saw international tourism increase to around 2.25 million international visitors in 1988, Australia's international tourism performance was more subdued in 1989 and 1990, with 2.08 million and 2.21 million visitors respectively.

This has been due to a number of factors, including the impact of the disruptions to domestic air services in the second half of 1989 caused by the actions of domestic pilots; recession in some of Australia's major source markets; and the effects of increased costs of travel and security concerns associated with the Gulf crisis.

Despite the steadying in the number of international visitors, in 1990 international tourism to Australia generated record tourism foreign exchange earnings of more than A$6.7 billion (about 9 per cent of Australia's total export earnings) due to increases in average expenditure largely as a result of longer average duration of stay rates.

While there are currently no accurate measures of domestic tourism expenditure, the volume of domestic travel has increased strongly during 1989 and 1990. In 1989 Australians undertook nearly 48.5 million domestic trips involving at least an overnight stay (5 per cent higher than in 1988) and spent 219 million nights away from home (1 per cent higher than in 1988). During 1990 nearly 49 million domestic trips were recorded although the number of visitor nights, at slightly more than 218 million, was lower indicating a tendency towards shorter trips.

During 1989-90 total expenditure derived from tourism was estimated at A$24 billion, with A$17.6 billion attributed to domestic tourism. It is estimated that the tourism industry contributed around 5.2 per cent to gross domestic product in 1989-90.

The tourism industry accounted for an estimated 453 000 jobs or 5.8 per cent of the total workforce and generated over 100 000 new jobs during the 1980s.

There is considerable optimism in the industry, stimulated by the strong inbound tourism performance over the 1986-88 period and in 1991. Tourism projects valued at more than A$ 9.2 billion are due for completion between 1991 and 1994.

Prospects for development

While Australia's tourism performance over the recent biennium has steadied, longer term forecasts of visitor growth by the Bureau of Tourism Research (BTR) and estimates by other authorities, indicate that sustainable growth of around 7 per cent per annum can be expected. This would result in around 5 million visitors by the year 2000.

Domestic tourism demand is expected to continue to grow slowly as prospects are largely dependent on disposable income and population growth. While the Australian economy continues to experience difficulties accompanied by relatively high levels of unemployment, the short to medium term prospects for sustained growth in domestic tourism appear to be constrained.

As price differentials are important in the allocation of consumer expenditure, the BTR has undertaken an analysis of the tourism components of the consumer price index (CPI) to compare the position of the tourism industry in competing for the expenditure of Australians.

The BTR found that between March 1986 and December 1990, price increases for holiday travel and accommodation within Australia continued to exceed those for overseas travel and goods and services in general. Continuation of this trend would affect the ability of the Australian tourism product to compete effectively within the Australian market against outbound travel and other outlets for discretionary expenditure will be eroded. However, increases in accommodation prices appear to have moderated and air transport prices actually declined in the period following the study.

Some changes have been experienced in the pattern of domestic travel, following the deregulation of Australia's domestic airline system late in 1990. The introduction of additional carriers and greater fare competition on domestic routes have stimulated non-business air travel and have altered transport mode shares for domestic travel.

The Australian Government is developing ecologically sustainable development strategies for Australia's major industry sectors, including tourism. The outcome of this process is to provide advice to Government on future policy options and to develop practical proposals for implementing them.

Another critical element in achieving and managing the growth rates projected for Australian tourism to the year 2000 will be in understanding tourism labour force needs and labour force planning. To this end, research is currently being undertaken to comprehensively analyse the tourism industry labour force needs and supply options to develop a labour force plan to the year 2000.

The study will:

- -- produce a tourism industry labour force plan to the year 2000;
- -- produce a report identifying and recommending solutions to critical education and training supply issues facing the tourism industry; and
- -- identify remaining information gaps needed to refine the labour force model of the tourism industry.

Link between tourism policy and other economic activity

To assist the policy development process, the Treasurer referred the travel and tourism industries to the Industries Assistance Commission for inquiry. The report from that inquiry, issued in September 1989, highlighted the regulation of transport services as a main impediment to the development of tourism. The Government has since deregulated the domestic aviation sector, and taken decisions to privatise its domestic carrier Australian Airlines and sell 49 per cent of Qantas. Further aviation initiatives will continue to be considered in the context of broader microeconomic reform.

Given the growing significance of foreign investment in the Australian tourism industry, the Government has commissioned two studies on the subject in the last two years. The first, "Foreign Investment in Australian Tourism", was released mid-1990. The report explores, at a theoretical level, arguments for and against foreign investment in tourism and its effects on employment, the balance of payments, the environment and society. The initial report also identified a theoretical framework for further examination of the impact of foreign investment, through several case studies - Cairns (QLD), the Gold Coast (QLD) and Sydney (NSW).

The second report "Impacts of Foreign Investment in Australian Tourism" was released in July 1991. It confirmed that overall the Australian economy benefits from foreign investment in tourism. Foreign investment enhances the competitiveness of the industry, therefore reducing costs to tourists and increasing tourism flows into Australia.

Government policy

In recognition of the growing economic importance of the tourism industry, the Government established a separate Ministry for Tourism in December 1991 and gave it Cabinet status.

To provide for a more co-ordinated approach to the development of the industry, work has progressed on the development of a National Tourism Strategy. A background paper "Towards a National Tourism Strategy" was released in September 1991 to generate discussion and industry/community output to the development of the Strategy.

The Strategy, which is expected to be finalised in early 1992, has three principal aims:

-- to provide all levels of government, the industry and other interest groups with a clear statement of the Commonwealth Government's objectives for the future development of the tourism industry;

-- to provide a sound basis for the formulation of government tourism policy and industry planning over the next decade; and

-- to enhance community awareness of the economic, environmental and cultural significance of the tourism industry.

The Strategy aims to achieve an integrated approach to industry development taking into account economic, environmental and social objectives with the view to creating a competitive and sustainable industry framework.

Issues to be considered in the Strategy include marketing, research, policy co-ordination, taxation, investment, industrial relations, transport, facilitation, employment and training, environmental and social issues, accommodation and attractions.

The Senate (upper house of the Federal Parliament) is also undertaking an inquiry into the role of the Commonwealth Government in the further development of the Australian tourism industry. In particular, the inquiry will focus on the environmental impact of tourism developments in coastal regions and national heritage areas, the co-ordination of foreign tourism development strategies between the States, the role of foreign investment in tourism developments and the net benefit to Australia of overseas tourism.

The Government has also embarked on a major review of Ecologically Sustainable Development (ESD). Working Groups have been established covering nine major areas or industries, including one group which is to report on ESD in relation to tourism and another on transport. The report was finalised in November 1991 for consideration by the government.

Other studies relevant to environmental concerns of the industry include inquiries by a House of Representatives (lower house of the Federal Parliament) Standing Committee and by the government's Resources Assessment Commission on coastal zone management.

In the past two years there have been no major changes to the institutional framework for national tourism administration, which had been subject to review and reorganisation in the preceding biennium. However, during 1990 and early 1991, an evaluation was undertaken of the Australian Tourist Commission's effectiveness in meeting its international marketing responsibilities. At the State level the Government of the north-eastern State of Queensland, which has been a major recipient of growth in both domestic and international tourism in recent years, carried out a review of its tourism administrative arm, the Queensland Tourist and Travel Corporation.

Tourism industry representatives continue to play a significant role in shaping policy at the national level through both formal and informal mechanisms. The Tourism Advisory Council is the major forum for consultation between the Federal Minister responsible for tourism and major industry representatives, unions and individuals with tourism interests. It provides a platform for members to express their concerns on policy issues and to assist co-ordination of the Government's tourism marketing responses.

The Council, which is chaired by the Minister, provided advice on the development of a major recovery programme for the tourism industry following the domestic pilots' dispute in 1989. Council discussions early in 1991 also assisted the development of a considered response to the impact of the Gulf War on Australia's tourism industry.

Action and measures taken in 1989 and 1990

Transport. The following measures were taken during 1989 and 1990 to increase the supply and reduce the cost of air transport both to and from Australia and within Australia:

-- the economic regulation of interstate air services within Australia ceased on 31st October 1990, with the termination of the two airlines agreement and the opening up of the domestic aviation market to new carriers;

-- in June 1989, the Government announced a more liberal approach to the negotiation of international aviation rights. Underpinning this approach is a greater recognition of market forces, more forward looking and flexible arrangements, particularly in relation to capacity, and greater receptiveness to requests by foreign carriers wishing to fly to Australia;

-- new air services agreements were put in place with Switzerland, the Republic of Korea, Zimbabwe, Brunei and Egypt; and

-- approval was granted for substantial charter programmes targeting inbound tourism, including two separate programmes of air charters by Britannia Airways.

A related initiative taken during the period was the decision to sell 100 per cent of Australian Airlines and 49 per cent of Qantas, both currently fully owned by the Federal Government.

The Government's major objective in deregulating domestic aviation was to create an environment which would foster:

-- increased responsiveness by airlines to consumer needs;

-- a wider range of fares and types of services to provide enhanced travel opportunities; and

-- increased competition and pricing flexibility leading to greater economic efficiency in the industry.

Following the first year of operations in a deregulated market, it would appear that Government objectives are being met and in particular, non business travellers have benefited from fare reductions and a greater range of discount fares.

In respect of international aviation, the Government was concerned to ensure that the approach adopted in the negotiation of aviation rights was able to meet the growing demand for travel, particularly visitor traffic. It recognised that greater emphasis needed to be placed on maximising the national interest while taking into account the bilateral nature of air services discussions and the needs of Qantas.

On 1st January 1989 new road funding arrangements were introduced by the Government under the Australian Centennial Roads Development Program.

The new programme replaces the previous scheme (Australian Bicentennial Road Development Program) which ended on 31st December 1989. It focuses Federal road funding on roads of national economic significance and introduces more efficient administrative arrangements.

During the period 1989 to 1995 more than $A6 billion will be provided under this programme for funding of roads of national economic importance (this includes National Highways and a new category of roads called National Arterials).

The introduction of the new road funding category of National Arterial Roads allows for the funding of projects in both rural and urban areas on routes that will yield benefits to the export and import-competing sectors of the economy, including tourism.

Environment. The Australian Government recognises the fundamental link between economic growth and the environment. It is also committed to the principle of ecologically sustainable development.

In his July 1989 Statement on the Environment, the Prime Minister acknowledged the role that Australia's unique environment - climatic, natural and cultural, plays in attracting tourists from both within Australia and from overseas.

It also recognises that tourism in some areas dramatically changes the size and nature of local communities, particularly in the more remote parts of the country. Careful and sensitive planning and management of growth will be required to ensure that the fragile resources which form the basis of much of the industry are not compromised.

The Australian Government is developing ecologically sustainable development (ESD) strategies for Australia's major industry sectors, including tourism. The outcome of the process is to provide advice to Government on future policy options and to develop practical proposals for implementing them. The four fundamental goals of the ESD process are:

-- improving individual and community well-being and welfare by following a path of economic progress that does not impair welfare of future generations;

-- providing for equity within and between generations;

-- recognising the global dimension; and

-- protecting biological diversity and maintaining ecological processes and systems.

Working Groups on ESD for all industry sectors (including tourism) were established, comprising representatives from all levels of Government, the Commonwealth Scientific and Industrial Research Organisation (CSIRO), industry, unions, conservation groups and the Australia and New Zealand Environment and Conservation Council. Final Working Group Reports were provided to Government in December 1991.

Tourism is not being examined in isolation. The ESD process is considering links between tourism and other industries including agriculture, forestry, fisheries, mining and transport.

The ESD process is also examining intersectoral issues which relate to tourism as well as other industry sectors. These include climate change, public health, population, waste disposal/recycling, urban issues, coastal zone management, employment, women's issues and Aboriginal issues.

Employment. A high priority has been given to improving the skills of the tourism industry's workforce. Commonwealth Government initiatives have included:

-- a research project which examined the tourism labour market and the constraints and attitudes to employment. The study's objectives were to indicate directions for the tourism industry to further develop career awareness programs and to identify training initiatives that may be required by the industry; and

-- a major survey of employees in the hospitality sector to gauge the attitudes to a range of training issues including career paths and structured training arrangements.

In response to the government initiatives encouraging structural efficiency, a restructuring of hospitality employment awards is in progress. The new classification structure is linked to a new training structure which allows for an employee to move through the levels on completion of training, development of skills, obtaining formal trade and non-trade qualification, taking greater career responsibilities or undertaking supervision of other employees.

Changes in work conditions associated with the restructuring of the hospitality awards include:

-- changes to the spread of hours worked;

-- additional part time employment provisions;

-- an exemption from the payment of penalty rates in certain circumstances; and

-- time off in lieu of overtime provisions.

Vocational training. In 1989 the government accepted a recommendation from the National Board of Employment, Education and Training that a Training Guarantee Scheme be introduced:

-- the Training Guarantee Scheme commenced operation 1st July 1990. The government's intention is to increase the training effort by employers. All employers whose payroll exceeds A$200 000 per annum are required to expend 1 per cent of their payroll on approved training in 1990-91, rising to 1.5 per cent in 1992-93.

The government encouraged employer participation on training through the Traineeship system, the Skills Share Centre programme and the Innovative Training Program.

Most States/Territories have introduced either general tourism studies or employment orientated courses into schools curricula.

Articulation between secondary, Technical and Further Education (TAFE) and university institutions is being addressed by the National Tourism Industry Training Committee (NTITC) which trades as Tourism Training Australia (TTA). The system of industry accreditation of training courses operated by NTITC should ensure that courses are relevant to students' needs.

TAFE colleges have introduced course changes in line with industry requirements and reviewed selection criteria to reduce attrition levels.

Cultural tourism. The Commonwealth Government commissioned a project, to be undertaken during 1990-91, to determine and quantify the economic, cultural and/or social benefits from cultural tourism. Factors that currently limit tourists' access to and participation in cultural experiences are being identified and strategies will be formulated to develop the market for cultural products.

Tourism shopping. Following an inquiry into tourism shopping, which reported in 1988, an implementation committee was established in 1989 to act on the recommendations. In light of concerns that Australia was failing to maximise revenue from overseas visitors, a range of measures was developed to promote tourism shopping opportunities and improve Australia's image as a unique shopping destination. The Committee's Report was presented in August 1990.

Taxation. To help facilitate the development of a taxation regime that does not disadvantage tourism relative to other industries or adversely affect the industry's competitive advantage, the government is developing a discussion paper on the impact of taxation issues on the tourism industry. The paper aims to:

-- identify the principal taxation issues relevant to the tourism industry;

-- facilitate discussions between the Government and the industry as a means of exploring the implications of these issues; and

-- provide the basis for an informed tourism input to the formulation of taxation policy.

Preliminary work on the taxation paper is expected to be completed around mid 1991.

Australian tourism investment database. The Australian Tourism Investment Database was launched in April 1991. For the first time the industry now has access to comprehensive details on the existing and projected stock of tourist accommodation. The database will provide valuable information in assisting the industry plan its future development and ensure that its potential is fully realised.

Marketing. During 1989 and 1990, further market research was conducted by the Australian Tourist Commission (ATC). The ATC is responsible for the promotion of Australia as an attractive tourist destination in all of our major international markets.

The tourism departments of the various Australian states and territories also undertook market research to obtain better knowledge of present and potential national demand. The ATC research focused mainly on present and potential international demand.

Market segmentation studies were completed in priority source markets within each major market area and segmentation studies will have been completed for all major markets by the end of July 1991. Tracking studies were also carried out for each and every television advertising campaign in order to determine the effectiveness of the message, and the media employed.

The ATC approaches its destination marketing in two major ways. The first is through consumer advertising campaigns using both electronic and print media. This advertising is conducted in all major markets, and the creative elements are developed and employed in response to market research initiatives such as those noted above. As an adjunct to this, the ATC also plays a facilitating role in servicing local travel trade suppliers by putting them in contact with similar tour operators and travel wholesalers in our overseas markets. The primary consumer fulfilment piece used in each of our overseas markets is a destination guide which carries price/product advertising on behalf of Australian travel suppliers in order to give them some access to consumers who have expressed an interest in travelling to Australia.

The ATC operates travel missions in each of our major overseas market segments. In some cases the ATC is responsible for organising the event, in other markets the ATC is responsible for coordinating an Australian presence in an existing travel trade fair such as Berlin's ITB.

The ATC operates a comprehensive public relations programme including a visiting journalists' programme which brings some 250 international journalists to Australia on general or special interest familiarisation. Its programme also uses the services of specialist consultants in each of our major overseas markets responsible for dissemination of audio, video and print news releases.

Following domestic pilots' industrial action which disrupted air services in the later months of 1989, the Commonwealth Government approved a major industry recovery programme which included an additional A$18.5 million in promotional funding to the ATC to assist recovery of its major international visitor markets. As a result a number of successful new promotional activities were launched in Australia's major source markets in the early months of 1990.

All of the Commission's activities were directed to international markets. The promotion of domestic travel remains the responsibility of various state and territory tourism authorities in Australia.

While the majority of the ATC's market research studies covered the holiday market, significant research was undertaken into the convention and incentives markets and their value to Australia. An evaluation of the ATC's effectiveness in meeting its international marketing responsibilities was undertaken during 1990.

Consumer protection. Tourism Training Australia has established two industry review panels, the Australian Travel Training Review Panel and the Australian Hospitality Review Panel, to provide recognition to training programmes which meet minimum national industry standards. Through these panels, tourism training is regulated and attempts are made to ensure that the consumer will receive a standardised high level of professional service.

The Australian Federation of Travel Agents (AFTA) has proposed the establishment of a new tourism industry compensation plan to be funded by consumers through a ticket tax. Under the proposed scheme consumers would be covered not only against failures by travel agents but also against defaults by transport operators.

Before the scheme can be introduced, AFTA will need to reach agreement with the participating transport operators and the relevant Government agencies on specific details.

Staggering of holidays. Schools in all States and Territories now operate on a four-term school year. Although there is some overlap of holidays, they are not totally aligned. Queensland education authorities agreed to rearrange school holidays so as to ensure minimum overlap with other States and Territories.

International co-operation. In recent years Australia has not initiated any tourism-specific bilateral agreements, although it has encouraged continuing international co-operation on tourism through regular formal and informal contacts with other countries.

Through its aid programme Australia continues to fund tourism and tourism-related projects and studies both bilaterally and regionally. These include planning studies and training assistance as well as related infrastructure support, such as airport upgrading.

AUSTRIA

Tourism as an economic activity

Expenditure on tourism and leisure activities had reached Sch 309 billion in 1989. According to estimates the share in value of the entire sector in GDP amounted to some 14 per cent. Expenditure by foreign and domestic tourists will continue to increase on average in 1990 and reach a volume of approximately S 330 billion.

Slightly less than half of the total expenditure is accounted for by foreigners. The major share of expenditure in tourism and leisure falls to domestic tourists (approximately 55 per cent), who spend almost 90 per cent of their leisure time budget on consumption at their place of residence or on one-day excursions, only a little more than 10 per cent is spent on holiday and recreational trips.

The major part of total expenditure in tourism and leisure goes to accommodation and restaurant facilities and to the transport sector.

28 per cent of total expenditure, or S 84 billion, was spent in restaurants in 1990, 61 per cent by foreign tourists and 9 per cent by Austrians travelling in their own country; the remaining 30 per cent was spent by Austrians during private daily excursions in Austria and for leisure time consumption at the place of residence. Expenditure on accommodation amounted to S 34 billion (11.5 per cent share), of which 86 per cent came from foreign tourists.

Expenditure on transport reached a volume of S 68 billion, or a share of 22.5 per cent in 1989, with expenditure on individual transport (S 46.9 billion) by far exceeding public transport.

At about 6-6.5 per cent per annum, total expenditure for tourism and leisure time has increased slightly more than GDP (in nominal terms) since 1980, with expenditure on leisure activities at the place of residence and daily excursions representing above average growth rates of approximately 7 per cent per annum.

Expenditure on tourism, however, contrary to expenditure on leisure activities at the place of residence and daily excursions, increased by almost one percentage point less than the nominal GDP from 1980 to 1988 (approximately 5 per cent per annum). It is noteworthy that, during the period 1980/88 turnover from inland travel lagged behind overall economic development as compared to demand from abroad. In 1988 tourism started to recover, attributable first of all to foreign tourists.

Prospects for development

Among the main topics the tourism industry will have to deal with in the 90s is maintaining the environment. Tourism policy will also have to concentrate on the following conditions:

-- as regards countries of origin: greater importance of the overseas markets: Japan, the Asian countries, Latin America, and Eastern Europe;

-- heavily increasing demand for health tourism facilities, cultural and educational facilities, sports (health and fitness and outdoor sports games);

-- favourable development of city tourism;

-- trend towards short trips;

-- the private car remains popular but other means of transport gain in importance. Increasing problems of traffic and congestion. Road and air traffic are faced with breakdowns;

-- marked differences in travel behaviour according to age groups and life cycles. A large increase in the share of the elderly, singles and couples without children necessitates corresponding facilities;

-- Continuous urbanisation. The population of built-up areas participates to an ever increasing extent in transport for pleasure;

-- New leisure time awareness -- trends towards cultivating a new leisure style. A dominant desire for social gatherings and adventure. Active leisure time projects -- to enjoy life and make the most of it;

-- New trends in winter activities. Rising interest in skiing tours, skiing variants, cross-country skiing and ski touring.

Government policy

The bases of general targets and priorities of Austrian tourism policy are:

-- the Government Programme of 17 December 1990;

-- the resolutions and the "Guidelines for Tourism Policy up to the Year 2000" as published at the 1989 "Österreichische Fremdenverkehrstag" - the Austrian Zoning Policy concept;

Focal points of tourism policy are as follows:

-- quality orientation in promotional policies, taking into account ecology and regional political aspects;

-- further attempts at a decongestion of domestic and foreign demand, i.e. by means of improved staggering of holidays;

-- environmental protection as an important economic basis of tourism;

-- improvement of conditions for those employed in tourism;

-- increased incorporation of new technological and social developments in tourism training (EDP, languages, psychology);

There has been no Austrian tourism concept on an overall federal basis; however several federal provinces have developed concepts of their own.

Institutional framework. In a number of federal provinces new provincial tourism laws transferred competence for marketing matters from official bodies to private legal persons.

The organisation of the Federal Ministry for Economic Affairs, the competent ministry for tourism in Austria, was expanded and now includes a state secretary.

The tourism industry is represented first of all by the Federal Chamber for Economy and/or the Provincial Chambers. The chambers and the independent industrial associations are represented in the co-ordination boards of Austrian tourism. One of the most important co-ordination boards is Österreichischer Fremdenverkehrstag already mentioned above.

The co-ordination of tourism policy with other policies is realised via the Österreichische Fremdenverkehrstag and the Curatorium of Austrian Tourism, but also via the Austrian Zoning Commission and if and when requested also by the Federal Ministry for Economic Affairs.

Action and measures taken in 1989 and 1990

Accommodation. The trend towards well furnished and specialised accommodation (special hotels, holiday apartments) is met by means of modern adaptation. Improved quality refers not only to installation and equipment but also to service, recreation and entertainment. Package offers are developed and promoted (by those providing the facilities) for certain target groups, i.e. tennis, golf, horse-riding, hôtels welcoming children.

Catering. Diversification in the food sector is promoted to give healthy nutrition with national dishes.

Marketing. In co-operation with the Federal Chamber for Economy and the National Austrian Tourism Office a study on the situation of the leisure industry was financed ("Leisure billions"). The scope of tourism and leisure and their importance for Austria's economy were investigated in the framework of this desk research study. The structure of expenditure in tourism and leisure was also examined. Following this study and in line with government agreement, a report on the situation of the tourism and leisure industry in Austria is prepared on an annual basis in Austria and submitted to the National Council.

Preparatory work for the 1991/92 "Guest interviews in Austria", co-financed by the Federal Chamber for Economy, the Austrian National Tourism Office, all Federal Provinces and the Federal Ministry for Economic Affairs, has been completed. In a number of selected communities both domestic and foreign guests will be interviewed on their travel habits during the 1991 summer season and the 1991/92 winter season. A repetition is envisaged in about three years' time. For the first time a so-called "life-style investigation" will be carried out as well. A special evaluation of Austrian guest interviews on health tourism is planned.

A random sample investigation with 1 500 Austrians on sports activities was carried out by the National Austrian Tourism Office.

Preparation and permanent up-dating of the "tourism indicator". This desk research study aims at completing measurements of the quantitative component (above all overnight stays) with the qualitative component (primarily turnover data) in tourism. The Federal Provinces, the National Austrian Tourism Office, the Provincial Chambers and the Federal Ministry for Economic Affairs contributed to the costs. The study is regularly revised.

Marketing strategies and measures, planning of new tourism products. Increased creation of packages in the following sectors: cultural holidays, active or personal experience holidays, sports holidays, adventure holidays, nostalgia holidays.

Transport. To improve staggering of holidays and longer seasons, transport decongestion measures in tourism centres are promoted.

Promotion of economic activities in sensitive areas. Alpine regions are increasingly visited during the summer season. Tourists stay in two types of accommodation: mountain inns and rescue huts which must be adequately modernised and restored (a long-term programme has been prepared in this respect) or rooms rented on a non-commercial basis in family farms which are given financial assistance by the Federal Ministry for Economic Affairs in co-operation with the Federal Ministry for Agriculture and Forestry within the framework of the "Farm Holidays" project.

Environment. The following steps were taken:

-- active participation in the preparation of the "Alpine Convention". Furthermore, a study on "Integrated Alpine Protection" was compiled;

-- the Austrian Association of Communities organised a campaign on "Maintenance of Environment, Culture and Village Style in Austrian Communities".

Employment. In the field of social policy in the tourism industry, initiatives for improved promotion of staff flats for employees in the hotel industry were launched.

Aids and incentives to enterprises for construction. The Austrian Zoning conference set up criteria for discerning tourism promotion areas to be recommended to the respective bodies for consideration for regional promotion.

Protection of the tourist as a consumer. General travel conditions are being re-examined with a view to increasing protection to tourists as consumers.

Staggering of holidays. School holidays were staggered in Austria in order to avoid overlapping with other European countries. The tourism industry also endeavours to better exploit free capacity by means of campaigns to extend the season.

BELGIUM

Tourism as an economic activity

Tourism accounts for 6.2 per cent of GNP (compared with 10.5 per cent for food, 8.1 per cent for transport, 7.5 per cent for housing, taxes and water, 7.2 per cent for health care and toiletries, 6 per cent for consumer durables and 4.8 per cent for clothing and personal items).

At this stage, no long-range forecasting is available.

Government policy

No significant tourism policy change has affected the Tourist Office for the Flemish Community of Belgium (VCGT) since the last Annual Report.

The Decree on enterprises supplying tourist accommodation entered into force on 6 June 1991. Under this Decree, licensed hotels must satisfy stricter fire safety standards. The Decree applies to any enterprise, however constituted, that can provide accommodation for ten or more persons, and all tourist accommodation enterprises have been graded.

On the institutional side, there has been no change in the responsibilities of the tourism authority. French-speaking Community and Flemish Community tourism services together with Sabena have set up BECIB for the purpose of attracting more conference tourism to Belgium.

Tourism policy for Flanders is determined in consultation with representatives of a number of sectors: tourism services at local and provincial level; social tourism, tourism for the young and for adults; camping site operators; travel agencies and enterprises providing tourist accommodation. Policy remains unchanged since 1 January 1989.

Action and measures taken in 1989 and 1990

Vocational training. Several universities have introduced courses in tourism and leisure activities. The French-speaking Community and Flemish Community tourism services have organised regular training courses for local and regional tourism promoters and managers.

Marketing. Since 1989, the tourism services of the two Communities have conducted research on the Spanish market in order to initiate actions in Spain.

In the domestic market, research has been conducted on a more modest scale into the effects of "Vlaanderen Vakantieland", a campaign to promote off-season holidays in Flanders hotels.

In 1991 a new three-year survey of the Belgian population's holiday patterns will be undertaken and in 1992 a new series of marketing surveys covering the Belgian, Netherlands, French, German, United Kingdom and Italian markets will be carried out.

The most important structural concern for the tourism industry is definitely the transition to the single European market, with its implications for competition. Many enterprises are readying themselves for this, especially by recruiting better-qualified personnel.

Protecting the tourist as a consumer. The Belgian authorities are co-operating to develop an EC Directive governing the activities of tour operators. Consumer protection is also receiving considerable attention in the preparation of amendments to update the travel agency legislation.

Staggering of holidays. In spite of pressure from the tourism authority, the Flemish Executive has decided to set the school holiday regulation for a longer period, leaving no scope whatever for holidays to be staggered. For some years, the tourism authority has been conducting its own campaign to promote off-season holidays in Flanders hotels. The results are very hard to measure but they do show that over the years, the custom of taking a succession of shorter holidays has grown.

Environment. Tourism policy is formulated inside a rather closed circuit. However, environmental concerns are being taken into account, with new facilities authorised only after a searching environmental impact study.

CANADA

Tourism as an economic activity

Tourism generated C$26 billion in revenues for Canada in 1990. This is the equivalent of 3.8 per cent of Canada's Gross Domestic Product. The tourism industry alone contributed C$26 billion in value added to the Canadian economy in 1990. This was more than the contribution of either the agriculture or automobile industries, and more than that of the electronics, textiles or steel industries combined.

The revenues generated by the industry have important economic spin-offs. They include C$4.1 billion of investment spending on tourism-related infrastructure across the country. Capital expenditures in hotels averaged C$816 million during 1989 and 1990.

Tourism adds to Canada's export earnings. In 1990, foreign visitors spent over C$7.4 billion in Canada. This makes the tourism industry the fourth largest earner of foreign exchange after motor vehicles, automobile parts, and communication and electronic equipment, ahead of wood pulp, newsprint, lumber and crude petroleum.

The industry employs one in every 20 Canadian workers, or approximately 615 000 persons. The accommodation, food services and transportation sectors dominate the industry labour force. Together, they account for nearly 82 per cent of the total.

Prospects for development

The international tourism market is not projected to grow as fast as it has in the past. The World Tourism Organisation's (WTO) optimistic forecast estimates that international tourist arrivals will grow by 4 per cent per year on average through the 1990s.

In line with these forecasts, the growth in the number of American visitors to Canada is also projected to be modest by past standards. Average annual growth of visits is projected at 1.3 per cent over the next five years.

The growth in non-American markets is expected to be more robust, especially France (6 per cent) and Japan (5.6 per cent). However, only modest growth is projected by the WTO for the United Kingdom (0.7 per cent) and no growth for Germany. International receipts are also expected to grow less rapidly than in the past, 4.9 per cent per annum during the same period.

Different factors come into play in these forecasts. Canada, the United States and the United Kingdom are in a recession and will slowly recover. The exchange rate between Canada and the United States is significantly less favourable to American tourists than it was a few years ago. Several international events will take place in Europe in 1992 which will increase competition. Germany, even with good economic conditions, has an enlarged population more preoccupied with their domestic situation than by international travel. In all overseas countries, fear of terrorism is always a major deterrent to travel.

Maintaining, let alone increasing, a share of overseas markets represents a significant challenge for the Canadian industry in an environment characterised by slowing demand. In the face of intensified competition, an objective clearly is to attract the high-yield, long-haul visitor.

Western Europe offers important opportunities, as does the Asia/Pacific region. Market research indicates that the United Kingdom, France, Germany and Japan are four international markets which show great promise for Canada. Long haul travel is expected to grow faster than intra-European travel. Further, interest in long international trips in this market has approximately doubled over the past three years. In Germany, the incidence has more than doubled from 9 per cent to 24 per cent.

Key Policy Issues.

Understanding the markets:

-- Undertake Research Analysis: the industry needs to research travellers' experiences, products sought and potential for visits within Canada. Cataloguing and assessing internationally competitive products available is also important, along with increased knowledge about the international economic and business developments which may affect tourism.

-- Information to Industry: industry associations can play an important role in disseminating information to smaller operators. The federal government can assist this undertaking by providing timely, analytical information as a business service to the industry through reports, seminars, workshops to assist planning and decision-making.

Developing the Right Products:

-- The Product: the tourism industry needs to continue to work to take advantage of opportunities to develop the products the customer demands, to further package Canadian experiences to create satisfied customers and to provide value for the right price.

-- Human Resource Development: excellent service will generate return visits and word-of-mouth advertising. The skill, knowledge, attitude and efficiency of industry employees determine the level of service. The industry needs to upgrade the labour force skills of its employees.

-- Sustainable Development: the tourism industry and the tourism research community need to work with other industry sectors to protect and upgrade Canada's tourism product -- the environment. The tourism industry must also develop principles and codes of practice to guide the future development of the tourism industry while preserving Canada's reputation for possessing a clean, unspoiled and uncrowded environment.

-- Transportation: the federal and provincial governments are working to ensure that transportation deficiencies do not hinder market access. For example, the federal government will negotiate a new bilateral air services agreement with the United States to improve transborder air services and provide greater access to the most lucrative tourist market in the world. The tourism industry needs to take advantage of new opportunities and work with the transportation industry to attract more tourists.

-- Financing: the tourism industry and the financial institutions need to work together to assist the industry to become better acquainted with business practices and financial planning to improve the prospects of securing financing.

-- Institutional, Regulatory and Legislative Climate: the tourism industry needs to work with federal, provincial and territorial governments to examine ways of reducing the cost of doing business in Canada, including an investigation of interprovincial barriers to trade, incentives for innovation, levels of taxation, etc.

Selling The Product:

-- Marketing: The sector needs to market its products more aggressively by, among other things, raising the awareness of Canada in potential market segments.

-- Reaching the Customer: the tourism industry needs to develop partnerships to establish distribution networks which respond to identified customer needs.

Link between tourism policy and other economic policies

The adoption of the new Federal Tourism Policy signalled the government's commitment to the tourism industry. It also guaranteed that the industry's voice would be heard and its concerns addressed by all federal government departments. For the first time, tourism policy will be taken into account in the development of other government policies.

Government policy

In September 1990, Canada announced its first-ever federal tourism policy. The policy was developed in consultation with provincial and territorial governments and representatives of the tourism industry. It commits the federal government to support the tourism industry in its efforts to achieve renewal and to improve its international competitiveness.

The four pillars of the policy are:

-- recognition of the tourism industry as a strategic sector of the Canadian economy;

-- confirmation of the international focus of federal activity in support of tourism;

-- co-ordination of federal efforts to enhance and improve international competitiveness; and

-- continuing co-operation between the federal government, provincial and territorial governments, and the industry itself.

The policy has these key objectives:

-- to increase international tourism revenues to Canada;

-- to ensure that Canada has the products demanded by the customer;

-- to ensure long-term growth and prosperity for Canadian tourism through a balance between tourism development and maintenance of Canada's physical and cultural environment;

-- to ensure that visitors from Canada's primary international markets can reach Canadian destinations;

-- to harness technology to the task of improved competitiveness;

-- to improve service to visitors through improved training of human resources;

-- to improve the flow of financing to the right demand-driven tourism products;

-- to facilitate the industry's ability to undertake more information-based advocacy and decision making.

The new policy recognises the important role the federal government plays in promoting and supporting excellence and international competitiveness of Canada as an international tourist destination. The government is in an ideal position to accumulate and disseminate the detailed information required to develop effective strategies for the tourism industry. At the same time, based on its information and its position, the government has a leadership role in identifying challenges, articulating concerns, mobilising efforts, and suggesting priorities. Government also promotes the interests of the tourism industry and helps to make Canadians aware of the contribution tourism makes to Canada's social and economic well-being.

In the area of market development, the federal government continues to deliver a comprehensive international tourism marketing programme in Canada's primary markets. The federal government also packages strategic marketing information for dissemination to industry to assist it to spend "smarter" in the markets of greatest potential. It is seeking additional partners to sell particular product lines to high-yield markets. It is exploring new ways of integrating the efforts and expenditures of the federal and provincial/territorial governments and the private sector in the international market place.

In product development, the federal government is encouraging consortia of product suppliers, tour operators, wholesalers and retailers both in Canada and abroad to develop new packaged products. The range of business services offered by the government is being increased and will include a data base on Canadian international-calibre tourism products and suppliers which will be accessible from all Canadian embassies and consulates. Seminars on new products and technologies will be offered and better commercial intelligence will be disseminated to industry decision makers.

The Action Plan for Tourism and Sustainable Development, which emanated from the Globe '90 Conference, outlines issues, principles and areas for action. Under the auspices of the National Round Table on the Environment and the Economy, the Tourism Industry Association of Canada is leading the development of codes of ethics and practices for the Canadian tourism industry. In co-operation with the World Tourism Organisation, Canada is inviting representatives of the international tourism community to discuss industry codes of practice. In addition, indicators are being developed to measure the health of the tourism product.

To improve the exploitation of technology by the tourism industry, the federal government has included the sector in its programming for technology diffusion. It will offer workshops and seminars on the application of new technology in the industry. It will monitor and inform industry partners on the implications of technology applications for human resource planning. It will work closely with industry owner/operators of international travel information networks to ensure that Canadian products are "on-line" with these sales and distribution systems.

The training needs of the industry have been incorporated into the government's Labour Force Development Strategy. A tourism industry representative has been placed on the Labour Force Development Board, which will advise the government on private sector training needs. The federal government will disseminate the results of its work on research standards and certification and career awareness.

To help the tourism industry secure appropriate financing, the federal government will develop an information programme to improve business planning in the industry and an understanding of the industry among financial institutions.

Institutional framework. Tourism Canada is a branch of the new Department of Industry, Science and Technology Canada (ISTC), which was created in 1989. The new department is characterised by its customer-oriented approach to its organisation and operations. Tourism Canada's support to the tourism industry falls within three areas: advocacy, business services and international marketing. The objective of advocacy activities is to position tourism industry considerations in the planning and policies of other federal departments and agencies having an impact upon tourism. Business services include those activities aimed at contributing to the strategic planning and decision- making of both the private sector and government. International marketing is that set of activities aimed at increasing the awareness of Canada in its primary markets, at developing new opportunities in selected markets, and at co-ordinating the marketing efforts of other partners.

The new federal tourism policy recognises that improving the international competitiveness of the tourism industry depends on co-operation among all interested parties to maximise the use of available resources. Industry representatives were consulted extensively in the development of the policy. The Tourism Marketing Council, which works to co-ordinate private and public sector marketing plans, is an example of industry-government co-operation.

The Tourism Industry Association of Canada has struck a task force to examine the key policy issues facing the sector in Canada with a view to influencing public policy.

Action and measures taken in 1989 and 1990

Transport. In 1989, an International Air Policy Task Force was set up to recommend to the government an appropriate international aviation policy in light of emerging global trade, cargo and travel patterns, and emerging trends in the airline industry world-wide. The Task Force is mandated to examine the role air services play in supporting Canada's tourism strategy. In addition, a Royal Commission on Passenger Transportation was formed in October 1989 to inquire into and report on a national integrated inter-city passenger transportation system to meet the needs of Canada in the 21st century. This review will include all modes of transportation - road, air, rail and marine. Also in October 1990, Canada and the United States announced their decisions to renegotiate a more liberalised transborder air services regime.

Employment. The Tourism Industry Standards and Certification Committee, chaired by Tourism Canada, was established to co-ordinate the development of occupational standards and nationally-recognised industry-based certification programs. To date, occupational standards and certification programs have been established for more than 20 occupations. Another 20 occupations are under development. A Federal-Provincial/Territorial Working Group on Tourism Industry Human Resource Issues was established to provide a forum for governments to share information on and co-ordinate their human resource policies and programs. The working group has undertaken a labour market study to document the size, structure, characteristics and growth patterns of the tourism industry labour force. It will also provide demand and supply projections for the labour force. A first draft report is expected this summer. With respect to training, more than 400 programmes in tourism-related subjects are offered in 28 universities and 93 community colleges. The majority of these are at the community college level -- 100 in hotel and restaurant management; 140 in cooking; 45 in the service of food and alcohol. There are 41 undergraduate university courses in tourism related studies.

Accommodation. In all regions of Canada, there is a growing recognition of the need to establish uniform grading standards for the accommodation sector. The Tourism Industry Association of Canada has commissioned a two-phase study which will research consumer and travel trade perceptions and expectations on accommodation grading and standards, and will establish a strategy and action plan for the implementation of a national programme. At the completion of the study in the fall of 1991, the various provincial and territorial jurisdictions will assess their level of participation with a view to implementing a national standards program in 1992-1993.

Marketing research. A syndicated survey of the United States' pleasure travel market (1989 U.S. Pleasure Travel Market - Canada's Progress and Challenges) was conducted in 1989. This was an update of a survey which has been the blueprint for Canada's advertising campaigns since 1985. The 1989 survey was designed to measure the impact of Canada's marketing efforts since 1985 and examine specific segments of the market in more detail.

The methodology used an occasion-based segmentation model which acknowledges the reality that the same people seek different vacation experiences at different times of the year and that the market is driven by different types of trips, not by types of travellers. The trip types previously identified as important for Canada included the touring trip, city trip and outdoor vacation. In 1989, a business/pleasure trip type was added to the segmentation analysis.

The findings of the 1989 study include:

-- overall potential pleasure travellers have grown from 130 million in 1985 to 139 million in 1989;

-- Canada's touring and city trip types have shown substantial growth during the four years;

-- Canada's image has been significantly enhanced - for touring, city and outdoor vacations. Canada is now seen as a more enjoyable place to visit than the United States;

-- the challenge that remains is to close the sale with retail advertising, focusing on price, product and packages.

As part of a continuing series of studies examining the pleasure travel market to North America and in co-operation with the United States Travel and Tourism Administration, a study of the markets in the United Kingdom, France, Germany and Japan was completed in 1989.

These four markets had been studied in 1986, but due to the fast growth of travel from these countries, it was decided to update and track the results from these markets somewhat earlier than originally anticipated.

The study uses a random probability cluster sampling procedure with respondents who were 18 years of age or older who had taken a trip of four nights or longer by plane in the past three years, or who intended to take such a trip in the next two years. For European travellers, trips were defined as being to destinations outside Europe or the Mediterranean. For Japanese travellers, trips were to destinations outside Japan and South Korea. Approximately 1 200 personal, in-home interviews averaging 50 minutes in length were conducted in each country.

The studies provide broad-based marketing information on the long haul pleasure travel market; identify and describe travel segments that are prime targets for travel to Canada and the United States; describe elements of the travel products required to meet the needs of the target market segments; and describe the ways in which the respective markets have changed since 1986.

Similar studies as described above have been completed in South Korea and Venezuela.

In addition to the two country specific market studies, a secondary analysis of the 1989 United Kingdom and Japanese data bases was conducted from the point of view of the city travel market and package tour travel market. Supplementary data collection was also used to complement the secondary analyses. The results of the 1990 work will be released over the next few months.

In 1990, a joint government-industry study was commissioned to better understand Canada's competitive positioning with respect to the price and the quality of its products.

The Price/Value Perceptions study involved an extensive multiphased research approach structured into four data collection components which were designed to confer with both actual and potential pleasure travellers at various stages of their travel decision-making process. Altogether, over 10 800 interviews were conducted from the United States and also from Canada. Visitors from Japan, Germany, the United Kingdom and France were also included in the study, because of the increasing importance of these non-American markets.

Overall, the results clearly indicated that Canada is in a favourable position with respect to its tourism products. All visitors in general, but American visitors in particular, are extremely positive about returning to Canada and, more importantly, about recommending it. Moreover, their level of satisfaction with their pleasure trip was extremely high.

With a few exceptions, prices in Canada were considered to be higher than in the United States for tourism products and services of comparable quality. Canadians perceived prices in Canada to be significantly higher than any of the United States and non-American group surveyed. Although prices were considered to be high, so were the corresponding quality ratings. The vast majority of American visitors considered the quality in Canada to be the same or better than in the United States.

The role of price was examined from a number of perspectives corresponding with the stages in the decision-making process. At the initial stage in selecting a destination, the study shows that prices were not the most important factor. Relatively speaking, however, they become more important depending on the destination selected. Compared to other destinations such as the United States, Europe and southern destinations, price was least important for travel to Canada. Prices were, however, considered to be much more important when selecting the various components of a trip such as transportation, accommodation, meals and shopping, and especially as it pertained to the selection of a travel package.

Marketing. While Tourism Canada's marketing priority continued to be the development of international markets, 1989 and 1990 were transition years for the federal tourism marketing program.

Recognising that the easy marketing days of double digit growth from international markets were drawing to a close, Tourism Canada and its public and private sector colleagues joined together to address challenges such as changes in demographics and travel patterns, rapid changes in the economies of primary markets, and an increasingly competitive market-place. The result was a series of significant changes in how the federal government operates, and with which partners.

In line with the new Federal Tourism Policy, Tourism Canada's marketing strategy will:

-- continue to deliver an international marketing program in Canada's primary international markets -- the United States, Japan, the United Kingdom, France and Germany;

-- package strategic marketing information for dissemination to industry in order that it can spend "smarter" in the markets of greatest potential;

-- seek additional partners in order to sell particular product lines, including a new emphasis on promoting getaway travel and Canada's fall and winter products, to high-yield, high-potential markets -- primarily touring, city, heritage/culture and outdoors travel experiences to up-scale senior citizens and double-income household families, and meetings, conventions and incentive travel experiences to business travel targets;

-- explore new ways of integrating the efforts and expenditures of the federal and provincial/territorial governments and the private sector in the international market-place.

As such, Tourism Canada's marketing objective is to contribute to an increase in tourism export revenue growth from the United States, the United Kingdom, Japan, Germany, France and selected emerging overseas markets:

-- by raising the awareness of Canada as an international travel destination;

-- by strengthening Canada's image as a major international travel destination with a distinct identity; and,

-- by assisting selected members of the Canadian and foreign tourism industries through a variety of trade development programs and the dissemination of market information and expertise.

Major marketing measures undertaken in 1989 and 1990 included:

-- development of a new medium-term (1990/91-1992/93) meetings, conventions and incentive travel (MCIT) program designed to increase foreign receipt earnings by enhancing the international competitiveness and export performance of Canada's MCIT industry in the United States and overseas;

-- implementation of a re-shaped 1990 United States multi-season television and print advertising program, including four new television commercials, designed to further break down existing stereotypes, to enrich favourable impressions of Canada, and to personalise the Canadian travel experience;

-- hosted in 1990, in co-operation with the respective Canadian provinces, cities and private sector:

  . the Pacific Asia Travel Association Annual Conference in Vancouver, British Columbia, and the Travel Mart in Edmonton, Alberta (2 000 delegates from 36 countries);

  . the National Tour Association Annual Convention and Tour and Travel Exchange in Montreal, Quebec (3 500 delegates - American market); and,

  . the American Bus Association Annual Convention and Market Place in Niagara Falls, Ontario (2 500 delegates - American market);

-- levered, over 1989 and 1990, approximately C$23.6 million from public and private sector partners for co-operative international marketing;

-- conducted a series of major program reviews in the primary market countries with the Department of External Affairs and International Trade (EAITC), which delivers local tourism programme activities at missions and posts abroad under Tourism Canada's direction, e.g., marketing, media relations;

-- opened up participation by the Canadian tourism industry in three EAITC market development programmes to develop their international sales opportunities:

  . New Exporters to Border States (NEBS), which provides businesses that have not previously been exporters to the United States market with initial information on how to develop markets and sales in the United States;

  . New Exporters to United States South (NEXUS), a complementary program to NEBS, designed to encourage small to medium sized companies, which have already demonstrated some success in their export efforts to border states, to expand their export markets to the American southwest and southeast; and,

  . New Exporters to Overseas (NEXOS), designed to encourage small and medium sized Canadian companies which have traded traditionally with the United States to expand their activities overseas into Western Europe;

-- established, with EAITC, an "Emerging and Secondary Market Opportunities" programme to assist the industry to take advantage of significant tourism marketing opportunities in secondary and emerging markets.

Environment. Following extensive consultations with industry, governments, associations and the Canadian public, the government issued a paper, entitled Canada Green Plan for a Healthy Environment in 1990. Included in the many proposals are the following goals relevant to tourism:

-- to expand Canada's national parks system by establishing new parks so as to set aside a protected space equal to 12 per cent of the country;

-- to maintain and enhance the health and diversity of Canada's wildlife and plants;

-- to commemorate and protect the historical heritage of Canada and to establish 15 new historic sites.

Canada's federal tourism policy approved by the government in 1990 supports the Canadian government policy of operating within a sustainable development philosophy. Increasingly, proposed tourism development projects are undergoing environmental impact assessments.

The Government of Canada organised Globe '90, the first in a series of biannual international conferences on environment and economy. The Conference comprised 18 different streams. The Tourism stream addressed the issue of integrated resource planning and demonstrated through practical case studies how competing industrial sectors can successfully coexist. The stream examined the environmental impact of other resource users on the tourism industry and suggested ways for the tourism sector to cope with the changes.

The Tourism Stream of Globe '90 produced a document entitled "An Action Strategy for Sustainable Tourism Development". This Action Strategy incorporates broad guiding principles, states measurable objectives and outlines specific actions and recommendations to be undertaken on a global basis by governments, businesses, industries and individual tourists to achieve sustainable tourism development goals.

The recommendations from the Tourism Stream of the Globe '90 Conference were passed to Canada's National Round Table on Economy and Environment which agreed later that year to launch a separate national dialogue on tourism and the environment which will last from February 1991 to February 1992. It is hoped to be able to reach consensus on developing several environmental codes of practice for several sectors of the tourism industry.

Taxation. The needs of the tourism industry were taken into account in the design of the new Goods and Services Tax. A non-resident rebate programme provides visitors to Canada with a rebate of the tax paid on accommodation and on goods taken out of the country. In addition, foreign convention organisers are eligible for a rebate of up to 70 per cent of the tax paid on conventions in Canada.

International co-operation. The Canada/USA Free Trade Agreement (FTA) is expected to produce important benefits for the tourism industry in all regions of the country. The Tourism Annex, together with other measures in the Agreement itself, will enable owners and operators of tourism services and facilities to benefit from increased opportunities and easier access to the United States by:

-- eliminating barriers to trade in goods and services;

-- facilitating conditions of fair competition;

-- liberalising conditions for investment;

-- establishing a dispute mechanism to resolve any future problems; and

-- laying a foundation for further co-operation.

The phased reduction of tariffs contained in the Free Trade Agreement will lead to lower costs for many aspects of the tourism industry. These tariffs, some as high as 25 per cent, add significant costs to many products and materials used in the industry, (e.g., food, hotel and restaurant equipment).

The liberalisation of investment rules between the two countries will also benefit tourism. Tourism entrepreneurs should find it easier to attract much needed investment capital from the United States to develop new products and expand and upgrade existing facilities.

The Tourism Annex of the FTA established a Canada-U.S. Working Group on Tourism. It provides for the parties to consult at least once a year to:

identify and seek to eliminate impediments to trade in tourism services, and

-- identify ways to facilitate and increase tourism between the two countries.

To date, two meetings have been held; the first in 1989 and the second in 1990. The first meeting focused on exchanging information and establishing lines of communication. The second agreed on several co-operative initiatives such as renewal of the Canada -- US. Memorandum of Understanding on Research and communicating information on Canada's Goods and Service Tax to the United States travel community.

In 1990, Canada signed a tourism co-operation agreement with Mexico to facilitate travel between the two countries. The agreement provides a vehicle to encourage projects of mutual interest to either governments or private-sector organisations in the two countries. It also recognises the benefits of eliminating obstacles affecting the movement of people and the operation of tourism and tourism-related businesses.

In October, 1990, Canada and the United States announced their intention to negotiate a new, more liberalised, bilateral air services agreement. The Canadian tourism industry has been recognised as an important stakeholder, whose interests will be taken into account in the course of the negotiations.

DENMARK

Government policy

There have been no changes in general tourism policy objectives and priorities since the 1st January 1989. Tourism has become even more important to the Danish economy and, as a result of this recognition, the Minister of Industry, presented in Spring 1991 an updated "Statement on Tourism Policy" to the Danish Parliament.

The tourism action plan, which was introduced in the very first "statement on tourism policy" in 1986, is still active, though some of the initiatives in the action plan have been changed. The aid scheme aiming at strengthening the marketing of Denmark to the Danes and the aid scheme encouraging product development within the tourism industry have been replaced by an aid scheme aiming at strengthening the co-operation between individual tourism industries and public or semi-public institutions. Although there is no specific aid scheme, the staggering of holidays or, as we prefer to say, the creation of new seasons is a priority area in tourism policy.

Actions and measures taken in 1989 and 1990

The Ministry of Environment, the Joint Council of the Danish Tourist Trade, which is an umbrella organisation for the professional associations within the tourist trade, and the National Tourism Council are co-operating in order to formulate a common strategy for a differentiated development in tourism in different regions of the country. The aim of this work is to allow the tourism industry an appropriate expansion without doing any damage to the environment.

Since August 1989, great efforts have been made by the educational secretariat, which is led by the Joint Council of the Danish Tourist Trade, to formulate education programmes in all levels to those who already have a job in the tourism industry and those who want to work in the tourism industry.

Market research. The Danish Travel Analysis was conducted in 1991 and surveyed the domestic market, its characteristics, travel practices and attitudes towards tourism in Denmark and abroad. The Norway analysis 1989 surveyed Norwegian families, their characteristics, and the significance of the marketing campaign. The Spanish, French and Italian markets were surveyed through the European Travel Monitor. The Japanese market has been analysed in a common Nordic survey.

Marketing. Over the period 1989-90, marketing efforts concentrated on eight markets: Denmark, Norway, Sweden, Germany, the Netherlands, the United Kingdom, Finland and the United States, labelled as primary markets. All major efforts were concentrated here.

Staggering of holidays. The Joint Council of the Danish Tourist Trade has taken several initiatives in order to achieve a better staggering of holidays in Denmark. Besides that, the Danish government seeks to stimulate holiday-making during the off-peak periods through activities within the tourism action plan, e.g. by giving high priorities to off-season projects within the aid schemes.

International co-operation. Denmark co-operates with the other Nordic countries in the field of tourism within the framework of the general Nordic co-operation.

FINLAND

Impact of tourism as an economic activity

In 1990, travel account receipts totalled MkF 4.6 billion, i.e. approximately 4 per cent of goods and services exports. Tourism ranks sixth among the export industries, behind manufacture of fabricated metal products, machinery and equipment (35.5 billion), manufacture of paper and paper products (31.7 billion), manufacture of chemicals (9.5 billion), basic metal industries (8.1 billion) and manufacture of wood and wood products (7.8 billion). The share of tourism receipts of the export of services was roughly 24 per cent.

According to a recent report, tourism generated employment equivalent to 76 000 man-years. The biggest employer in tourism is the transport sector with 26 000 jobs, followed by the accommodation and catering sector with 19 000 jobs.

Prospects for development

The biggest problem at present for the Finnish tourism industry is the decreased price competitiveness of the industry. Of vital importance is therefore an economic policy which would lower the price level in Finland as compared to other countries.

In its budget proposal for the years 1991-1995 the Finnish Tourist Board has set as its goal to increase income from tourism by 1 billion FIM in real terms during the planning period. The precondition for achieving this goal is however, *inter alia*, that the conditions of competition for the Finnish tourism industry are made identical with the conditions in the EC-countries. In the long run Finland, like the other Nordic countries, has good potential for increasing tourism from abroad. A relatively well preserved environment, plenty of space, a high level of services are the among the features which form the basis for the optimistic view for tourism in Finland in the future.

Link between tourism policy and other economic policies

The Ministry of Trade and Industry has set up a follow-up group on tourism policy representing nine ministries; this group will co-ordinate the tourism-linked measures and projects in the various administrative sectors. In addition, co-ordination of tourism policy and economic policy is being carried out by the Advisory Board for Tourism.

Government policy

The general tourism policy objectives and priorities from 1989 onwards followed the guidelines set up in the "Council of State guidelines for the development of tourism in 1989-1992" from December 1988, (as described in the Annual report of 1989).

The new Finnish government, which was installed in April 1991 declared in its programme that the price competitiveness of the tourism industry will be improved as tourism is an activity which creates foreign currency and substitutes import of services.

A development plan for tourism in Finland to the year 2000 - "Tourism 2000" - was finalised during 1991. The plan, which concentrates on the most vital questions for the future development of tourism in Finland, could lead to a renewed version of the "Council of State guidelines for the development of tourism".

Institutional framework. The Finnish Tourism Board was reorganised in 1989 to reflect the role of the board as a marketing organisation. A new post of deputy director general, with the overall responsibility for marketing activities, was created. The former three-departement organisation was changed to a two-department organisation, giving the marketing department a better organisational structure. The marketing activities abroad and in Finland were organised to the benefit of groups which, in the case of foreign markets means a group of several countries with similar market conditions. This means *inter alia* that decision making has been delegated downwards in the organisation as the profit groups have quite far-reaching powers to decide how to use their marketing budget.

In March 1991 the number of Finnish Tourist Board offices abroad was increased by an office in Tokyo, which means that the tourist board at present has 14 offices abroad. Besides Japan the office in Tokyo is also responsible for marketing activities in Hong Kong, South Korea, Taiwan and also Australia.

The tourism industry is represented in the Board of Directors of the Finnish Tourist Board by four members of a total of nine members. The state administration is also represented by four members and the ninth member is the director general for the Finnish Tourist Board.

For the purpose of the general promotion and development of tourism and the related industries, as well as of the co-operation taking place in that field, the Ministry of Trade and Industry appoints an Advisory Board for Tourism for three years at a time on which the various sectors of the tourism industry are represented.

Action and measures taken in 1989 and 1990

Accommodation. A new Decree on the Accommodation and Catering Business (19 April 1991; 727/91) will take effect as from the beginning of 1992. This amendment means cancelling the present system of business licences and permitting operation of a business merely on the basis of registration. The administrative procedure connected with the starting of operations will be facilitated and, at the same time, the supervision of the accommodation and catering business will be essentially eased.

Catering services. Following the Council of State guidelines some licences for food imports have been granted direct to restaurants.

Travel agencies. In 1991, an amended decree on travel agencies, co-ordinated with the 1990 EC directive concerning conducted tours, was under preparation. The decree will probably come into effect during 1992.

Research. The two most important studies carried out by the Finnish Tourist Board is a holiday survey concerning the national market and a visitor survey concerning markets abroad.

The holiday survey has been carried out biannually, but from 1991 on it is a continuous (every four month) survey which will also include business travel. By modifying the frequency of the travel monitor, changes in demand and patterns of travel can be observed more rapidly, which is vital for marketing planning.

The most important study on the international market is the annual visitor survey, in which about 4 000 foreign tourists are interviewed when leaving Finland. The survey includes questions on decision making, use of travel agency, type of trip (business, congress, leisure), reasons for choosing Finland as a holiday destination, places visited in Finland, etc. and the expenditure pattern for tourists from the different markets. The information on expenditure patterns is especially important for the measurement of the economic result of the marketing activities carried out by the Finnish Tourist Board and the tourism industry.

Marketing. To make the marketing activities more effective a strategic marketing planning system was introduced in 1990. Special attention was paid to the measurement of the effectiveness of marketing.

The main strategy concerning the domestic market is to create new tourism demand for domestic holidays and to inform the domestic customer about the possibilities Finland can offer as a holiday destination; several tools are used:

-- The most important one is the Holiday-Finland brochure, which is distributed to 1.5 million households twice a year (summer and winter).

-- To create new demand for holidays in Finland, a short-break holiday project was started in 1989 together with the tourism industry. As a result of the project, product development and marketing of short break holidays has increased significantly.

-- A farmhouse holiday and car tourism project were started on the domestic market to increase domestic tourism.

-- In the winter season downhill skiing in Finland was promoted heavily as during the last few years it has become more and more popular. The emphasis in the marketing was in particular to promote the shoulder months of the winter season for which there is already sufficient demand.

In 1989 and 1990 the marketing activities of the Finnish Tourist Board were further concentrated on those tourism products which are strong areas in Finnish tourism. These were, *inter alia*, farmhouse holidays, activity holidays, round-trips in Finland, car tourism, combined tours Finland/Scandinavia and Finland/Soviet Union, incentive travel and congresses.

To increase product development and strengthen the marketing of the above-mentioned areas, projects with the tourism industry were started.

In 1989 and 1990 the Finnish Tourist Board together with the tourism industry participated in a great number of tourism fairs and exhibitions. Together with the other Nordic countries the board arranged and took part in the Fifth Nordic Travel Mart in Reykjavik in 1991. In Finland the most important sales meeting was the Finland Purpuri Travel Market, which was arranged in Helsinki in May 1990.

Around 1 000 representatives for foreign media were annually invited to Finland, partly in close co-operation with the Finnish Foreign Trade Association, the Foreign Ministry, Finnfacts and the tourism industry.

Together with the other Nordic countries, Finland started a big marketing campaign in the United States, "Focus on Scandinavia", which was partly financed by the Nordic Council of Ministers. This campaign is continuing into 1992.

Protection of the tourist as a consumer. The Ministry of Trade and Industry has appointed a working group to prepare an amendment to the trade legislation; this working group is also working on the Amendment to the Decree on Travel Agencies. The amendment aims at improving consumer protection.

International co-operation. Finland (The Finnish Tourist Board) participated in the programme of the European Year of Tourism 1990. Co-operation with other Nordic countries continued in the Nordic Tourist Board, which is an organisation for the Nordic NTO's. The most important field of co-operation was the "Focus on Scandinavia" marketing campaign in the United States.

On the governmental level Finland participated in the work of the Nordic Council of Ministers Tourism Committee. The Committee is a forum for co-operation for the Nordic countries with the aim of promoting tourism to and within the Nordic countries and to further develop the tourism industry in the Nordic countries.

To achieve these goals the committee works in close co-operation with the Nordic Tourist Board. It initiates and finances projects with the above mentioned goals and is a forum for the co-ordination of tourism policy in the Nordic countries and for Nordic co-operation in international organisations.

FRANCE

Tourism as an economic activity

In France 1989 and 1990 were particularly good years for tourism. Domestic tourism consumption amounted to FF 436 billion in 1989 and FF 460 billion in 1990. At this figure, tourism is contributing as much as agriculture to the country's economy, representing over 7 per cent of gross national product and as much as 9 per cent if tourism-related consumption is included.

In 1990 France consolidated its position as second-ranking tourism country, behind the United States but ahead of Spain. The surplus on tourism account which was some FF 24 billion in 1988 rose to FF 39.6 billion in 1989 (admittedly the bicentenary year), FF 42 billion in 1990 and close to FF 50 million in 1991. Thus tourism is making an essential contribution to France's foreign trade equilibrium.

The industry employs about 900 000 people, over 500 000 of them as wage-earners. Net job creation is in the region of 30 000 per year.

Prospects for development

An industrial strategy group has been formed. With six workshops, its task is to study major developments that could affect the tourism industry.

Aspects selected for investigation are:

-- consumer behaviour;

-- tourism consumption forecasts;

-- analysis of foreign competition: customer profiles of France's main rivals, their policy as concerns products, and product promotion and marketing. Also studied are the part played by government and the tax and legal environment;

-- avenues for development and policies to be applied; the aim is to propose tourism strategies for France;

-- training and organisation of work: this Workshop deals with training and certification issues and also with school holiday calendar scheduling as a constraint on the industry

-- Promotion and marketing: the focus here is on methods of marketing the more promising products;

The Ministry for Tourism has to date entered into four formal agreements with other government departments. Among those agreements, attention may be drawn in particular to:

-- an agreement with the Ministry for Culture on a number of joint activities: a competition for the most welcoming museum or monument, joint creation of cultural tourism products,

-- an agreement with the Ministry for the Environment, in which the main purpose is to promote nature tourism, protect the country's environmental heritage and encourage local development by fostering tourism-related activities.

Even in the absence of formal agreements, a number of joint activities are being carried out: with the Ministry of Transport, for example, on such matters as tourism-related road signs and the classification of motor coaches for tourism purposes.

Government policy

In a communication to the Cabinet on 10 October 1990, the Minister for Tourism defined three major priorities for action:

-- devoting particular attention to man and his relationship with his environment

-- exploiting the diversity of the tourism heritage

-- promoting quality

The three priorities are reflected in 12 activities:

1. Continued promotion abroad of French tourism, by the Maison de la France

2. Establishing a tourism observatory in the form of an association of government departments, local authorities, representatives of the industry, universities and researchers who are well placed to observe developments in France. The observatory's purpose will be to collect all available tourism-related data, analyse them and circulate the findings.

3. Updating the range of tourism products.

4. Training, with four priority aspects: hospitality, management, marketing and foreign languages, paying special attention to the self-employed.

5. Upgrading of jobs by encouraging collective bargaining in order to retain high-quality personnel in the tourism industry.

6. Modernisation of the independent hotel sector. This is expected to involve 5 000 hotels.

7. Exploiting French know-how in tourism infrastructure by providing technical back-up for exporting it.

8. Promoting "social" tourism (for lower-income groups), by redefining support for construction to take account of change in the economic and social environment and by providing more assistance to the individual.

9. Supporting tourism in the overseas departments and territories.

10. Developing inland tourism, especially its two main components, rural tourism and cultural tourism.

11. Encouraging change in mountain tourism, by extending the season and diversifying activities.

12. Promoting high-quality coastal tourism, especially by making the local authorities concerned more aware of their responsibilities in the matter.

A Parliamentary Bill laid before the Cabinet on 10 April 1991 would amend the 1975 Act in order to incorporate the EC Directive on package travel. The Bill would:

-- make the regulations concerning the marketing of tourism products less restrictive, by entitling certain categories of operators (hotels, carriers) to market products on behalf of their clients, subject to certain conditions;

-- strengthen consumer protection, by stiffening penalties and controlling access to the profession more strictly.

Proposed legislation on the territorial organisation of tourism has also received Ministry backing. Territorial units would be created to award labels for tourism products in three categories: holiday resorts, conference-centre cities, and inter-communal rural tourism groupings (GITER).

They would fulfil a variety of functions: in the welcoming of tourists (especially by developing accommodation capacity), in devising attractions, in maintenance, information and promotion, also security (especially by making resources available as appropriate for the numbers of tourists).

Institutional framework. A Decree of 30 August 1989 made certain changes to the administrative structure of the Ministry for Tourism.

A new Directorate for Tourism Industries is in most respects successor to the former Directorate for the Tourism Industry. The new Directorate has three Sub-Directorates:

-- general administration;

-- economic monitoring, research and forecasting;

-- tourism professions, tourism policy, together with a Department for International Affairs and Reception.

A Delegation for Tourism Investment and Products encourages the development and adaptation of tourism facilities and products. The Delegation has three divisions:

- -- a technical division, consisting of a technical development and product service and an R&D service for mountain tourism (SEATM);
- -- a sub-directorate collecting policy data from relevant public sector agencies (local authorities, other government departments);
- -- a financial consultancy department to advise on arranging finance for tourism development and the export of French know-how.

In addition, the Maison de la France, established in 1987 as a "groupement d'intérêt économique" (GIE), operates abroad to promote France as a tourism destination.

The National Tourism Council, an advisory body to the Minister for Tourism is the structure which enables industry representatives to be associated, in accordance with the regulations, in the framing of tourism policy.

The Council has a wide field of competence. It can advise on:

- -- any matter referred to it by the Minister for Tourism, or recommended to him by the "Steering Committee" as a question for review;
- -- tourism-related objectives of the Plan, receiving progress reports;
- -- long-range forecasting;
- -- by government departments, on laws or regulations that might have an impact on tourism.
- -- the Council receives reports on national and regional programmes to promote France abroad as a tourism destination;
- -- the Council provides a forum for the discussion of agreements negotiated between branches of the tourism industry and providers of tourism services.

The Council is chaired by the Minister for Tourism. It comprises 182 full members:

- -- 27 representatives of tourism committees etc. in the regions;
- -- 71 representatives of tourism organisations;
- -- 23 qualified persons appointed by the Minister for Tourism;
- -- 61 technical advisors appointed by the Minister for Tourism.

During the difficult Gulf crisis, the Council established a liaison committee to maintain close contact with every part of the industry, as a way of assessing the conflict's immediate repercussions on tourism and devising appropriate, widely-agreed measures.

Another development has been the formation within the National Tourism Council of a National Committee for Foreign Trade in Tourism, whose function is to build up tourism's contribution to the balance of payments. This Committee consists of representatives drawn from all the leading tourism exporting companies.

Actions and measures taken in 1989 and 1990

Development of supply. On the supply side, tourism services as well as tourism products have been receiving attention, while action has also been taken in certain special fields, such as environmental protection and social tourism.

Reference has already been made to updating the stock of independent hotels as one of the Ministry's twelve priorities. This concerns about 15 000 hotels and 300 000 rooms, which the industry might otherwise lose in the short or medium term.

Under a three-part "renovation, training, production" scheme, the individual hotelier would finance 70 per cent of the cost of renovation, with government and local authorities covering the remaining 30 per cent.

With better-performing, more profitable tourism companies in view, the Ministry for Tourism has been keen to develop training. It is mainly concerned with in-service training, since initial training is a matter for the Education Ministry. The Tourism Ministry has been developing a policy of encouraging the various branches of the industry, its companies, its institutional networks, to work out what they really need in terms of qualifications and training. The Ministry has entered into planning contracts with tourism associations, and is making similar arrangements for the hotel and catering side.

The Ministry for Tourism has also funded development of national training guidelines for the Fédération Nationale des Offices de Tourisme et Syndicats d'Initiative, and a training plan for the Fédération Nationale des Gîtes de France (self-catering, farmhouse or bed and breakfast accommodation in rural areas).

The Ministry also supports training for seasonal workers, who account for one third of employees, especially in hotels and catering, through a variety of courses which the industry provides.

The Ministry is taking considerable pains to promote the tourism trades, by funding explanatory brochures on the different trades and sending representatives to support members of those trades at the major fairs and shows open to young people and students.

A number of tourism products have received development support:

-- rural tourism: 50 million nights spent, 20 per cent by foreign visitors. The aim is to develop product ranges (rambling, nature parks, fishing);

-- mountain tourism: following difficulties in recent years, policy is shifting towards product diversification and extending the season, while seeking to maintain orderly growth in property development;

-- waterway tourism: this is growing, with 120 companies recorded in 1989 and 170 000 locations;

-- golf: a fast-growing sector, with 305 golf courses in 1989 as against 136 in 1981, and an expected 560 by the end of the decade. Growth prospects are good as France has excellent potential for developing golf;

-- leading national beauty spots: current policy to enhance these covers, among others, the Ardèche gorges, the Cirque de Gavarnie, Cap Fréhel and the Pointe du Raz;

-- business tourism: in this key sector, promotion trips are receiving special attention.

Tourism policy has taken three main practical forms up to now:

-- Provision of tourism facilities and moderately priced accommodation in underprivileged areas;

-- Assistance to the individual, and particularly, since 1982, the holiday voucher scheme (3 million recipients in 1991);

-- Help for construction, FF 33.3 million in grants to associations during 1991.

Present trends are to step up assistance to the individual, by extending the holiday voucher scheme (especially to SMEs) and by introducing a second reduced-fare ticket, subject to a ceiling.

Another trend is to step up public support for certain underprivileged or marginalised groups (young people in suburbs, the handicapped). It is also policy to provide back-up for associations as they evolve, particularly by helping them with management and with product diversification.

Marketing. Since 1990, tourism observation has been substantially improved. In 1991 a permanent frontier survey was introduced; previously such surveys had been only occasional. Since April 1990 a monthly survey has been conducted of residents' travel, with a "residents' holidays" survey twice a year. A survey of hotel occupancy is carried out every month, and of camping sites every season. In order to adjust its strategy to changes in international demand, the Maison de la France systematically collects and utilises data to improve its understanding of foreign markets and identify potential customers. Data are analysed by the Marketing Department, which formulates broad promotion strategy together with individual market approaches and produces country studies. For remoter markets, the strategy is to make

Paris the point of entry into Europe and then encourage tourists to discover the regions. For nearer markets, France is promoted as the No. 1 short-stay destination on grounds of its favourable price/quality ratio. In accordance with the specific strategy for each market a promotion campaign is planned in each country. This consists of joint operations in the form of advertising, public relation exercises, press conferences, trade fairs, workshops and translations. Priority markets are Germany, the United Kingdom, the United States, Japan and Italy.

Environment. Environmental concerns are increasingly reflected in approaches to tourism issues. A seminar on the topic at La Rochelle on 13 and 14 May 1991 attracted 400 elected representatives.

On the other hand developing nature tourism has been the main policy thrust for protecting rural and coastal areas from uncontrolled building or other development. In addition the "labelling" concept, along the lines of the existing "Pavillon bleu" ("blue flag") scheme.

Protecting the tourist as a consumer. This is a constant concern for the tourism authorities and is reflected in the various regulations applying to the industry. Laws and regulations governing the marketing of tourism products require tour operators and suppliers of accommodation to comply with certain conditions and meet certain obligations, thereby providing consumers with the necessary guarantees. Existing legislation stems from the Act of 11 July 1975 and amendments are in preparation to strengthen consumer protection.

The parliamentary Bill in preparation would introduce all the provisions of the EC Directive on package travel of 13 June 1990 and to this end, redefines the general conditions of sale and the tourism supplier's liability vis-à-vis the customer. It would also strengthen penalties for engaging illegally in the travel agency business, while the financial guarantees required to cover reimbursement and repatriation if necessary would be increased.

Staggered holidays. During the period under consideration, this has mainly involved school winter holidays. The way these are concentrated in the month of February has several undesirable consequences:

- for companies, which cannot operate their facilities profitably;
- for families, especially those on lower incomes, whose only chance of a winter holiday is during the peak-rate season;
- for holiday-makers generally, as transport networks become congested or seize up altogether at this time.

A joint working party drawn from the Education Council and the Tourism Council, called upon to suggest changes to the school calendar, has made two recommendations:

- dividing the country up into three distinct geographical areas for school calendar purposes;
- bringing the Spring holidays forward.

In a Decree of 4th April, the Minister for Education gave effect to these recommendations.

International co-operation. The Department's main international activity has been in following up a) EC matters, b) development of bilateral co-operation and c) development of multilateral co-operation.

a) EC matters: in 1990, France participated actively in preparing and organising the European Tourism Year which formally closed in Nice on 30 May 1991.

   The Ministry for Tourism oversees implementation of the different proposed EC directives having implications for tourism industries (harmonisation of indirect taxation, "atypical" employment, working hours, impact of development on the environment, recognition of diplomas, etc.)

   An important decision on improving tourism statistics was taken by the Council of European Ministers for Tourism on 29 November 1990.

b) Bilateral co-operation: following visits by tourism ministers and industry leaders from abroad, and recent visits by Mr Baylet (to the USSR, Tunisia and Morocco), co-operation on tourism was strengthened, as reflected in the signature of agreements between France and 15 other countries. As well as the co-operation represented by those agreements, several requests for assistance, especially with training, are under consideration.

c) Multilateral co-operation: Participation by the Ministry for Tourism in the work of international organisations fostering tourism is essential if France is to retain its leading rank in the world.

   The World Tourism Organisation (WTO). France plays an especially important role in this international organisation. Because of its responsibilities, especially in budgeting and in the statute reform process currently under way, the Ministry for Tourism is regularly present at meetings of the WTO's Council and Commissions. France has also contributed effectively to the work of the WTO's various technical commissions, especially those whose purpose is to facilitate the growth of international tourism and improve the quality of the services offered to travellers.

   In late June 1991 at an important conference in Ottawa, Canada, on world tourism statistics, France made a presentation drawing on its wealth of experience in this field.

   The Organisation for Economic Co-operation and Development (OECD): the Ministry for Tourism contributed to the OECD's annual tourism report and provided a Vice-Chairman for its Statistical Working Party.

GERMANY

Tourism as an economic activity

The Federal Government estimates that the tourism industry accounts for 5 per cent of Gross Domestic Product. Altogether, around 2 million people earn their living directly or indirectly from the tourism industry.

Prospects for development

Many studies of tourist development prospects have been undertaken by public and private enterprises and research institutions. Tourist activity is expected to expand at an annual rate of around 4-8 per cent in the 1990s.

The real challenges for tourism will be the advent of the Single Internal Market and developments in the new Länder as well as in the Central and Eastern European countries. The quality of the tourism supply has still to be upgraded and greater attention will have to be paid to the ecological aspect.

In the general policy framework, tourism policy is indissociable from the other sectoral policy objectives.

The Federal Government attaches ever greater importance to the interface between tourism and the ecology; there is hence no divergence between tourism and environmental policy aims.

Government policy

Since 1 January 1989, Germany's tourism policy priorities and directions have had to be reconsidered in the light of the changes that have taken place in Germany and Europe. The chief objective of tourism policy is now to develop the industry in the new Länder. Consideration is also being given to exigences of the Single Internal Market due to become a reality in 1993 and to the commitment needed by the Central and Eastern European countries in effecting the transition from a centrally-planned to a market economy. In view of the growing number of tourists seeking an unspoilt environment, policy-makers are also seeking to alert the tourism industry to environmental concerns.

The medium- and long-term objective is sustained modest growth with due regard to the need for an unspoilt environment. To this end, the Federal Minister of Economics organised a conference in September 1991 on the environment and tourism, which aroused keen interest. Draft regulatory provisions also exist in this area.

Since January 1989, the institutional framework of the tourism industry in Germany has been expanded with the creation of new administrative bodies and structures in the new Länder.

In January 1991, the Tourism Sub-Committee of the "Deutsche Bundestag" was replaced by a Tourism Committee. In addition to the tourism policy department in the Federal Ministry of Economics in Bonn, another department has been set up whose special concern is the tourism industry in the new Länder.

In Germany, tourism industry representatives participate in all major deliberations on tourism policy. In 1991, the Federal Ministry of Economics again convened a a consultative tourism board comprising 30 of the main representatives of the tourism industry; an expert working party was set up on tourism and environmental issues. The responsible Minister and Secretary of State hold regular talks with the tourism industry.

Actions and measures taken in 1990 and 1991

Development of supply. The development of tourism supply in the new Länder has proved problematic. In order to improve the tourism situation as speedily as possible, a whole package of measures have been brought in; these were published in a handbook "Economic promotion of the new Länder". In Germany, incentives have also been introduced in other areas, notably in the context of the joint scheme for the improvement of regional economic structures.

Market research. The Federal Government does not itself undertake any market research. It relies on the official tourism statistics and on the research findings of private institutions. In 1989 and 1990, research projects were mainly directed to studying the situation in the new Länder.

According to the statistics, foreign visits to Germany from other European countries reached the record figure of 19 million, up 9 per cent year-on-year.

As a result of the opening up of the East European market the Deutsche Zentrale für Tourismus e.v. (the German National Tourist Office) set up offices in Poland, Hungary and The Czech and Slovak Federal Republic with the object of promoting Germany as a tourist destination.

Consumer protection. In June 1990, the EC Council published a Directive on package travel, package holidays and package tours. This Directive is to be embodied in Member States' national laws before the end of 1992. It affords tourists greater protection by ensuring that they are better informed before and when they sign the contract, in the event of a change in the services supplied, failure to perform or insolvency of the tour operator.

Staggering of holidays. The Federal Government is seeking to improve the German system of staggering school holidays. For instance, it is planned that school holidays should henceforth start on a weekday. Tour operators have accordingly been encouraged to offer more holidays beginning midweek and so help to ease the pressure on weekend travel.

International co-operation. Since 1989, the Technical Co-operation Ministry has not brought in any new technical and financial co-operation measures in the field of tourism, with the exception of measures to admit skilled personnel through the Zentrum für Internationale Migration und

Entwicklung (ZIME -- the centre for international migration and development), and training and further training for hotel school lecturers and hotel managers provided by the Carl-Duisberg company (CDG).

At 30 September 1991, ten people had participated in ZIME training courses which cost around DM 1 million per year. Participants are tourism consultants to government, hotel school lecturers, training instructors, etc.

Carl-Duisberg (CDG) organises training courses and sessions for hotel school lecturers, hotel managers, etc. A 4-year course is organised in a Kenya college providing training and further training for 25-30 people working in the tourism industry; this includes 6 months' training in Germany. In 1989 and 1990, the CDG arranged workshops in Germany for hotel school lecturers, attended by some 15 to 20 participants. The CDG also paid for the training of 15 tourist sector personnel from several countries, in the Lufthansa-Beijing Centre set up by Lufthansa. It also funded the activity of two tourism planning experts in 1991.

The Deutsche Investitions- und Entwicklungsgesellschaft (DEG -- the German investment and development corporation) in Cologne, for its part, provided resources totalling DM 21.8 million for seven tourist projects (including six new ones) in Portugal, Jamaica, Kenya, Thailand and Gambia.

Last, Germany participated in activities by EC Member States in connection with European Tourism Year.

GREECE

Tourism as an economic activity

As is well known tourism constitutes a very important economic activity and a valuable source of foreign exchange for Greece. International tourist receipts in Greece amounted to 1 976 million US$ in 1989. In 1989 the share of foreign exchange earned by tourism was 46.5 per cent in invisibles and 6.6 per cent in GNP. In 1990 international tourist receipts amounted to 2 575 million US$ with a participation of 42.5 per cent in invisibles and 6.3 per cent in GNP. In the period 1989-90 approximately 350 000 persons were directly or indirectly employed in the field of tourism in Greece.

Prospects for development

A key issue for tourism after 1992 will be the Single Internal Market within the framework of the EEC, which will have its impact also on Greek Tourism.

Government policy

The policy of the Ministry of Tourism and of the National Tourist Organisation of Greece, after the change of government of April 1990, can be summarised as follows:

-- Upgrading of Greek tourism, on the one hand, by planning and constructing works of general infrastructure and, on the other hand by creating the specific tourist infrastructure which will contribute to the development of new forms of tourism (marinas, spas, golf courses, convention centres, ski resorts, etc.).

The development of specific tourist infrastructure will be effected:

. by transferring the enterpreneurial activities of the National Tourist Organisation of Greece, through multi-annual leasing (no selling) of NTOG tourist installations or suitable land, to the private sector, which will undertake to self-finance the modernisation or completion of the facilities or the construction of new works, and

. by private investors themselves on their own land, profiting from various incentives provided by the Law.

-- Improvement of the tourist services by activating and increasing control mechanisms.

-- Updating and adjustment of the tourist legislation to the new realities and the new needs.

-- Assignment to KEPE (Greek Centre of Programming and Research) of the elaboration of the master plan for tourist development of the country, which will at the same time safeguard respect for the environment.

-- Creation of a climate of confidence between the state and the private sector, encouragement of private initiatives and close co-operation with entrepreneurs and employees of the tourist industry.

-- Development of underdeveloped tourist regions, which possess important natural and cultural resources, through appropriate incentives.

-- Broadening of the spectrum of services provided by the Greek hotels and similar establishments with an emphasis on the restoration and conversion of traditional settlements and mansions.

A draft law for the amendment and completion of the tourist legislation is under examination by Parliament. This, when approved, will constitute the legal framework for the implementation of Government policy in the field of tourism. The draft law provides, among other things, for the establishment of new organs and mechanisms, through which the co-operation of the state and the private sector will be institutionalised. Such envisaged organs are the "National Council of Tourism" and the "Council for the promotion of Greek Tourism abroad". The draft law also enhances decentralisation through the establishment of "Prefectural" and "Local Tourism Committee". The Greek Commercial Attachés, in countries where there are no NTOG Offices, will be utilised in favour of Greek Tourism in a more systematic way. New rules are established for joint advertising (co-operation tour). The legislation for travel agencies is updated and the procedure for approving the suitability of the site, for granting operation licences and for issuing technical specifications for accommodation units is stipulated.

There are also provisions for the characterisation of tourist zones as saturated ones, for the classification of hotels by Presidential Decree according to the star system and for the updating of the legislation on tourist guides.

Finally, the draft law protects tourists from exploitation, regulates matters concerning the NTOG personnel in Greece and abroad and the School of Tourist Guides and amends the legislation on the Greek Chamber of Hotels.

Apart from this draft law, in the period 1989-90 the law 1892/90 on "Incentives for investments in Greece" was promulgated, to which reference is made below.

Institutional framework. Since March 1989 when the Greek Ministry of Tourism was established it has been the appropriate authority for laying down the tourist policy of the country, for planning tourist development within the framework of the overall government policy and for enhancing the necessary institutional and legislative measures for their implementation. The Ministry of Tourism also draws up short-term or long-term plans for tourist development and provides the guidelines to the competent authorities for their execution.

The services of the Ministry of Tourism are not fully developed as yet. The National Tourist Organisation of Greece works under the supervision of the Ministry of Tourism.

When there are matters of common competence of the Ministry of Tourism and other Ministries, a commonly acceptable policy is laid down after consultations with all competent authorities and representatives of the private sector.

The implementation is effected either by draft laws signed by all competent Ministers or by common Ministerial Decisions.

At the level of the Council of Ministers, the Minister of tourism presents his proposals for the tourism policy and government decisions are made, taking into consideration the views of other Ministers concerned.

The draft law on "The amendment and completion of the tourist legislation" mentioned above establishes the National Council of Tourism, where high officials of all Ministries having a direct or indirect involvement in Tourism matters participate under the Minister of Tourism or the President of the NTOG, who replaces him, and have the task of co-ordinating their activities, safeguarding the implementation of decisions taken and avoiding duplication.

Whenever there is the need for a decision to be taken affecting a branch of the tourism industry, the necessary consultations take place between the Ministry of Tourism and NTOG, on the one hand, and the representatives of the trade unions of the branch concerned.

When there is a general problem concerning the tourism industry as a whole the representatives of all trade unions (employers and employees) of the tourism sector are consulted. Usually representatives of trade unions in the field of tourism are appointed members of the Administrative Council (or Board of Directors) of the NTOG. Also two representatives of the NTOG, the Director and Chief of Section of the appropriate Directorate, are ex-officio members of the Board of Directors of the Greek Chamber of Hotels.

The new draft law on "The amendment and completion of the Greek tourist legislation" mentioned above institutionalises the participation of the representatives of the main trade unions of the tourist sector in the new organs that it is creating.

Thus, the above representatives will participate ex-officio in the National Council of Tourism which has an advisory role for the laying down of the strategy in the field of Tourism, for defining the framework of the tourist policy, for fixing the priorities for tourist development and for taking the necessary administrative or legislative measures.

They will also participate in the "Prefectural Committees", which will follow the implementation of the tourist policy at the prefecture level and will locate problems and suggest relevant measures.

Finally they will participate in the new "Council for the promotion of Greek Tourism abroad" which has an advisory competence in matters of promotion, localising of financial resources and evaluation of suggested advertisement programs.

Action and measures taken in 1989 and 1990

Accommodation. The elaboration of the technical specifications for the convention centres, which started in 1990, has been completed and the specifications were published in the Official Government Gazette at the beginning of 1991.

The technical specifications for marinas and golf courses are also under elaboration.

Transport. The contracts were signed for establishing at all Greek airports ultra-modern radars and digital systems for the processing of flight information.

The telecommunications system of the country is being updated with the installation of digital circuits.

During 1990 all the procedures were accelerated and in 1991 the contracts were signed for the construction of two more lines of the underground (metro) of Athens.

The operation of the customs offices has been upgraded for better and more rapid service to passengers.

The necessary procedures are being followed for the selection of the contractor who will build the new Athens international Airport at Spata.

The Authority of the Port of Piraeus has created a new terminal for cruise-ship passengers which has regular connections to Athens and the airport with luxurious coaches.

Promotion of economic activity in sensitive areas (rural and mountain areas, etc.). Law 1892/90 on "Incentives for investments in Greece" stipulates bigger subsidies for investments in less developed areas. It also provides for the subsidisation of the improvement or construction of new ski resorts in the mountains.

The programme of social tourism of the NTOG and the General Secretariat of Youth provides for subsidised holidays for young people in the mountains.

The Agricultural Bank of Greece has elaborated, submitted and managed to include in the "Mediterranean Integrated Programmes" of the EEC integrated rural development programs in mountain areas which concern in particular he mountain areas of Arcadia, Eboea, Skyros, Evrytania, Fthiotis and Fokis, N.W. Macedonia, Epirus and Cephalonia.

In the above areas accommodation units, infrastructure, small handicrafts, revival of old customs, baby care etc. are created in an integrated way and have a multiplier effect on the local economies.

Moreover, an effort is being made to link rural tourism in Greece with the LEADER programme (Liaison Entre Actions de Développement de l'Economie Rurale) at the EEC, according to which local groups will be financed directly by the EEC for effecting investments, for tailoring small public infrastructure works to the needs of tourist demand, for the restoration and conversion of buildings and rural settlements which have a tourism interest, for the promotion of sales of tourist products, for market research, for the establishment of reservation systems and for measures aiming at the lengthening of the tourist season.

Protection of the environment. The Interministerial Decision published in the Official Government Gazette of 25/10/90 aims at the application of sections 3, 4 and 5 of the Act 1650 of 1986 on " Environmental protection" and simultaneously at the adoption and application of the regulations of the EEC (Directive 64/360 concerning the "suppression of air pollution due to industrial installations" and Directive 85/337/85 on the "Evaluation of the consequences of some public and private work projects on the environment".

In 1989 the "Pomme d'or" was awarded to the NTOG by FIJET (International Federation of Tourism Journalists) for the restoration of the traditional settlements on Mount Pelion.

In 1990 a "Blue Flag" was awarded by the EEC to 82 beaches and six marinas in Greece.

Also in 1990 a pilot project named "Golden Starfish" was conducted in Greece and Great Britain following a proposal by HELMEPA (the national operator of the Blue Flag campaign). It consists of a "mark of excellence" for beaches fulfilling basic requirements of amenities to bathers, hosting a small or medium number of bathers, having natural beauty and complying with objective criteria of clean water (absence of urban or industrial pollution, self cleaning of the waters). The "Golden Starfish" has been awarded to 267 Greek beaches.

As was mentioned above, the Greek Centre of Programming and Research has been assigned the task of elaborating the master plan for the tourist development of Greece which will particularly respect the environment.

According to Law 1892/90 on "Incentives for investments in Greece" bigger grants are given to investments aimed at protecting the environment, reducing pollution of the soil, subsoil, water and air, restoring the natural environment and recycling water.

Vocational training. Initial training: during 1990, courses on confectionery were established by the Greek School of Tourist Professions in three areas in Greece to meet growing demand in this field. The Greek Ministry of Education has created in certain Greek Islands the first professional Lyceums (High Schools) of touristic orientation comprising three years of studies.

Continuing training: during 1989/90, continuing training of a duration of 5 1/2 months has been applied all over the country for people already working in tourist professions.

Apart from the above, the study of the EEC programme entitled "Archipelago" has been completed. Greece, Spain and Portugal participate in this programme which provides distance training using multiple educational high technology methods. It is aimed at owners and employees of small and medium size tourist enterprises which are located in areas situated far from schools and training centres in the field of tourism. This programme will start in October 1991.

Under the auspices of the President of the NTOG, an expert group was established in 1990 for the evaluation and review of the educational system in the field of tourism. The group has completed its work and the conclusions, if and when adopted by the Administrative Council of the School of Tourist Professions, will have an impact on the educational programmes.

Also during 1989/90, Greece has co-operated with all members of the EEC, within the framework of CEDEFOP (Centre de Formation Professionnelle) with regard to the equivalence of the diplomas of the Schools of Tourist Professions of the EEC. The job profiles for eight tourist professions have already been established.

Aids and incentives. Law 1892/90 on "Incentives for investments in Greece" divides the country into four areas (A, B, C, D) on the basis of economic and regional development. The incentives are provided on a rising scale from area A to D. The Law provides particularly attractive incentives for the region of Thrace. Tourist facilities, hotels, camp sites, spas and winter tourism centres are, among others, eligible for being granted the above incentives. The Development Law provides five main types of incentives: grants, interest rate subsidies, tax allowances, increased depreciation rates and reduced tax on profits.

The prospective investor is entitled to choose one of the following combinations:

- -- investment grant, interest rate subsidy and increased depreciation rates, or

- -- tax allowances and increased depreciation rates.

Enterprises operating marinas, conference centres and golf courses, as well as hotel enterprises effecting investments which involve the manufacture, expansion and modernisation of marinas, conference centres and golf courses in any area except area A are entitled to a grant of 25 per cent. This also applies to enterprises operating spas and winter tourism centres.

Social tourism. The NTOG and the "Workers Home" (for workers and employees of the private sector) organised during 1989 and 1990, as in previous years, programmes of "social tourism" for persons of all ages on low incomes (below a certain limit set each year).

These persons can enjoy seven-day holidays, half-board, at a nominal price, subsidised by the NTOG or the "Workers Home". Beneficiaries of the programme also get reductions in transport and museum charges during their holidays.

Special low prices were offered within the framework of the programme of "social tourism" for holidays in Cyprus. For young people in particular, there were winter tourism programmes, spring tourism programmes and summer tourism programmes organised by the NTOG and the General Secretariat of the Young Generation. The winter tourism programmes were of a duration of five days at Christmas or three days (Friday, Saturday and Sunday) and comprised half-board accommodation at low prices in ski resorts, mountain refuges and youth hostels, combined with, depending on the location, ski courses, mountaineering or speleology. There was also a spring programme for young people of the G.S.Y.G. (General Secretariat of Young Generation) which included a five-day Easter holiday and three-day week-ends. The summer programmes of NTOG and G.S.Y.G. provided for three, five or seven days holidays in the case of NTOG, and seven days holidays, in the case of G.S.Y.G., in hotels or camping sites at low prices. Finally there is an exchange programme of the G.S.Y.G. with Cyprus, which concerns 2 500 young people between 18-25 years of age. The eligible young people get air transport, six days half-board accommodation and guided tours at a low prices. The programme was applied between 25 November 1990 and 14 December 1990.

Marketing. During the years 1989-90, and within the framework of the NTOG programme for the promotion of Greek tourism, an "Annual Report 1988-89" was published, containing data on tourist flows to Greece for the years 1987-89 as well as information on the main tourism generating markets and on Greek Tourism in general.

Moreover, in the same period the NTOG financed a study-survey conducted by KEPE (Centre of Research and Programming) in two Greek Prefectures published under the title "Basic Characteristics of foreign tourists in the prefectures of Lasithi and Kerkyra (Corfu)".

The NTOG Research and Marketing Dept., in collaboration with the NTOG Offices abroad, also conducted various surveys on the foreign tourism generating markets.

In July 1989 the Final Report of the "Study of Tourism Promotion Means to increase tourism" was published by J.I.C.A. (Japan International Co-operation Agency). The study was conducted in collaboration with NTOG and aims at indicating measures that are necessary to be taken for increasing the flow of Japanese tourists to Greece. During 1989-90 the main objective of the NTOG promotion policy was to attract tourists of a high social and financial level without excluding mass tourism.

The market segments were different in every foreign country according to the prevailing conditions and market research conducted in each of them.

As to the way of assigning the advertising campaigns of NTOG abroad, it should be noted that in 1989-90 the same policy was applied as in previous years. That is, every NTOG Office abroad presented to the NTOG Headquarters various proposals submitted by advertising companies of the country in which they are located and the final selection was made in Athens.

This policy changed in 1991. The publicity campaign of the NTOG all over the world was assigned to six of the biggest advertising companies worldwide which have subsidiaries in Athens. This policy allows a concerted and co-ordinated effort to be undertaken and the Greek message to be the same in all markets. It also has the advantage that payments are made in Athens in drachmas rather than in foreign exchange.

Another new feature is that for the first time a logo and a slogan for Greek Tourism have been established which will foster one and the same image of Greece in all foreign markets.

Consumer protection. The Directorate of Inspection of the NTOG has been re-established as a separate Directorate. The NTOG inspectors control tourist enterprises in order to ensure that they adhere to the tourist legislation. It also investigates complaints by tourists about the services rendered to them by the various Greek tourist enterprises. Moreover, the Tourist Police was re-established by Presidential Decree 508/89. The Tourist Police, working within the structure of the Ministry of Public Order and consisting of officers speaking one or more foreign languages, assists tourists in the main places of tourist interest, provides information and guidance on matters of tourist interest by telephone on a 24-hour basis and suggests and applies measures for the protection of tourists in collaboration with the Ministry of Tourism, the NTOG and all the other appropriate Authorities.

Finally, the Ministry of Commerce has brought to the Parliament a draft law for the protection of the consumer, which also concerns tourists.

Staggering of holidays. Hotels and similar establishments, also operating during the winter in tourist zones, were subsidised as in previous years. Law 1892/90 provides for the subsidisation of the construction or improvement of hotels serving winter tourism.

Greek bank employees are encouraged to take part of their holidays off-season by being granted some additional days leave (one additional day for every five days of off-season holidays).

The NTOG's social tourism progamme for young people and the General Secretariat for Youth aim at encouraging the mobility of young people off-season. As mentioned above, there was a winter tourism programme for young people in the period January-March and there was an exchange programme with Cyprus from 24 November to 14 December 1990 and from 12 January to 29 March 1991.

International co-operation. On the 25 January 1989 Agreed Minutes were signed in Athens following a Greek-Tunisian meeting of experts in the field of tourism. The minutes provide, among others things, for the exchange of information and co-operation in the field of education and training, in marketing, in management and control matters as well as technical co-operation.

On 20 February 1989 the second session of the Greek-Italian joint commission of tourism co-operation took place in Cortina d'Ampezzo, where information was exchanged on the development of tourism in the two countries, bilateral relations were reviewed and proposals were discussed for the further strengthening of co-operation at the bilateral and European Communities level, which are included in the Agreed Minutes signed on that day.

On 14 June 1989 a meeting of a Greek-Italian working group, on the definition of tourist cultural itineraries between Greece and Southern Italy and Sicily (Magna Grecia) was convened in Athens and Agreed Minutes were signed mentioning, among others things, that these itineraries will link the main Greek metropolis and western colonies.

In view of their common heritage, the two countries will endeavour to organise package tours of 8 or 15 days which will include Greek and Italian destinations as outlined above. The details of implementation of this project and its marketing will be examined in collaboration with the appropriate authorities and the private sector.

ITALY

Tourism as an economic activity

Long term trends suggest that supply and demand are moving in a broadly favourable direction, represented by increases in nights spent and in overall turnover (which reached some L 80 000 billion in 1989), by the lengthening of the period of facility use (from about 27 per cent to 33 per cent) and by the larger average size of enterprises in the sector.

Conversely, assessing the same data comparatively suggests that growth has not been sufficient to enable Italy to retain its share of the world market.

This slower growth and consequent loss of position are the result of changes in the tourism market due to the general economic, social and cultural conditions for the services offered, all of which substantially affect the supply side, determining volume on the demand side, competitiveness on the supply side, and the broader background to the tourism industry as such. Measures thus need to be programmed and implemented at the three distinct though related levels at which problems arise:

i) The country as a whole

-- The environment. In recent years, successive incidents have been much publicised abroad, from industrial pollution and city centre traffic jams to eutrophication of the Northern Adriatic. This is damaging to a country like Italy, where tourism has flourished because of its environment and the artistic heritage of many of its cities.

-- Transport. This is a key factor. The lack of alternatives to motoring and industrial disputes in certain transport sectors tarnish Italy's image and can make travel difficult for the tourist.

  A reorganisation of the transport system making for better connections is long overdue.

-- Prices. In foreign currency terms, Italy has difficulty in remaining competitive because its prices appear rather high compared with those of direct competitors. Also the tourism industry is often criticised because the charges a tourist has to pay during his stay in Italy are sometimes far from clear.

-- Access to cultural attractions. At present, even in the leading cities it is hard to gain access to them, and the many smaller places with a valuable artistic and cultural heritage are hardly even included on tourism circuits.

-- The Mezzogiorno. Southern Italy is particularly seriously affected by the problems that beset the country as a whole (poor infrastructure and services, difficulty in accessing cultural attractions, inadequate transport).

ii) Image promotion:

Promotion is at present somewhat fragmentary and weak in certain respects, partly because of the regional system and partly because of structural shortcomings in ENIT, the agency responsible for tourism promotion abroad.

iii) Supply:

Factors of production and the location of activities are in the hands of private initiatives, which can only be partly guided by government. Location in particular is very important in ensuring a more even territorial distribution of all the benefits of tourism development and in relieving congestion in saturated areas.

Attention must also be drawn to the burden of social charges and the application of VAT to tourism services, both of these having a definite influence on prices.

The figures for 1990 as a whole confirm the favourable trend of domestic tourism, which is growing in particular in the hotel sector.

The more detailed figures show that total internal flows reach 38 192 000 arrivals (up 3.4 per cent) and 167 453 000 nights spent (up 5.2 per cent). Final figures for the hotel sector are 33 739 000 arrivals (up 3.1 per cent), with 124 757 000 nights spent (up 5.0 per cent). For the non-hotel sector, arrivals increase by 6.7 per cent and nights spent decline by 5.9 per cent, giving 4 453 000 arrivals and 42 696 000 nights spent.

Foreign tourist arrivals increase by 1.4 per cent, to 20 876 000 and nights spent decline by 2.5 per cent to 84 471 000. In the hotel sector, foreign tourist arrivals increase by 1.2 per cent to 17 888 000 and nights spent decline by 3.3 per cent to 65 671 000.

For the non-hotel sector, the pattern records an increase of 2 per cent in arrivals and 0.3 per cent in nights spent. It should be mentioned that data for non-hotel sector do not cover private flats and secondary residences.

For 1990 overall, the figures are 59 068 000 (up 2.7 per cent) for arrivals and 251 924 000 (up 2.5 per cent) for nights spent.

For travel abroad by Italian tourists, 1990 confirms the previous year's trend, with an increase of over 8 per cent on 1989. Notably, there is a very slight reduction in destinations to Europe (up 7.9 per cent) and Africa (up 7.6 per cent), in favour of the American continent (up 10.3 per cent) and Asia (up 9.5 per cent).

For the tourism foreign exchange balance, final figures (produced with new, more accurate techniques, though this makes it impossible to compare the 1990 outturn with previous years' outturns) suggest receipts of L 23 654 billion against expenditure of L 16 569 billion, a balance of L 7 085 billion.

Prospects for development

Tourism remains an important sector of Italy's economy: for 1989, the tourism-related foreign exchange figures as percentages of Italy's GNP are:

-- Tourism receipts/GNP = 1.38 per cent (down 8 per cent on 1988)
-- Tourism expenditure/GNP = 0.83 per cent (up 15 per cent on 1988)
-- Tourism balance/GNP = 0.6 per cent (down 21 per cent on 1988)

For 1990, the same ratios using new foreign exchange figures are:

-- Tourism receipts/GNP = 1.8 per cent
-- Tourism expenditure/GNP = 1.26 per cent
-- Tourism balance/GNP = 0.54 per cent

Note that 1990 figures are not comparable with previous years.

Overall turnover for 1990 is estimated at around L 80 000 billion.

The tourism sector's importance can also be seen from research publications such as the annual reports on tourism (the fourth is in preparation) and the many conferences organised by high-level bodies, most recently by the CNEL. Tourism is still an important government policy issue, though responsibility for it was of course devolved to the regions by Delegated Decrees No. 6 of 14 January 1972 and No. 616 of 27 July 1977. The latest annual Finance Act No. 405 of 29 December 1990, provides financial reserves for the three-year period, under the heading of the Refinancing Act No. 217 of 1983 establishing a framework regulation for the tourism sector and for national and international tourism-related measures. For the current three-year period, the Act provides sums of L 50 billion in respect of 1991, L 75 billion for 1992 and L 100 billion for 1993. Another important measure concerns the ENIT, for which over the current three-year period the Finance Act provides L 56 billion in respect of 1991 and L 67 billion for both 1992 and 1993. This shows the great importance attached to promotional advertising of tourism as a product. Supplementary resources are being made available for the full range of ENIT activities because the new Act, No. 292 of 11 October 1990, empowers it to use faster, direct procedures, even in support of private initiatives.

The need for centrally programmed support policies has prompted the Cabinet to adopt a bill significantly amending the tourism Framework Act, No. 217 of 17 May 1983, on procedures for central government intervention, notably as to discretion to fund national projects (80 per cent of the Finance Act appropriations), the introduction of a crisis contingency fund (5 per cent of the appropriations), promotion for tourism and enhancement of cultural heritage and the environment (10 per cent). On the basis of experience in implementing Act 217/83, the bill lays down a different set of guideline and co-ordination standards for the classification of hotels, for prices, for promotion abroad and for tourism enterprises (defining and extending the concept of tourism enterprise).

This legislation has had the effect of providing the industry, much of it highly fragmented, with a better basis for linkage with Italy's institutional system, under which independent bodies can be related to central government in a variety of ways through a set of defined and codified instruments (programming, directives, guidance and co-ordination functions).

Other targeted measures appear in Table D of the Finance Act providing for fresh funding of Article 1 Paragraph 1 of Act 424 of 1989, on support measures for economic activities in areas affected by the exceptional eutrophication of 1989 in the Adriatic Sea; L 20 billion are allocated for 1991. Act No. 195 of 3 July 1991 allocates L 40 billion for such measures in 1992 and L 50 billion in 1993.

The Ministry of Tourism and the Performing Arts is particularly attentive to the interaction between policies in matters affecting tourism such as transport, environment, cultural goods, being implemented by other ministries, with which all possible forms of co-operation are sought. Other every-day concerns are decongestion and seasonal spreading of tourism flows, addressed by an Act amending the tourism Framework Act 217/1983 and establishing a fund for bringing minor centres more to the fore. Over the last few years, tourism demand and motivations have changed considerably and its pattern is now so intricate, with so many different features that it seems doubtful whether one can still speak of motivations purely in terms of tourism. For example, there is business tourism, study tourism etc. Tourism is tending to spread out over the year, with two consequences: the end of long holidays spent in just one location and the emergence of a much wider choice of objectives for the individual tourist. Competition between the different forms of tourism has become keener and substitution processes have become less frequent. Italian tourism is sensitive to all these current and impending developments. Changes in motivation and sociological behaviour have been allowed for in the framing of legislative and administrative measures to make Italy competitive again in the tourism sector.

Government policy

The Act reforming the ENIT (Ente Nazionale Italiano per il Turismo) was promulgated on 11 October 1990. It gives the agency greater operational independence for promotion purposes, in which it had not been very effective because:

- -- its structure and organisation were insufficiently adapted to the rapid change in the international market;
- -- it had inadequate resources;
- -- ENIT's promotional activities were difficult to co-ordinate with those of the regions.

The reform Act dealt effectively with these problems by reorganising the agency along lines that will certainly make it more able to perform the institutional tasks assigned it.

In particular, Section 2 empowers the ENIT to co-operate with the regions or other entities to create and even to participate in private companies for the promotion of Italy's tourism image abroad, supporting the promotional initiatives of private companies, in compliance with EC regulations and with general guidelines for the promotion of Italy as a destination established by the Ministry of Tourism and the Performing Arts.

The ENIT is also empowered to support the activity of public and private bodies interested in the promotion and marketing of Italian tourism products, while Section 6 of the Act empowers the Minister of Tourism and the Performing Arts to co-ordinate promotional initiatives on the part of the regions.

Overall the reform Act reflects a long-held intention to give the ENIT more operational scope so as to strengthen its position on foreign markets.

Action and measures taken in 1989 and 1990

Environment. The 1989 eutrophication crisis in the northern Adriatic prompted the adoption of Act No. 424 of 30 December 1989 to provide support for economic activities in the affected areas. To refurbish the Adriatic coast's image as a seaside resort, Section 2 authorised expenditure of L 10 billion for 1989 on a special publicity campaign abroad. Of that sum, L 500 million was earmarked for an information campaign about the environmental control operations, the main purpose being to provide rapid, full information, especially on water quality for bathing. An ad hoc Committee to promote the Adriatic, chaired by the Minister for Tourism and the Performing Arts, supervised the campaign and set guidelines for it.

Vocational training and employment. Section 11 of the tourism framework Act No. 217 of 17 May 1983 provided in paragraph 13 that for access to occupations associated with tourism (guide, interpreter, tour conductor or courier, professional conference organiser, sailing instructor, skiing instructor, Alpine guide or porter, speleological guide, group organiser or any other tourism-related occupation) nationals of EC member States had the same rights as Italian nationals, subject to reciprocity. Under Section 11 of Community Act No. 428 of 29 December 1990 that paragraph was amended to provide that nationals of EC member States should have equal rights of access to those occupations unreservedly.

Act 428/90 also amended Section 9, paragraph 10 of the framework Act to provide that for foreign nationals or corporate persons not belonging to an EC member State, entitlement to exercise these occupations should be subject to the issue of the State "nulla osta" permit under Section 58 of DPR No. 616 of 24 July 1977.

Consumers. The definition of tourist protection (as a consumer of the tourism product) covers all initiatives intended to protect both Italian tourists travelling abroad and Italian or foreign tourists staying in Italy. The former are the responsibility of the Foreign Affairs Ministry, but it is the Ministry of Tourism and the Performing Arts that is responsible for updating a list, based on Foreign Ministry information, of countries where there may be any kind of political, social or health hazard. The Tourism Ministry immediately warns the FIAVET (travel agents' federation) of such hazards, at the same time passing on information supplied by the Ministry of Health on epidemic disorders, protective measures and health requirements in the various countries. For VAT reimbursement to foreign tourists, provided for under DPR No. 38 of 26 October 1972, the Minister approaches the bodies concerned when there is delay or any other difficulty in implementing the procedures laid down by law.

Users may also contact directly the Ministry of Tourism and the ENIT at central level or tourism promotion offices at local level.

JAPAN

Government policy

With the aim of bettering international understanding, contributing to the economic growth of other countries and improving the international balance of payments in Japan, the Ministry of Transport (MOT) launched the "Ten Million Programme" in September 1987. The target of this programme is to double the annual number of Japanese tourists going abroad, which stood at 5 520 000 in 1986, to 10 million in 1990.

The number of Japanese outbound tourists exceeded 10 million in 1990, which means that the Ten-Million target has been realised one year earlier. Accordingly the MOT reviewed its policy objective and launched, in July 1991, the "Two way Tourism 21", which is meant to expand both inbound and outbound tourism, in order to further mutual understanding internationally.

In 1990 the international tourism deficit amounted to US$21 350 million, contributing to a 33.6 per cent reduction in the trade balance. The total expenditure of the Japanese traveller increased by 10.8 per cent over the previous year.

In the field of international tourism in Japan, the Department of Tourism in the Transport Policy Bureau of MOT functions as the central administrative agency, playing an important role in international co-operation relating to tourism. Regarding domestic tourism, other governmental agencies are highly involved within their respective fields of activity. These include the Environment Agency, Ministry of Health and Welfare, Ministry of Construction and National Land Agency.

Action and measures taken in 1989 and 1990

Accommodation and catering. In 1990, the number of government-registered international tourist hotels increased from 597 to 619 whereas that of registered international tourist ryokan increased from 1 629 to 1 639. As of 31st December 1990, the number of registered international tourist restaurants was 146.

Transport. In fiscal year 1989, the domestic passenger transport volume registered, in items of total volume transported, 77.3 billion passengers or 5.6 per cent increase over the previous year. In items of total passenger-kilometers transported, 1 267 billion passenger-kilometers or 6.4 increase. As for the sharing ratio by transport mode of passenger-kilometers transported for domestic passengers, passenger cars stood at 58.1 per cent, railways 29.1 per cent, bus 8.6 per cent, air 6.1 per cent and sea 0.5 per cent.

Vocational training. Although all vocational training in the tourism sector is in the hands of private enterprises, there are two national qualifying examinations for guide-interpreters and certified travel service supervisor. In 1990, 633 candidates qualified as guide-interpreters, 3 111 as general (international and domestic) and 4 656 as domestic certified travel service supervisor.

Aid and incentive. The government provides financial assistance for the construction and expansion of hotels, ryokan and restaurants which meet specific standards. During the fiscal year 1990, total loans made by the government financing institutions amounted to approximately Y 31 billion.

Other. The MOT has been developing "Family Travel Villages" to encourage the people to engage in recreational activities. There are 33 Family Travel Villages now open to the public. The Law for Development of Comprehensive Resort Areas was promulgated in 1987, and the framework of 30 development plans for resort areas has been authorised as of April 1991.

Marketing. There are no marketing research studies at governmental level.

Consumer protection. The "Have a nice trip '90" and "Have a nice trip '91" campaigns, which were aimed at preventing difficulties while travelling, were undertaken jointly by the MOT, local governments, the Japan Association of Travel Agents (JATA) and the Japan Association of Domestic Travel Agents, from 2nd to 22nd March 1990 and from 1st to 31st March in 1991.

International co-operation. Group training courses entitled "Seminar on Comprehensive Tourism" continued to be conducted by the Japan International Co-operation Agency (JICA) in collaboration with the MOT and International Tourism Development Institute of Japan (ITDIJ) from October to December in 1989 and 1990. Junior staff from the Malaysian travel industry have been trained within JICA's individual training arrangement on the request of the Malaysian Government, reflecting its "Look East Policies" in 1989 and 1990. The Japanese government dispatched tourism experts to the secretariat of the U.N. Economic and Social Commission for Asia and the Pacific (ESCAP), Fiji, India, Indonesia, Maldives, Malaysia, Mexican States and Panama in 1989 and 1990 as a part of JICA's technical co-operation. The ITDIJ subsidised by the MOT accepted trainees and dispatched experts in the travel industry. Y 965 million of the budget of the ASEAN Centre (Asociation of South-east Asian Nations) was contributed by the Japanese government.

LUXEMBOURG

The prospects for development and the main lines of government policy have not changed since the last OECD annual report (1989 edition).

Action and measures taken in 1989 and 1990

Promotional activities by the Ministry of Tourism take three forms:

a) agencies and agents abroad;

b) fairs and exhibitions, promotion days abroad;

c) specific activities such as production of video-cassettes, brochures, etc.

In addition the National Tourist Office is endeavouring to develop tourism between seasons and attract a quality clientele; with this in mind it has encouraged the development of flat charges in hotels offering a long weekend combined with special offers in the spring and autumn. The results are more than satisfactory.

1990 saw the setting up of a Société des Congrès (public limited liability company), shares in which are held by the Luxembourg State, the city of Luxembourg, and the private and semi-private sector, the aim being to promote Luxembourg as a Conference centre and consequently ensure that the best possible use is made of existing infrastructures.

The Minister for Tourism carried out a wide-ranging consultation at national level in 1990 and 1991 with a view to the entry into force as from 1st January 1993 of the EC Directive on package travel, including package holidays and package tours.

International co-operation. Bilateral co-operation between Lorraine and Luxembourg has been established in the framework of Sarre-Lor-Lux; this should encourage common interests and the beginnings of joint action.

The working party on "Benelux hotel harmonisation" is continuing to analyse the criteria for the classification of tourist accommodation establishments and seeking to adapt them to general trends in the hotel industry.

The co-operation agreement between the two Luxembourg, bringing together the tourist Federation of Belgian Luxembourg on the one hand and the Ministry of Tourism and the National Tourist Office of the Grand Duchy on the other hand, is continuing in the form of joint participation in fairs and exhibitions to attract the general public and in the field of advertising.

The Ministry of Tourism has taken an active part in the preparatory work for the creation in 1991 of a European Institute for Tourism at the University of Trier (Germany). This is a joint project of the Rhineland-Palatinate, the German-speaking Community of Belgium, the Grand Duchy of Luxembourg and the University of Trier. The three main tasks of the Institute will be research, re-training and advisory activities.

NETHERLANDS

Tourism as an economic activity

Consumption in the tourism and leisure sector and the production and employment related to it is concentrated in four major categories of company within the commercial service sector. These categories account for 93 per cent of total direct employment. The majority of direct employment (66 200 man-years) is connected with the catering trade.

If part-time employment is taken into account the total employment effect of spending on tourism and leisure can be estimated at 230 000 jobs.

It is noteworthy that part-time jobs in the tourist sector grow much faster than full-time jobs. (Figures have been taken from the report "Business development in tourism and recreation 1986-90").

Direct and indirect employment created by spending on tourism and leisure in 1989, per category of company

Category of company	Employment (man-years)	
	Direct	Direct and Indirect
Catering trade	66 200	84 600
Transport/communication	28 900	34 300
Culture/recreation	17 900	23 300
Trade	16 700	20 400
Other categories	9 200	14 900
Total	138 900	177 400

Prospects for development

In 1991 a study was completed on the "Toer model", a simulation model of the tourist market, in which the tourist sector is analysed in detail.

The purpose is that the model can approximately reproduce the developments of various indicators of the tourist market (such as demand, supply or prices of holiday types) given information on the development of the variables that are exogenous to the world of tourism.

Some results of this research are:

-- holiday expenditure in the Netherlands, of Dutch and foreign tourists together, will increase 19 per cent during the period 1989-94. For the Dutch the increase will be 13 per cent; for foreigners the increase will be as much as 23 per cent;

-- the developments in various sub-areas within the tourist sector are very different. Some figures: long holidays in hotels will grow by 23 per cent, and long holidays in rented accommodation by 11 per cent.

The Toer model has also been used for the calculation of new trends. On this basis alternative prognoses are drafted. The following four new trends have been discerned: people intend

-- to take more short holidays;

-- increasing importance of culture as choice criterion;

-- increase of Italian and Spanish incoming tourism;

-- increase and changes in holiday-participation of elderly people.

Government policy

In May 1990 the paper "Enterprise in Tourism" was published and has been approved and adopted by parliament.

This paper is the third successive policy paper to discuss tourism policy in the Netherlands and follows the 1985-89 Tourism Policy Paper which was brought out at the end of 1984. The main pillars for the 1985-89 Paper were: intensified promotion, a stronger infrastructure for tourism, improved services and increased awareness of the importance of tourism among other government agencies.

Since the beginning of the period following the adoption of the second paper the Ministry of Economic Affairs has conducted a series of policy evaluation studies, focusing particularly on areas in which policy was intensified or in which new policy was initiated. Partly on the basis of these studies, it was decided to continue and intensify the main lines of policy already implemented, although some further tightening and adjusting was necessary. In the third Policy Plan, called "Enterprise in Tourism", tourism policy for the 1990s is sketched out. The aim of this paper is to maintain, and where possible increase, the Netherlands share in total expenditure on tourism and leisure. To this end, the policy is geared at strengthening the Dutch tourism and leisure industry (supply) on the one hand and at stimulating both domestic and incoming tourism, as well as maximising profit from outgoing tourism on the other hand (demand).

In order to strengthen the Netherlands' competitive position and to achieve sustainable economic growth, four main themes can be distinguished: These are:

-- professionalisation;

-- co-operation;

-- consideration of issues concerning the environment and nature sites;

-- priorities.

Concerning priorities the Ministry of Economic Affairs has given attention to those aspects of tourism in the Netherlands which can be used to give the country the opportunity to stand out in international terms. On the basis of market research four priority themes have been selected: Holland - Waterland, Cultural Heritage, the Coast and the Urban Centres.

In order to implement the goals put forward by these four themes, the following important action points for the coming years are formulated:

1. Policy on national and international co-operation;

2. Improvement of management in the tourist and leisure industry;

3. Tourism policy aimed at consumers;

4. Infrastructure;

5. Policy on tourist information and promotion.

6. Expanding knowledge through research and statistics.

The prime responsibility for tourism policy falls to the State Secretary of Economic Affairs. However, co-operation with other Ministries takes place, for instance with the Ministry of Agriculture, Nature Management and Fisheries. This Ministry is conducting a policy to promote open air recreation, in which the recreational needs of the domestic population are of central importance. Co-operation and policy-influencing also takes place in policy governing tourism and recreational mobility (Ministry of Transport and Public Works) and in cultural policy operated by the Ministry of Welfare, Public Health and Culture.

In the government sphere the 12 provinces and 647 local authorities also play a role.

There are a number of authorities handling the promotion of tourism and tourist information which rely heavily on government funding. The most important is the NBT (Dutch Tourist Board) (50 per cent government funding) which is aimed at tourism promotion abroad and the encouragement of domestic tourism.

It should be pointed out that the Dutch government does not have a separate service for the general Holland promotion. The NBT therefore partly fills this role. For the provision of information about domestic tourism and leisure attractions, there are over 400 local VVV's and 15 regional so-called 'promotional' VVV's.

Finally there is the ANWB Royal Netherlands Tourist Association, the largest consumer organisation for tourism and leisure (2.8 million members). This organisation provides information and services about tourist destinations both in Holland and abroad.

On the international level as well the Netherlands wishes to contribute to the development of tourism.

Institutional framework. No significant changes have affected the institutional framework since 1st January 1989.

The representatives of the tourism industry have been consulted by means of the paper "Enterprise in Tourism". The initial development of the action-programme will be carried out in close co-operation with these representatives.

Action and measures taken in 1989 and 1990

Development of supply. In the Netherlands, tourism policy is part of general economic policy aimed at promoting sustainable growth. The Ministry of Economic Affairs is pursuing this task along two main lines of policy: macro-economic policy and company-orientated (industry-orientated) policy. Company-orientated policy is aimed at the industrial (manufacturing industry) and commercial service sector, with particular attention being given to small and medium-sized enterprises. In total the Ministry's annual budget is almost 3 billion Gld.

Within the Ministry of Economic Affairs, tourism policy is handled as part of services policy. Services policy aims at good co-operation with the service industry to remove unnecessary obstacles to growth and innovation and to encourage the maximisation of opportunities. Central themes are:

-- promoting a good investment climate, both nationally and internationally (improving infrastructure; opposing unnecessary regulations; training, etc.);

-- stimulating continuous innovation, both from a technological and an organisational point of view (stimulating information technology, promoting quality and environmental care, etc.).

Budget: It is unique that the tourist sector is the only sector within the services policy for which separate financial resources are set aside. A total budget for tourism of 75 million Gld. for 1991 is made available on the basis of the policy paper "Enterprise in Tourism" .

In contrast with the countries surrounding the Netherlands there are no special financial, fiscal or labour costs instruments available to support individual companies. Companies in the tourism sector can, just as companies of other sectors, use the so-called "generic" instruments.

Breakdown of the Netherlands' budget for tourism (millions of guilders/year)

	1989	1990	1991
NBT promotion and information supplies	34.2	35.9	38.5
Product improvement (including public infrastructure)	7.5	16.0	16.5
Management improvement, services automation and international activities	4.6	1.9	7.5
Attraction of more international congresses	2.5	4.0	4.0
Research and statistics	1.5	1.5	2.5
Promoting developments in provincial tourism	4.0	2.5	5.0
Other	1.0	1.0	1.0
Total	55.3	61.8	75.0

Marketing. The market research department of the Netherlands Board of Tourism conducts approximately 75 research projects each year. Apart from special surveys in 1989 and 1990 on, e.g., yachting, mobility, environment, incentive travel, senior citizens, the Single Internal Market and measuring the effectiveness of promotional campaigns. In principle all the tourist markets are monitored via research regularly.

Regarding the measurement of the present and potential demand more generally, three types of survey are used: holiday surveys, image-research and research on the motives of tourists travelling to the Netherlands. Image and motivation studies are carried out at regular intervals, but as changes are relatively small, only every five years.

Motivation studies in 1989 and 1990 were conducted for the French, Northern American, British, Scandinavian, Belgian, German, Spanish and Italian market.

Image surveys were carried out in Spain, Germany and the Brussels agglomeration.

To have better knowledge of the present state of tourism via holiday-surveys, special attention was given to the Swedish, German and Belgian markets. These studies were commissioned from specialised research institutions on tourism.

For the domestic market the Continuous Holiday Survey (CVO) is used. CVO is a structural survey of the Dutch population carried out every quarter. A panel is used with a net number of respondents of 3 500 as the yearly average. In total the research objective is to have relevant data for marketing use preferably no more than five years old, but on average three years in principle.

The marketing strategy of the Netherlands Board of Tourism on the domestic market emphasises the possibilities for second and third holidays, in particular in the off-season. In combination with that, special attention is given to stimulate day-tripping. Home to home brochures and free publicity via television in particular are used, apart from more common marketing instruments such as fairs, advertising etc. Four main areas of supply are focused upon: water-sports, culture, the cities and the Dutch coast.

The four main areas of supply are also used in marketing the Netherlands abroad, within the total mix of available instruments. In order to attract more foreign tourists the target is to have a mega-event every two years. The Van Gogh exhibition was an example of that. Of the 600 000 visiting foreign tourists, approximately 300 000 would not have visited the country if the event had not taken place.

Concerning market priorities the neighbouring countries (Germany, Belgium/Luxemburg and the United Kingdom), with a share of 60 per cent in arrivals, rank first. The remaining European countries rank second with 35 per cent of all the registered arrivals. The inter-continental market ranks third.

The general marketing approach gives special attention to stimulating the quality of the tourist industry. In order to market the industry in the country itself and abroad it is essential to combine it in groups which co-operate regionally or sectionally. As the majority of supplying businesses are small firms the promotional impact increases when they unite and are marketed in joint schemes with the Tourist Board.

Protection of the tourist as a consumer. Via a consumer interest approach, industry can be stimulated by devoting more attention to the market, a development which will have beneficial effects for both the employer and the consumer. The main effort will concentrate on stimulating self-regulation, for instance in the following areas:

-- complaints and disputes;

-- guarantees and general conditions of supply;

-- the travelling expenses contingency fund.

In a European context, the main focus of attention is to achieve balanced regulations governing package holidays and over-booking, which will then need to be set down in the New Civil Code. Also included in this context are the questions of the staggering of holidays, regulations for consumers in the Law on Open Air Recreation and action in the field of recreational criminality and pollution.

Within the Netherlands several parties are discussing the staggering of holidays: the appropriate educational and touristic groups together with four Ministries discussed three parts of this subject and recommendations will soon be made. The first concerns the staggering of the summer holidays, the second concerns the staggering of the "other" holidays and the last is the introduction of the so-called "snipper" days, which means that parents are allowed to ask the school authorities for one or more days off for their children outside the normal holidays. In the European context attention is paid to this subject, too.

International co-operation. Tourism appears increasingly on the international policy agenda. The Dutch Ministry of Economic Affairs is trying to actively maintain contact with policy-influencing and/or policy-making bodies such as the WTO, OECD and the EC. Particular priority is being given to the development of a overall EC tourism policy.

For instance, during the Dutch presidency of the EC in the second half of 1991, the Ministry of Economic Affairs organised an international conference on staggered holidays in conjunction with the EC.

NEW ZEALAND

Government policy

The National Government which took office in October 1990 has proceeded to restructure the government's role in tourism significantly. On 1 November 1991, an Act of parliament abolished the former New Zealand Tourism Department and replaced it with two separate agencies reporting to the Minister of Tourism. They are the Ministry of Tourism and the New Zealand Tourism Board.

The Ministry of Tourism's principal role is to provide advice to the Minister of Tourism and the Government on policy issues relevant to the tourism sector.

The Cabinet has specified the major functions of the Ministry of Tourism as:

-- providing advice to the government on policy and regulatory issues relevant to tourism;

-- advising departments and the government about how the activities of other departments affect tourism;

-- representing the government's tourism interests on interdepartmental and intergovernmental activities;

-- managing the Tourism Facilities Development Grants programme;

-- managing and reviewing Crown land and Acts of Parliament for which it has responsibility;

-- advising the government on the outputs it purchases from the New Zealand Tourism Board;

-- providing services including information for Parliament and the Minister of Tourism.

Work areas that the Ministry of Tourism is involved in include:

-- Aviation: The Ministry is a member of the External Aviation Policy Committee. It attends formal government to government air services negotiations where these have implications for tourism;

-- Air facilitation: The Ministry plays an active role in airport facilitation issues to ensure that there are minimum restrictions on travellers;

-- Crown owned lands: The Ministry manages Crown owned land included in the Wairakei Tourist Park and reserve land in Rotorua;

-- Government policies: The Ministry seeks to ensure that policies adopted by the government have regard to the impacts on tourism;

-- Human resource development: The Ministry seeks to ensure that government policies on training and education are consistent with the needs of the tourism industry;

-- Intergovernmental relations: The ministry represents government on tourism interests to other governments and to intergovernmental organisations;

-- Investment: The ministry seeks to ensure that government investment policy encourages investment which adds value to the New Zealand tourism product;

-- Ministerial services: The ministry provides briefing papers, parliamentary information and other material for the Minister of Tourism as required;

-- Resource development: The ministry interprets and monitors resource management legislation as it applies to the development of tourism in New Zealand.

-- Sustainable tourism: The ministry is working towards sustainable tourism which will meet the needs of tourists and host regions now, while protecting and enhancing opportunities for future generations.

-- Tourism facilities development grants programme: The ministry runs a programme providing grants to non-income tax paying organisations. It aims to increase the range of nationally significant tourism facilities which enhance overseas visitors' understanding and enjoyment of New Zealand;

-- Vote tourism: The ministry administers Vote: Tourism. This includes the amount appropriated for the ministry itself, plus various payments to others on behalf of the Crown. It advises the minister on outputs purchased from the Board and their contribution to the tourism outcomes sought by the government.

The functions of the New Zealand Tourism Board as set out in the New Zealand Tourism Board Act 1991, are:

-- to develop, implement and promote strategies for tourism; and

-- to advise the government and the New Zealand tourism industry on matters relating to the development, implementation and promotion of these strategies.

The Board's objective is to ensure that New Zealand is so marketed as a visitor destination to maximise the long-term benefits to New Zealand.

Actions and measures taken in 1989, 1990 and 1991

Development of supply. The New Zealand Government has followed a non-interventionist approach to the economy, including the tourism sector. The previous Labour government's Budget of 1986 phased out most of the grants and incentives available, including for tourism, as of 1 April 1988.

The government has had a major change in emphasis in its involvement in tourism, as determined by the restructuring of its state agency, the New Zealand Tourism Department.

The former department's three commercial units were privatised and sold in 1989-90; these were the NZTP Travel Offices in Auckland, Rotorua, Wellington, Christchurch, Dunedin and Queenstown; the National Film Unit and the National Publicity Studios. As indicated earlier, the former Department has been abolished and replaced by a small Ministry and a Tourism Board. Staff numbers have been reduced as the private sector is expected to assume a greater share of tourism marketing and promotion. The Tourism Board has reduced the number of staff based in New Zealand and increased staff involved in promotions off-shore. The Tourism Board also intends to open new promotional offices in Osaka, Chicago, Melbourne and Brisbane.

Transport. There has been further liberalisation in air transport and the emphasis has been to deregulate and encourage increased private sector competition.

Environment. The government passed the Resource Management Act in 1991. The new legislation requires all aspects of air, land or water to be managed in a more integrated way. The focus of the Act is on the environmental effects of activities, rather than the activities themselves. This means that planning controls no longer direct development activities. For example, areas will be zoned according to environmental effect, not type of land use.

Development is less restricted, provided any damaging effects on the environment are avoided, or minimised to levels determined by the community (as specified in policy statements and plans).

The central concept of the Act is sustainable management of natural and physical resources, a broad philosophy which reflects aspects of use, development and protection.

The Act replaces 59 statutes and 19 regulations on town and country planning, water and soil management pollution (land, water, air and noise pollution) and waste disposal, hazardous substances control, coastal management and geothermal consents.

Employment. The Employment Contracts Act was passed by Parliament in 1990 to change from the previous system of award negotiations to encourage the negotiation of individual contracts between staff and employers. The emphasis is on reducing wage demands and reducing inflation.

Vocational Training. The government is placing a lot of emphasis on vocational training and is keen to ensure that New Zealand qualifications are designed to be internationally portable and internationally competitive.

Qualifications are being reformatted into a standardised system of units of learning, enabling greater access to training and the ability to acquire a greater range of skills. Legislation has been passed to make industry become more responsible and accountable for the provision and funding of training for their sectors.

Marketing. The New Zealand Tourism Board is responsible for the marketing and promotion of New Zealand as an overseas visitor destination. Its goal is "to successfully position New Zealand as a distinct and competitive visitor destination and to achieve results in terms of visitor numbers, length of stay, visitor expenditure and industry profitability in line with specific targets".

The previous New Zealand Tourism department used the following mix of activities in its marketing strategy:

-- Market review, assessment and identification research: The undertaking of commissioned or in-house research to review market performance in terms of outbound travel generally, to determine the potential for travel to New Zealand and to identify and describe in detail the characteristics, location and behaviour of market niches which offer the greatest potential;

-- Market strategy development: The development of a means of presenting New Zealand in terms of a communications theme and the determination of how this theme might be most appropriately directed at target groups. This involves determining an appealing image and theme for New Zealand and developing an integrated marketing campaign incorporating this theme using a mix of advertising, promotions, public relations and information distribution;

-- Consumer advertising: The specification and management of contracts to develop creative material and place it in media appropriate to each target group. The encouragement of private sector participation in these activities.

-- Consumer promotion: The undertaking of, or participation in, exhibitions, contests and other activities directed at target groups. Encouragement of private sector participation in these activities.

-- Trade promotion: The undertaking of, or participation in, travel shows, exhibitions, advertising, contests and other activity directed at targeted trade personnel. The encouragement of private sector participation in these activities.

-- Trade education: The planning and implementation of familiarisation visits to New Zealand for targeted trade personnel. The undertaking of educational seminars about New Zealand for targeted trade personnel. The encouragement of private sector participation in these activities;

-- Public relations: The initiation and organisation of media visits to obtain favourable publicity of New Zealand which will reach targeted consumer and trade groups. The preparation and distribution of press releases to reach target groups;

-- Information distribution: Response to inquiries (whether by telephone, written or in person) from consumers and trade about New Zealand and about specific aspects of the New Zealand travel product (accommodation, transport, attractions, etc.). Development and distribution of audio-visual materials appropriate to the needs of targeted trade and consumers.

-- Evaluation of the effectiveness of marketing activity: The establishment of monitors of awareness of New Zealand and intentions to travel to New Zealand in targeted market segments. The commissioning of surveys of knowledge of New Zealand and confidence in selling New Zealand for targeted trade personnel. The measurement of the return on investment for marketing activity.

Staggering of holidays. The school year was reformatted into four, instead of three, terms. This, however, is not considered to have any noticeable effect on tourism.

International co-operation. The Ministry of Tourism is closely associated with the Pacific Asia Travel Association and the Asia-Pacific Economic Council.

NORWAY

Tourism as an economic activity

The value of gross sales by the travel and tourism industry rose by 6.1 per cent or NKr 2.4 billion from 1989 to 1990, to reach NKr 41.8 billion in 1990, or 3.2 per cent of GDP.

Prospects for development

Norway sees the greatest potential for growth in the international holiday market, where favourable developments are expected over the next few years.

Norway's competitiveness in foreign markets has improved in the past two years; the reasons include the relatively favourable domestic price inflation, the restructuring in the industry aimed at improving its products, educational and competence-enhancing efforts, intensive marketing, and increased productivity.

Foreign markets appear increasingly to be demanding values for which Norway is known and which are being focused on, like a healthy environment, "clean" surroundings, fresh air, and qualified personnel.

Government policy

Tourism policy is an extension of the guidelines drawn up in Report n° 14 (1986-87) to the Storting on Travel and Tourism. Its principal objective is to develop tourism into a growth sector and increase the industry's profitability.

In 1989, the government drew up a national strategy for travel and tourism, in which national attractions were selected for international marketing and the criteria were defined for establishing priorities among target sectors for product development.

The main aim of the national strategy for travel and tourism is to achieve better co-ordination and greater concentration of the public instruments used in the sector, so that investments produce greater economic effects than before.

The national strategy defines the following target sectors:

-- Research and education;

-- Marketing and sales;

-- The travel and tourism infrastructure.

As part of the strategy, a number of projects/activities have been initiated in the 1989-91 period:

-- Research and education:

. A research programme has been established for travel and tourism in which priority has been given to three research projects: the measurement of effects in the market, the market-consciousness of the Norwegian tourist industry, and the development of local tourist destinations;

. A company scholarship scheme has been set up under academic auspices.

-- Marketing and sales:

. NORTRA, the national tourist marketing organisation in Norway, has received increased allocations, both for its general promotion of Norway and for marketing;

. The tourist industry and the authorities have agreed to give priority to establishing commercial regional marketing companies with close geographic contacts with the tourist industry and its products;

. Funds have been spent on developing an information system with regard to the Norwegian and foreign markets.

-- The travel and tourism infrastructure:

. The Industrial Fund has given priority to stimulating international sales by means of its restructuring grants;

. Support for single projects has been reduced in favour of joint measures, i.e. infrastructure projects which are necessary for the development of the industry, especially in the designated target sectors;

. An experimental programme has been established relating to the travel and tourism infrastructure;

. To promote the development of tourism in rural communities, a competence centre has been established in Roros.

Institutional framework. Particular emphasis is being put on ›rdination, aimed at developing comprehensive packages which are in demand he market.

The government-appointed Co-ordinating Committee for Travel and Tourism, hich eight Ministries are represented and which has been at work for nearly years, has defined its major tasks as:

-- An overall assessment of the use of instruments aimed at travel and tourism. The aim is to encourage co-ordinated use of, and priorities among, such instruments, with a view to improving the productivity and profitability of the industry.

-- Achieving more concentrated and specifically targeted use of the various systems of public grants.

-- Channelling instruments away (from company-specific and towards joint measures (enhancing knowledge, marketing, and infrastructure measures).

Travel and tourism has been defined as a private industry, to be developed along commercial lines, with prominent roles given to individual companies and industrial organisations.

Action and measures taken in 1989 and 1990

Development of supply. Norway has designated travel and tourism as a growth sector. The authorities are seeking to provide suitable conditions for growth by their use of instruments.

This use is taking a new direction, with public funds increasingly being allocated to local authorities, including the counties and municipalities which are taking part in the greater local autonomy experiment. Of the funds allocated to the Regional Development Fund, 60 to 70 per cent are now managed by county municipalities.

Preparations are in hand for the 1994 Winter Olympics in Lillehammer. A central government guarantee amounting to NKr 7 billion has been given. The central authorities are especially eager to see the arrangements for the Games bearing fruit in the form of after-use of the facilities.

It has been viewed as an important task to make Norwegian travel and tourism products more accessible. The conditions have been created for increasing charter tourism into Norway. Two new airfields linked to the most important tourist areas were built relatively recently. Plans are currently being developed for a new main airport which will be of great importance to travel and tourism.

The number of man/years worked in the industry fell by 9.5 per cent in the 1987 to 1990 period. Despite the reduction, the industry's gross turnover rose over the same period. That suggests that productivity improved, thanks to more efficient use of the workforce.

Student places at colleges which provide courses in travel and tourism have been increased.

A national strategy is in place for the development of information technology in travel and tourism. Priority is being given to developing an up-to-date information system with international communication links.

Marketing. At the international level NORTRA conducted extensive research programmes on: summer tourism in Sweden, Denmark and Japan; winter tourism in the United Kingdom, Germany, the Netherlands, Denmark and Sweden; Incentive travel in Italy.

On a national level NORTRA conducted one major market research, and in addition started an ongoing (structural) market research programme (Norwegian Travel Monitor).

NORTRA's major marketing strategy is directed towards the following target groups:

-- 45 years and upwards (both couples and singles), characterised by being independent of children, flexible, healthy financial situation, well educated and interested in nature and the environment. Travel is a high priority, and they travel several times a year.

-- 20-30 years (couples and singles), characterised by being independent of children, affluent economy, flexible, well educated and interested in leisurely outdoor activities, the environment and cultural activities. They want to travel before they settle down with small children.

-- Families with children seeking adventurous holidays with emphasis on outdoor activities and culture.

-- Life-style and special interest groups travelling to pursue their major interests.

-- "Narrow" families, like one adult travelling with one or more children, seeking an adventurous holiday based on natural attractions and environment.

A study on health tourism and the market potential has been conducted by the Norwegian College of Hotel Management.

Consumer protection. EC legislation is taken into account in the tourist sector and protects the interests of consumers.

Staggering of holidays. Trends in holiday travel show an increase in the number of short holidays being taken at all times of the year. Summer holidays appear to have levelled off, whereas increasing numbers of holidays are being taken in the autumn. There has been a slight decline in the duration of summer holiday trips. Social changes in recent years are one reason why holidays are now more widely distributed. NORTRA's market plans include more emphasis on extending the typical holiday periods.

International co-operation. Both the government administrations and the tourist industries of the Nordic countries co-operate on tourism, both in projects and marketing, as in the major promotion campaign "Focus on Scandinavia" presented over a three-year period in the United States. A similar campaign has been planned for Japan.

PORTUGAL

Tourism as an economic activity

Tourism is regarded as a key factor in the process of national economic development, aside from its social and cultural role.

Its economic impact may be measured by:

- -- the improvement of external account deficits;
- -- the percentage of gross value added (GVA) by tourism in gross domestic product (GDP)
- -- the multiplier effect of tourist activities on other economic sectors;
- -- the volume of employment created.

Indeed, over the last few years, tourism receipts have constantly covered the negative trade balance by over 34 per cent; in 1990, the rate of coverage was 41.2 per cent.

Regarding the current transactions balance (excluding tourism), the rate of coverage by the tourism operations balance was 102.7 per cent for the period January to December 1990, as against 108.4 per cent the year before.

At the same time, research by the General Directorate for Tourism shows that:

- -- the impact of the gross value added by tourism on GDP (7.9 per cent) is greater than that of other major industries or sectors such as textiles, agriculture, construction and banking;
- -- the demand induced (directly or indirectly) for various industries by tourism activities leads to a rise in total resources throughout the economy which is never less than 1.5 times total resources (e.g. a "purely" tourism sector such as 5-, 4- and 3-star hotels shows a multiplier of 1 684, while "tourist restaurants" show an even higher multiplier of 1 949, which means that every Esc. 1 000 of demand directed at restaurants prompts a rise in resources of Esc. 1 949 throughout the economy);
- -- the demand for tourism goods and services does not have a higher imported content than non-tourism demand; if one looks at "private tourism consumption" by residents, the amount of imports induced by the former is seen to be slightly less than that induced by the latter (0.218 and 0.283 respectively);
- -- consumption by foreign tourists never accounts for more than 15 per cent of the total expenditure on imports by the economy as a whole;

-- investment in the tourist industry is well above Esc. 50 billion (1986 figure), underlining its dynamic effect on other industries such as building and public works, engineering and transport equipment.

Prospects for development

At national level, and in the light of the main statistical indicators, the following conclusions may be drawn for 1990:

-- arrivals of foreign visitors totalled nearly 18.4 million, an increase of 11.8 per cent over 1989; the trend was not uniform throughout the year, a faster growth rate being observed in the second half (+ 13.5 per cent) than in the first -- with varying increases for all means of arrival, the highest percentage rise for 1990 over 1989 being for arrivals by air (+ 15.9 per cent);

-- in 1990, as in the years immediately preceding, actual tourist movements increased (+ 12.7 per cent over 1989 in the end-of-year count, with just over 8 million arrivals) at the expense of excursionists, whose number went up slightly less (+ 11.2 per cent);

-- average length of stay fell again in 1990 (to 7.4 days from 7.7 the year before), resuming the downward trend which had only been interrupted in 1989;

-- the shorter average stay meant that there was a lower rate of increase (1990-89) in nights spent by foreign tourists in all means of accommodation than in the number of tourists themselves (+ 8.7 per cent as against + 12.7 per cent);

-- again in the field of external demand, according to the provisional figures provided by the National Statistics Institute (INE), nearly 16.8 million nights were spent in hotels during the year; if the difference between this and the final figure is not very substantial, the percentage of nights spent in hotels in 1990 will be the same as the 28 per cent or so in 1989;

-- nights spent by Portuguese residents in hotels amounted to nearly 7.2 million in 1990 (provisional figure), which was an 8.7 per cent increase over the previous year, thus maintaining an uninterrupted rise from 1986;

-- there was a slight increase in hotel occupancy over 1989 (48.4 per cent, compared with 48.3 per cent, in the rate of bed occupancy for the country as a whole, excluding boarding houses and inns), which interrupted the annual series that had been falling since 1986;

-- gross tourism receipts were almost Esc. 506 billion, i.e. a 19.1 per cent increase at current prices over the preceding year; at constant prices, the rise in receipts fell by 5 per cent, while average expenditure per tourist/day dropped for the third year running;

-- this fall in real average expenditure per tourist had its full impact on hotels, where the average price per night has gone down in real terms over the last two years (- 2.9 per cent from 1989 to 1990 and - 0.7 per cent from 1988 to 1989) to an absolute level below 1987 (constant prices).

Thus, there was a clear rise in the physical indicators, counterbalanced by the declining purchasing power of tourists; it is precisely in this area that action must be taken urgently to develop "quality" tourism rather than quantity alone. But "quality" does not only mean luxury; in its economic interpretation, it is much closer to the capacity to anticipate potential demand, satisfying it and making it effective.

The 1991 results confirm what was observed at the end of 1990, i.e. that Portugal was not affected by the Gulf crisis as a tourist destination. Indeed, total foreign tourist arrivals reached 8.8 million, (+ 10.0 per cent over 1990) while nights spent in all means of accommodation amounted to 65.1 million (+ 9.4 per cent over the same period).

On the other hand, the macroeconomic projection model on which the tourism indicator forecasts are based -- and which is used to compare the foreseeable GDP trends (of the main departure markets) and tourism prices with the respective demand elasticities -- can be used to make the following preliminary forecast to 1995:

	1995 million	1990-95 Average annual per cent
variation		
Total arrivals of foreign visitors	29.2	+ 9.7
Tourist arrivals	13.7	+ 11.2
Total nights spent by foreigners	94.3	+ 9.6
Nights spent in hotels	23.7	+ 7.6

Arrivals in 1995 will therefore probably total 29.2 million and tourist flows will continue to rise more quickly than excursionist arrivals, whose proportion might be 47 per cent (13.7 million in 1995).

The trend also indicates that external demand for hotel accommodation might be responsible for some 23.7 million nights in 1995, which, although stemming from the significant average annual growth rate (1990-95) of 7.6 per cent, will not be on the same scale as the non-hotel increase.

Given the expected rise in hotel demand, Portuguese capacity must be increased by around 3 per cent in order to reach the 208 000 rooms required in 1995 (normal projection hypothesis, with no significant increase in occupancy rates and reduced seasonal occupancy).

Finally, it must be added that, according to WTO forecasts, international tourist arrivals throughout the world should amount to 515 million in 1995 (an average annual increase of 3.5 per cent), with Europe channelling 294 million (an average annual rise of 1.4 per cent). This opens up prospects for an improvement in Portugal's position, and it is probable that by 1995 Portuguese shares of world and European tourist flows will be 2.7 per cent and 4.7 per cent higher respectively.

Government policy

The growing influence of the private sector in Portuguese tourism, which should increase still more in the future, has allowed the government to confine its own action to specific essential aspects, thus implementing in this sector too the principle demanded for all State intervention: "less government, better government".

Action already taken will be stepped up, while the government will also launch other activities, with the accent mainly on:

-- improving the information and scientific knowledge on which decisions are based, in both the public and private sectors;

-- providing more investment for recreational facilities and infrastructure, including sports, cultural and social facilities, not only for the local population but also for tourists;

-- reviewing the environment and the aesthetic quality of the facilities at tourist resorts, in accordance with the Land-Use Development Plans, and renovation of the less successful as far as possible;

-- strengthening, decentralising and stepping up inspection in agreement with local authorities so as to keep better check on the quality of tourism products (kitchens, quality of meals, prices, hygiene of infrastructures and quality of products);

-- diversifying the supply of tourism products, notably by investing in and promoting rural tourism, religious tourism, conference and incentive tourism, cultural tourism, sea tourism, golf, spa treatment, environmental tourism, hunting and fishing tourism, and gastronomic and wine tourism;

-- playing up the factors connected with reception of the visitor, especially such traditional features as the hospitable, friendly, likeable and communicative nature of the Portuguese people;

-- continuing the modernisation of infrastructures, especially transport, communications, drainage, telecommunications, etc.

The choice of targets must be confined to those best suited to Portuguese economic policy which, as far as possible, contribute to a harmonious and coherent tourism development policy.

In this perspective and in the light of the major 1989-92 Plan options, the following priorities have been defined:

-- to contribute to balance-of-payments equilibrium by increasing the relative importance of tourism in the national accounts;

-- to help reduce regional disequilibria and discrepancies;

-- to help improve the quality of life of the Portuguese people;

-- to help protect the environment and enhance the value of the cultural heritage.

Institutional framework. No significant changes have been made in the structure of the State Secretariat for Tourism. The resources of the Institute for the Promotion of Tourism, on the other hand, have been increased with the creation of the post of Vice-President, the opening of two more tourist offices abroad, in Japan and Austria, and closer co-operation with the Tourist Regions.

The private tourism sector is well represented both in the Tourist Regions and in the National Tourism Council. There have been no significant changes since 1989 since the existing structure has proved perfectly operational.

Action and measures taken in 1990 and 1991

Accommodation and catering. Supported by the outright grants from the EEC's ERDF structural fund and the Tourism Fund, supply has grown constantly. This incentive programme, called SIFIT, to which the EEC contributes 70 per cent and the Portuguese Government 30 per cent through the Tourism Fund, has provided very attractive financial incentives for areas regarded as having priority for the development of tourism, amounting in some cases to as much as 50 per cent of the total investment for specific types of facility.

SIFIT has been widely publicised and both Portuguese and foreign private investors have responded by submitting projects which are now being implemented and which, in addition to creating many jobs, will in fact largely fill the existing gaps in Portuguese tourism supply, especially in the areas of accommodation, catering and recreation.

At the same time, the Tourism Fund has improved its direct funding terms by raising the ceilings, with interest rates lower than those of the commercial banks and allowing up to 15 years for reimbursement.

The Hotels and Catering Act is being amended with a view to simplifying the procedures for the approval of projects and laying down stricter rules on the quality of supply.

Transport. One of the reasons why private operators are interested in the hinterland was given in the 1989 edition (accommodation and catering): the excellent terms offered by SIFIT and the Tourism Fund. The new land transport network completed by the government, and which is now "changing the appearance" of the country, has also had a positive impact in this connection. With the opening of new sections of motorway, main roads and other means of communication, both within the country and for its road and rail links with the rest of Europe, the traditionally less developed inland areas will have a transport network which will eliminate the disadvantages of isolation.

This development in the inland areas has been accompanied by the opening of a number of universities and higher education establishments, job creation and population settlement. It is therefore natural that tourist agencies should make their contribution by ensuring tourism supply.

Stimulation of economic activity in sensitive areas. The support measures described above for accommodation and catering are applied to rural tourism, which takes various forms:

-- "Turismo de habitaçâo": in houses of special architectural and historical interest. The existing network is all privately owned and its quality is comparable with the Portuguese State-owned "Pousadas";

-- "Turismo rural": accommodation in country-style houses in country towns or their vicinity;

-- "Agro-turismo": accommmodation on farms, with participation by tourists in farming activities;

-- Hunting areas for tourists: development of possibilities;

-- Rural hotels: with between 10 and 30 rooms and situated in non-urban areas.

Environment. The fact that Portugal is a member of the European Economic Community obliges the government to comply with EEC directives on environmental protection. The authorities have always been sensitive to this aspect since there is no future for tourism in derelict areas. The special case of the Algarve, where too many apartment blocks were built (approved not by central government but by the local authorities during the period of political instability resulting from the change of regime in April 1974) has not been emulated. On the contrary, it was a "lesson" to the government on the need to take special steps to protect the environment, obliging the town authorities to draw up urban guidelines, defining protection standards for the whole coastal area and the most sensitive inland regions (lakes, waterways, mountains, etc.) and laying down very strict standards on the location of tourism projects outside urban areas.

Employment. Tourism has created about 144 000 permanent jobs for the various related activities; with 131 000 jobs created, "hotels and catering" count for some 91.4 per cent of the total. In the high season, when demand is at its peak, this last figure tends to rise significantly: the data available show an average rise of 22 per cent compared with the off-season. Assuming this percentage roughly reflects the reaction of the "hotels and catering" sector to the demands of the high season, it can be fairly safely concluded that, during the period of peak demand, total employment in tourism (which of course includes insecure jobs) must be about 175 000 jobs, some 31 000 of which are seasonal.

Vocational training. Initial vocational training was provided for 541 trainees in all, comprising 291 senior managers and 250 middle managers. In the area of continuing training, the Mobile Brigade Schools received 1 758 workers. Several private schools offering tourism and hotel training have also made their appearance, but as they are of recent creation no one has as yet qualified. This also applies to the new Polytechnic Institutes set up under the development programme for inland areas, whose first graduates will only be leaving in 1993/94.

Aid and investment incentives. Decrees on this sector were published between 1989 and 1991.

Spa treatment. In addition to social financial incentives which have prompted the refurbishment, modernisation and extension of the operating period of many thermal spas, a programme has been launched to create a new image of spa treatment, adopting new forms of promotion at home and abroad, involving the following surveys:

- a comparative survey of the competing foreign and Portuguese supply of thermal treatment;
- a survey of the international and domestic market for spa treatment in Portugal, and the implications for the definition of target groups;
- a survey of the image of spa treatment among the Portuguese population;
- a preparatory survey with a view to creating new thermal products and appropriate distribution channels;
- a survey of promotion campaigns to launch the new concept of "Spas in Portugal".

Marketing. The CTPs undertake regular market research on present and potential international demand with an eye to adjusting promotional strategy. The methods used include surveys in some cases, while in others existing information is collected and analysed for items of direct interest to Portugal. Market research does not cover fixed periods, but these are usually not more than 3 years.

The CTPs engage in trade-related activities in advertising, public relations, and trade and other fairs, and organise meetings in order to reach not only the general public on certain markets but also the better-off classes for the supply of the national tourism product.

Over the period 1989-91 tourism promotion enjoyed EEC aid for activities on non-Community markets. CTPs have also been opened in Japan and Austria.

A campaign to promote the image of Portugal has been launched in the Republic of South Africa. Promotion campaigns have also begun on non-EEC markets where Portuguese tourism is represented, appropriate additional resources having been allocated for this purpose.

Tourists from these new markets have been targeted and action stepped up on the traditional markets, with emphasis on the "products" regarded as supply priorities, in the hope of attracting socio-economic groups of more interest to Portugal. These activities have been jointly organised by the tourist regions and central government.

Consumer protection. As a member of the European Economic Community, Portugal endorses all the measures taken by the EEC in this area, including the following:

-- strengthening of safety precautions in hotels, etc., with the installation of special equipment to deal with fire, flood, earthquake and other risks;

-- briefing for architects working in the private sector on the needs of the physically handicapped regarding access, movement and comfort.

-- special increased policing in the high season in areas with a heavier concentration of tourists;

-- publication of leaflets in foreign languages warning tourists about health protection, theft, etc.;

-- a complaints book provided in all hotels, restaurants and other tourist facilities. Complaints are immediately examined by a group of inspectors from the General Directorate for Tourism and by staff in the tourist areas;

-- at EEC level, Portugal has taken an active part in drafting the Travel Directive which is due to come into operation in January 1993.

Staggered holidays. Unfortunately, not much progress has been made in this area and any action taken by the State Secretariat for Tourism -- such as domestic tourism campaigns, a special low-season prices policy, etc. -- has had little effect.

Since this is a European problem which cannot be solved by the tourism industry alone, the question of EEC measures is part of the 1991-93 Community Action Programme, in which Portugal is actively involved.

In Portugal, the school year, which traditionally used to begin in mid-October, will start this year on 15th September and the Christmas, Shrove Tuesday and Easter holidays will be longer. It is not known whether this will increase the tourist supply, but a slight improvement is expected.

International co-operation. Several agreements on tourism have been signed by Portugal with countries in the Mediterranean basin, Latin America and Africa.

Apart from the Outline Agreement signed in May 1991 with Brazil which will certainly have a considerable impact, it is interesting to note the co-operation and technical assistance agreements that have been negotiated with the five African countries whose official language is Portuguese: Angola, Cape Verde, Guinea Bissao, São Tomé and Principe, and Mozambique.

Agreements, with strong implications for tourism, were signed when the respective political regimes were moving towards pluralism and the peace negotiations were progressing (already completed in the case of Angola and well advanced in the case of Mozambique). As well as sending multidisciplinary missions of Portuguese technicians to these African countries, various services in the State Secretariat for Tourism have taken trainees, mainly in the areas of legislation, inspection, hotels and catering, project evaluation, economic research, statistics, etc. The cost of this co-operation is borne by the Institute for Economic Co-operation, an agency of the Ministry of Finance, the Ministry of Foreign Affairs and the official tourism offices of the countries which have sent trainees to Portugal. This programme was stepped up in January 1991 and it is still too early to take stock of it. However, it is currently one of the Tourism Secretariat's priorities.

In 1989 and 1990, the National Institute for Tourism Training awarded 40 scholarships to trainees from the Portuguese-speaking African countries.

SPAIN

Tourism as an economic activity

In 1989 the Spanish economy experienced a notable boom - unemployment figures improved, together with consumption and export figures. On the other hand, economic results from tourist activities overall suffered a decrease as the consequence of the pattern of international demand. However the demand within Spain showed an important increase.

As a result of these circumstances, the final economic contribution from overall tourist activities showed a decrease of a few tenths of a percent, positioning itself around 9 per cent in its contribution to the Gross National Product and 11 per cent with respect to the total for the working population.

Income for international tourism reached 36.4 per cent of the exports of goods and services (in US dollars) in 1989 and 33.3 per cent in 1990.

The ranking occupied by the economic contribution from tourist activities (8.7 per cent of the GNP in 1989) is above that of construction (8.3 per cent) and banking services (6.8 per cent). Activities in the industrial sector, excluding construction, contributed 27.1 per cent in the same year.

Tourism is intimately connected with other sectors, especially transport, territorial planning, health, city safety and the environment.

In these fields and in the last two years, the Spanish Government, together with the governments of the different autonomous communities, has worked extensively.

The creation of secondary and charter airline companies (Binter, air Europa ...) will facilitate the movement of passengers at lower prices; the intensive construction of dual carriageways (without tolls) and the elimination of the need for travellers to cross through cities (such as Valencia) will facilitate tourism by road travel, which in Spain supposes 62 per cent of the total; the demand for larger areas per person in tourist accommodation -- the Community of the Balearic Islands now demands 60 m2 per person in newly constructed hotels -- and the construction of installations for leisure, recreational and sports equipment is under way in all tourist towns. The improvement in environmental cleanliness is clear and is corroborated by the increase in the number of beaches flying the blue flag, which the EEC granted to Spain in 1991. In the high season, the increase in the police force in tourist areas is one of the norms of the Ministry of the Interior and the environment has been improved to a considerable degree by the creation of the Secretariat of State for Environment, within the Ministry of Public Works and Transport.

The collaboration between the General Secretariat for Tourism and the Secretariat of State for the Environment has been very close during the last few months. At the present time both organisms have shown their willingness to carry out certain initiatives jointly. Among these the most important are those connected with education and making tourists aware of the products available and those referring to the prevention of damage to, and the restoration of, the environment in areas that are essentially tourist areas. In order to carry this out both secretariats will work together to strengthen the present lines of collaboration described above.

Prospects for development

In general, the perspectives for 1992 are good: the national tourist market continues to develop strongly and the international market is showing signs of overcoming the relative slump experienced in 1989-1990. The important events anticipated for 1992 - Expo 92 in Seville, the Olympics in Barcelona and the year in which Madrid is the Culture Capital of Europe - will surely contribute very notably to the new surge in the international tourist market.

The key questions for the tourist industry in 1990 are the development of infrastructures - mainly transport and investments in improving the environment; the cultural heritage for tourists and the development of alternative tourist products.

Government policy

The Spanish Tourism Administration, following the pattern laid down in previous years, has established a series of priorities which are laid down in the White Book of Spanish Tourism and which refer to:

-- the updating of the hotel infrastructures;

-- the boosting of quality tourism in order to improve competitiveness;

-- the segmentation of the market with a view to promotion;

-- capture of the extra-community market, especially the recovery of the United States market and the opening up of the Japanese market;

-- significant boosting of cultural tourism: the Pilgrims' Way to Santiago, the Silver Trail, the Silk Route, the Celtic Route, etc.

-- tourist development in accordance with environmental protection;

-- action giving support to rural tourism and alternative tourism;

-- adaptation to the liberalisation of transport, as demanded within the EEC (travel agents, air travel, etc.).

Institutional framework. Responsibility for tourist matters is shared between the central administration and the various autonomous administrations, in application of the Decretos de transferencias to the autonomous communities passed in 1978, 1979, 1982, 1983 and 1984.

At the central level, tourist policy is the responsibility of the Secretary General for Tourism whose role is that of co-ordination, harmonisation of the legal order and promotion at international level.

On this point it is necessary to indicate that on the occasion of the reorganisation of the ministries effected in 1991, the Secretary General for Tourism instead of forming part of the Ministry of Transport was moved to the Ministry of Industry, Commerce and Tourism.

However, the 17 autonomous communities that form the Spanish State all have tourist responsibilities in their respective territories with regard to promotion at national level, infrastructures and the existing legal order which now covers ample legislation on the classification of hotels, camping sites, tourist professions, travel agencies, territorial legislation and tourist protection. It should be made clear that the different regulations on the activities of the travel agents are at present being revised in order to adapt them to EEC guidelines.

With regard to plans and programmes, the autonomous communities have legislated on various matters. Those of most importance are the plans for modernising tourist accommodation anticipated by the Autonomous Communities of the Balearic Islands, Castilla-La Mancha, Castilla-Leon, Extremadura and Navarre. Where rural tourism is concerned the Communities of Aragon, Catalonia, Castilla-Leon and Asturias among other all have programmes.

Finally, all the autonomous communities have drawn up rules for regulating the awarding of aid (credits and subsidies) destined to improve tourist infrastructures and the level of training. In this way, it is the various communities which have the task of elaborating operative programmes within the different community support frameworks. These programmes are subject to the approval of the central administration which sends them to the EEC Commission for final approval.

With regard to the state, it should be pointed out that its aim is to stimulate the private sector so that this will determine the standards of quality in tourist establishments. There also exist programmes relating to technological innovation, anticipating the creation of information networks and automation systems in the different tourist establishments. Together with this action it is planned to boost initiatives for environmental protection.

However, where plans are concerned, the most outstanding is the Integral Tourist Plan, which contains all the initiatives proposed by the administration which have an effect on the tourist environment. An Interministerial Commission will watch over the development of said initiatives.

Also worthy of note, in the area of promotion, is the Triennial Marketing Plan of 1991-93.

Tourist policy is effected through close collaboration between the central administration and the various autonomous administrations.

In this way since 1989, the establishment of greater co-ordination with the private sector has been encouraged and this is the object of special attention on the part of the central administration.

Contact with the professional sectors is constant. Proof of this has been the celebration of the "Meetings on Spanish Tourism" which have been held for two consecutive years. Some organisations such as the Confederacion Espanola de Organizaciones Empresariales (C.E.O.E.) (Spanish Confederation of Business Organisations) have a Tourist Committee which deals exclusively with this sector.

Mention should also be made of the contacts that have been made between the public administrations and the private sector. This is the case of the "Crisis Committee" formed to follow up the consequence of the Gulf crisis and its impact on tourism.

Also worthy of note are the relations established between the tourist administration and the private sector within the Commission for Industry, Public Works and Services to Parliament. At the end of last year the "Committee for analysing the tourist situation in Spain" was set up within the said Commission. This committee has been called upon on a number of occasions by parliamentary groups those in positions of high responsibility in the tourist administration and other organisms of the administration related to tourism such as civil aviation, ports, coasts, etc. and also representatives of the private tourist sector have appeared before it.

Action and measures taken in 1989 and 1990

Accommodation. This covers measures for limiting the supply, and measures for the reclassification and identification of the illegal supply which is undeclared, with the consequent failure to comply with the fiscal laws. Aid for modernisation for modernisation is also covered.

Restoration. Vigilance regarding the quality and inspection of same and the imposition of sanctions in the case of non-fulfilment.

Transport. Air transport is in a stage of liberalisation within the framework of the EEC. Transport on land, both by road and rail, has been the object of great investment in such schemes as the plan for dual carriageways and the high-speed train. No particular measures exist with regard to river transport.

An estimate of the economic activity in *sensitive areas* (rural areas, mountain areas, etc.). Within the policy of diversification of the Spanish tourist product, the development of rural tourism is receiving priority attention on the part of the Secretary General for Tourism.

The autonomous communities have established various types of financial aid for the creation of accommodation in rural tourist areas, together with the regulations which determine the characteristics of this offer.

There also exists economic aid for agrotourism developed by the Ministry of Agriculture, Fisheries and Food by means of the Royal Decree 808/1987 on aid for the improvement in the efficiency of structures. This was modified in 1990.

Mention should also be made of the work carried out by the Ministry of Commerce and Finance through the Directorate General for Regional Incentives, although in the field of rural tourism subsidies granted by the said Directorate General have been few in number. The Secretary General of Tourism, in his work of co-ordination and promotion of rural tourism has developed the following strategy:

-- Concession of credit at a preferential interest rate.

-- With regard to co-ordination it is worth mentioning the recent international Seminar on Rural Tourism which took place on 21st and 22nd March 1991, to which those responsible for the 17 autonomous communities, in the Secretariat General for the Environment, in the Secretariat General for Agrarian Structures and for the private sector were invited. As a conclusion to this Seminar, the Secretary General for Tourism agreed to carry out a study on comparative legislation to serve as a basis for establishing the regulatory framework for the development of rural tourism in Spain. In the field of training, a study is being drawn up to provide a knowledge of the needs at national level and will offer a programme which is easily applicable in the various regions of the country.

-- Promotional activities will be channelled through action programmes agreed with the autonomous communities, participating technically and economically in those projects which may act as catalysts in the development of rural tourism in Spain.

-- Ultimately, it is intended to strengthen the necessary channels of information at both the national and international level, which will allow an effective co-ordination in this matter.

-- An area of particular interest for the Secretary General of Tourism is the introduction of advanced technologies for information in the rural areas. In this connection, particular mention should be made of the experiences in the province of Almeria, with the setting up of the community programme STAR.

-- The Secretary-General for Tourism also carries out the task of propagation of community aid referring to this sector. He makes studies and informs the organisms that manage this aid at central level on the suitability and viability of the projects presented. Special attention is now being paid to the operative programmes of the CEC (objective 5b) which are in the preparatory stage, to aid requested under the leadership initiative programme and to those programmes which will shortly be presented with the incentive of the EEC bid for pilot projects for rural and cultural tourism.

-- Finally, mention must be made of the task of promoting specific products such as "El Camino de Santiago" (The Pilgrims' Way to Santiago) or "La Ruta de la Plata" (The Silver Trail) which to a large degree are influenced by the rural environment.

Environment. The agents that intervene in this field are many. The general framework is established in the Law on Conservation of Natural Spaces and Wild Flora and Fauna of 27 March 1989, in the regulations for the creation of the 10 national parks and in those for natural parks which make up in their entirety 10 per cent of the total area of Spain. To the above must be added a meticulous and lengthy legislation which includes the Law on Water of 2 August 1985, the Law on the Coastline of 26 July 1988 and the Royal Decree 738/88 of 1 July in which are established regulations on the quality of seawater for bathing, etc.

The Secretary General for Tourism collaborates in the activities for the protection of the environment and also in making the sector aware of the inter-relations that exist between tourism and the environment, regarding which the following activities may be highlighted:

-- The organisation of seminars and publications as a means of making the sector aware and amongst which should be mentioned the meetings on Spanish tourism of 1989 and 1990.

-- Insistence on a technical file of environmental conditions in projects for new investment that are subject to public subsidies.

-- Compilation of documents, analyses and research.

-- Participation in seminars and international organisms, in particular the Environment Committee of the World Tourism Organisation (WTO).

-- Co-operation with the Secretary of State for the Environment.

-- Consideration of environmental factors on the rest of the policies developed by the Secretary General for Tourism and in particular in the diversification and non-seasonal quality of the tourist products available, boosting the creation of alternative products.

Employment. There have been no significant changes. Emphasis should be placed on the preoccupation that exists over tourism-related professions (guides, posts, etc.), given the standards demanded by the EEC.

Education on tourism. Education on tourism is carried out in the Schools of Tourism. At present there are three Official Schools (Madrid, Gerona and Palma de Mallorca); the first is dependent on the Central Tourist Board and the other two on the respective autonomous communities. There are also private schools which provide this education.

The National Institute of Employment also provides training in the different professional fields related to the tourist sector, basically in the hotel business and in restaurants.

With regard to specialist courses and master's degrees in tourism, mention should be made of the courses provided by the Official School of Tourism in Madrid and the Universities of Madrid, Malaga and Las Palmas in the Canary Islands.

Concerning the Official School of Tourism in Madrid, it should be pointed out that its legal standing will shortly be modified to make it a public entity. On the other hand, it is at present also revising its study plan with the intention of creating two courses: an initial specialisation course and another on hotel and travel agency management.

Aid and incentives. The aid granted by the Spanish Administration to the tourist sector is: subsidies that are written off, by virtue of the Law on Regional Economic Incentives, and credit for tourism.

Regional Economic Incentives have been granted since 1988 and are conceded by the state administration, in collaboration with the Autonomous communities, for determined areas as a function of its GNP par inhabitant and the level of unemployment. They cover 83 per cent of the country with a maximum value of up to 75 per cent in the least favoured areas and an average of up to 25 per cent of the cost of the investment.

New installations, extensions and modernisation of hotels are all subsidised. Support is given for the establishment of new hotels, tourist camping sites and complementary installations for leisure activities of particular interest to the development of the zone concerned. Excluded are saturated areas, apartments and restaurants.

With regard to tourist credit, one is speaking of a soft credit with an interest of 13.5 per cent authorised by the Banco Hipotecario. The Board limits itself to declaring the value of the tourist interest. This credit is applied to the modernisation of the tourist supply and technological innovation.

Social tourism. The programmes offered by the Instituto Nacional de Servicios Sociales (National Institute of Social Services) are noteworthy and are, in turn, related to the holidays for senior citizens and single parent holidays for mothers and children.

Various autonomous communities collaborate with both projects such as Andalusia, Murcia, the Balearic Islands, Catalonia and Valencia for programmes for senior citizens and Castilla-La Mancha, Extremadura, and Madrid in the case of single parent vacations together with Andalusia, Valencia and Castilla-Leon.

Youth tourism. This is carried out via the network TIVE, Oficina de Tourismo Juvenil (Youth Tourism Office) where various tourist services, help and advice are offered (Travel, studies, exchanges, etc.).

Spas. The General Secretary for Tourism has available credit of Ptas 2 billion subject to preferential interest for the promotion of thermal establishments. The autonomous communities also authorise subsidies such as in Cantabria where financing has been obtained from the European Tourist Year to promote tourism in spas.

Marketing. Studies and investigations have been carried out in the demand area in order to understand the holiday habits of Spaniards, week-end trips and other tourist travel in Spain, the journeys the Spaniards make abroad and their spending habits, their motivation and degree of satisfaction. This study is biannual and the last one was carried out in 1990.

Studies have been effected to find out the degree of satisfaction over international demand for the Spanish tourist product; the possible technical, legal, political and economic circumstances which influence Spanish tourism, the construction of a matrix for the forecasting of the origin/destination of tourists for 1995 and another for the evaluation of the economic efficiency of foreign tourist demand.

These efforts represent a continuous endeavour to investigate the tourist market and the methods employed vary according to the subject of the study.

The Direccion General de Politica Turistica (Directorate General for Tourist Policy) has elaborated a study on the flow of tourists in Europe and the Mediterranean with a projection to 1995. In this study it has been decided to use the flow of tourists as detailed by the actual countries of origin using the opinion polls carried out on the whole population. These are considered the most reliable variables because the traditional "Income" and "Relative Prices" variables which, in principle, explain the demand for any goods, are subject to a fair amount of uncertainty when other sociological or cultural factors (difficult to quantify or predict) intervene.

When it comes to the average amount spent per tourist the amount stated in the study are supported by the statistics drawn up by CMT and others by OECD and PMI. In this context and with respect to Spain as the destination, by applying an economic model and taking as countries of origin Germany, the United Kingdom, Holland, France, Belgium and Switzerland it can be deduced that in the year 1995 holiday tourism will experience an annual increase of between 1.7 and 4 per cent, excluding factors difficult to predict. As for the real income from tourism, the values are also positive and vary between 4.1 and 7.9 per cent if the predictions for the arrival of visitors are achieved. It should be noted, however, that the predictions effected refer to the tourists who remain four nights or more but, taking into account the fact that the duration of a stay in this type of tourism is tending to diminish in favour of short duration tourism, and it is not unrealistic to venture that the overall positive increments in tourism will be exceeded.

With respect to the marketing and commercialisation strategies of the Spanish tourist industry abroad, these revolve around various elements:

-- Publicity: this may be international or local. The first is primarily directed towards the European markets and to a lesser degree to the Far East and Australian markets with the slogan of "Spain, everything under the sun". Local publicity is carried out by 27 Spanish Tourist Offices in their respective countries.

-- Fairs: the different Spanish Tourist Offices participate in the most important tourist fairs which take place annually: BIT in Milan, BIF in Brussels, ITB in Berlin, WBI in London and FITUR in Madrid.

-- Workshops and professional meetings: here it is necessary to make contact with foreign travel agencies and tour operators. Specific products are presented (the Green Country of Spain, Sporting Tourism, Golf). This is directed at Europe and is marketing high quality, and at promotions in the United States and Japan.

Where conferences, conventions and incentive travel are concerned, contact is maintained with large European and North American companies so that they will choose Spain as the place for their business trips.

-- Public relations: this covers relations with journalists and with travel agents who come to Spain in order to familiarise themselves with the tourism that is on offer. Support for promotion covers printing (brochures, posters and other publications), the maintenance of photographic files and the production of audio-visual material among others things. Collaboration is also ensured with public and private organisations for the development of specific promotions. In this way the TURESPANA-IBERIA-American Express campaign for the promotion of Spain in the United States and the TURESPANA-Daimler-Benz campaign for the promotion of the Pilgrims' Way to Santiago were brought about.

Consumer protection. The autonomous communities have legislated on matters of inspection and the imposing of sanctions in the tourist environment but, moreover, their laws in defence of the consumer, and thus the Decree 63/1982 in the Principality of Asturias or the Law 1/1990 of 6th January, are applicable to tourists as consumers. At the national level the General Law on the Defence of Consumers and Users of 1984 is also applicable to tourists given its general character.

The existence of private and public consumer organisations (OMIC) that monitor adherence to the legislation should also be mentioned. If necessary they will take judicial action against the offender.

In all tourist establishments there are claim forms on which the user may point out that, in his opinion, the regulations in force have not been adhered to in matters of cleanliness, economic conditions, etc. These forms are in three copies: one for the tourist, one for the company and a third to be sent to the organism within the administration that is responsible for tourist affairs in the area where the establishment is located. This organism will be responsible for dealing with the complaint and, where necessary, imposing a sanction. Any tourist who makes a complaint will be informed of the result of his claim.

On this point it is fitting to indicate the support given by the Secretary General for Tourism to the WTO for the holding of a Seminar on "Security in Tourism" which took place in Madrid in September 1990. Also Spain forms part of the Group of Experts formed within the WTO which is proceeding to draw up two documents, the first referring to "Security in Tourism" and the second to a "Deontological Code for Handicapped Tourists".

Lastly, it is necessary to indicate the importance of the Directive of the European Community Council of 3 June 1990, regarding combined travel, combined holidays and combined circuits. This Directive necessitates the adoption of a series of liberalisation measures in view of the proximity of the single European market, assuring a high level of protection for the consumer vis-à-vis the disparities that exist among the various national regulations.

Staggering of holidays. Problems due to seasonal holidays have forced the main transport companies to take measures to ease transport congestion during holiday periods. Iberia follows a policy of launching specific products during low seasons offering destinations which are different from the traditional ones, such as the case of South America in the winter period. The company also establishes lower flight prices in periods of lower demand. Iberia, together with organisms such as tourist boards, tourist consultants, etc. sets up promotions in the country of origin with the aim of establishing specific traffic in low season periods.

Another means of combating the problem of seasons is that of incentive travel for companies and similar groups that are experiencing increasing development. On its part, Renfe (Spanish National Railway Company) has developed a programme called "The Four Seasons" with the aim of attracting travellers outside the holiday season. The programme covers 2/3 day holidays at a price that includes train, transfer from train to accommodation, accommodation and visits. Lastly, it should be noted that the Marketing Plan for 1991 contemplates the end of emphasis on the holiday season as one of its main objectives. For this the Plan states the intention of promoting traditional tourism in the form of sun and beaches in periods outside the summer season, where possible by means such as tourism for retired persons on the coast, together with the promotion of other tourist attractions such as culture, touring holidays, cities, sports, religion, languages, etc. It also encourages camping at weekends in off peak seasons.

International co-operation. The Secretary General for Tourism is carrying out a task of international co-operation which consists basically in encouraging the signing of agreements on co-operation in tourism with the countries that are interested in this and also in sending support missions, that is, groups of experts on specific subjects, to the country in question. This work is carried out in collaboration with the Agencia Espanola de Cooperacion Internacional (Spanish Agency for International Co-operation). Financing is the responsibility of this Agency.

With regard to agreements, the signing of a tourist co-operation agreement between Spain and the USSR in October 1990 may be cited and, with regard to support missions and technical aid, an agreement which has been made with Ecuador and Guatemala (Maya Route, the Trifinio Region) and the Dominican Republic (legislation and classification of hotels) in 1989.

On the other hand, grants are provided annually for tourist studies in Spain, the value of which was 34 870 500 Ptas in 1989 and 37 215 000 Ptas in 1990. Grants were also given to Spanish students for studying tourism abroad. These reached a total of 5 000 000 Ptas in 1989 and 6 000 000 Ptas in 1990.

SWEDEN

Tourism as an economic activity

Total earnings of Swedish tourism are estimated at some 80 billion SKr, of which foreign travel currencies amounted to 16.3 billion SKr in 1990. In the list of export sections -- according to the SITC standard -- Swedish tourist income in 1990 ranked in the sixth place corresponding to 4.5 per cent of total export value. Tourist income in foreign travel currencies (16.3 billion SKr) represented some 15 per cent of the total invisible income in Sweden 1990. According to an analysis, carried out by the National Board of Taxation in 1990, 63 per cent of all tourist spending in Sweden is constituted of taxes and different kinds of social charges.

The number employed in the Swedish tourist industry is estimated at some 200 000 individuals totally, out of which some 100 000 are full-time employed. Some 63 000 individuals are employed in hotels and restaurants. The general rate of unemployment in Sweden is around 2 per cent. Although no corresponding figure is available for the tourism sector as a whole, unemployment within this industry has been rising steadily. Tourism in Sweden has declined in numbers for the first time since the seventies. In the year 1990 as compared to 1989 there is a decrease of 7 per cent. Some areas of the travel market have reacted negatively to the increased price level and some tourist establishments, primarily restaurants, have left the market.

The general tax reform, introduced by the government in January 1991, with a transformation of the tax system aimed at, among other things, reducing income taxes by higher VAT rates, worsened the situation for the Swedish tourist industry, due to the effects on consumer prices for hotel, restaurant and transport services and the resulting effect on business volume.

On prospects for development, no forecasts on the demand and/or supply of tourism for 1992 or beyond have been undertaken by the Swedish Tourist Board (STB).

Government policy

After the ministerial re-organization in late 1988, when the responsibility for tourism and recreation was transferred to the Ministry of Industry, no change has been formally decided regarding the governmental policy on tourism.

However, a governmental investigation has recently been undertaken with the aim of reconsidering governmental tourism policy as well as the objectives and the organization of the Swedish Tourist Board (STB).

According to the report from the investigation committee, published in mid-June 1991:

-- the general objectives of the governmental tourism policy, being to promote and develop tourism into and within Sweden, should be operationally described;

-- the objectives of the STB should be more clearly formulated, separating tourism policy and recreation policy;

-- the distribution of responsibilities between STB and other bodies, involved in tourism, should be more clearly stated, with the aim of making the tourist industry more aware of their responsibilities for an extended financial contribution to the joint promotion abroad of Sweden as a tourist destination;

-- extended co-operation is recommended between the STB and other institutions and authorities, dealing with information abroad, such as the Swedish Institute, the Swedish Export Council and the Ministry of Foreign Affairs as well as regional tourist organizations and the travel trade, so as to reach a better co-ordination and a greater efficiency/effectiveness of information and promotion activities;

-- the consequences of EEC policies and activities on European tourism must be taken into account.

As to the responsibilities and actitivies of the STB, the governmental committee is proposing the following guidelines:

-- the main task of the STB should be to promote travel to Sweden from abroad, primarily by carrying out information and marketing activities in co-operation with the tourist industry whereas the responsibility for domestic tourism should be laid upon the local and regional authorities;

-- by increasing its knowledge of tourism and markets, the STB should try to improve the awareness of the need for co-operation and consultation among tourist agents inside the private and public sectors in order to create and develop tourist products of a high quality;

-- the STB should support the coordination of regional tourist activities;

-- increased efforts should be given to the sectoral tasks, e.g. the establishment and maintenance of adequate relations with relevant authorities and organizations on the national and international level in order to secure good working conditions for the tourism industry;

-- in principle, the government and the private industry should take equal responsibility for the financing of joint tourist promotion activities.

Furthermore, the committee is proposing the reconstruction of the STB into a governmentally owned company which, however, should be open to private shareholders such as interested partners from the tourist industry.

The Government is expected to decide on these proposals through a bill to Parliament in the early part of 1992.

Institutional framework. The situation regarding public finance has in some parts of the country caused a reconsideration by the authorities of the maintenance of local and/or regional tourist organizations. Some of them have been closed down, some others have been re-constructed. A general tendency is to demand an improved financial contribution from the local tourist industry.

In 1989 the Swedish Travel Federation (RRF) was formed as a common organization for the different branches of the travel trade. Thereby a forum has been established for an intensified dialogue and co-operation between the different sectors of the travel trade, and with the STB, which is an associated member of the RRF.

In order to create better inter-sectoral communication with different partners involved in tourism, special consultative groups have been initiated by the STB with representatives for the tourist industry, the public sector and regional tourist organizations, respectively.

Action and measures taken in 1989 and 1990

Transport. In 1989-90 deregulation of coach traffic was carried out in Sweden, which led to a better and more competitive supply of regional and inter-regional coach services.

In 1990-91 the Swedish taxi system was liberalised. As a consequence, the supply has increased markedly and the competition between different taxi companies has hardened. Now, varied pricing systems have been introduced, sometimes confusing the customers.

For coach as well as for taxi traffic permission is required from the regional authority, which has to consider the appropriate total capacity for the area. In practical terms, the reform means that the former monopolistic situation is abolished.

Protection of the environment. From 1990, higher taxes had to be paid by industries causing environmental pollution.

Employment. Although the general rate of unemployment in Sweden is very low, some 2 per cent, the situation within the hotel and restaurant sector has worsened, due to the present situation of the Swedish tourist industry. The rate of unemployment for people working in hotels and restaurants was 9 per cent in May 1991 as compared to 5.4 per cent in May 1990.

Vocational training. On the basis of a report from a governmental investigation on the supply of personnel and the demand for vocational training for the tourist sector, carried through 1988-89, a special programme for education and training in the tourism sector has been decided by the Government and will be elaborated by a state authority.

Aids and incentives to enterprises. The policy of granting loans and subsidies to tourist projects by public means has been continued after 1989, the overall purpose being to uphold employment in less populated areas. For certain regions, e.g. the Island of Gotland, development programmes have been elaborated with direct governmental support and supervision.

Social tourism. A pilot programme with government financial support, started in 1989 by the STB in co-operation with the Trade Union Federation, has continued through 1990-91. The aim is to extend the possibilites for trade union members to experience suitable holiday recreation facilities.

Marketing. A market study of travel patterns, motivation, expenditure, length of stay, types of accommodation, etc. was carried out by the STB among European car tourists in the summer of 1989. The study was conducted in co-operation with some of the largest ferry companies.

A study on foreign coach tourists in Sweden was carried out in 1989 with the aim of improving the knowledge of this market segment. Information was collected on nationality, length of stay in Sweden, distance driven, shown monthly over the year.

In co-operation with the other nordic tourist boards (Denmark, Finland and Norway) and Scandinavian Airlines (SAS), the STB has carried through a study of the Japanese market, giving travel trade facts, expected travel trends, and operational suggestions for the planning of a future marketing strategy.

Within the STB "Tourism Data Base" (TDB) Programme systematic studies are permanently carried out on a stratified sample of 24 000 individuals per annum, representing the entire Swedish population. On the basis of the material collected, analyses are made of the changes in different types of travelling and travel patterns, actual and planned.

Protection of the tourist as a consumer. The Swedish Travel Guarantee Act of 1972 is still in force, and no change nor development worth mentionning has occurred.

International co-operation. Within the frame of the European Year of Tourism (EYT) 1991 a special pan-European project on tourism for disabled people was carried through by the STB in co-operation with the English, Finnish and Norwegian Tourist Boards. The project culminated with a "Tourism for All" Conference in Gatwick with some 200 participants from 18 different countries.

SWITZERLAND

Tourism as an economic activity

Tourism occupies a prime position in Switzerland's economy. A study by the Federal Office for Industry, Arts and Crafts (OFIAMT) gives detailed information for the first time on the ways in which tourism is adding value and on how important tourism is to other branches of the economy. The study shows that tourism provides 8 per cent of Gross Domestic Product for a turnover of SF 34 billion in 1989, and value added of SF 22 billion. Tourism ranks fifth in the economy after the public sector, banking, the wholesale trade and the retail trade.

A number of sectors depend heavily on tourism: mountain railways, cable cars and ski lifts (83 per cent of turnover), the hotel industry (79 per cent) and air travel (69 per cent). Tourism contributes less but still appreciably to catering (35 per cent), rail travel (29 per cent) and waterways (25 per cent). And tourism exerts an economic impact well beyond its own branches; nearly half of total value added comes from the other branches of the economy (retailing, construction, private schools etc.).

Prospects for development

The OFIAMT has made long-range forecasts of the future for Swiss tourism. Study techniques included surveys, econometric modelling and expert qualitative analysis. Transfrontier tourism in particular was scrutinised quantitatively. The most significant findings are that effective flows of foreign tourism will grow at an average rate of 2.8 per cent between 1990 and the year 2000, so more slowly than during the 1980s, and that real expenditure abroad by the Swiss population will also grow more slowly during the 1990s, by an annual 4 per cent.

The effects of the single European market on Swiss tourism were also analysed. Switzerland's participation in the EC single market would contribute to the growth of tourism, though not very significantly (by an additional 0.2 per cent annually).

On the supply side, the trend towards concentration is expected to become more marked. The fact that smaller enterprises in particular are not very market-oriented is one of the weak points of tourism supply in Switzerland. The present lack of co-ordination in the sales strategies of the different bodies concerned, tourism offices, hotels and travel companies needs to be put right by co-operation.

Government policy

The objectives of national tourism policy are laid down in the Swiss Tourism Strategy, which the Federal Government in 1981 declared should determine all matters relating to tourism. That strategy, still in force, is geared to qualitative growth.

A working party is currently determining new tourism policy orientations to be presented in two years to replace the strategy in force today. As a key sector of the Swiss economy, tourism has to become a more central policy concern, with greater emphasis on international competitiveness. The revision process concerns cantons and communes just as much as the private tourism bodies.

Since 1989, there have been no organisational or institutional changes, either governmentally or in the private sector. Private bodies and interest groups systematically take part in the formulation of national tourism policy. The Federal Council has established a Consultative Commission for Tourism comprising representatives of tourism organisations and the regions.

Action and measures taken in 1989 and 1990

Hotel trade. In 1989, the Swiss Hotel Credit Association (SCH) provided a record SF 66.6 million in loans and guarantees. For 1990, the total was SF 65.1 million. The reduced rate for 1990 varied from 5.75 per cent to 6.5 per cent. This constitutes a type of subsidy, unlike the loans which are repayable.

Aid and investment incentives. In 1989 and 1990, projects worth some SF 55 million were supported under mountain region development programmes. The tourism infrastructures concerned were sports facilities, SF 16 million; swimming pools, SF 1 million; cable cars, ski lifts, SF 34 million; museums, SF 3 million; conference centres, SF 1 million. Financial assistance takes the form of long-term interest-free loans from the Confederation, generally matched by equivalent contributions from the Cantons.

Environmental. Lack of snow in winter has increased the need for snow-making equipment in ski resorts but environmental protectionists have been seeking to ban the installation of such equipment. That conflict prompted the Federal government to produce an analytical report on the effects of snow-making equipment and to base tourism policy on its findings. Since snow-making equipment was not proved to have any adverse environmental impact, the Federal government concluded that using it temporarily, to alleviate shortage of snow in a clearly defined area, could be reasonable and ecologically justifiable.

Employment. New figures indicate that tourism provides 290 000 jobs, representing 9.1 per cent of Switzerland's employment. Of those, 90 000 are indirectly tourism-related. As in previous years, there was a serious labour shortage in 1989 and 1990, only offset to some extent by recruiting foreign workers. However, the unemployment rate in hotels and catering (1.1 per cent), the main branches of tourism, was well above the average rate, which remained unchanged at 0.6 per cent throughout the period covered by the report.

Indeed, as in all highly developed countries, Switzerland's workers are moving away from low value-added sectors of activity, especially hotels and catering. In recent years, labour shortages have been the main curb on the growth of tourism.

Vocational training. In 1989 and 1990, OFIAMT invested some SF 6 million in tourism-related initial and further training. Support for initial and further training took the form of contributions to training establishments, some operated by the cantons, some by professional associations. Switzerland is actively encouraging the foundation of higher schools of tourism. In 1991 OFIAMT will award higher school status for the first time to tourism schools in Zurich, Chur, Samedan and Thun.

Transport. At the end of May 1990, the high speed rail service was inaugurated in Zurich. This extended the Swiss rail network by 14 per cent in the most densely populated regions. Moreover, the downward trend in public transport prices continued. Supply mainly takes the form of season tickets for a widening range of public transport systems. In early 1990 the CFF season ticket was valid on 24 urban transport networks. The relative reduction in prices has stimulated demand, with the result that on some systems capacity limits are being reached. In the long term "Rail 2000", the current railway extension project, can be expected to remedy these capacity shortages.

Marketing. Surveys, financed by private organisations, are regularly conducted among tourists in Switzerland. Every two years the "Swiss Tourism Market" survey investigates the preferences of the Swiss population travelling at home and abroad. This survey has shown that 81 per cent of Swiss had been on trips of four days or longer, a new record internationally. The survey also showed that the trend towards taking several shorter holidays has continued.

In a second survey, "Study of the Swiss Tourism Market (Tomas)", Swiss and foreign tourists are interviewed on the spot. This survey is also conducted every two years at 140 resorts. Foreign visitors expressed astonishingly high levels of satisfaction. Many return to spend holidays in Switzerland. Nationals and foreigners alike report choosing Switzerland as their holiday location mainly because it is so restful and relaxing.

Alongside these two-yearly surveys have been market studies of specific aspects. A survey on winter sports conducted in Germany, the Netherlands, the United Kingdom and Switzerland studied prospects for winter sports following the succession of winters with little snow-fall. The study has shown that as in the past, these countries still enjoy considerable potential for winter sports holidays. However, international competition in this area has not only increased but has become increasingly quality-oriented.

An extensive survey of the German market, Switzerland's largest, sought to identify Germans' image of Switzerland. Positive aspects mentioned were style and quality, ecological awareness, cleanliness, shopping opportunities and stability. Negative points were the high exchange rate (prices), the uncommunicative character of the people and a lack of amusements for the young.

Every year the Swiss National Tourism Office devises an action and promotion programme. In 1989, Switzerland was promoted as a tourist destination under the theme "Swiss towns". In 1990, the slogan was "Lakes and rivers, Switzerland's pearls". These advertising messages are delivered in Switzerland and abroad in numerous campaigns using a variety of media.

TURKEY

Tourism as an economic activity

Economic contribution comparisons with the other sectors highlight the following features:

-- in 1990 the share of tourism receipts in GNP was 2.2 per cent;

-- in 1990 the share of tourism receipts in the export earnings was 25.5 per cent;

-- by the end of 1990, the share of tourism investments in total investments was 0.7 per cent.

-- in 1990, the share of tourism, according to the number of Encouragement Certificates issued, was 4.4 per cent and is fourth in rank after animal husbandry, food and weaving industries. The share of the tourism sector in the total amount of investments with Encouragement Certificates is 7.4 per cent and together with the Service Sector Investments with Encouragement Certificate is 47 per cent.

-- in 1990, the share of tourism in the total amount of foreign capital is 15 per cent, that in service sector is 50 per cent.

-- in 1990, the share of tourism receipts in (balance of payments) the Current Account Income is 10.9 per cent.

-- in 1990, the share of labour employed in hotels, restaurants and places of entertainment, in the total labour force as registered by the trade unions, was 3.8 per cent.

Prospects for development

According to the Research and Evaluation Department in the Ministry, the number of beds will be 247 000 and 431 000 in 1991 and 1993 respectively while the number of foreign visitors is expected to be 4.6, 6.1 and 6.6 million in 1991, 1992 and 1993 respectively; tourism receipts are estimated to reach US$2.9 in 1991 and US$4.2 billion and 1993; in addition, according to the results of another research (see "Employment" below), the number of personnel needed in hotels, restaurants and travel agencies with operating certificates, are estimated as 74 186, 84 675, 96 674, 110 512 in 1991, 1992 1993 and 1994 respectively.

Government policy

Tourism policy objectives have been determined by five-year plans. The sixth plan came into force in 1990 to cover the period 1990-1994. According to this sixth Five-Year Plan (1990-1994) the number of foreign visitors' arrivals is expected to reach 7.4 million with an annual increase rate of 8.2 per cent up to 1994. During the same period, Turkish citizens travelling abroad are estimated to rise to 2.2 million with an annual increase rate of 4.8 per cent at the end of this period. Expected tourism receipts and expenditures respectively with about 13.6 per cent and 18.4 annual increase rates, are US$5.5 billion and US$1 billion.

It is projected that accommodation capacity registered by the Ministry of Tourism will exceed 350 000 beds at the end of this period.

The principles of the policy given below are determined by annually prepared programmes:

-- General tourism policy will be prepared in co-operation with the tourism-related bodies and private entrepreneurs.

-- Priority will be given to the protection of the environment, natural and cultural assets.

-- Facilities will be further provided for Turkish nationals to take holidays under favourable conditions.

-- Present accommodation will be given momentum to operate under proper health standards, provided that their infrastructures are completed.

-- Infrastructural improvement, vocational training and marketing studies will be encouraged.

-- New measures will be taken to introduce second homes on to the tourist market and to encourage marketing companies.

-- Tourist management will be improved and small-sized management and family management will be supported.

-- Measures will be taken for increasing occupancy rates and quality of existing accommodation. Incentive policies will be developed based on variation and diversification of existing and potential tourism supply. Further studies will be made to spread the tourist season throughout the year.

-- Charter transportation will be improved and Turkish travel agencies will be encouraged to improve their competitiveness among foreign tour operators.

-- Improvement of cruise tourism will be supported and related infrastructural systems will be established according to priorities.

-- Co-operation between the public and private sector will be encouraged for marketing and promotion of the tourism services.

-- Rapid collection and evaluation of statistical data will be provided according to the needs for the orientation of the tourism sector.

-- For professional tourism training, training centres will be modernised, hotel-school systems will become widespread to meet the demands of contemporary tourist accommodation, and foreign language teaching will be practised in these institution.

-- The resources of the Turkish Development Bank will be utilised so that the productivity and the volume of private investments can be enhanced.

-- Tourism Co-operation Agreements with countries with well developed tourism will be concluded and relations with international institutions will be improved.

Action and measures taken in 1989 and 1990

Accommodation. As a result of the incentives provided for local and foreign entrepreneurs, at the end of 1990, the number of beds in establishments which have operating licences given by the Ministry, reached 173 227, and the number of beds in establishments with investment licences, reached 325 515. This implies a 41.6 per cent increase in the number of beds with operating licences, compared to the end of 1988.

According to the results of a study, there is already a capacity of 102 400 second homes in Turkey potentially available. Now it seems necessary that a field survey will have to be made to see how many owners are eager to open their homes for public use and what kind of management model would be beneficial.

Environment. The activities of the Ministry for the protection of the environment gain more importance for the elimination of the deficiency and inadequacy of infrastructure which is the cause of the pollution.

In this direction, drinking water supply, sewerage and waste water treatment plants, sea fall discharge, electrification and telecommunication investments are completed in the tourism areas and centres on the Aegean and Mediterranean coastlines which are planned and opened to investments. These investments are financed by the Ministry of Tourism and Prime Ministry Mass Housing Fund.

While infrastructure investments of tourism development projects with 10 000 beds, have started on the Aegean coast, "Master Plans" are being prepared to control over-construction on the Aegean and Mediterranean coastlines. In addition, in order to obtain a licence from the Ministry, it is mandatory for establishments to have waste water treatment plants.

Twelve areas of ecological importance which are sensitive to environmental pollution have been declared "Special Protection Zones", and the Ministry Counsellor is a member of the "Special Environment Protection Committee". In addition, work is under way on the protection of sea turtles and Mediterranean seals, in co-ordinatation with the WWF and the Environment Counsellor.

In order to prevent environmental pollution, particularly coastal water pollution and to find solutions to the existing problems, the Ministry has started to carry out the "South and West Anatolia Environmental-Tourism Infrastructure Project".

This project is carried out by the Ministry with contributions from the World Bank and the Japanese government. The objectives of the project cover a wide range of subjects such as planning, designing and construction of water supply and sewage systems, treatment and disposal facilities, solid waste collection and disposal systems, pollution control studies, financial and institutional framework studies, etc.

The main purpose of the project is to eliminate current waste-water disposal deficiencies and to prevent future ones which cause pollution and health hazards that threaten local populations and the tourist industry.

For this project 58 municipalities were selected along approximately 2 000 km of the Mediterranean and Aegean coast from the town of Garipasa in the east to the north western town of Altinoluk.

Assessment of the present and future infrastructural need of selected municipalities will be completed during the second half of 1991. These high priority locations will be selected and the designs for implementation of urgent infrastructure facilities for these locations will be contracted. This project which is planned to be finished in 1995, will be financed from local sources and foreign credits.

In addition, starting from 1992, it is planned to carry out "Blue Flag" implementation along our coastline.

Transportation. For the construction of highways in accordance with the yearly investment programmes, co-ordination with the relative governmental institutions is being established.

In order to overcome the problems encountered in the field of air transportation, close co-ordination is provided with the related institutions. Studies to increase the capacity of Atatürk airport have started and the construction of a conventional airport in Mugla-Milas is included in the investment programme. Additionally, in order to provide air transport to all provinces, attempts to improve or establish small airports and to open military airports to civilian transport have been carried out.

Marketing. In order to prevent concentration on the coast, plans are being made to provide tourism in mountain, health, highland and hunting activities. In this respect, studies are carried out to select areas suitable for highland, tracking, mountain, winter and hunting tourism in the East Black Sea region; infrastructure investments are carried out related to "Nigde-Nevsehir-Kaysseru (Cappadocia) Development Project", "Erciyes-Mountain Tourism Development Project", "Terme-Karakurt Thermal Project".

Work is also being carried out to develop camping and caravan tourism and to establish Leisure Centres (13 centres in Antalya are planned) golf links (ten in Antalya, one in Izmir) and land has been allocated for Health centres with tourism in mind (two health centres in Antalya are planned).

Additionally, in order to establish the priorities on a provincial basis, Provincial Tourism Master Plans are being prepared.

Market research has been planned, first of all in Germany, to obtain information on the travel habits of a sample of people.

Employment. In 1989, a study was conducted by the Ministry of Tourism in co-operation with an ILO expert as technical advisor, with financial support from UNDP, to investigate the number and qualifications of the personnel employed in hotels, restaurants and travel agencies registered by the Ministry.

As a result of this survey, it is understood that the number of employed persons in registered hotels is 36 427, in 3 687 restaurants and in travel agencies 9 910; in total 50 024.

In 1989, according to the Ministry of Labour's figures, 134 034 persons were employed in hôtels, restaurants and entertainment places.

UNITED KINGDOM

Tourism as an economic activity

The tourism industry in the United Kingdom contributes at least £24 billions to UK GDP; this represents nearly 5 per cent of the total UK GDP and it is the most important export earner amongst service industries and fifth overall.

Visits to the UK by overseas residents amount, according to revised estimates for 1990, to 18.0 millions -- up 4 per cent on 1989, fourth record year in succession. The US market is the single most important with 2.8 million visits (16.4 per cent of the total) in 1989, followed by France (13 per cent), Germany (11.7 per cent) and Ireland (7.5 per cent).

Earnings from overseas tourism according to revised estimates for 1990, are £7.7 billions, an 11 per cent increase on 1989.

Spending by UK residents involving an overnight stay corresponds to a total expenditure of £10.9 billion in 1989.

Employment, about 1.5 million employees, 6 per cent of employees in employment in Great Britain.

- -- 191 000 self-employed, 6 per cent of all self-employed in Great Britain.
- -- Number of employees has grown by 30 per cent (between December 1981 and December 1990) compared to 5 per cent for all employees in employment.
- -- Number of self-employed has grown by 17 per cent (1981-89) compared to 57 per cent for all self-employed.

Prospects for development

The British Tourist Authority (BTA) expects that markets with rapidly expanding economies and/or increasingly liberal political regimes will show the highest average spending growth rates. This will include Japan, South Korea, Taiwan and Eastern Europe. In terms of size, however, the United States will continue to be Britain's single largest market generating about 3.5 million visitors, spending around £2 billion by 1995. BTA project that by 1995, over 22 million visitors per annum will visit the United Kingdom, spending £11.6 billion.

This assumes continuing economic growth in key markets and further development of UK facilities and infrastructure. This will be particularly important with greater liberalisation of intra UK air traffic with the completion of the European single market and the opening of the Channel tunnel.

Key policy considerations will be continuing negotiation between relevant government departments and within the EC to ensure that the tourism case is heard and understood and that policy development in other policy areas takes full account of tourism. Improving skill levels in the UK industry, particularly in languages, is a key policy aim.

The formal mechanism for influencing government departments in the United Kingdom is the Tourism Co-ordinating Committee, chaired by the Secretary of State for Employment, which includes Ministers responsible for policy areas impacting on tourism. On an ad hoc basis particular issues are discussed between Ministers and officials in different Departments when appropriate.

Tourism also features on the agenda of the National Economic Development Council -- a tri-partite body comprising Government, Employers and Trade Unions.

Within the European Community, the United Kingdom has pressed for greater co-ordination of tourism issues within different parts of the European Commission so that tourism interests are fully represented in other policy areas interfacing with tourism.

Government policy

General tourism policy objectives and priorities remain generally as reported in previous OECD annual reports. Implementation of the findings of the review of the Government's role in tourism is now virtually completed with increased emphasis given to the work of the overseas offices of the British Tourist Authority (BTA) and increased funding by the English Tourist Board (ETB) to the 12 non statutory regional tourist boards in England.

The BTA and ETB have drawn up corporate plans governing their activities and focusing them towards meeting policy aims and objectives. These incorporate performance measurement systems to demonstrate the effectiveness of their operations.

Since the members of the Tourist Board are drawn from the industry and BTA has a number of Committees looking at different aspects of the industry, which include industry representatives, this gives the opportunity for the industry to influence the detailed work of the Boards. In addition Ministers are keen to hear industry views and maintain a number of ad hoc contacts with leading industry figures and bodies as do Employment Department officials.

A major new policy initiative has been in the field of tourism and the environment. This was launched by the Secretary of State for Employment, Michael Howard, in August 1990. A task force was set up specifically to examine how visitor management techniques can be used to ensure that tourism continues to develop in harmony with the environment on which it depends for its success. The task force presented its findings in a report issued at a Conference in May 1991.

No laws or regulations are contemplated. Ministerial agreement to the Board's corporate plans and evaluation of performance will ensure adherence to policy aims and objectives.

Action and measures taken in 1989 and 1990

Accommodation. The National Tourist Boards continued to develop the national scheme for classification of serviced and self-catering accommodation to include a quality assessment dimension. This enables both domestic and overseas visitors to identify places to stay which will meet the level of service and comfort that is required as well as being an indication of the facilities available. The scheme for classifying holiday-home parks has been further developed and the two leading trade associations have made participation by parks in the scheme a condition of membership thus contributing to a general raising of standards in this sector.

Catering. The Food Safety Act 1990 has had far-reaching implications in the tourism sector by placing a number of requirements on operators relating to the storage, preparation and serving of food. All premises handling food are required to be registered with their Local Authority and obligations of proprietors and managers of food establishments have been considerably increased with severe penalties for non-compliance. Shortly, a regulation requiring everyone handling food for public consumption to be trained in food hygiene will come into force.

Transport. The renegotiation of air transport agreements with the United States and changes related to operations at Heathrow Airport have allowed additional airlines into London's major airport. This, combined with the opening of a new terminal at Stanstead Airport (which has a direct rail link to central London) is gradually changing the patterns of use of London's airports. However, a projected serious shortfall of capacity in the airports serving London has led to the establishment of a government working party with wide representation from the industry to develop a strategy for London's airports in the next century.

The regulations for road signs directing visitors to tourist amenities have been refined and developed following their initial introduction in 1986. A network of white or brown tourist signs is now found nationwide in Britain.

British Rail has continued to promote initiatives involving tourist and leisure travel, particularly encouraging off-peak travel. Many promotions have taken place, often in partnership with local interests, including tourist boards, to publicise specific scenic routes or facilities. These have been very successful and have generated excellent sales in many areas. A Bill to allow for construction of a fast service rail access between Heathrow Airport and central London has recently completed its progress through parliament and journey times will be reduced to as little as 17 minutes.

Rural tourism. The English Tourist Board has worked closely with organisations such as the Countryside Commission and the Rural Development Commission to develop sensitive visitor management schemes for tourism in environmentally sensitive areas. Concern about damage to the environment by large numbers of visitors has become a major issue which the English Tourist Board addressed at a major environmental conference entitled: "Shades of Green" held jointly with the Countryside Commission and the Rural Development Commission.

Protection of the environment. The Government has worked closely with the Tourist Boards and environmental agencies; a Task Force was established in August 1990 which reported in Spring 1991. The four guiding principles which the Government has adopted in supporting tourism are:

-- to look to support the development of the industry in ways to contribute to, rather than detract from, the quality of our environment;

-- to promote environmental quality issues within the industry as well as issues concerned with the quality of its services and products;

-- to ensure through the Tourist Boards and Training and Enterprise Councils that managers in tourism become increasingly aware of visitor management techniques and ways of protecting the environment whilst promoting their industry;

-- to look particularly to encourage and disseminate those types of tourism which in themselves aim to safeguard the environment.

The report of the Task Force was contained in the document entitled: "Tourism and the Environment -- Maintaining the Balance".

Tourism for people with special needs. The National Tourist Boards in Britain have worked hard to develop the market for people with special needs (disabled people and those with other disadvantages) under the general campaign title of "Tourism for All". A booklet giving design advice and practical suggestions for making accommodation premises accessible to disabled people has been distributed to over 20 000 operators in Britain and a conference reviewing best practice in tourism provision for disabled people in Europe was organised by the English Tourist Board, (ETB) with EC support.

High priority is given to advising tourism providers on how they can make their premises more accessible in the broadest sense to people with special needs.

ETB has piloted a scheme for two years to provide holidays at very low cost for families or others on low incomes utilising capacity at hotels, guest houses and visitor attractions during the offpeak period. The principle operated is that voluntary agencies identify groups of people unable to take holidays because of low income (typically disabled people, single parent families and elderly people) in a particular town and coach transport is provided to take them to the holiday destination where the groups are deliberately mixed and integrated. The coach company, accommodation providers and visitor attractions offer their facilities at a considerably reduced cost (but still receive some income) and the low income families pay a very reduced sum for the holiday. The scheme has been immensely successful and will be developed in the future.

Employment. Employment in the industry stands at about 1.5 million people. No figures are available for unemployment rates in industry sectors.

Vocational training. The establishment of the network of 82 Training and Enterprise Councils (TECS) across England and Wales is providing the industry with a major opportunity to ensure its training and skills needs are met at the local level. Regional Tourist Boards receive funds from the English Tourist Board specifically to ensure effective liaison between the industry and TECS. Work is well advanced on the development of competence-based qualification structures, particularly in the travel trade as hotel and catering sectors; the importance of management training is also gradually being recognised. The links between training and both quality of service and product quality are now increasingly being made, and businesses are also realising the benefits which effective training can bring to staff recruitment and retention.

Market research. The following annual market research surveys were conducted:

-- United Kingdom Tourism Survey; measures the volume, value, purpose, timing etc, of domestic tourism trips lasting one night or more.

-- British National Travel Survey; measures the extent of holidays taken in Britain and abroad by British residents.

-- International Passenger Survey; measures incoming tourism to and outgoing tourism from the United Kingdom.

The United Kingdom tourist boards have produced the following strategy documents, to advise the tourist industry and Government:

-- Guidelines for Tourism to Britain, 1991-95 (BTA)

-- Strategy for the Development of Tourism, 1991-95 (BTA)

-- 1993 Cross Channel Marketing Strategy (BTA)

-- Tourism: People and Places (ETB)

-- Tourism in Northern Ireland, A View to the Future (NITB)

-- Annual Marketing Plan (WTB)

-- Tourism in Wales - Developing the Potential (WTB)

-- Prospect of Prosperity - Scottish Tourism in the 1990s (STB)

Marketing. BTA's specific marketing objectives for the British tourism industry are to:

-- increase visits to Britain from abroad by an average of 4 per cent per annum;

-- generate an increase in overseas visitor spending by an average of 8 per cent per annum;

-- maintain a good spread of markets: 21 per cent of earnings from North America, 44 per cent of earnings from Europe, 35 per cent of earnings from rest of the world;

-- maintain out-of-London overseas nights at a minimum of 60 per cent of total nights;

-- continue to address seasonality, seeking to fill troughs wherever and whenever they occur, and encourage better utilisation of the tourism product;

-- encourage the industry to continue to raise standards and improve welcome.

European markets, the United States and Japan will continue to be given high priority. The business travel sector will also receive high priority -- especially with regard to encouraging 'extenders', spouse traffic, conference business and visits to trade fairs/exhibition.

The English, Scottish and Welsh Tourist Boards undertake marketing campaigns to promote their country to the British. Their marketing initiatives are designed, for example, to encourage seasonal/geographical spread; improve visitor management; promote high standards and improved value for money (through award schemes etc); expand national accommodation classification schemes; encourage "Tourism for All" (i.e. for disabled, low income people, etc.,) and provide tourist information.

Protection of the tourist as a consumer. The United Kingdom is a party to the European Community's Package Travel Directive, adopted by Ministers in June 1990.

International co-operation. During 1989-90, the United Kingdom offered technical assistance, through the Overseas Development Administration, to the following countries:

-- a grant to Kenya of £122 589 to employ a game warden;

-- a grant to St Helena of £65 119 for hotel/accommodation on Ascension Island;

-- a grant to St Kitts-Nevis of £4 293 for hotel maintenance and personnel;

-- a grant to Turks and Caicos Islands of £63 745 for a consultant to make a feasibility study of tourism on behalf of the ODA and a feasability study of casino registration;

-- a grant to Zimbabwe of £2 024 for monitoring wildlife.

UNITED STATES

Tourism an an economic activity

Various agencies and Departments of the Government have asked the US Travel and Tourism Administration (USTTA) to provide measurements for the economic impact on individual States, as well as on national interests. Working co-operatively with Canada and Mexico, USTTA is now able to provide measurements on total US expenditures (inbound and outbound). From this data the economic impact on individual US States is being measured on expenditures, employment and payroll, as well as for regional and local internal tax revenues which are being generated by visitors from abroad.

In 1990, the tourism surplus was US$4.7 billion. 1989 foreign visitor travel generated US$9.6 billion in payroll, US$4.8 billion in tax receipts and 760 700 jobs in public transportation, auto transportation, lodging, food service, entertainment and recreation, and general retail trade.

Prospects for development

USTTA uses its historical arrivals data and an econometric model to forecast arrivals to the US.

The US Department of Transportation (DOT) is presently analysing available in-flight data to establish the purposes of US international travel (inbound and outbound) as well as traveller expenditures, the type of tickets and days of airline travel, to distinguish leisure travel from business travel, student travel and other purposes. The DOT objective for this analysis is to provide information on the impact of travel between city-pairs as well as types or purposes of travel.

The number of international visitor arrivals is expected to reach 44.5 million in 1992, an increase of 7 per cent over the preceding year, while the tourism surplus is expected to total US$6.5 billion the same year.

Government policy

The International Travel Act of 1961 (thereafter referred to as "The Act"), as amended, requires the Tourism Policy Council (TPC) to submit an annual report to the President for transmittal to the Congress. The report is required to contain four items: a summary of the Council's activities and its accomplishments for the year; the results of the Council's co-ordination efforts; an analysis of problems referred to the Council along with the actions taken to resolve such problems; and such recommendations as the Council deems appropriate.

The Act established the TPC in 1981 as an interagency co-ordinating council to assure that the national interest in tourism is fully considered in Federal decision-making. The TPC consists of the Secretary of Commerce, who serves as Chairman; the Under Secretary of Commerce for Travel and Tourism, who serves as Chairman "pro tem"; the Director of the Office of Management and Budget; a representative of the International Trade Administration; the Secretary of Energy; the Secretary of State; the Secretary of Interior; the Secretary of Labour; and the Secretary of Transportation. The heads of agencies which are not members of the TPC may be invited to attend meetings whenever matters affecting the interest of those agencies are discussed. In 1990, representatives were invited from such agencies as the Minority Business Development Agency, the Departments of Justice and Agriculture, the US Customs Service, and the Small Business Administration. In addition, the Secretary of Agriculture, and the Administrators of the Tennessee Valley Authority and the Small Business Administration were invited to serve on the Council on the recommendation of the Federal Task Force on Rural Tourism. This was done to facilitate co-ordination of federal programmes and policies affecting the development of rural tourism.

The Act directs the TPC to "co-ordinate policies, programmes and issues relating to tourism, recreation or national heritage resources involving Federal departments, agencies, or other entities." The TPC is also directed to "seek and receive concerns and views of State and local governments and the Travel and Tourism Advisory Board with respect to Federal programmes and policies deemed to conflict with the orderly growth and development of tourism." The TPC is not empowered to co-ordinate State, local or private sector policies, only those at the Federal level.

In 1990, the TPC addressed policy issues ranging from rural tourism development and legislation, to implementation of the Visa Waiver Pilot Program, bilateral civil aviation negotiations and the impact of the European Single Internal Market on inbound tourism. The TPC and its policy committees have been active contributors to the work accomplished on essential issues for the international tourism industry, including elimination of travel-related impediments, principles of liberalisation affecting travellers and travel businesses domestically, trade in services and air transportation.

The Council's Policy Committee on Trade Barriers met three times in 1990. Its most significant task was to co-ordinate US Government (Office of the US Trade Representative, Departments of Commerce, State, and Transportation) efforts to assist a US travel agency (American Travel Abroad) in obtaining the same right to conduct business in Poland as Poland's tourism office (ORBIS) enjoys in the United States. The Policy Committee on Rural Development met once; and the Policy Committee on Passenger Facilitation met twelve times at the staff level and once at the executive level.

Actions and measures taken in 1990

Visa Waiver Pilot Program. The Visa Waiver Pilot Program (VWPP) created in 1986 authorises the Attorney General and the Secretary of State to waive the non-immigrant visitor visa requirement for the nationals of eight countries. By the end of July 1989, the programme was in effect in the United Kingdom, Japan, Germany, France, Sweden, Switzerland, Italy and the Netherlands.

The Justice Department (Immigration and Naturalisation Service or INS), State Department, Customs Service, Transportation Department, Commerce

Department, Air Transport Association, and others actively discussed the implementation process throughout the year to ensure optimal co-ordination and a successful programme. Discussions included issues related to security, facilitation, drug trafficking and terrorism.

Trends indicate that this programme has generated significant incremental tourist traffic, especially from Japan. USTTA believes that the number of visitors from the eight countries now participating in the VWPP will substantially increase.

On 29 May 1990 the State Department and the Justice Department jointly submitted a report to Congress on the VWPP as required by section 405 of the Immigration Reform and Control Act of 1986. The report evaluated the implementation of the VWPP and expressed the Administration's view that the programme has been highly successful. The report recommended that the VWPP be extended for three years beyond its legislative sunset date of 30 September 1991, be revised in light of our experience with it, and be expanded to other countries to be selected by the Attorney General and the Secretary of State. Without Congressional approval and extension, the VWPP would have expired in September 1991.

Section 201 of the Immigration Act of 1990 extended and revised the VWPP. Section 201 authorises the State and the Attorney General to continue the programme through 30 September 1994 and to expand it to include additional countries.

Interagency Border Inspection System. The INS is co-ordinating with the Customs Service and the State Department the establishment of a single query system for all persons arriving in the United States. This System is known as "IBIS" (Interagency Border Inspection System) and includes document readers to query the various data bases. The system has already been installed in few airports and will be at all major airports in the near future.

Pre-inspection and pre-clearance programmes. The INS has implemented pre-inspection procedures (inspection of travellers at point of embarkation for admissibility) in Aruba and Shannon, Ireland. INS has begun testing a pre-inspection programme in London's Heathrow and Gatwick Airports. The London programme was launched 25 September 1990, being the first site for a test of pre-inspection at two major European gateway airports.

Pre-clearance (inspection of travellers for customs and immigration purposes at point of departure) was initiated in 1952 to help relieve congestion at major US airports by clearing low-risk flights before their arrival. Since 1989, the Customs Service has been using a new strategy for processing air passengers at major domestic airports. The strategy is based on selectivity and has replaced traditional inspection techniques. Resulting improvements in facilitation promise to benefit the tourism industry in view of projected increases in air passenger traffic and already-crowded terminal conditions.

Facilitation of Inbound Tourism. During the TPC's meetings there have been comprehensive discussions on strategies to improve the processing of travellers upon arrival. There have been discussions on how to better co-ordinate US government agencies so that they could function effectively together, including specific master plans for air passenger processing for the 1990s. Input from members of the Council was collected in order to develop coherent policies vis-à-vis international tourism facilitation committees and to enhance efforts in negotiating bilateral tourism agreements and liberalising air transport agreements. The Council continues to work with federal inspection agencies to address this issue.

Liberalisation in tourism. The Council has served as a forum for preparation of US positions on issues before inter-governmental organisations such as the European Community (EC) and the Organisation for Economic Co-operation and Development (OECD). The EC Single Internal Market and tourism have been a standing item on the TPC's agenda because of the significance of the single European integrated market to US tourism competitiveness.

Transport. Bilateral Civil Aviation Agreements: Throughout the year the Departments of State and Transportation regularly reported to the Council on the progress of bilateral civil aviation negotiations. Talks focusing on the expansion of the international aviation markets were held with such countries as Saudi Arabia, Turkey, Kuwait, Poland, Japan, France, Germany, Italy, Canada, United Kingdom, Australia, Singapore, South Korea, the Netherlands and Thailand.

Airlines Competitiveness Study: The Department of Transportation briefed Council members on its airline competition study which was completed in February 1990. This study, the most comprehensive since the airline industry was deregulated, analysed domestic and international airline competition and involved a number of experts from the Departments of Transportation and Justice, the Council of Economic Advisors and other interested agencies.

Policy Committee on Passenger Facilitation (PCPF): The Department of Transportation Facilitation Committee (TFC) and the Policy Committee on Passenger Facilitation (PCPF) meet jointly when passenger issues are dealt with. The Assistant Secretary of Transportation for Policy and International Affairs chairs both committees. Key passenger facilitation issues examined by the TFC/PCPF in FY 1990 included:

-- London pre-inspection test program;

-- visa Waiver Pilot Program;

-- Guam Visa Waiver Program;

-- new Customs passenger inspection programmes to speed processing;

-- updating the Airport Federal Inspection Facilities Design Guidelines;

-- expansion of automation to speed passenger processing;

-- expansion of machine readable travel documents; and,

-- matters before the International Civil Aviation Organisation, International Maritime Organisation and Economic Commission for Europe facilitation activities.

Tourism and rural development. In 1989, the Congress directed USTTA to conduct a study to determine whether tourism could contribute to the development of small businesses in rural communities. As part of this study, USTTA requested that a Task Force on Rural Tourism Development be formed by the TPC to examine federal programmes affecting rural tourism development and to recommend an appropriate federal response to rural tourism development needs. As a result of the Task Force's study, the TPC established the Policy Committee on Rural Tourism Development to:

-- monitor policies affecting rural tourism development;

-- recommend the modification of federal policies which impede that development;

-- facilitate co-operation and co-ordination between federal agencies involved in rural tourism-related activities;

-- make recommendations on rural tourism development to the TPC.

In January 1990 President Bush ordered the implementation of a series of recommendations of the Economic Policy Council's Working Group on Rural Development. Among other things, he asked for a study of the "feasibility of designating tourism development zones within federal rural enterprise zones to encourage the orderly planning, development, and clustering of necessary tourism services and to facilitate the establishment of enterprises of high economic impact such as year-round resorts and retirement communities."

The TPC instructed the Policy Committee on Rural Tourism Development to study the feasibility of rural tourism enterprise/development zones (EZs), to report its findings, and to include in its inquiry a review of the concept of Tax Increment Financing. Final findings and recommendations of the Policy Committee on Rural Tourism Development are to be submitted to the TPC at its first meeting in 1991.

YUGOSLAVIA

Tourism as an economic activity

Tourism plays a significant role in the Yugoslav economy. In all documents defining economic policy, tourism is given priority treatment. The development of priority sectors (tourism, transport, agriculture) is based on an integral concept. In 1990 registered foreign exchange earnings from international tourism amounted to US$2,77 billion or 24.4 per cent more compared to the previous year. The share of tourism in the total value of exports of goods and services increased from 11.5 per cent in 1989 to 13.14 per cent in 1990. Its share in total export of services amounted to 40.19 per cent, in Gross National Product to 3.1 per cent, in total employment in the social sector to 4.1 per cent.

In the tourism sector 2 111 private enterprises were established, which represents 4 per cent of the total number of private enterprises.

Prospects for development

The future tourism development policy will be determined by:

-- international tourist demand, specific requirements and traditional travel habits;

-- protection and sustainable use of the environment;

-- strengthening and maintaining the competitiveness of Yugoslav tourism on the world market;

-- different forms of enterpreneurship and the restructuring of the tourist industry and complementary sectors;

-- quality growth;

-- permanent training and specialisation of staff.

The Project of Classification and Categorisation of tourist facilities in Yugoslavia that has recently been completed, covers three areas of tourism: accommodation and catering facilities, tourist agencies and marinas.

Government policy

The main aims established by the "Strategy of the Development of Tourism" are still valid and in accordance with the general economic policy and reforms (see the 1989 edition of the Annual Report). As set by the Yugoslav Federal Executive Council the priority has been given to the development of international tourism.

Action and measures taken in 1989 and 1990

Development of supply. In 1990, the most important action taken by the authorities responsible for tourism and other complementary sectors was in the area of promotion of the quality of services.

Within the overall economic reforms, in 1989 and 1990 the development of tourism was particularly stimulated by the following measures taken by the Federal Government: convertibility and exchange rate of the national currency dinar, liberalised import of goods and liberalised system of payments, credit facilities, permanent funds for promotion of Yugoslav tourist product abroad, financial support for export of tourist services, tax reduction on cold drinks in catering facilities, reimbursement of sales tax on purchases of goods for export of value over 1 000 dinars per item, toll coupons for vehicles with foreign number plates, lower prices for fuel oil used in hotels and restaurants, liberalised legislation to encourage foreign investments etc.

Besides the Foreign Investment Law, the Law on Amendments to the Basic Property Law Relations Act, that entered into force on 7 July, 1990 is of importance because it enables foreign natural and legal persons, who operate in Yugloslavia on the reciprocity basis, to own business premises, buildings, flats and apartment buildings, etc. This law also regulates the time-share, so the Time-Share Law ceased to be valid on 7 July, 1990.

Under the provisions of the Law on Foreign Credit Transactions, which was recently adopted, it is possible for enterprises to take loans abroad without the state guarantee.

Market research. Tourist Association of Yugoslavia which is in charge of overall tourism promotion abroad, has paid special attention to tourism market research with the aim of establishing adequate estimates for future tourist traffic.

Market research is particularly directed to the traditional tourist generating countries by conducting yearly studies of the United Kingdom, Germany, Netherlands, Belgium, Switzerland, Austria, Sweden and Denmark.

Tourist Association of Yugoslavia has 16 representative offices and bureaux in 13 European countries and in the United States.

Consumer protection. The Law on Trade, for the first time in Yugoslavia, introduces provisions for the protection of the tourist as a consumer, similar to those existing in other countries.

A Commission for Protection of Consumers was established by the Federal Secretariat for Trade.

Staggering of holidays. A number of usual measures have been undertaken to encourage off-season holidays: lower prices for off-peak packages, special rates at hotels, adjustment of school calendars and vacations in order to spread the holiday season, etc.

International co-operation. Yugoslavia, as a member of the European Travel Commission, has joined EEC and other European countries in the activities undertaken in the framework of the European Year of Tourism 1990. Yugoslavia has formed the National Committee and made a specific Yugoslav National Programme for the European Year of Tourism, aiming at the improvement of the quality of tourist services and offers, promotion and facilities for international tourism.

The National Committee undertook numerous measures and actions, the most important of which was the adoption of the Law on Facilities for Arrival of Foreign Tourists into Yugoslavia, providing that foreign tourists can enter Yugoslavia with any valid identity card, not necessarily a passport, without a visa.

Yugoslavia is constantly developing international co-operation in the field of tourism on the bilateral, multilateral and regional basis.

CHAPTER II

INTERNATIONAL TOURIST FLOWS IN MEMBER COUNTRIES

This Chapter brings together, in the form of summary tables, the most recent data available on international tourist flows to the Member countries of the Organisation for Economic Co-operation and Development and Yugoslavia. The tables give regional totals for each of the three geographical areas of the OECD -- Europe, North America and Australasia-Japan -- plus the OECD total.

Annual data by country of origin of foreign tourists or visitors, for 1989 and 1990, are set out in the Statistical Annex.

Section A outlines the general trends noted in 1990 for the OECD area as a whole.

Section B records changes in international tourist flows in individual Member countries and Yugoslavia in 1990. The data cover:

a) Arrivals at frontiers either of tourists (persons spending more than one night in the country being visited) or, where such figures are not available, all visitors (tourists plus excursionists). For further details of how travellers are classified please refer to Chart A in the Statistical Annex.

b) The number of nights spent by foreign tourists in hotels and similar establishments (generally speaking, hotels, motels, inns and boarding houses).

c) The number of nights spent in all forms of accommodation without distinction.

For further details of the types of accommodation covered by the data for each receiving country, please consult Table C in the Statistical Annex.

Lastly, Section C describes international flows from the OECD's main generating countries: Canada, France, Germany, Italy, Japan, the Netherlands, the United Kingdom and the United States.

A. INTERNATIONAL TOURISM IN THE OECD AREA

In observing international tourism trends in the different oecd regions, the reader must bear in mind two major occurrences in 1990 that had an obvious impact on tourist demand. These are discussed in greater length in the introduction along with other elements that help to elucidate developments over the year.

First, the upheavals in Central and Eastern Europe and the beginnings of the transition of these centrally-planned economies to a market economy meant that Member countries needed to embody this new dimension in their tourist policies. The changes are on many fronts, involving inter alia the privatisation of tourist enterprises, air links, the establishment of tourist offices and marketing. On the demand side, these changes have had implications for demand from the central and eastern european countries which, though still low, is steadily rising for most member countries. Similarly, the opening up of frontiers and growth in trade with the developed countries has meant that more nationals from the OECD Member countries are visiting the Central and East European countries.

Second, the Gulf crisis that broke in August 1990 has also had an impact on the volume of international tourist flows. The general effect of the crisis was to exacerbate economic tensions, restrict personal movements, instil a sense that it was unsafe to travel, and raise air fares for scheduled flights. On the demand side, its main effect was to boost domestic tourism at the expense of foreign tourism, with preference being given to closer destinations over more remote ones (enhancing the regional integration of tourism) and others being avoided.

Definitive 1990 data bear out the initial estimates made at the beginning of 1991: international tourism in the OECD area is flourishing. In 1990, indicators of trends in international tourist flows were positive for all OECD regions.

Europe:

-- Arrivals at frontiers: + 4 per cent (against + 9 per cent in 1989);

-- Nights spent in hotels and similar establishments: + 3 per cent (against + 7 per cent);

-- Nights spent in all forms of accommodation: + 3 per cent (against + 1 per cent).

North America:

-- Arrivals at frontiers: + 5 per cent.

Australasia-Japan:

-- Arrivals at frontiers: + 11 per cent (against +6 per cent);

-- Nights spent in all forms of accommodation: + 13 per cent.

Arrivals at frontiers (Table 1)

Table 1 sets out the figures for 15 Member countries plus Yugoslavia. Arrivals at frontiers were up overall by 4 per cent in 1990, though growth was slower in Europe than in the other OECD regions.

Of the 19 European Member countries, only 12 compile statistics on tourist or foreign visitor movements at frontiers. Two of these 12 countries, Austria and Germany, record all traveller arrivals at frontiers, a much broader yardstick than that used for analysing tourist flows, since it includes travellers in transit (for information see Table A of Statistical Annex). These figures have not therefore been included in Table 1, but are shown for information in Table 6 of the Statistical Annex.

In **Europe** growth was twice as slow as in 1989 for several reasons. For one thing, one of the main European receiving countries, Spain, experienced a sharp drop in visitors in 1990 (- 4 per cent) but growth declined as well in other major receiving countries: France (+ 7 per cent against + 29 per cent in 1989), the United Kingdom (+ 4 per cent against + 10 per cent), and even Switzerland (+ 5 per cent against + 8 per cent). Italy saw a noticeable turnaround (+ 3 per cent against - 1 per cent), while arrivals in Turkey and Yugoslavia (+ 21 per cent and + 16 per cent) rose appreciably over the year.

North America was up by 5 per cent due in particular to the excellent outturns for the United States (+ 7 per cent). This destination became quite cheap in 1990 owing to the weakening of the US dollar against most other currencies which gave a special boost to intra-regional flows (from Canada and South America, for example).

Australasia-Japan, where growth was buoyant, received 11 per cent more visitors in 1990, benefiting from the expansion in Asian markets. In Japan, which posted the steepest increase (+ 14 per cent), arrivals from Asia-Oceania and South America surged by 17 per cent and 49 per cent respectively. Altogether, arrivals at frontiers rose faster in the first half of 1990, before the onset of the Gulf crisis, than later in the year.

Nights spent in hotels and similar establishments (Table 2)

Seventeen European countries plus Australia compile data on nights spent in hotels and similar establishments; generally speaking these data concern nights recorded in hotels, motels, boarding houses and inns (see Table C in the Statistical Annex).

In **Europe**, the number of nights spent in hotels and similar establishments rose by 3 per cent in 1990 (against + 7 per cent the year before). This slowdown was ascribable to a variety of developments across countries. Italy, where some 66 million nights were spent, recorded a decline for the second year running of 3 per cent, with the number of nights spent down 4 million between 1988 and 1990. Yugoslavia was in a similar position in 1990 with the number of nights spent down 3 per cent. The outturns for

Table 1. **Annual growth rates of number of arrivals of foreign tourists at frontiers**[1]

	T/V	% 88/87	% 89/88	% 90/89	1990 Millions of arrivals
Austria					
Belgium					
Denmark					
Finland					
France[4]	T	3.6	29.4	7.3	53.2
Germany					
Greece	T	2.7	3.9	9.8	8.9
Iceland	T	–0.6	–0.4	8.2	0.1
Ireland	V	15.0	16.5	12.3	3.1
Italy	T	1.6	–0.8	2.9	26.7
Luxembourg					
Netherlands					
Norway					
Portugal	T	8.6	7.4	12.7	8.0
Spain	V	7.2	–0.2	–3.7	52.0
Sweden					
Switzerland[2]	T	0.0	7.7	4.8	13.2
Turkey[3]	V	46.1	6.9	20.9	5.4
United Kingdom	V	1.5	9.7	3.9	18.0
EUROPE[1]		5.0	8.9	3.6	
Canada	T	3.4	–2.7	1.0	15.3
United States[5]	T	–4.6	33.5	6.7	39.1
NORTH AMERICA		–1.9	20.5	5.0	
Australia	V	26.0	–7.5	6.5	2.2
New Zealand	T	2.4	4.2	8.3	1.0
Japan	V	9.3	20.4	14.2	3.2
AUSTRALASIA-JAPAN[1]		14.3	6.3	10.5	
OECD[1]		3.7	11.1	4.1	
Yugoslavia	V	13.3	15.1	16.0	39.6

V Visitors.
T Tourists.
Note: Canada, Italy and Portugal dispose of both series (V and T); see annex.
1. Overall trend for all countries with data available from 1987 to 1990.
2. Estimates.
3. Travellers.
4. Change of series in 1989: new frontiers' survey.
5. New series from 1989.

Table 2. **Annual growth rates of nights spent by foreign tourists in hotels and similar establishments**[1]

	% 88/87	% 89/88	% 90/89	1990 Millions of beds-nights
Austria	1.7	9.0	0.8	61.9
Belgium	2.0	21.2	4.5	6.9
Denmark	–2.3	11.6	11.1	5.4
Finland	4.1	9.5	–2.0	2.5
France	14.1	24.4	8.2	55.9
Germany[3]	3.4	12.5	4.9	29.8
Greece	–1.2	–1.2	6.3	35.0
Iceland		1.8		
Ireland	11.9	20.2	5.2	7.8
Italy	–0.4	–3.2	–3.1	66.0
Luxembourg	2.9	5.0	5.8	1.1
Netherlands	–4.0	6.2	12.9	8.1
Norway	–13.2	2.2	3.1	3.5
Portugal	3.3	3.1	8.0	16.7
Spain	–4.4	–11.4		
Sweden	–1.6	5.5	–5.2	3.2
Switzerland	–2.2	7.3	2.7	21.0
Turkey	44.6	3.3	5.7	10.3
United Kingdom				
EUROPE[1]	3.1	7.2	3.2	
Canada				
United States				
NORTH AMERICA				
Australia[2]	37.3	–24.8	18.1	13.5
New Zealand				
Japan				
AUSTRALASIA-JAPAN[1]				
OECD[1]	4.3	5.6	3.7	
Yugoslavia	–0.4	–1.1	–3.3	27.0

1. Overall trend for all countries with data available from 1987 to 1990.
2. New series from 1989.
3. From October 1990, excluding movements of visitors from eastern Germany.

Table 3. **Annual growth rates of nights spent by foreign tourists in all means of accommodation** [1]

	% 88/87	% 89/88	% 90/89	1990 Millions of beds-nights
Austria	2.2	8.4	-0.2	94.8
Belgium	5.1	14.8	6.1	12.9
Denmark	-1.0	5.6	8.9	9.3
Finland				
France [4]	2.1	-6.4	4.4	339.3
Germany [3]	3.5	11.5	3.8	34.8
Greece	-2.7	-1.8	6.3	36.3
Iceland				
Ireland	15.8	19.9	7.2	33.7
Italy	-0.7	-5.9	-2.9	84.4
Luxembourg	-1.4			2.4
Netherlands		12.1	15.6	16.4
Norway	-1.3	2.8	5.4	5.8
Portugal	4.0	2.5	6.1	19.3
Spain				
Sweden	0.3	6.6	-13.3	6.6
Switzerland	-0.4	4.4	2.6	36.9
Turkey	40.0	1.8	11.8	13.3
United Kingdom	-3.0	8.4	4.8	196.4
EUROPE [1]	1.3	0.8	3.4	
Canada	8.3	-2.0		
United States				
NORTH AMERICA				
Australia [2]		-1.3	13.6	70.9
New Zealand	2.0	1.8	9.5	20.7
Japan				
AUSTRALASIA-JAPAN [1]		-0.6	12.6	
OECD [1]	5.7	0.7	4.2	
Yugoslavia	0.1	-6.1	-11.8	43.4

1. Overall trend for all countries with data available from 1987 to 1990.
2. New series from 1989.
3. From October 1990, excluding movements of visitors from eastern Germany.
4. Change of series in 1989: new frontiers' survey.

these two countries which are at oddswith the number of arrivals at frontiers may in part be explained by shorter lengths of stay and an increase in the number of excursionists.

Growth is also slowing in some major receiving countries, notably Germany, France, Austria and Switzerland. But Greece performed well (+ 6 per cent after two years of minus figures), as did the Netherlands and Portugal (+ 13 per cent and + 8 per cent respectively) where growth was faster than in earlier years.

In Australia, the number of nights spent was almost up to the 1988 peak, rising by 18 per cent in 1990.

Nights spent in all forms of accommodation (Table 3)

Nights spent in all forms of accommodation are available for 19 Member countries and Yugoslavia; this category includes both hotel and non-hotel accommodation (see Table C in the Statistical Annex).

Nights spent in all forms of accommodation were up 4 per cent overall in 1990, a higher pace of increase than in previous years but consistent with the rise in nights spent in hotels and similar establishments.

The main receiving countries recorded a modest increase in nights spent except for Austria (- 0.2 per cent), Italy (- 3 per cent) and Yugoslavia which lost the most ground (- 12 per cent); the latter destination's competitiveness was eroded by the economic and political problems besetting the country.

Australia and New-Zealand both performed buoyantly, posting increases of 14 per cent and 10 per cent respectively.

B. INTERNATIONAL TOURISM IN INDIVIDUAL MEMBER COUNTRIES

Australia. After a poor year, international tourism picked up in 1990 and growth was brisk, with nights spent in all forms of accommodation up 14 per cent, in hotels and similar establishments up 18 per cent and arrivals of foreign visitors at frontiers up 7 per cent.

Following a change in the method of calculating nights spent, 1989 and 1990 cannot be compared to earlier years and figures are broken down only for the major markets.

Measured by arrivals of foreign visitors at frontiers, the most buoyant markets were Japan (+ 37 per cent), Asia-Oceania (+ 6 per cent), the European countries (+ 4 per cent) and non-Member countries (+ 6 per cent). However, some markets are still contracting after significantly regressing in 1989, notably the United States (- 4 per cent) and New Zealand (- 7 per cent).

The first half of 1990 saw a surge in arrivals in Australia, though they fell off markedly in the second half.

Austria. In 1990, for the first time since 1986, the number of nights spent in all forms of accommodation was slightly down (- 0.2 per cent); nights spent in hotels, on the other hand, were up 1 per cent.

The two chief markets, namely Germany (with a relative share of 60 per cent) and the Netherlands (10 per cent) shrank by 5 per cent and 6 per cent respectively, giving a decline of 3 per cent for OECD-Europe as a whole. However, these outturns were mitigated by a greater influx of tourists from the United States (+ 26 per cent) and Japan (+ 27 per cent) and, within Europe, from Italy and Switzerland (+ 11 per cent and + 8 per cent respectively).

On a more general note, the tourist season in Austria suffered from the lack of snow over the winter 1989/1990, though it benefited from the growth of cultural tourism (mainly city-based) and from the launching of new tourist products during the summer season.

Belgium. The rates of growth for nights spent in all forms of accommodation and in hotels and similar establishments have continued to grow in 1990 (+ 6 per cent and + 5 per cent respectively) after a very good year in 1989.

In Europe, the main markets are growing well, in particular the Netherlands, the main market (+7 per cent) and the United Kingdom (+14 per cent), with one exception, however: Germany, its second market (-1 per cent).

Outside Europe, North America (+7 per cent) and the non-member countries are growing more rapidly than the OECD zone. Japan, however, had bad results (-6 per cent).

Canada. The number of foreign tourists edged up 1 per cent in 1990; this sluggish growth may be ascribed in part to the slowdown in economic growth and a loss of confidence by consumers in the major tourism generating countries, notably on grounds of aviation security.

The number of American tourists rose by just 1 per cent. This poor performance reflects migratory movements to the South and and South-West of North America, as well as a shift to other destinations by this customer group. Cyclical factors, such as slower economic growth and exchange rate fluctuations, also played a part.

While, overall, growth in the number of overseas tourists (+ 1 per cent) was slower than in the 1980s, there were major differences across the main markets. It was negative for the United Kingdom (-0.3 per cent) and Western Germany (the Federal Republic of Germany before unification) (- 3 per cent). In the former case the reason was primarily the weakness of the economy, while in the latter it was unification and the opening up of the East European countries which affected travel from Germany. Tourist flows from the Pacific region, a feature for several years past, continued steeply up, with Japan (+7 per cent) and Hong Kong (+ 6 per cent) among the star performers.

At the time of going to press, 1990 figures on arrivals of tourists and visitors at frontiers and nights spent in all forms of accommodation broken down by country of origin were not yet available.

Denmark. International tourism, measured by nights spent in all forms of accommodation and of nights spent in hotels and similar establishments, continues to flourish and posted a significant increase for the second year running (+ 9 per cent for the former in 1990 against + 6 per cent in 1989 and + 11 per cent for the latter against + 12 per cent in 1989). In 1990 it was up by over 10 per cent for Germany and Sweden, Denmark's two main markets, though the number of nights spent by tourists from Japan declined by 8 per cent and by 3 per cent from both the United States and the Netherlands.

Finland. Nights spent in hotels and similar establishments were slightly down (-2 per cent). Among the OECD regions, only Australasia-Japan performed well, up 5 per cent; among the other regions, Europe (accounting for 63 per cent of the market) declined by 6 per cent, and North America by 3 per cent.

Among the countries recording a decline, were Sweden (- 11 per cent) -- Finland's main market accounting for 21 per cent, -- and Germany (- 4 per cent); figures for Norway were also down for the second year running (- 14 per centin 1990 and - 5 per cent in 1989). The USSR, Finland's fourth largest market, gained considerable ground for the second year in succession (+ 13 per cent in 1990 and + 46 per cent in 1989).

France. Nights spent in all forms of accommodation were up 4 per cent in 1990, but this was a smaller rise than for arrivals of tourists at frontiers(+ 7 per cent); nights spent over the same period in hotels and similar establishments in France (excluding three regions, the Loire, Champagne-Ardennes and Corsica) rose more briskly (+ 8 per cent). 1990 may thus be considered a good year, given that 1989 was exceptional on account of the French Revolution Bicentenary celebrations.

This growth in the number of nights spent in all means of accommodation was due primarily to the buoyancy of the country's second main market, the United Kingdom (+ 8 per cent), a good two years before the opening of the Channel Tunnel. Also noteworthy is the firmness of the African market which is growing by 9 per cent. Of the Southern European countries, Portugal is noteworthy for a fall of 1 per cent in visitors.

Finally, in terms of nights spent in hotels and similar establishments, the only data available for the Japanese market, a fall of 7 per cent is seen after an exceptionally large rise in 1989 (+68 per cent).

Germany. The tourism statistics data for 1990 refer only to the territory of the Federal Republic of Germany prior to unification.

Germany recorded around 15 million visitors in 1990 (7 per cent more than in 1989); at the same time the number of nights spent in all forms of accommodation rose by 4 per cent, much slower growth than in 1989 (+ 12 per cent), with 35 million nights spent, of which 30 million in hotels and similar establishments.

Growth in demand, measured by nights spent, was primarily attributable to the expansion in the number of tourists from the United States (+ 11 per cent), the United Kingdom (+ 10 per cent) and Japan (+ 9 per cent). On the other hand, Germany's main market, the Netherlands, declined by 3 per cent while there was a fall-off of 23 per cent in the number of visitors from Iceland.

The fall in nights spent by visitors from the eastern European countries (- 17 per cent) was due in part to the unification of Germany as well as to the fact that tourists from Eastern Germany (151 000 in 1989) since 1990 count as domestic tourists.

Greece. In 1990, Greece received almost 9 million tourists, 10 per cent more than in the previous year. Greece's two main markets, Germany and the United Kingdom (which together account for 40 per cent of tourist flows to Greece), posted increases of 16 per cent and 1 per cent respectively year on year. The largest percentage increases were in arrivals from Yugoslavia (+ 57 per cent), Norway (+ 32 per cent), Belgium and Luxembourg (+ 24 per cent) and Spain (+ 23 per cent). On the other hand, there was a significant decline in the number of arrivals from Denmark (- 11 per cent) and Portugal (- 24 per cent) within Europe as well as from North America (- 3 per cent), and Australasia-Japan (- 4 per cent).

Iceland. After remaining flat in 1989, arrivals of tourists at frontiers rose by 8 per cent in 1990. An increase was posted only for Europe (+ 11 per cent), while the other regions recorded a decline: North America (- 2 per cent) and Australasia-Japan (- 1 per cent). Among non-Member countries, Europe again posted the highest growth (+ 90 per cent). Iceland is experiencing a boom in arrivals from the East European countries (with the exception of Romania, down 42 per cent).

Developments differ across the major markets, with Germany and Sweden up by over 13 per cent and the United States and Denmark losing ground (- 3 per cent and - 6 per cent respectively).

Ireland. In Ireland, 1990 was a year of continuing brisk growth, though somewhat slower than in 1989, both as regards nights spent in hotels and similar establishments (+ 5 per cent against + 20 per cent in 1989) and arrivals of visitors at frontiers (+ 12 per cent against + 17 per cent).

1990 was the third year in a five-year plan designed to double the number of overseas visitors and to boost tourist receipts and expand employment. The year's excellent performance ought to help achieve these goals.

In terms of nights spent, outturns varied according to generating country: in Europe, the United Kingdom, Ireland's main market, plummeted by 9 per cent, after performing buoyantly in 1989 (+ 38 per cent). On the other hand, the French and German markets both expanded apace, up 101 per cent and 41 per cent respectively. As for North America, the pattern was also uneven, with the United States up 5 per cent and Canada down 57 per cent.

Italy. Arrivals of visitors at frontiers grew by 9 per cent (against - 1 per cent in 1989), while nights spent in hotels and similar establishments continued downwards (- 3 per cent in both 1990 and 1989). In terms of nights spent -- the most reliable yardstick for measuring tourist flows -- the figures for Europe which accounts for 76 per cent of nights spent in Italy were lacklustre, down 6 per cent. The World Football Cup did not produce the hoped for results. Italy's main European markets (Germany, the United Kingdom and France) are all contracting and it is the smaller Southern European markets that are expanding -- Spain (+ 8 per cent), Greece (+ 4 per cent), Portugal (+ 17 per cent), Yugoslavia (+ 53 per cent) and Turkey (+ 34 per cent) -- primarily because the Italian tourist industry has become more competitive.

The other non-European markets stood up well. The North American market continued to expand (+ 3 per cent in 1990 and + 6 per cent in 1989) as did that of Australasia-Japan (+ 24 per cent and + 8 per cent).

Growth was on the whole more rapid (+ 10 per cent) for non-member countries (12 per cent of the market).

At the time of going to press, 1990 figures on arrivals and nights spent in all forms of accommodation broken down by country of origin were not yet available.

Japan. International tourist demand continued to rise in 1990 (+ 14 per centagainst + 20 per cent in 1989(measured by arrivals of visitors at frontiers. This was mainly due to growth in tourism from non-Member countries (accounting for 64 per cent of the market and up 18 per cent year on year). Among the best performers were Latin America (+ 49 per cent) and Asia-Oceania (+ 17 per cent). The Republic of Korea and Taiwan, which together account for 42 per cent of arrivals, were up 21 and 15 per cent respectively. Among the OECD countries (average growth 8 per cent), Japan's chief European market, the United Kingdom, was buoyant (+ 21 per cent).

Netherlands. International tourism in the Netherlands is flourishing for the second year running and nights spent in all forms of accommodation were 16 per cent up in 1990 to 16 million. Around half this number were spent in hotels and similar establishments (+ 13 per cent on 1989).

In 1990 the Netherlands not only enjoyed good weather but also benefited from the impact of the Van Gogh Exhibition as regards arrivals from neighbouring countries (Germany: + 17 per cent; France: + 19 per cent; and Belgium: + 8 per cent) as well as from its other major markets (the United Kingdom: + 13 per cent; the United States: + 13 per cent).

The only markets to show a decline were the Scandinavian countries (Norway: - 16 per cent; Sweden: - 3 per cent; and Denmark: - 2 per cent).

New Zealand. In 1990, New Zealand received 976 000 tourists, with arrivals, 8 per cent up on 1989. Growth was faster in the first half year (especially in January with the holding of the Commonwealth Games). Of the four main countries that together account for 69 per cent of the market, three are vigorously expanding -- Australia (+ 9 per cent), Japan (+ 11 per cent) and the United Kingdom (+ 17 per cent) -- whereas the United States gained only 2 per cent. Germany, the country's second largest European market, was particularly buoyant (+ 26 per cent).

Almost 60 per cent of nights spent were recorded between May and September, of which 22 per cent by visitors from Scandinavia and 32 per cent by visitors from Europe (excluding Scandinavia). The number of nights spent in camping sites rose faster (+ 11 per cent) than nights in hotels and similar establishments.

Norway. Foreign visitors totalled 3.5 million nights in hotels and similar establishments in 1990 (up 3 per cent on 1989). More nights were spent by visitors from France (+ 22 per cent), the Netherlands (+ 7 per cent), the United States and Japan (+ 5 per cent), as well as from Norway's Scandinavian neighbours, Sweden (+ 9 per cent) and Finland (+ 7 per cent). However, among its main markets, Germany was sluggish, though it remains the country's largest market, while Denmark was down 4 per cent.

Finally, the number of nights spent in camping sites over the summer season was up 10 per cent on the previous year.

Portugal. Growth in Portugal was twice as fast in 1990 as in 1989 on most indicators: nights spent in all forms of accommodation + 6 per cent), nights spent in hotels and similar establishments (+ 8 per cent) and tourist arrivals at frontiers (+ 13 per cent).

The European countries accounted for 90 per cent of nights spent in all forms of accommodation. Among Portugal's five main markets, only France showed a slight decline (- 1 per cent); but growth in nights spent by tourists from other OECD regions was also sluggish, mainly because of a 1 per cent decline in tourists from the United States and Australia.

A look at the figures for Spain, the country's prime market (accounting for 49 per cent of tourists and 75 per cent of visitors) reveals that stays of less than 24 hours (excursions) were losing ground in favour of stays of more than one night. As a result the number of Spanish tourists expanded by 21 per cent in 1990 and that of excursionists by around 11 per cent.

Spain. In 1990 Spanish tourism showed contrasting developments between the domestic and foreign sectors. Domestic tourism was considerably more buoyant than foreign tourism, though here discussion is limited to foreign tourism.

Data on nights spent in hotels and similar establishments show a 9 per cent decline; but in Spain, only 20 per cent of nights spent are in hotel accommodation, since the supply of other forms of accommodation is very plentiful and highly popular with non-residents.

Measured by arrivals of foreign visitors at frontiers - the only 1990 data available that are broken down by country of origin -- Spain recorded a 4 per cent decline. This was due to a sharp drop in visitors from North America (- 12 per cent in 1990 against + 10 per cent in 1989) as well as to a slight fall for the second year running (- 3 per cent in 1990, - 0.4 per cent in 1989) in arrivals from Europe (91 per cent of the Spanish market). While France, Spain's main market, was down 3 per cent and the United Kingdom down 14 per cent, some other major markets picked up, such as Germany and Portugal (+ 1 per cent).

At the time of going to press, 1990 figures on nights spent in hotels and similar establishments broken down by country of origin were not yet available.

Sweden. While growth of tourism in Sweden has been fairly stable over the past ten years, in 1990 nights spent in all forms of accommodation plummeted by 13 per cent. This surprising outturn may be explained in part by the rather high level of tourist prices and by the tax reforms that are coming into force in 1991 and 1992. Value-added tax payable by hotels and restaurants was virtually doubled in January 1990 to 25 per cent. The number of hotels and restaurants going out of business was up 50 per cent in 1990.

Several customer groups reacted negatively to these price hikes; a 24 per cent decline was recorded for the Scandinavian countries, with Norway, Sweden's chief foreign market accounting for 24 per cent of the total, down 32 per cent. Germany, Sweden's next largest market, was also down 7 points. However, it is felt in Sweden that in the long run the tax reforms will be beneficial and promote domestic demand for tourism-related services. More public investment in the transport sector -- such as the construction of a bridge linking Sweden and Denmark -- ought too to foster the long-term growth of tourism in Sweden.

Switzerland. In 1990, Switzerland enjoyed greater popularity with international tourists than in 1989, with nights spent in all forms of accommodation and in hotels and similar establishments both up 3 per cent. The main beneficiaries were "holiday houses and flats and rented rooms" (+ 4 per cent) and camping sites (+ 10 per cent). Given the rather adverse conditions generally (a poor start to the season because of lack of snow, the rise of the Swiss franc, the political upheavals in Germany and the Gulf crisis), performance may be deemed satisfactory in terms of numbers of visitors.

The number of nights spent by Europeans staying in Switzerland increased a good deal more slowly (+ 1 per cent) than the number of nights spent by tourists from other OECD regions: North America (+ 11 per cent) and Australasia-Japan (+ 5 per cent). This increase may well be due to the changes in the political arena in Europe as well as to the Oberammergau Passion Play, an event which takes place every ten years in Bavaria.

Of the major markets, Germany (- 1 per cent) and France (- 2 per cent) are contracting, while tourist flows from the United Kingdom, the United States and Italy are expanding (+ 2 per cent, + 12 per cent and + 11 per cent respectively).

Turkey. The positive developments on the international tourism front in the early part of 1990 were halted in August when the Gulf crisis flared up. Many bookings were cancelled, particularly from Western Europe; the cancellation rate -- 5 per cent in August -- was up to 20 per cent in the ensuing months. However, despite alll this, nights in all forms of accommodation and in hotels and similar establishments rose by 12 per cent and 6 per cent respectively and arrivals of foreign visitors at frontiers by 21 per cent.

Developments in the East European countries also had a beneficial impact on the Turkish tourist industry. Visitor arrivals from these countries were up 136 per cent compared to only 7 per cent for the OECD countries. In terms of number of nights spent, Turkey's two main markets, Germany and France, were both buoyant, expanding by 15 per cent and 7 per cent respectively. Growth of the Austrian (+ 69 per cent) and Benelux (+ 30 per cent) markets was particularly spectacular. But for the second year running, Turkey's popularity with British tourists waned (- 20 per cent in 1990 and - 14 per cent in 1989).

United Kingdom. Demand expressed in terms of nights spent in all forms of accommodation rose by 5 per cent in 1990; the number of arrivals of foreign visitors at frontiers was also up 4 per cent. Demand from the OECD countries expanded by 4 per cent mainly as a result of the buoyancy of two markets: Australasia-Japan (+ 18 per cent) and North America (+ 5 per cent). European demand, however, was almost flat (+ 1 per cent). The largest increases were recorded by the Southern European countries: Yugoslavia (+ 235 per cent), Turkey (+ 34 per cent) and Portugal (+ 25 per cent). But other markets contracted -- Finland (- 30 per cent), Norway (- 21 per cent) and Austria (- 16 per cent), in contrast to the brisk growth of 1989.

United States. In 1990, the number of tourist arrivals at frontiers topped 39 million, up 7 per cent year on year, due in part to the weaker dollar which enhanced America's appeal as a tourist destination and in part to the major promotional campaigns launched to attract visitors from abroad.

Visits from OECD-Europe were sharply up (+ 6 per cent), with Spain and Belgium leading the way (both + 20 per cent), followed by Italy, Austria and Germany (all + 12 per cent). Tourism from the East European countries also expanded (+ 27 per cent). But the United States above all gained from the buoyant growth of tourist flows from neighbouring markets such as Canada (+ 12 per cent) and the South American countries (+ 17 per cent); one exception was however the marked drop in visitors from Mexico (- 7 per cent).

Yugoslavia. International tourism in Yugoslavia continued to lose ground in 1990 for the second year in succession; the number of nights spent in all forms of accommodation dropped 12 per cent (- 6 per cent in 1989) while nights spent in hotels and similar accommodation were down 3 per cent (- 1 per cent in 1989). Over the period 1988-1990, some 10 million fewer nights were spent in Yugoslavia.

The steepest declines were recorded for Europe, where the country's main markets are located and which accounts for 86 per cent of all nights spent: Germany, - 20 per cent, Austria, - 23 per cent and Netherlands, - 11 per cent. Only the numbers of Italian and British tourists were up for the second year running (+ 5 per cent and + 1 per cent respectively). Among the other OECD regions, the only bright note was struck by Canada (+ 1 per cent).

C. MAIN GENERATING COUNTRIES

This part sets out recent developments in the main international tourism generating countries to the OECD area (Tables 4, 5, 6 and 7), namely Canada, France, Germany, Italy, Japan, the Netherlands, the United Kingdom and the United States. In the Annex, summary tables covering the period 1979-1990 give an historical overview of the trends in the main generating countries.

These countries were selected not at random but on the basis of the contribution they have made to the development of international tourism as

Table 4. **Annual growth rates of number of arrivals at frontiers from main generating countries**

	T/V	Total Variation % 90/89	From France		From Germany		From United Kingdom		From United States	
			Relative share % 89	Variation % 90/89	Relative share % 89	Variation % 90/89	Relative share % 89	Variation % 90/89	Relative share % 89	Variation % 90/89
Austria										
Belgium										
Denmark										
Finland										
France (R)	T	7.3			21.4	14.2	14.3	3.6	4.4	–4.4
Germany										
Greece (N)	T	9.8	5.9	18.3	20.5	16.1	20.2	0.9	3.5	–1.8
Iceland (N)	T	8.2	6.4	22.4	14.4	11.6	9.3	14.6	17.9	–1.5
Ireland (R)	V	12.3	5.0	44.1	5.5	13.9	61.1	7.1	13.9	4.2
Italy (N)	V	9.4	17.0	–1.8	18.4	5.4	3.5	7.4	2.5	4.7
Luxembourg										
Netherlands										
Norway										
Portugal (N)	T	12.7	8.6	1.1	7.9	10.0	14.4	3.3	2.6	–1.5
Spain (N)	V	–3.7	22.2	–3.1	12.5	1.4	13.6	–14.4	1.8	–12.3
Sweden										
Switzerland										
Turkey (N)	V	20.9	6.4	9.6	20.1	8.6	9.1	–13.4	4.6	0.6
United Kingdom (R)	V	3.9	13.0	2.1	11.7	–7.3			16.4	7.3
EUROPE		5.2	12.7	–1.2	16.5	7.4	10.6	–2.6	4.2	0.8
Canada (R)	T	1.0	1.6	6.9	1.7	–2.9	3.7	–0.3	80.6	0.7
United States (R)	T	6.7	1.8	9.5	2.9	11.8	6.1	1.0		
NORTH AMERICA		5.0	1.7	8.8	2.6	8.9	5.4	0.7	23.5	0.7
Australia (R)	V	6.5	1.0	5.0	3.3	9.0	13.1	1.8	12.5	–3.8
New Zealand (R)	T	8.3	0.5	–15.8	2.6	26.2	8.2	17.4	15.3	1.6
Japan (N)	V	14.2	1.7	7.9	2.2	5.9	6.3	21.0	18.8	4.4
AUSTRALASIA-JAPAN		10.5	1.2	5.8	2.6	10.4	9.0	10.5	16.0	1.6
OECD		5.3	10.2	–0.9	13.4	7.4	9.5	–1.9	8.4	0.8
Yugoslavia (N)										

V Visitors.
T Tourists.
(R) Tourist count by country of residence.
(N) Tourist count by country of nationality.

expressed in terms of dollar expenditures, the standard unit of account for the "Travel" item in the balance of payments. These eight countries together accounted for about 77 per cent of total expenditure by the 24 OECD Member countries in 1990. The data in the summary tables were compiled by adding up the totals for arrivals in the individual countries. Although gross national statistics are not always comparable with one another, they do give an order of magnitude and an idea of recent trends.

The number of nights spent by **Canadians** in Europe rose 9 per cent in 1990. Fairly high average incomes and the firmness of the Canadian dollar against the US dollar for the second year running encouraged the flow of tourists across the border into the United States. They also travelled more to the European countries, Portugal, Austria and the United Kingdom being particularly popular destinations. On the other hand, they tended to desert Finland and Turkey (- 4 per cent and - 8 per cent). Outside Europe, Canadian tourist arrivals in the United States, where Canada accounts for 42 per cent of the market, were up 12 per cent.

Nights spent by **French** tourists and visitors in European destinations rose 8 per cent. In 1990 popular destinations with the French were Finland (+ 17 per cent), Ireland (+ 45 per cent), the Netherlands (+ 19 per cent) and Norway (+ 22 per cent). Other countries suffered a loss in popularity: Yugoslavia (- 13 per cent). Switzerland (- 2 per cent) and Portugal (- 1 per cent). Outside Europe, the number of French visitors expanded in all Member countries except in New Zealand where the figures were sharply down (- 16 per cent). In considering French travel to the United States (+ 10 per cent), it must of course be remembered that since 1990 visas have been waived reciprocally, partly at least to encourage tourism.

In Europe, the predominant **German** market was virtually flat in 1990 in terms of nights spent (+0.7 per cent). 1990 was of course the year of unification, an event which probably played a part, in the last quarter, in the smaller number of trips abroad by German nationals. Austria, Yugoslavia (where German tourists account for 63 per cent of the market) and Sweden all recorded fewer visits (- 5 per cent, - 20 per cent and - 7 per cent). On the other hand, visits to the Netherlands (+ 17 per cent) and Denmark (+ 12 per cent) were strongly up. Outside Europe, arrivals at frontiers from Germany increased in all Member countries except Canada (- 3 per cent) and were up 26 per cent in the case of New Zealand.

In the case of **Italy**, generally believed to be one of the most promising markets, the number of nights spent by its nationals in Europe rose by 6 per cent. The largest increases were recorded in the Netherlands (+ 43 per cent,), Portugal (+ 16 per cent), Denmark, Austria and Switzerland (all over 10 per cent). Only in Finland was there a significant decline (- 9 per cent). Italian tourism to Australia and New Zealand was also sharply up (+ 19 per cent) as it was to Japan and the United States (+ 8 per cent and + 12 per cent respectively.

Under the impetus of Japan's healthy economy and the government's active encouragement of travel abroad, **the Japanese** are travelling overseas in ever larger numbers. The number of nights spent were up for virtually all the European countries, headed by Austria (+ 27 per cent), the United Kingdom (+ 20 per cent), the Netherlands (+ 16 per cent) and Sweden (+ 16 per cent),

Table 5. **Annual growth rates of number of arrivals at frontiers from main generating countries**

	T/V	Total Variation % 90/89	From Japan		From Netherlands		From Canada		From Italy	
			Relative share % 89	Variation % 90/89	Relative share % 89	Variation % 90/89	Relative share % 89	Variation % 90/89	Relative share % 89	Variation % 90/89
Austria										
Belgium										
Denmark										
Finland										
France (R)	T	7.3	1.6	–2.7	8.0	0.2			10.6	7.9
Germany										
Greece (N)	T	9.8	1.3	3.6	5.3	15.8	1.0	–6.1	7.0	9.1
Iceland (N)	T	8.2	1.0	–7.2	2.0	19.0	1.0	–11.8	2.3	21.2
Ireland (R)	V	12.3					1.4	2.7		
Italy (N)	V	9.4	0.8	39.5	3.3	15.3	0.8	12.4		
Luxembourg										
Netherlands										
Norway										
Portugal (N)	T	12.7	0.4	8.5	4.5	–5.6	1.2	0.2	2.3	13.3
Spain (N)	V	–3.7	0.4	12.6	3.8	–4.0	0.3	–8.5	2.8	9.6
Sweden										
Switzerland										
Turkey (N)	V	20.9	0.7	9.5	2.4	40.9	0.7	9.5	3.5	1.5
United Kingdom (R)	V	3.9	2.9	13.3	5.4	5.4	3.7	9.9	4.1	0.8
EUROPE		4.4	0.9	21.1	3.9	6.1	1.0	6.9	2.1	7.3
Canada (R)	T	1.0	2.6	6.6	0.6	–0.6			0.6	0.4
United States (R)	T	6.7	8.4	4.9	0.7	8.9	42.0	12.3	1.0	11.6
NORTH AMERICA		5.0	6.7	5.1	0.7	6.5	29.7	12.3	0.9	9.3
Australia (R)	V	6.5	16.8	37.3	1.0	5.0	2.6	–0.9	1.0	19.0
New Zealand (R)	T	8.3	10.8	10.8	0.8	9.2	3.4	9.9	0.3	19.9
Japan (N)	V	14.2			0.6	6.9	2.1	6.9	1.0	7.7
AUSTRALASIA-JAPAN		10.5	7.7	31.5	0.8	6.4	2.5	4.6	0.9	12.9
OECD		4.8	2.6	11.4	3.0	6.1	8.3	11.8	1.8	7.6
Yugoslavia (N)										

V Visitors.
T Tourists.
(R) Tourist count by country of residence.
(N) Tourist count by country of nationality.

though nights spent in Denmark and Yugoslavia were down 8 per cent. Outside Europe, over 3 million Japanese tourists visited the United States (+ 5 per cent on 1989) though the biggest increases were posted by the countries of the Pacific region: Australia (37 per cent more visitors than in 1989) and New Zealand (11 per cent more).

The number of nights spent by **Dutch** nationals in Europe remained the same in 1990. They spent fewer nights in Austria (- 6 per cent), Germany (- 3 per cent) and Yugoslavia (- 11 per cent), a popular destination with the Dutch, and rather more in the Northern European countries (Finland, Norway and the United Kingdom) and Switzerland. In terms of arrivals at frontiers, the only data available for most of the non-European Member countries, the Netherlands market is growing apace, expanding by around 6 per cent.

The **United Kingdom,** one of the major OECD generating countries, gained ground in most European destinations, despite the economic recession. Nights spent in Europe were up 5 per cent. The British went in larger numbers to France (+ 8 per cent), Germany (+ 10 per cent), the Netherlands (+ 13 per cent) and Portugal (+ 4 per cent), a country where they account for 29 per cent of all nights spent and which had suffered a loss of popularity in 1989. But numbers were down for Ireland (- 3 per cent), for which the United Kingdom constitutes the main market, and for Turkey (- 20 per cent).

Nights spent in Europe by **United States** nationals were up 5 per cent. Among the major destinations where they constitute a large share of the market, Germany received 11 per cent more US tourists, Norway 5 per cent more and the United Kingdom 4 per cent more. In Ireland their numbers diminished (- 2 per cent) as they did in Yugoslavia and Turkey (- 12 per cent and - 8 per cent) for cyclical reasons. Outside Europe, arrivals were up 1 per cent in Canada where they account for 80 per cent of all foreign tourist arrivals at frontiers. Australia, however, recorded a 4 per cent drop in the number of US visitors.

Table 6. **Annual growth rates of nights spent in the various means of accommodation from main generating countries**

	H/A	Total Variation % 90/89	From France		From Germany		From the United Kingdom		From the United-States	
			Relative share % 89	Variation % 90/89	Relative share % 89	Variation % 90/89	Relative share % 89	Variation % 90/89	Relative share % 89	Variation % 90/89
Austria (R)	A	–0.2	3.1	6.2	63.1	–5.2	5.0	4.5	1.8	26.0
Belgium (R)	A	6.1	10.0	4.3	16.1	–0.9	9.7	14.1	4.9	7.4
Denmark (N)	A	8.9	1.7	3.6	35.1	11.5	4.2	9.7	5.1	–3.4
Finland (R)	H	–2.0	2.8	17.4	14.0	–4.3	5.6	0.6	8.0	–2.5
France (R)	A	4.4			19.1	3.2	15.1	7.8	5.5	5.1
Germany (R)	A	3.8	4.9	5.7			8.8	10.1	12.6	11.4
Greece (N)										
Iceland	H		4.3		11.2		7.2		7.0	
Ireland (R)	A	7.2	6.9	44.6	7.1	24.5	51.4	–3.4	14.5	–2.4
Italy (N)	A	–2.9	7.3		36.9		7.4		6.0	
Luxembourg (R)										
Netherlands (R)	A	15.6	4.7	18.6	45.0	16.9	11.9	13.4	6.4	13.1
Norway (N)	H	3.1	4.1	21.9	16.9	–0.1	9.8	1.0	10.1	5.0
Portugal (N)	A	6.1	7.3	–1.0	15.1	7.7	28.7	3.5	3.8	–0.8
Spain (N)	H		9.0		27.8		32.3		2.3	
Sweden (N)	A	–13.3	2.2	9.5	20.0	–7.4	4.5	–1.5	4.6	–1.6
Switzerland (R)	A	2.6	6.9	–1.6	41.6	–0.7	7.6	2.2	6.9	11.7
Turkey (N)	A	11.8	12.4	7.4	39.7	15.2	7.1	–19.8	3.3	–8.1
United Kingdom (R)	A	4.8	8.7	4.8	9.5	–1.8			14.7	3.6
EUROPE		4.2	3.9	7.5	22.6	0.7	10.9	5.0	7.9	5.0
Canada (R)	A		3.2		3.6		7.6		59.5	
United States										
NORTH AMERICA										
Australia	A	13.6			4.1	40.5	22.4	17.6	9.2	9.3
New Zealand	A	9.5			3.9	19.5	15.2	11.7	10.7	5.3
Japan										
AUSTRALASIA-JAPAN										
OECD		4.2	3.9	7.5	22.6	0.7	10.9	5.0	7.9	5.0
Yugoslavia (N)	A	–11.8	2.3	–12.8	35.6	–20.0	12.0	1.1	1.3	–11.6

H Hotels and similar establishments.
A All means of accommodation.
(R) Tourist count by country of residence.
(N) Tourist count by country of nationality.

Table 7. **Annual growth rates of nights spent in the various means of accommodation from main generating countries**

	H/A	Total Variation % 90/89	From Japan		From Netherlands		From Canada		From Italy	
			Relative share % 89	Variation % 90/89	Relative share % 89	Variation % 90/89	Relative share % 89	Variation % 90/89	Relative share % 89	Variation % 90/89
Austria (R)	A	–0.2	0.4	26.5	10.2	–5.7	0.2	12.7	2.9	10.9
Belgium (R)	A	6.1	1.4	–6.3	36.9	7.2	0.9	7.9	3.0	7.2
Denmark (N)	A	8.9	1.4	–8.0	6.1	–3.0			1.9	12.6
Finland (R)	H	–2.0	2.4	4.6	2.1	5.6	1.3	–3.5	3.5	–8.8
France (R)	A	4.4			10.0	3.3	1.6	5.6	9.1	3.2
Germany (R)	A	3.8	3.8	9.2	17.8	–3.4	1.2	5.9	5.0	7.1
Greece (N)										
Iceland										
Ireland (R)	H	5.2			2.7	9.0	3.4	–57.5		
Italy (N)	A	–2.9	1.7		3.7		0.8			
Luxembourg (R)										
Netherlands (R)	A	15.6	1.2	16.2			1.5	5.1	3.8	43.3
Norway (N)	H	3.1	2.3	5.5	3.4	6.6				
Portugal (N)	A	6.1	0.4	6.2	9.6	6.1	1.9	10.4	2.5	15.5
Spain (N)	H		1.1		3.6		0.2		5.9	
Sweden (N)	A	–13.3	1.1	15.9	5.3	–4.8	0.4	3.8	1.8	3.7
Switzerland (R)	A	2.6	2.3	4.5	8.8	3.9	0.7	6.0	4.8	10.7
Turkey (N)	A	11.8	1.1	–0.1			0.3	–7.5	4.1	9.0
United Kingdom (R)	A	4.8	1.8	20.2	2.8	6.3	4.6	9.0	4.4	1.1
EUROPE		3.5	1.5	15.1	7.5	0.4	2.5	8.8	3.9	6.4
Canada (R)	A		2.8		1.3				1.1	
United States										
NORTH AMERICA										
Australia	A	13.6	6.1	14.9			1.7			
New Zealand										
Japan										
AUSTRALASIA-JAPAN										
OECD		3.5	1.5	15.1	7.5	0.4	2.5	8.8	3.9	6.4
Yugoslavia (N)	A	–11.8	0.1	–7.7	7.1	–10.7	0.2	1.0	12.5	4.8

H Hotels and similar establishments.
A All means of accommodation.
(R) Tourist count by country of residence.
(N) Tourist count by country of nationality.

Trends of international tourism in Europe, from:

(Overnights in accommodation, indices 1977=100)

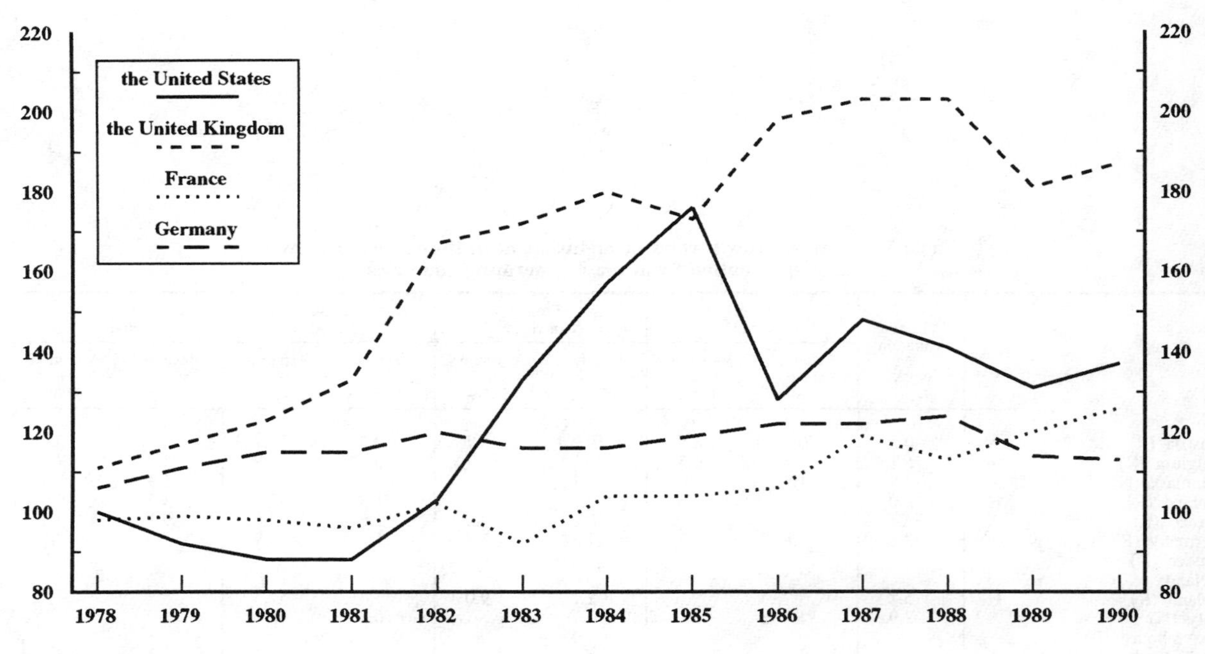

Source: OECD

Trends of international tourism in Europe, from:

(Overnights in accommodation, indices 1977=100)

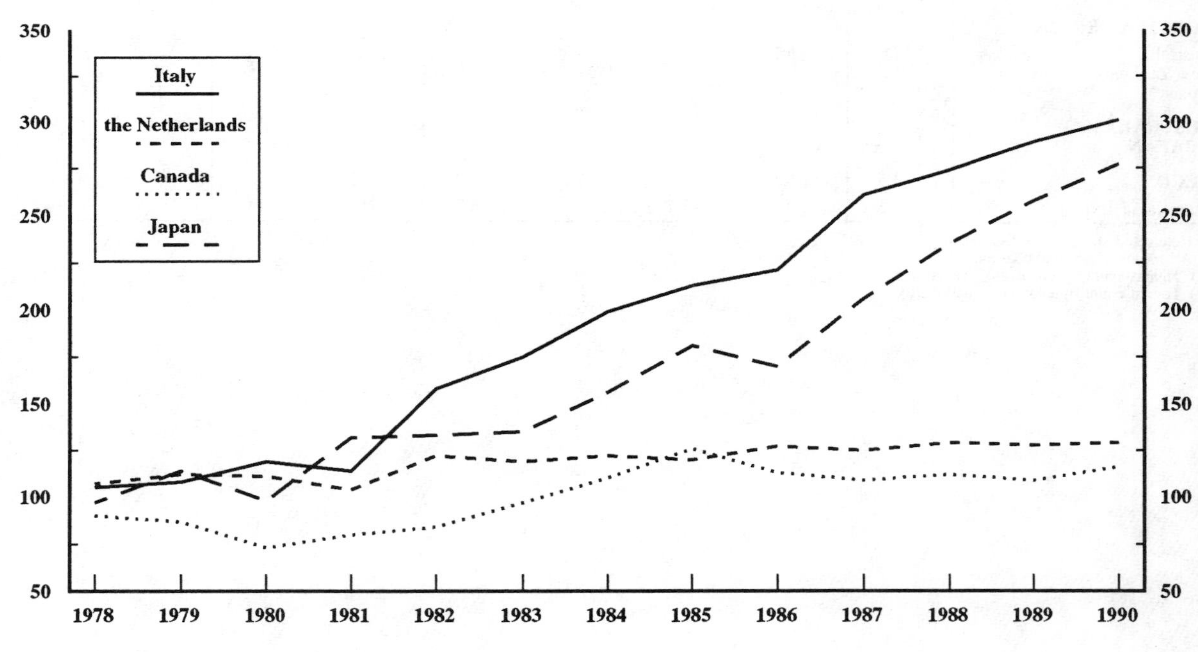

Source: OECD

Trends of international tourism in North America, from:

(Arrivals at frontiers, indices 1977=100)

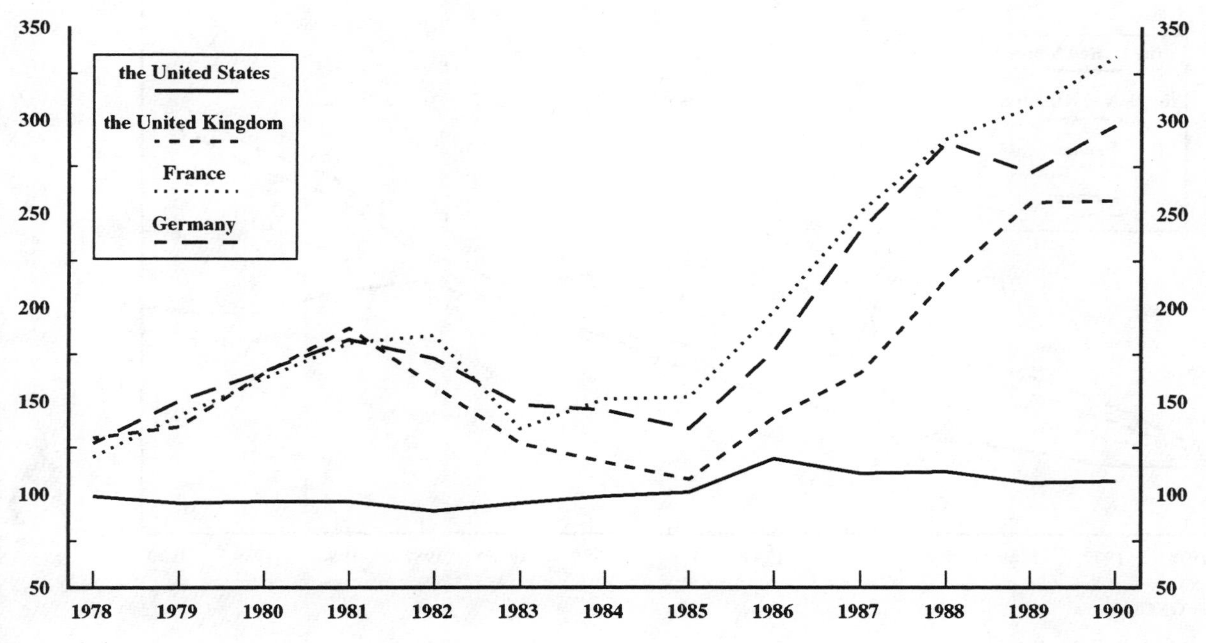

Source: OECD

Trends of international tourism in North America, from:

(Arrivals at frontiers, indices 1977 = 100)

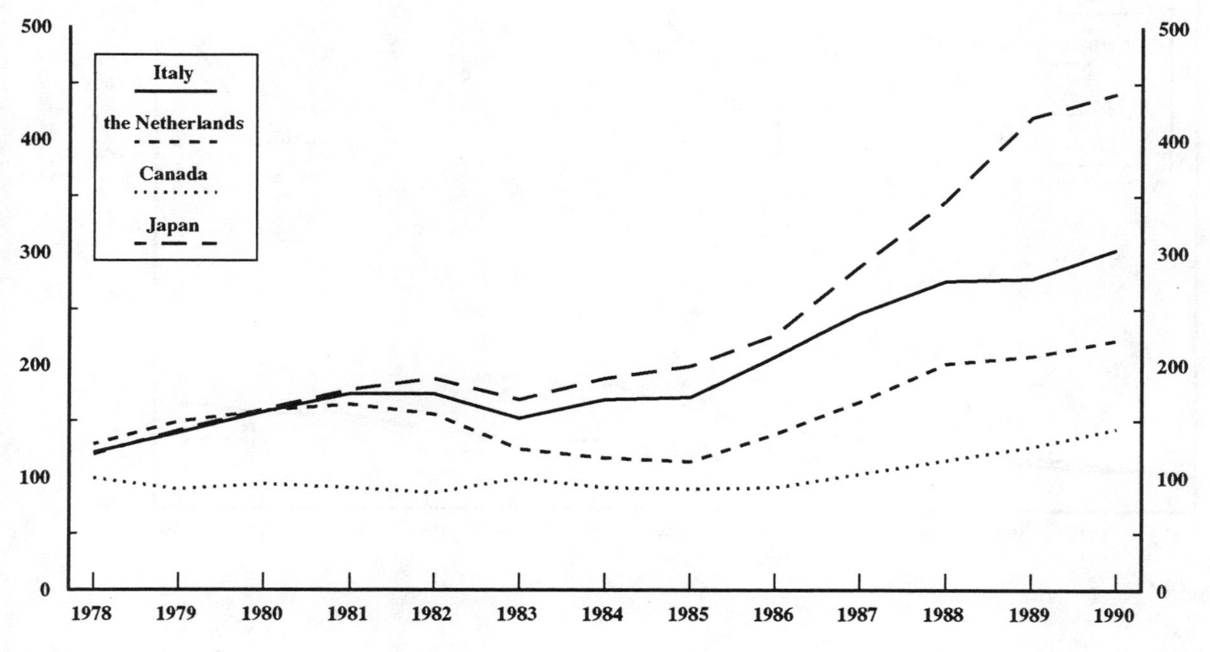

Source: OECD

Trends of international tourism in Australasia-Japan, from:
(Arrivals at frontiers, indices 1977=100)

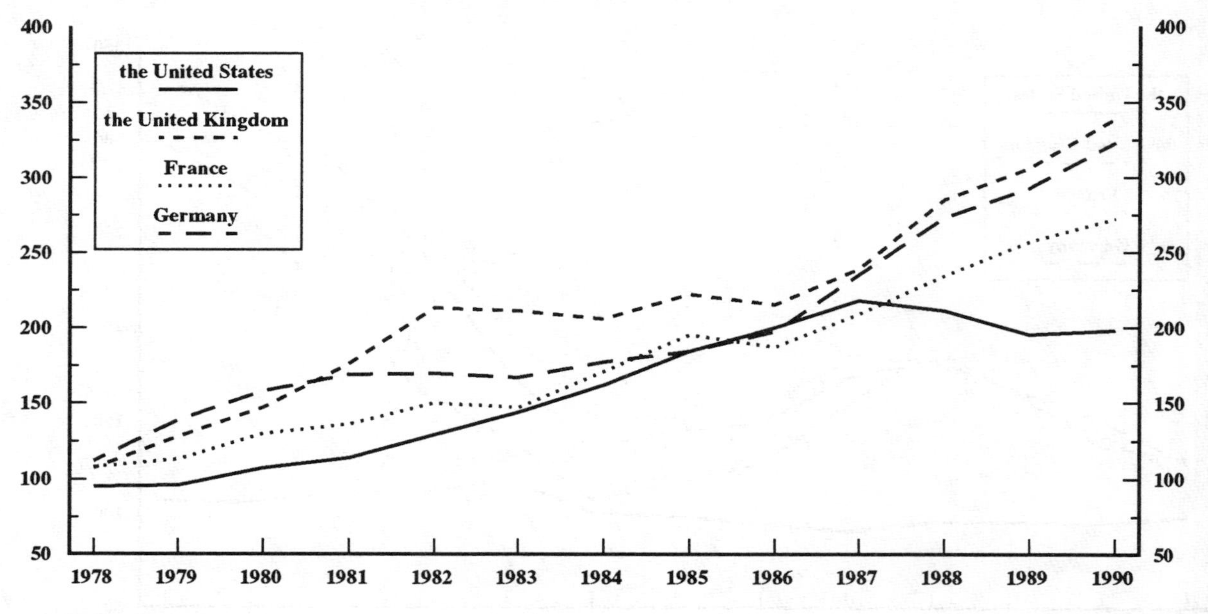

Source: OECD

Trends of international tourism in Australasia-Japan, from:
(Arrivals at frontiers, indices 1977=100)

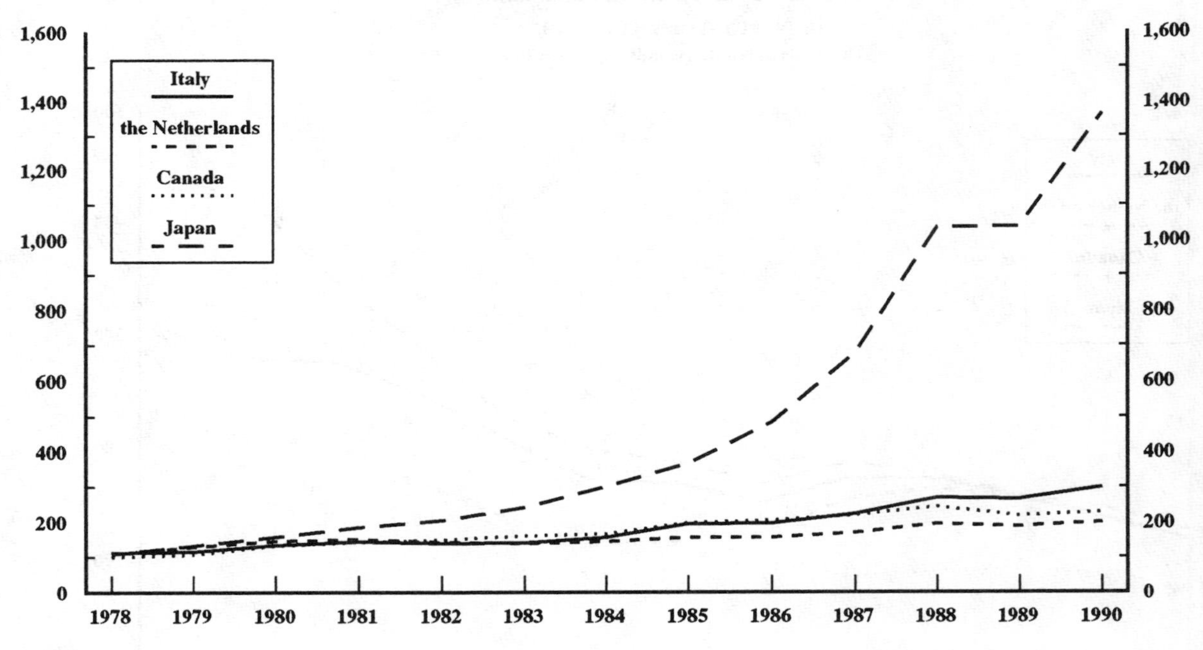

Source: OECD

CHAPTER III

THE ECONOMIC IMPORTANCE OF INTERNATIONAL TOURISM IN MEMBER COUNTRIES

This Chapter brings together the most recent data available on international tourism receipts and expenditure in 1990 for the 24 OECD Member countries and Yugoslavia. The figures do not include international fare payments, except where explicitly stated (see Table 18 in the Statistical Annex).

The first part of the Chapter (Section A) considers:

a) receipts in both national currencies and US dollars, first in current terms and then in real terms, i.e. adjusted for the effects of inflation and for changes in parities between the dollar and national currencies;

b) expenditure, again in both national currencies and US dollars, in current terms;

c) the tourism balance sheet for the OECD area and its three constituent regions.

The US dollar was used as the common unit of account to evaluate trends for a range of countries. However, when considering the tables which give figures in "current dollars", the reader must take into account the marked fluctuations that have taken place in recent years in most OECD currencies against the dollar. In contrast with 1989, in 1990 the dollar fell against the currencies of most (17) OECD countries. In Europe, the only currencies against which the dollar appreciated were the Icelandic krona (2 per cent) and the Turkish lira (23 per cent). As for the non-European Member countries, the relative weakness of the Australian dollar (1 per cent) and the yen (5 per cent) against the US dollar may be noted. Lastly, in Yugoslavia the exchange rate of the dinar continued to fluctuate, plunging even further against the dollar (by 250 per cent, after falling by 1057 per cent in 1989) (see Table 17 in the Annex). The limits to the use of these figures are thus obvious and great care must be taken in drawing any conclusions based on data expressed in dollars.

Section B compares the data on receipts and expenditure with a number of major macroeconomic indicators -- gross domestic product, private final consumption and exports and imports of goods and services. They cover the period 1987-1989, as comprehensive data on these indicators for 1990 are not yet available.

The comparability of the figures provided by Member countries on receipts and expenditure for international tourism is still insufficient and its improvement is a continuing priority for the Statistical Working Party of the OECD Tourism Committee.

The main source of divergence lies in the different survey methods used. Most countries use the "bank reporting method", which is based on the sales and purchases of foreign currency before or after travel abroad. The main drawback of this method is that it gives data on the currency concerned but not on the country visited. The "estimation method" is based on sample surveys carried out among residents at entry or departure points. Such surveys can provide extensive information but because of their cost are conducted by only a few countries. Lastly, some countries use a "mixed method" involving limited surveys to give adjustment factors to apply to bank-derived data. Progress towards data comparability is being made, however, (for further information, the notes in the Statistical Annex should be consulted).

A. INTERNATIONAL TOURISM RECEIPTS AND EXPENDITURE

Dollar receipts and expenditure for the OECD area as a whole were up by 21 per cent, i.e. four times the rate of increase in 1989 (respectively 5 per cent and 4 per cent); this was due to the fact that virtually all the Member country currencies rose against the dollar.

Receipts and expenditure grew most rapidly in Europe (by about 25 per cent), but at only half that rate (about 13 per cent) in North America and Australasia-Japan. In real terms, receipts for the OECD area were up by 5 per cent as in 1989.

International tourism receipts

Expressed in national currency (see Table 1), earnings from international tourism rose in all countries with the exception of Spain (down by 2 per cent). They fell slightly in Spain after having already fallen by 1 per cent in 1989. The largest increases were recorded by Yugoslavia (333 per cent), Turkey (58 per cent) and Greece (25 per cent); however, these increases were rendered almost meaningless by the soaring inflation in these countries (respectively 585 per cent, 60 per cent and 20 per cent) (see Table 22 in the Statistical Annex). The 1990 data for Austria were not used because they are provisional and not comparable with the 1989 figures; the data for Italy were not used either because a change in methodology meant that they were not comparable from one year to the next.

Expressed in current dollars (see Table 2), receipts increased in all OECD countries, partly on account of the weakening of the dollar against most national currrencies. The largest increases were recorded by Denmark (44 per cent), Ireland (+ 35 per cent), Portugal (31 per cent), Turkey and Greece (29 per cent). In volume terms, the countries that earned the most from

Table 1. **International tourist receipts and expenditure in national currencies**

In millions

	Currency	Receipts 1989	Receipts 1990	Receipts %90/89	Expenditure 1989	Expenditure 1990	Expenditure %90/89
Austria[1]	Schilling	141 780	133 660	-5.7	82 900	70 641	-14.8
Belgium-Luxembourg	Franc	121 452	123 613	1.8	170 921	181 985	6.5
Denmark	Krone	16 894	20 548	21.6	21 407	22 727	6.2
Finland	Markka	4 359	4 440	1.9	8 748	10 530	20.4
France	Franc	103 646	109 924	6.1	63 997	67 656	5.7
Germany	Deutsche Mark	16 454	17 262	4.9	44 506	48 210	8.3
Greece	Drachma	324 700	407 800	25.6	133 300	172 900	29.7
Iceland	Krona	6 143	7 121	15.9	10 053	12 690	26.2
Ireland	Pound	755	875	15.9	698	701	0.4
Italy[2]	Lira	16 443 000	23 658 000	43.9	9 291 000	16 569 000	78.3
Netherlands	Guilder	6 405	6 576	2.7	13 680	13 348	-2.4
Norway	Krone	9 218	9 492	3.0	19 678	21 367	8.6
Portugal	Escudo	424 759	502 470	18.3	92 316	122 841	33.1
Spain	Peseta	1 924 200	1 878 400	-2.4	364 700	429 300	17.7
Sweden	Krona	16 400	17 140	4.5	32 032	35 908	12.1
Switzerland	Franc	9 155	9 540	4.2	8 100	8 355	3.1
Turkey	Lira	5 518 967	8 728 509	58.2	1 206 511	1 361 117	12.8
United Kingdom	Pound	6 945	7 785	12.1	9 357	9 916	6.0
Canada	Dollar	5 936	6 138	3.4	8 726	9 843	12.8
United States	Dollar	34 432	39 253	14.0	34 229	38 376	12.1
Australia	Dollar	3 990	4 684	17.4	4 869	5 309	9.0
New Zealand	Dollar	2 277	2 551	12.0	1 525	1 672	9.6
Japan	Yen	435 462	518 756	19.1	3 111 633	3 526 342	13.3
Yugoslavia	Dinar	7 220	31 234	332.6			

Notice: for statistical coverage, see notes in table 18 in annex.

1. Preliminary data for 1990.
2. New series from 1990.

Table 2. **International tourist receipts and expenditure in current dollars**

In millions

	Receipts			Expenditure		
	1989	1990	%90/89	1989	1990	%90/89
Austria	10 716.2	11 753.8	9.7	6 265.8	6 212.0	–0.9
Belgium-Luxembourg	3 082.6	3 698.5	20.0	4 338.1	5 445.1	25.5
Denmark	2 311.1	3 321.5	43.7	2 928.4	3 673.8	25.5
Finland	1 016.5	1 161.5	14.3	2 040.1	2 754.7	35.0
France	16 245.1	20 184.8	24.3	10 030.7	12 423.3	23.9
Germany	8 752.3	10 683.1	22.1	23 673.9	29 836.2	26.0
Greece	2 003.3	2 577.3	28.7	822.4	1 092.7	32.9
Iceland	107.6	122.0	13.4	176.0	217.4	23.5
Ireland	1 070.0	1 447.2	35.2	989.2	1 159.4	17.2
Italy	11 987.4	19 741.7	64.7	6 773.4	13 826.2	104.1
Netherlands	3 019.9	3 611.6	19.6	6 450.0	7 330.9	13.7
Norway	1 335.3	1 516.7	13.6	2 850.5	3 414.2	19.8
Portugal	2 703.8	3 530.8	30.6	587.6	863.2	46.9
Spain	16 252.0	18 426.1	13.4	3 080.3	4 211.2	36.7
Sweden	2 544.1	2 896.1	13.8	4 969.1	6 067.3	22.1
Switzerland	5 597.8	6 869.2	22.7	4 952.7	6 015.9	21.5
Turkey	2 603.3	3 348.8	28.6	569.1	522.2	–8.2
United Kingdom	11 359.6	13 828.3	21.7	15 304.8	17 613.6	15.1
EUROPE	102 708.0	128 719.1	25.3	96 802.5	122 679.3	26.7
Canada	5 013.3	5 259.6	4.9	7 369.6	8 434.3	14.4
United States	34 432.0	39 253.0	14.0	34 229.0	38 376.0	12.1
NORTH AMERICA	39 445.3	44 512.6	12.8	41 598.6	46 810.3	12.5
Australia	3 154.7	3 654.2	15.8	3 849.6	4 141.8	7.6
New Zealand	1 360.2	1 520.4	11.8	911.0	996.5	9.4
Japan	3 156.1	3 582.7	13.5	22 552.3	24 354.0	8.0
AUSTRALASIA-JAPAN	7 671.0	8 757.3	14.2	27 312.9	29 492.3	8.0
OECD	149 824.3	181 988.9	21.5	165 714.1	198 981.9	20.1
Yugoslavia	2 228.4	2 773.9	24.5			

International tourist receipts in real terms

(Shares of the various regions within the OECD)

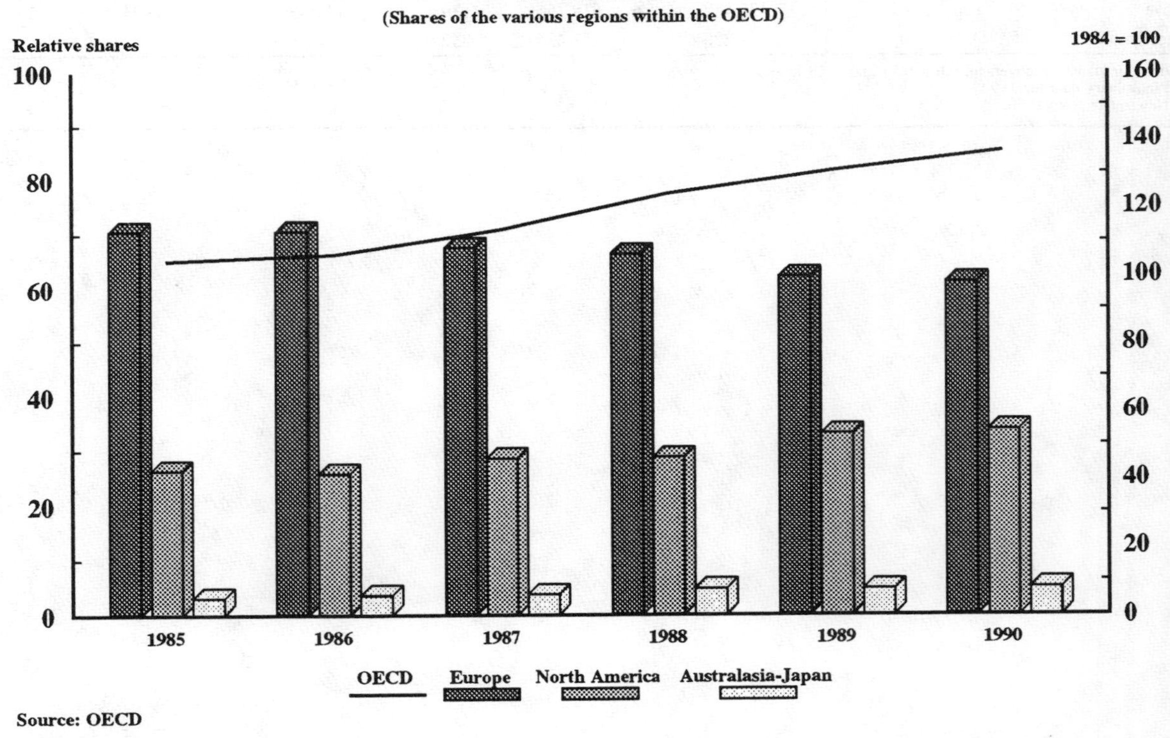

Source: OECD

tourism were the United States, France, Italy, Spain and the United Kingdom, which together accounted for 61 per cent of total OECD receipts (US$ 182 billion in 1990).

On the preliminary estimates of the World Tourism Organisation (WTO), international tourism receipts in 1990 amounted to US$230 billion, or 10 per cent more than in 1989. On this basis, in 1990 the OECD countries accounted for 79 per cent of world international tourism.

In real terms (see Table 3), i.e. after adjustment for the effects of inflation and changes in exchange rates against the dollar, international tourism receipts grew more rapidly in Australasia-Japan (11 per cent) than in the other regions. This was ascribable partly to the increase in Japan's receipts (16 per cent). The increase in Europe (3 per cent) was still below the OECD average (5 per cent) because trends differed quite sharply across countries: the largest increases were in Denmark (18 per cent) and Ireland (12 per cent), followed by Greece and Portugal (4 per cent), but receipts fell by 9 per cent in Spain, 5 per cent in Sweden and 4 per cent in Finland. Yugoslavia's receipts fell by 68 per cent in 1990.

International tourism expenditure

Expenditure in national currencies (see Table 1) was up in 22 of the 24 OECD countries. Only the Dutch spent slightly less abroad than in 1989. The largest increases were recorded by Portugal (33 per cent), Greece (29 per cent) and Iceland (26 per cent).

Expressed in current dollars (see Table 2), the increase in Europe's expenditure (27 per cent) was twice as rapid as that by North America (13 per cent) and Australasia-Japan (8 per cent), while expenditure by countries like Portugal, Spain, Finland and Greece rose by between 30 and 50 per cent. However, Turkey's expenditure fell by 8 per cent, as compared with an increase of 13 per cent in terms of national currency; this was due to the Turkish lira's steep depreciation against the dollar. All told, international tourism expenditure by the OECD area amounted to nearly US$200 billion, i.e. up by more than 20 per cent on 1989. Three countries -- the United States, Germany and Japan -- accounted for nearly half the total expenditure (47 per cent).

The tourism balance sheet

In 1990 the OECD tourism balance worsened slightly to about $17 billion (see Table 4). Over the period 1988-1990 expenditure by Australasia-Japan grew the most rapidly (up by 30 per cent), as a result of which the region's deficit widened by 38 per cent (compared with an increase of 10 per cent in the overall OECD deficit). In contrast, the deficit in North America fell by 50 per cent. In Europe the surplus increased slightly, rising to US$6 billion in 1990.

Table 3. **Trends in international tourist receipts in real prices**[1]

	1985 = 100					Relative share in percentage of total	
	1986	1987	1988	1989	1990	1989	1990
Austria	99.0	103.5	112.9	125.2	114.3	6.3	5.5
Belgium-Luxembourg	99.1	110.9	123.3	115.0	113.2	1.9	1.8
Denmark	98.0	100.5	103.0	101.9	120.6	1.3	1.5
Finland	94.9	107.7	115.8	115.0	110.4	0.6	0.5
France	91.9	94.4	105.9	129.1	132.5	10.2	10.0
Germany	98.2	98.8	105.0	112.9	115.4	5.3	5.2
Greece	106.7	107.6	109.7	90.6	94.5	1.3	1.3
Iceland	114.1	130.2	149.8	162.8	163.4	0.1	0.1
Ireland	95.3	101.5	115.3	127.7	143.3	0.7	0.7
Italy[4]	87.0	89.1	86.8	83.0	112.6	6.9	8.9
Netherlands	98.7	99.3	102.4	114.2	114.5	1.9	1.8
Norway	107.1	100.8	107.0	98.7	97.7	0.7	0.7
Portugal	104.9	126.0	133.5	144.2	150.5	1.6	1.6
Spain	111.8	115.9	117.8	109.1	99.8	8.8	7.7
Sweden	103.8	114.7	120.7	129.3	122.3	1.5	1.4
Switzerland	97.8	101.3	103.9	109.8	108.6	3.5	3.3
Turkey	87.7	117.6	156.9	148.7	146.7	2.2	2.1
United Kingdom	97.7	106.1	101.1	104.4	106.9	7.3	7.1
EUROPE[1]	97.9	102.9	107.5	111.3	114.8	62.2	61.2
Canada	121.3	114.6	119.7	119.5	117.9	3.7	3.5
United States	112.1	124.3	148.3	166.8	180.4	29.4	30.3
NORTH AMERICA	113.4	122.9	144.0	159.7	171.1	33.1	33.8
Australia[3]	114.8	168.3	217.7	190.7	208.7	2.1	2.2
New Zealand[2]	133.8	136.2	222.8	211.6	225.3	0.9	0.9
Japan	89.6	111.1	136.9	157.1	181.5	1.8	2.0
AUSTRALASIA-JAPAN[1]	106.9	138.7	183.7	179.5	199.5	4.7	5.0
OECD[1]	102.3	109.3	119.6	126.2	132.3	100.0	100.0
Yugoslavia	95.4	127.6					

1. After correcting for the effects of inflation in each country. For the regional and OECD totals, the receipts of the individual countries are weighted in proportion to their share in the total expressed in dollars.
2. Changes of series in 1986 and in 1987.
3. Change of statistical coverage in 1987.
4. New series from 1990.

Table 4. **Tourism balance sheet**

In billions of current dollars

	1988	1989	1990
EUROPE			
Receipts	100.2	102.7	128.7
Expenditure	96.1	96.8	122.7
Balance[1]	4.1	5.9	6.0
NORTH AMERICA			
Receipts	33.8	39.4	44.5
Expenditure	38.4	41.6	46.8
Balance[1]	–4.6	–2.2	–2.3
AUSTRALASIA-JAPAN			
Receipts	7.7	7.7	8.8
Expenditure	22.7	27.3	29.5
Balance[1]	–15.0	–19.6	–20.7
OECD			
Receipts	141.7	149.8	182.0
Expenditure	157.2	165.7	199.0
Balance[1]	–15.5	–15.9	–17.0

1. Minus signs indicate deficits. Due to rounding of figures, balances are not always equal to difference between receipts and expenditure.

B. THE ECONOMIC IMPORTANCE OF THE "TRAVEL" ACCOUNT IN THE BALANCE OF PAYMENTS

For some years, the Tourism Committee's Statistical Working Party has been working to apply the tried and tested approach of the System of National Accounts (SNA) to pinpoint the economic importance of tourism. The SNA is the only available framework for coherent analysis of the economic contribution of tourism because it brings together commodities, supply and use, and sets them against activities and final users. It also allows links with other parts of the system, such as income and outlays.

The Manual on Tourism Economic Accounts was adopted in April 1991 by the OECD Council and is now available free of charge from the Secretariat. It will be tested over a three-year period. It will undoubtedly be very useful for assessing the role that tourism plays in the economies of Member countries, since it takes both domestic and international tourism into account.

As not enough data are available at present, the Secretariat is still using other indicators which, albeit less satisfactory, are the only ones that give an idea of the macroeconomic importance of tourism.

The final section of this chapter considers the importance of tourism in individual Member countries as measured by four indicators. The Tables cover the period 1988 to 1990, with the exception of Table 7 for which 1990 data are not yet available. Admittedly, it would have been useful to include international passenger transport payments, but as only a few Member countries break down their "transport" account in this way (see Table 16 in the Statistical Annex), the data would not be comparable.

Share of "travel account" receipts in gross domestic product

"Travel account" receipts (see Table 5) amounted to 1 per cent of GDP for the entire OECD area. The increase in receipts as a proportion of GDP from 1988 to 1990 was particularly marked in Austria (from 8.0 to 8.5 per cent), in Iceland (from 1.8 to 2.2 per cent), and in Ireland (from 3 to 3.4 per cent) In contrast, the share of receipts in GDP fell fairly sharply in Greece (from 4.5 to 3.9 per cent) and Spain (from 4.8 to 3.8 per cent), two countries in which tourism plays a major role in the economy.

Share of "travel account" expenditure in private final consumption

From 1988 to 1990 "travel account" expenditure as a proportion of private final consumption in the OECD area rose from 1.9 to 2.1 per cent (see Table 6). The largest increase in this share was in Australasia-Japan (from 1.2 to 1.6 per cent) over the last three years. The steepest increases were in Iceland (from 6.1 to 7.2 per cent, Italy (from 1.2 to 2.0 per cent) and Finland (from 3.3 to 3.8 per cent). In contrast there was a marked decrease in the share of Norway (from 7.5 to 6.7 per cent) and of the Netherlands (from 5 to 4.5 per cent).

Share of "travel account" receipts in exports of goods and services

In 1989 (1990 figures were not available) the share of international tourism receipts in exports of goods and services for the OECD area fell slightly to 4.7 per cent (see Table 7). From 1987 to 1989 it fell in most European Member countries, particularly in Greece (from 22.2 to 17.7 per cent) and Spain (from 25.7 to 22.5 per cent). It was flat in Australasia-Japan (1.5 per cent over the same period). The main increases were in Turkey (from 10.2 to 13.6 per cent), Iceland (from 4.4 to 5.5 per cent) and France (from 5.4 to 5.9 per cent).

Share of "travel account" expenditure in imports of goods and services

In 1990 "travel account" expenditure accounted for 5.4 per cent of imports of goods and services, slightly down on 1988 (5.4 per cent). However, the picture varied from one region to another. In Australasia-Japan, following big increases in previous years, the share of travel account expenditure in imports was down (from 6.4 to 6.3 per cent) and similarly, for Europe (from 5.4 to 5.2 per cent). In contrast, the share of North America has increased slightly (from 5.1 to 5.5 per cent).

Increases occurred in the case of Canada (from 5.2 to 6.3 per cent) and Australia (from 5.3 to 6.3 per cent). There were significant falls in the case of Norway (from 9.1 to 7.8 per cent), Austria (from 11.7 to 10.7 per cent) and Germany (from 7.6 to 6.6 per cent).

Table 5. **Ratio of the "Travel" account receipts to the gross domestic product (%)**

	1988	1989	1990
Austria	8.0	8.5	8.5
Belgium-Luxembourg	2.3	2.0	1.9
Denmark	2.2	2.2	2.5
Finland	0.9	0.9	0.9
France	1.4	1.7	1.7
Germany	0.7	0.7	0.7
Greece	4.5	3.7	3.9
Iceland	1.8	2.0	2.2
Ireland	3.0	3.1	3.4
Italy	1.5	1.4	1.8
Netherlands	1.3	1.4	1.3
Norway	1.7	1.5	1.4
Portugal	5.8	6.0	6.0
Spain	4.8	4.3	3.8
Sweden	1.3	1.3	1.3
Switzerland	3.9	4.0	3.8
Turkey	3.3	3.2	3.0
United Kingdom	1.3	1.4	1.4
EUROPE	1.8	1.8	1.9
Canada	1.1	1.1	1.1
United States	0.6	0.7	0.8
NORTH AMERICA	0.7	0.7	0.8
Australia	1.3	1.1	1.2
New Zealand	2.4	2.4	2.5
Japan	0.1	0.1	0.1
AUSTRALASIA-JAPAN	0.2	0.2	0.3
OECD	1.0	1.1	1.2

Source: OECD, Balance of Payments Division and *National Accounts of OECD Member Countries.*

Table 6. **Ratio of the "Travel" account expenditure to the private final consumption (%)**

	1988	1989	1990
Austria	8.9	8.9	8.9
Belgium-Luxembourg	4.9	4.6	4.6
Denmark	5.4	5.2	5.4
Finland	3.3	3.4	3.8
France	1.7	1.7	1.7
Germany	3.8	3.7	3.7
Greece	2.0	2.1	2.3
Iceland	6.1	6.5	7.2
Ireland	4.9	5.1	4.9
Italy	1.2	1.3	2.0
Netherlands	5.0	4.9	4.5
Norway	7.5	6.6	6.7
Portugal	2.0	2.0	2.3
Spain	1.1	1.3	1.4
Sweden	4.8	5.0	5.1
Switzerland	5.6	5.7	5.6
Turkey	0.8	1.2	0.8
United Kingdom	2.8	2.9	2.9
EUROPE	3.0	2.9	3.1
Canada	2.8	2.9	3.2
United States	1.0	1.0	1.1
NORTH AMERICA	1.2	1.2	1.2
Australia	2.0	2.3	2.4
New Zealand	4.8	4.9	5.0
Japan	1.1	1.4	1.5
AUSTRALASIA-JAPAN	1.2	1.5	1.6
OECD	1.9	1.9	2.1

Source: OECD, Balance of Payments Division and *National Accounts of OECD Member Countries.*

Table 7. **Share of "Travel" account receipts in exports of goods and services**

	1987	1988	1989
Austria	19.0	18.9	18.6
Belgium-Luxembourg	2.4	2.4	1.9
Denmark	6.1	5.9	5.3
Finland	3.4	3.5	3.4
France	5.4	5.5	5.9
Germany	2.1	2.1	2.1
Greece	22.2	21.1	17.7
Iceland	4.4	5.3	5.5
Ireland	4.5	4.5	4.4
Italy	7.8	7.3	6.4
Netherlands	2.2	2.1	2.1
Norway	3.9	4.1	3.3
Portugal	16.6	16.2	15.5
Spain	25.7	24.9	22.5
Sweden	3.6	3.6	3.7
Switzerland	8.5	8.1	7.7
Turkey	10.2	13.1	13.5
United Kingdom	4.0	3.8	3.5
EUROPE	5.6	5.5	5.2
Canada	4.1	4.0	4.2
United States	5.4	5.4	5.8
NORTH AMERICA	5.1	5.1	5.5
Australia	6.0	7.5	6.5
New Zealand	9.3	8.5	8.3
Japan	0.7	0.8	0.8
AUSTRALASIA-JAPAN	1.5	1.7	1.5
OECD	4.9	4.9	4.7

Source: OECD, Balance of Payments Division.

Table 8. **Share of "Travel" account expenditure in imports of goods and services**

	1988	1989	1990
Austria	11.7	11.0	10.7
Belgium-Luxembourg	3.3	2.7	2.7
Denmark	7.5	6.7	6.8
Finland	6.1	5.9	6.9
France	3.9	3.7	3.6
Germany	7.6	6.8	6.6
Greece	4.6	4.6	5.0
Iceland	10.3	10.1	11.0
Ireland	4.2	3.9	3.9
Italy	3.4	3.4	5.3
Netherlands	5.2	4.7	4.5
Norway	9.1	7.5	7.8
Portugal	2.6	2.7	3.0
Spain	3.3	3.5	3.9
Sweden	7.3	7.1	7.2
Switzerland	7.7	7.0	7.0
Turkey	1.9	2.6	1.8
United Kingdom	4.7	4.4	4.4
EUROPE	5.4	5.0	5.2
Canada	5.2	5.5	6.3
United States	5.1	5.0	5.4
NORTH AMERICA	5.1	5.1	5.5
Australia	5.3	5.6	6.3
New Zealand	9.8	9.1	9.0
Japan	6.5	6.4	6.2
AUSTRALASIA-JAPAN	6.4	6.4	6.3
OECD	5.5	5.2	5.4

Source: OECD, Balance of Payments Division.

STATISTICAL ANNEX

TRANSPORT

EMPLOYMENT

PRICES

INTERNATIONAL TOURIST FLOWS FROM MAIN GENERATING

INTERNATIONAL TOURIST FLOWS BY RECEIVING COUNTRY

NOTES

This Annex reproduces the main international tourism statistical series available in Member countries. For 1990, data are in certain cases provisional. It illustrates recent tourism developments in the OECD (over a two or three-year period).

Some of the data contained in the text itself may not always correspond exactly to that included in the Annex: the discrepancies can be explained by a different statistical coverage (e.g. the use of GNP instead of GDP) or by the use of material of a more analytical nature (data derived from gross figures).

Finally, certain tables are prepared from data available for other OECD work (e.g. Balance of Payments and National Accounts). In some cases, these statistics, which have been standardised to follow existing international guidelines, may differ from the ones supplied by countries in response to the annual questionnaire of the Tourism Committee.

Three tables of general interest for the use of the statistical series are presented at the beginning of the Annex:

A. Classification of travellers;
B. Series available by countries;
C. Types of establishments covered by the statistics.

Main elements of the terminology used

This section indicates the main methods used for collecting statistics and deals with international tourism.

Table A gives an overview of the international classification of travellers.

International inbound tourism (i.e. tourism performed in a given country by non-residents) is usually measured by the receiving country as monthly, quarterly or annual number of arrivals and/or nights spent, using one of three methods:

- *Border controls*: these can provide only a limited amount of information about volumes, means of transport, etc. (as used in Japan, New Zealand and Spain);
- *Sample surveys*: these provide a large amount of quantitative and qualitative information (as used in Canada, Portugal and the United Kingdom);

-- *Registration in means of accommodation*: this method, which is used in Finland, Italy and Switzerland among others, provides more accurate information, but with a more limited scope. However, by definition, it excludes excursionists and certain types of accommodation that are not registered for tax or other reasons, such as that provided by relatives or friends.

In estimating tourism supply, it is necessary to take account of all the goods and services required by tourism i.e. the resources, infrastructure and industries producing such goods and services, whether in the tourism field itself or indirectly related to the tourist industries.

The various means of accommodation are an essential part of this supply. They can be divided into two broad categories: hotels and similar establishments, and supplementary means of accommodation.

The first category (hotels and similar establishments) normally covers four types of establishments: hotels, motels, boarding houses and inns. However, in order to reflect the actual situation in a country more accurately, similar establishments are also often included (in which case the statistical coverage is indicated in Table C or in the methodological notes for each country).

The second category (supplementary means of accommodation) can include seven types of establishemnt: youth hostels, camping sites, holiday villages, mountain hust and shelters, rented rooms, houses and flats, sanatoria and health establishments and children's holiday camps. The list can also be extended in some cases.

The data on international tourism receipts and expenditure are those found under the "travel" heading in the Balance of Payments. They are available in varying degrees of disaggregation by country/region of origin or country/region of destination.

Data concerning international tourism payments follow, in practice, the recommendations of the World Tourism Organisation.

International tourism receipts: they are defined as the receipts of a country resulting from consumption expenditures, i.e., payments for goods and services, made by visitors out of foreign currency. They should, however, exclude all forms of remuneration resulting from employment, as well as international fare receipts.

International tourism expenditure: they are defined as consumption expenditures, i.e., payments for goods and services, made by residents of a country visiting abroad. They should, however, exclude all forms of remuneration resulting from employment, as well as international fare payments.

Three different methods are currently used by the Member countries.

In most countries, data are collected by the central bank using a method called the *bank reporting method*. When a traveller purchases or sells currency before or after a trip abroad, the bank or authorised agency records the transaction. Under this method, data are broken down according to the currency used and not according to the traveller's country of origin or destination.

The *estimation method* is based on sample surveys that are usually carried out at the points of entry or departure for non-residents, or at the re-entry points for returning residents. Data are broken down according to tourists' country of origin or destination. These surveys provide the most reliable and most detailed statistics.

The *mixed method*, which is used by only a few countries, was developed to remedy the shortcomings of the bank reporting method. It uses parallel sources (surveys of visitors, comparison with data provided by receiving countries, etc.), allowing the statistics obtained by the bank reporting method to be adjusted.

However, these data have their limitations. First, the volumes obtained by the bank reporting method in most countries are not an accurate measure of international tourist trade, since they represent net balances and not gross volumes; tourist transactions therefore tend to be understated. Second, it was noted that items unrelated to international tourism were included under the "travel" heading. Third, large discrepancies are found when any attempt is made to compile bilateral balances by comparing a given country's receipts, broken down by country of origin, with the expenditure reported by generating countries, broken down by country of destination.

Geographic coverage

Belgium-Luxembourg: Balance of payments statistics refer to the Belgo-Luxembourg Economic Union.

Other OECD-Europe: include OECD European countries for which no breakdown is available.

Other European countries: include non-OECD European countries for which no breakdown is available.

Origin country unspecified: includes non-OECD countries which cannot be broken down into any specific large geographic (other European countries, Latin America, Asia-Oceania, Africa).

Conventional signs:

/ *Break of series.*

SOURCES

The principal national bodies for each OECD Member country dealing with tourism statistics are as follows:

Australia

Bureau of Tourism Research
Australian Bureau of Statistics

Austria

Osterreichisches Statistisches Zentralamt
Osterreichische Nationalbank

Belgium

Institut National de Statistiques
Banque nationale de Belgique
Institut Belgo-Luxembourgeois du Change

Canada

Statistics Canada, International Travel Section
Industry, Science and Technology Canada, Tourism

Denmark

Danmarks Statistik
Danmarks National Bank

Finland

Central Statistical Office
Bank of Finland

France

Ministère du Tourisme, Direction des Industries touristiques
Banque de France

Germany

Statistisches Bundesamt
Deutsche Bundesbank

Greece

National Statistical Service of the National Tourist Organisation of Greece
Bank of Greece

Iceland

Icelandic Immigration Authorities
Iceland Tourist Board
Central Bank of Iceland

Ireland

Central Statistics Office
Irish Tourist Board (Bord Failte)

Italy

Ministero del Turismo e dello Spetacolo
Istituto Centrale di Statistica
Banca d'Italia

Japan

Ministry of Transport, Department of Tourism
Japan National Tourist Organisation
Bank of Japan

Luxembourg

Service Central de la Statistique et des Etudes Economiques (STATEC)
Institut Belgo-Luxembourgeois du Change

Netherlands

Ministry of the Economy
Central Bureau of Statistics
Dutch Central Bank

New Zealand

New Zealand Tourism Department

Norway

Central Bureau of Statistics
Bank of Norway

Portugal

Direcçao-Geral de Turisme
Instituto Nacional de Estatistica
Banco de Portugal

Spain

Instituto Nacional de Estadisticas
Banco de Espana

Sweden

Central Bureau of Statistics
Swedish Tourist Board
Central Bank of Sweden

Switzerland

Office Fédéral de la Statistique, Section du Tourisme

Turkey

Ministry of Tourism
Central Bank

United Kingdom

Department of Employment, Office of Population Censuses and Surveys
British Tourist Authority

United States

Department of Commerce, United States Travel and Tourism Administration (USTTA)
Department of Commerce, Bureau of Economic Analysis

Yugoslavia

Federal Bureau of Statistics
National Bank of Yugoslavia

Graph A. **Classification of international visitors**

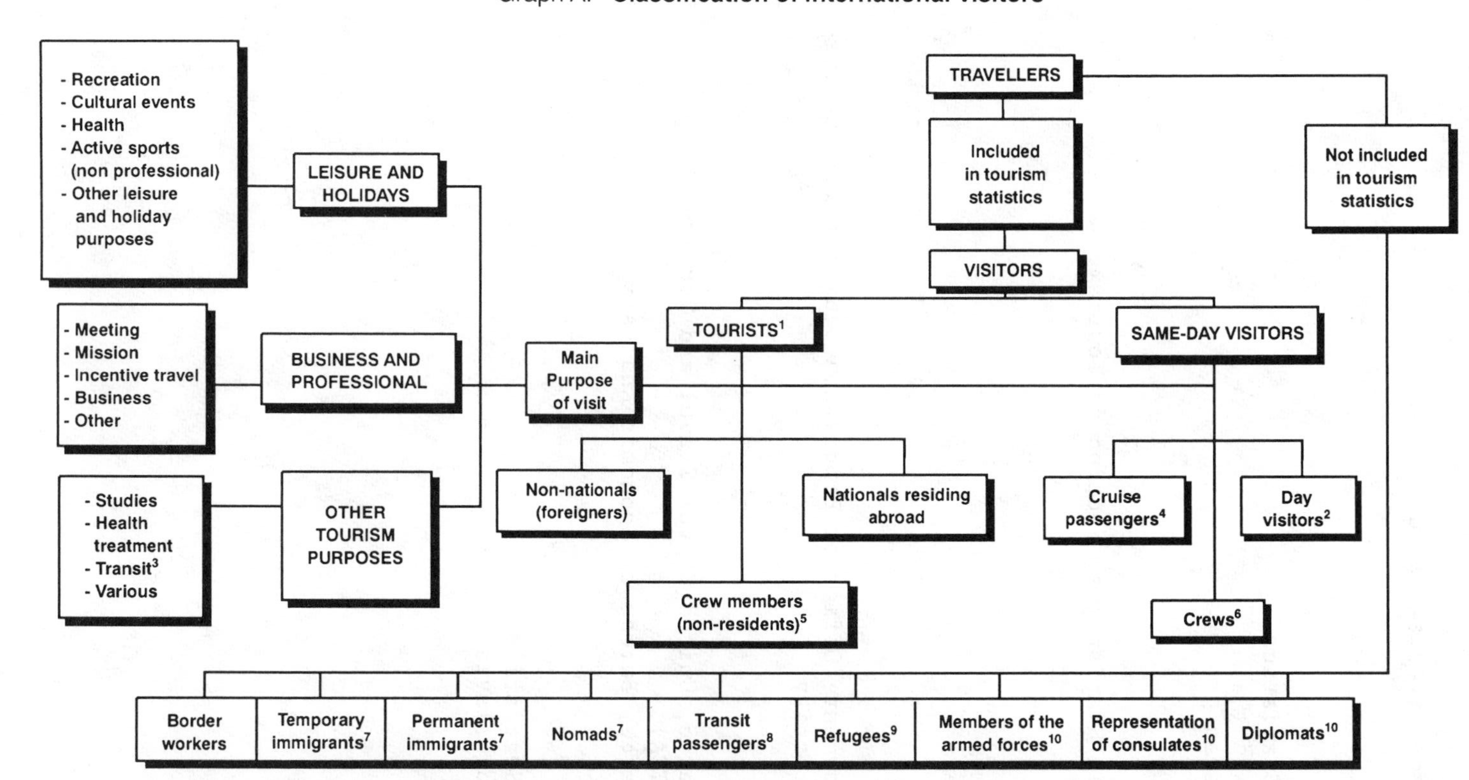

1. Visitors who spend at least one night in the country visited, but less than one year.
2. Visitors who arrive and leave the same day for pleasure, professional or other tourism purposes including transit day visitors en route to or from their destination countries.
3. Overnight visitors en route to or from their destination countries.
4. Persons who arrive in a country aboard cruise ships (as defined by the International Maritime Organization (IMO), 1965) and who spend the night aboard ship even when disembarking for one or more day visits.
5. Foreign air or ship crews docked or in lay over and who use the accommodation establishments of the country visited.
6. Crews who are not residents of the country visited and who stay in the country for the day.
7. As defined by the United Nations in the Recommendations on Statistics of International.
8. Who do not leave the transit area of the airport or the port, including transfer between airports or ports.
9. As defined by the United Nations High Commissioner for Refugees, 1967.
10. When they travel from their country of origin to the duty station and vice-versa (including household servants and dependants accompanying or joining them).

Source: World Tourism Organisation.

B. Series available by country

ARRIVALS OF FOREIGN TOURISTS AT FRONTIERS

Canada
France
Greece
Iceland
New Zealand
Portugal
United States

ARRIVALS OF FOREIGN VISITORS AT FRONTIERS

Australia
Canada
Ireland
Italy
Japan
Portugal
Spain
Turkey (travellers)
United Kingdom

ARRIVALS OF FOREIGN TOURISTS AT HOTELS AND SIMILAR ESTABLISHMENTS

Austria
France
Germany
Ireland
Italy
Netherlands
Portugal
Spain
Switzerland
Turkey
Yugoslavia

ARRIVALS OF FOREIGN TOURISTS AT ALL MEANS OF ACCOMMODATION

Austria
Germany
Italy*
Netherlands
Portugal
Switzerland
Turkey
Yugoslavia

NIGHTS SPENT BY FOREIGN TOURISTS IN HOTELS AND SIMILAR ESTABLISHMENTS

Australia
Austria
Belgium
Denmark
Finland
France
Germany
Ireland
Italy
Netherlands
Norway
Portugal
Spain*
Sweden
Switzerland
Turkey
Yugoslavia

NIGHTS SPENT BY FOREIGN TOURISTS IN ALL MEANS OF ACCOMMODATION

Australia
Austria
Belgium
Canada*
Denmark
France
Germany
Italy*
Netherlands
Portugal
Sweden
Switzerland
Turkey
United Kingdom
Yugoslavia

* As 1990 statistical series are not available, these tables show 1988 and 1989 data.

C. Types of accommodation covered by the statistics

Countries	Hotels and similar establishments					Supplementary means of accommodation							
	Hotels[1]	Motels[2]	Boarding houses[3]	Inns[4]	Others[5]	Youth hostels[6]	Camping and caravan sites[7]	Holiday villages	Mountain huts and shelters	Rented rooms, flats and houses	Sanatoria, health establishments	Recreation homes for children[8]	Others[9]
Australia	X	X	X		X	X	X			X			X
Austria[10]						X	X	X	X	X	X	X	X
Belgium	X				X		X			X	X	X	X
Canada	X	X					X						X
Denmark[10]						X	X						X
Finland	X		X		X		X						
France	X						X						
Germany	X		X	X	X	X	X	X		X	X		X
Greece	X	X	X	X	X		X						
Ireland	X		X										
Italy					X	X	X			X			X
Netherlands	X		X		X	X	X						
Norway[10]						X	X						
Portugal	X	X	X	X	X		X					X	
Spain	X						X						
Sweden	X	X	X			X	X	X					
Switzerland	X	X		X		X	X			X	X		X
Turkey	X	X	X	X	X		X	X					
Yugoslavia	X	X	X	X	X	X	X	X	X	X	X		X

Countries not listed in this table do not dispose of data by type of accommodation.

1. Includes: Germany: hotels serving breakfast only; Belgium: motels, boarding houses and inns; Finland: motels; France: motels; Ireland: motels; Portugal: studio-hotels; Spain: "Paradores" and boarding houses ("Fondas" and Casas de Huespedes"); Sweden: motels; Switzerland: boarding houses; Turkey: thermal hotels.
2. Includes: Greece: bungalows.
3. Includes: Finland: inns; Ireland: inns; Sweden: resort hotels.
4. Includes: Portugal: private and state-owned inns.
5. Includes: Australia: hotels and motels without facilities in most rooms and not necessarily providing meals and alcoholic drinks; Belgium: non-licensed establishments; Finland: lodging houses and part of youth hostels; Greece: bungalow-hotels, studio-hotels and recreation homes for children; Netherlands: youth hostels in Amsterdam; Portugal: holiday flats and villages; Spain: fondas; Sweden: boarding houses, inns, and resort hotels; Turkey: special licensed hotels and studio-hotels.
6. Includes: Germany: mountain huts and shelters.
7. Includes: Australia: cabins and flats; Finland: holiday village cottages.
8. Includes: Portugal: youth hostels.
9. Includes: Australia: rented farms, house-boats, rented camper-vans, boats, cabin cruisers, camping outside commercial grounds; Austria: mountain huts and shelters; Belgium: youth hostels, holiday villages and social tourism establishments; Canada: homes of friends or relatives, private cottages, commercial cottages and others (universities, hostels); Germany: recreation and holiday homes, institutions providing educational services; Greece: holiday centres; Italy: recreation homes for children, mountain huts and shelters, holiday homes and religious establishments; Spain: secondary residences, private appartments, chalets and bungalows; Switzerland: dormitories in recreation homes for children, tourist camps, mountain huts and shelters, holiday villages; Yugoslavia: children and student homes, sleeping cars, cabins on ships, mountain huts and shelters.
10. Total available without breakdown for "hotels and similar establishments".

1. Tourism from European Member countries[1]

	Arrivals at frontiers[2]			Arrivals at all means of accommodation[3]			Nights spent in all means of accommodation[4]		
	Volume 1990 (thousands)	% 90/89	% 89/88	Volume 1990 (thousands)	% 90/89	% 89/88	Volume 1990 (thousands)	% 90/89	% 89/88
Austria				16 020.7	0.0	9.7	86 737.4	- 2.8	8.2
Belgium							10 984.2	5.8	14.8
Denmark							8 364.7	10.1	6.4
Finland							1 542.9	- 6.0	6.1
France	32 301.0	7.9	- 8.2			16.4	270 609.0	3.8	- 4.4
Germany[5]				9 965.9	4.6	10.1	22 299.5	3.5	10.1
Greece	7 028.5	8.5	4.2						
Iceland	112.4	10.8	7.8						
Ireland	2 516.0	14.1	18.4	2 480.0	11.3	17.6	5 175.0	22.6	29.5
Italy	45 225.5	1.9	- 2.6			- 3.0			- 8.9
Luxembourg									
Netherlands				4 325.9	4.9	7.7	14 082.1	16.3	13.7
Norway							2 833.6	4.7	2.0
Portugal	7 371.0	13.4	7.3	3 790.0	7.1	4.5	17 477.0	6.3	2.4
Spain	47 243.9	- 2.8	- 0.4	9 008.5	- 14.3	- 6.3			- 12.8
Sweden							5 233.0	- 16.0	5.8
Switzerland				7 464.8	2.1	6.5	29 920.8	1.4	3.3
Turkey	2 886.3	7.3	4.6	3 036.8	2.8	9.5	11 485.2	14.1	2.9
United Kingdom	10 445.0	- 1.0	10.6				89 901.0	1.4	6.3
Canada	1 545.6	1.0	3.5						- 2.4
United States	6 460.0	6.2	7.9						
Australia	529.8	3.7	- 0.1				16 180.2	41.2	33.6
New Zealand	164.4	15.6	5.0						
Japan	484.2	13.1	12.2						
Yugoslavia				6 300.2	- 9.8	- 4.7	37 399.9	- 12.0	- 6.1

1. Derived from tables by receiving country (see corresponding notes).
2. *Tourist* or *visitor arrivals.* When both available: *tourist arrivals.*
3. Arrivals *in all means of accommodation* or *in hotels and similar establishments.* When both available: arrivals *in all means of accommodation.*
4. Nights spent *in all means of accommodation* or *in hotels and similar establishments.* When both available: nights spent *in all means of accommodation.*
5. The data relate to the territory of the Federal Republic of Germany prior to 3rd October 1990.

2. Tourism from Canada and the United States[1]

	Arrivals at frontiers[2]			Arrivals at all means of accommodation[3]			Nights spent in all means of accommodation[4]		
	Volume 1990 (thousands)	% 90/89	% 89/88	Volume 1990 (thousands)	% 90/89	% 89/88	Volume 1990 (thousands)	% 90/89	% 89/88
Austria				989.2	29.1	8.7	2 388.0	24.5	5.7
Belgium							748.1	7.5	4.9
Denmark							421.3	- 3.4	9.4
Finland							229.4	- 2.7	0.9
France	2 072.0	- 4.4	- 5.5			16.1	24 202.0	5.2	- 28.1
Germany[5]				2 642.2	16.8	10.5	5 143.6	11.0	9.7
Greece	348.1	- 2.8	- 10.9						
Iceland	23.8	- 2.0	- 19.2						
Ireland	434.0	4.1	4.0	443.0	3.7	1.9	2 148.0	- 2.5	- 2.0
Italy	1 896.1	6.5	4.3			4.1			5.5
Luxembourg									
Netherlands				609.2	8.1	1.3	1 250.3	11.6	8.2
Norway							364.5	5.0	- 0.2
Portugal	267.1	- 1.0	- 0.2	365.1	0.2	6.6	1 075.4	3.0	5.4
Spain	994.0	- 11.7	9.7	856.7	- 5.0	5.7			3.8
Sweden							371.4	- 1.2	2.7
Switzerland				1 419.7	14.9	10.5	3 052.4	11.1	8.3
Turkey	240.4	1.8	21.3	174.5	- 6.2	40.9	386.6	- 8.1	19.1
United Kingdom	3 751.0	7.8	6.4				37 973.0	4.9	5.3
Canada	12 267.0	0.7	- 4.5						- 4.6
United States	17 262.0	12.3	11.0						
Australia	304.4	- 3.3	- 19.0				5 908.5	22.5	- 14.2
New Zealand	173.6	3.1	- 17.7						
Japan	618.6	4.6	3.0						
Yugoslavia				279.5	- 6.6	- 12.7	662.5	- 9.9	- 13.2

1. Derived from tables by receiving country (see corresponding notes).
2. *Tourist* or *visitor arrivals.* When both available: *tourist arrivals.*
3. Arrivals *in all means of accommodation* or *in hotels and similar establishments.* When both available: arrivals *in all means of accommodation.*
4. Nights spent *in all means of accommodation* or *in hotels and similar establishments.* When both available: nights spent *in all means of accommodation.*
5. The data relate to the territory of the Federal Republic of Germany prior to 3rd October 1990.

3. Tourism from Australia, New Zealand and Japan[1]

	Arrivals at frontiers[2]			Arrivals at all means of accommodation[3]			Nights spent in all means of accommodation[4]		
	Volume 1990 (thousands)	% 90/89	% 89/88	Volume 1990 (thousands)	% 90/89	% 89/88	Volume 1990 (thousands)	% 90/89	% 89/88
Austria				350.4	19.2	19.7	731.1	20.2	19.5
Belgium							162.2	- 6.3	38.1
Denmark							108.0	- 8.0	9.0
Finland							63.7	4.6	9.1
France	750.0	- 2.7	- 18.8	1 445.7	1.1	56.4	3 083.1	- 5.3	62.3
Germany[5]				1 006.4	9.8	22.6	1 694.0	8.9	20.3
Greece	221.8	- 4.4	4.5						
Iceland	1.8	- 1.3	10.2						
Ireland	66.0	11.9	40.5	69.0	11.3	34.8	500.0	- 50.5	49.3
Italy	916.9	25.4	19.4			22.0			22.3
Luxembourg									
Netherlands				190.7	16.3	0.4	376.9	14.7	7.6
Norway							84.5	5.5	20.1
Portugal	54.1	8.0	8.4	60.2	5.6	3.7	135.7	3.9	1.3
Spain	314.6	9.5	21.2	498.0	5.6	32.3			34.1
Sweden							97.1	15.9	9.5
Switzerland				670.8	5.3	18.2	1 177.8	4.9	18.7
Turkey	85.3	13.0	13.3	96.4	7.3	20.7	171.3	3.1	10.6
United Kingdom	1 327.0	14.1	16.4				21 433.0	17.7	2.3
Canada	562.1	4.9	18.9						11.0
United States	3 871.0	6.0	20.9						
Australia	898.3	12.5	- 9.9				8 085.9	- 0.7	0.7
New Zealand	463.9	8.1	13.9						
Japan	72.4	1.8	17.8						
Yugoslavia				57.8	2.1	5.5	108.9	- 3.7	7.8

1. Derived from tables by receiving country (see corresponding notes).
2. *Tourist* or *visitor arrivals.* When both available: *tourist arrivals.*
3. Arrivals *in all means of accommodation* or *in hotels and similar establishments.* When both available: arrivals *in all means of accommodation.*
4. Nights spent *in all means of accommodation* or *in hotels and similar establishments.* When both available: nights spent *in all means of accommodation.*
5. The data relate to the territory of the Federal Republic of Germany prior to 3rd October 1990.

4. Tourism from all OECD countries[1]

	Arrivals at frontiers[2]			Arrivals at all means of accommodation[3]			Nights spent in all means of accommodation[4]		
	Volume 1990 (thousands)	% 90/89	% 89/88	Volume 1990 (thousands)	% 90/89	% 89/88	Volume 1990 (thousands)	% 90/89	% 89/88
Austria				17 360.3	1.6	9.8	89 856.4	- 2.1	8.2
Belgium							11 894.6	5.7	14.4
Denmark							8 894.0	9.1	6.6
Finland							1 836.0	- 5.2	5.5
France	35 123.0	6.9	- 8.3			13.3	294 811.0	3.9	- 8.8
Germany[5]				13 614.5	7.2	11.0	29 137.1	5.0	10.6
Greece	7 598.3	7.5	3.3						
Iceland	138.0	8.2	1.4						
Ireland	3 016.0	12.5	16.3	2 992.0	10.1	15.1	7 823.0	5.2	20.2
Italy	48 038.5	2.4	- 2.0			- 1.1			- 7.3
Luxembourg									
Netherlands				5 125.8	5.6	6.7	15 709.3	15.9	13.1
Norway							3 282.6	4.7	2.1
Portugal	7 692.3	12.8	7.0	4 215.3	6.4	4.7	18 688.1	6.1	2.5
Spain	48 552.6	- 2.9	- 0.1	10 363.2	- 12.8	- 4.3			- 12.1
Sweden							5 701.5	- 14.8	5.7
Switzerland				9 555.2	4.0	7.7	34 151.0	2.3	4.1
Turkey	3 212.0	7.0	5.9	3 307.7	2.4	11.3	12 043.1	13.0	3.6
United Kingdom	15 523.0	2.2	10.0				149 307.0	4.3	5.5
Canada	14 374.7	0.9	- 3.0						- 3.3
United States	27 593.0	9.9	11.6						
Australia	1 732.5	6.6	- 9.1				30 174.6	23.5	9.6
New Zealand	801.9	8.4	3.2						
Japan	1 175.2	7.7	7.3						
Yugoslavia				6 637.5	- 9.6	- 5.0	38 171.3	- 11.9	- 6.2

1. Derived from tables by receiving country (see corresponding notes).
2. *Tourist* or *visitor arrivals.* When both available: *tourist arrivals.*
3. Arrivals *in all means of accommodation* or *in hotels and similar establishments.* When both available: arrivals *in all means of accommodation.*
4. Nights spent *in all means of accommodation* or *in hotels and similar establishments.* When both available: nights spent *in all means of accommodation.*
5. The data relate to the territory of the Federal Republic of Germany prior to 3rd October 1990.

5. Tourism from non-Member countries[1]

	Arrivals at frontiers[2]			Arrivals at all means of accommodation[3]			Nights spent in all means of accommodation[4]		
	Volume 1990 (thousands)	% 90/89	% 89/88	Volume 1990 (thousands)	% 90/89	% 89/88	Volume 1990 (thousands)	% 90/89	% 89/88
Austria			9.1	1 651.1	48.3	9.8	4 931.8	55.5	16.4
Belgium							991.7	8.2	23.6
Denmark							444.1	5.2	- 9.8
Finland							632.2	9.0	25.5
France	18 034.0	8.1	583.8			- 0.3	44 452.0	7.8	14.3
Germany[5]				2 012.4	3.3	17.2	5 704.5	- 2.3	16.0
Greece	1 275.0	25.8	8.3				35 012.1	6.3	1538.6
Iceland	.8	8.2	- 75.4						
Ireland	52.0	4.0	25.0	104.0	19.5	33.8			
Italy	12 257.5	49.2	5.4			7.1			8.3
Luxembourg									
Netherlands				300.2	0.9	- 9.4	668.6	8.6	- 6.1
Norway							254.0	- 14.5	3.7
Portugal	327.7	10.4	17.5	219.4	8.2	- 1.2	661.3	7.0	1.4
Spain	3 491.4	- 13.7	- 1.4	1 237.4	- 4.6	7.2			1.5
Sweden							874.1	- 2.0	14.5
Switzerland			7.7	968.7	7.0	10.9	2 724.7	6.1	7.6
Turkey	2 177.3	49.4	8.8	561.5	1.5	8.8	1 227.6	1.6	- 11.8
United Kingdom	2 492.0	16.0	7.7				47 075.0	6.4	18.6
Canada	845.8	- 1.7	8.7						6.1
United States	11 496.0	- 0.3	133.9						
Australia	482.4	5.9	- 1.4				6 183.7	7.1	- 6.1
New Zealand	174.1	7.9	8.9						
Japan	2 061.5	18.2	30.3						
Yugoslavia			15.1	1 242.1	- 4.5	1.1	5 199.2	- 11.1	- 5.0

1. Derived from tables by receiving country (see corresponding notes).
2. *Tourist* or *visitor arrivals*. When both available: *tourist arrivals.*
3. Arrivals *in all means of accommodation* or *in hotels and similar establishments.* When both available: arrivals *in all means of accommodation.*
4. Nights spent *in all means of accommodation* or *in hotels and similar establishments.* When both available: nights spent *in all means of accommodation.*
5. The data relate to the territory of the Federal Republic of Germany prior to 3rd October 1990.

6. Tourism from all countries[1]

	Arrivals at frontiers[2]			Arrivals at all means of accommodation[3]			Nights spent in all means of accommodation[4]		
	Volume 1990 (thousands)	% 90/89	% 89/88	Volume 1990 (thousands)	% 90/89	% 89/88	Volume 1990 (thousands)	% 90/89	% 89/88
Austria[5]			9.1	19 011.4	4.4	9.8	94 788.3	- 0.2	8.4
Belgium							12 886.2	5.9	15.0
Denmark							9 338.0	8.9	5.6
Finland							2 468.1	- 2.0	9.5
France	53 157.0	7.3	29.4			12.4	339 263.0	4.4	- 6.4
Germany[7]				15 626.9	6.6	11.7	34 841.5	3.8	11.5
Greece	8 873.3	9.8	3.9				35 012.1	6.3	- 1.2
Iceland	138.8	8.2	- 0.4						
Ireland	3 068.0	12.3	16.5	3 096.0	10.4	15.6	7 823.0	5.2	20.2
Italy	60 295.9	9.4	- 1.0			- 0.2			- 6.0
Luxembourg									
Netherlands				5 426.0	5.4	5.6	16 377.9	15.6	12.1
Norway							3 536.6	3.1	2.2
Portugal	8 019.9	12.7	7.4	4 434.7	6.5	4.4	19 349.4	6.1	2.5
Spain	52 044.1	- 3.7	- 0.2	11 600.6	-12.0	- 3.3			-11.4
Sweden							6 575.7	-13.3	6.6
Switzerland[6]			7.7	10 524.0	4.3	8.0	36 875.6	2.6	4.4
Turkey[5]	5 389.3	20.9	6.9	3 869.2	2.3	10.9	13 270.6	11.8	1.8
United Kingdom	18 015.0	3.9	9.7				196 382.0	4.8	8.4
Canada	15 220.5	0.7	- 2.4						- 2.0
United States	39 089.0	6.7	33.5						
Australia	2 214.9	6.5	- 7.5				36 358.3	20.4	6.2
New Zealand	976.0	8.3	4.2						
Japan	3 236.8	14.2	20.4						
Yugoslavia			15.1	7 879.5	- 8.8	- 4.1	43 370.5	-11.8	- 6.1

1. Derived from tables by receiving country. See corresponding notes, except for the countries mentioned in notes 5 and 6 below.
2. *Tourist* or *visitor arrivals.* When both available: *tourist arrivals.*
3. Arrivals *in all means of accommodation* or *in hotels and similar establishments.* When both available: arrivals *in all means of accommodation.*
4. Nights spent *in all means of accommodation* or *in hotels and similar establishments.* When both available: nights spent *in all means of accommodation.*
5. *Traveller* arrivals at frontiers.
6. *Tourist* arrivals at frontiers: estimates.
7. The data relate to the territory of the Federal Republic of Germany prior to 3rd October 1990.

7. Tourism from the United States
Expenditure of US residents travelling abroad
In millions of dollars

	1986	1987	1988	1989	1990
Expenditure abroad[1]	26 746	30 022	33 098	34 548	38 671
Canada[2]	3 030	2 935	3 228	3 390	3 499
Mexico	3 579	3 975	4 828	5 657	5 999
Total overseas	20 137	23 112	25 042	25 501	29 173
Western Europe	9 069	9 979	11 052	11 625	14 002
United Kingdom	3 003	2 971	3 324	3 319	3 664
Germany	1 913	2 203	2 423	2 664	2 862
France	1 002	1 138	1 233	1 552	1 868
Italy	1 337	1 447	1 669	1 408	1 659
Eastern europe	117	230	261	299	401
Carribean, South and Central America	4 195	4 663	4 988	4 921	5 101
Japan	1 336	1 572	1 803	1 872	2 151
Australia	459	622	694	726	886
New Zealand	157	204	226	256	265
Other	4 804	5 842	6 018	5 802	6 367
Fare payments					
Foreign-flag carriers	6 666	7 411	7 932	8 387	8 890

1. Excludes travel by military personnel and other Government employees stationed abroad, their dependents a United States citizens residing abraod; includes shore expenditure of United States cruise travellers.
2. Excluding fare payments and crew spending.
Source: US Department of Commerce, Bureau of Economic Analysis.

8. Tourism from the United States
Number and expenditure of US residents travelling overseas

	Number of travellers In thousands			Total expenditure Millions of dollars[1]			Average expenditure per traveller		
	1988	1989	1990[2]	1988	1989	1990[2]	1988	1989	1990[2]
Total overseas	14 443	14 786	15 990	25 042	25 501	29 173	1 733	1 725	1 824
Europe	6 488	6 912	7 529	11 313	11 924	14 403	1 744	1 725	1 913
South and Central America	1 457	1 453	1 643	2 591	2 416	2 411	1 778	1 663	1 467
Caribbean	3 831	3 707	3 927	2 397	2 505	2 690	626	676	685
Other overseas countries	2 667	2 714	2 891	8 741	8 656	9 669	3 277	3 189	3 345

1. Excludes travel by military personnel and other Government employees stationed abroad, their dependents a United States citizens residing abroad and cruise travellers.
2. Includes shore expenditure of cruise travellers; excludes fares.
Source: US Department of Commerce, Bureau of Economic Analysis, based on data of the *US Department of Justice, Immigration and Naturalization Service.*

9. Average length of stay of foreign tourists

	Tourists from all foreign countries			Tourists from Europe (OECD)			Tourists from North America (OECD)			Tourists from Pacific (OECD)		
	1988	1989	1990	1988	1989	1990	1988	1989	1990	1988	1989	1990
	Average length of stay in tourist accommodation[1]											
Austria	5.3	5.2	5.0	5.6	5.6	5.4	2.6	2.5	2.4	2.1	2.1	2.1
Germany[3]	2.3	2.3	2.2	2.3	2.3	2.2	2.1	2.0	1.9	1.7	1.7	1.7
Italy	4.5	4.2	3.7	5.0	4.7	4.1	2.6	2.6	2.4	2.1	2.1	2.1
Netherlands	2.6	2.8	3.0	2.8	2.9	3.3	1.9	2.0	2.1	1.9	2.0	2.0
Portugal	4.5	4.4	4.4	4.7	4.6	4.6	2.9	2.9	2.9	2.3	2.3	2.3
Spain[2]	6.5	5.9		7.2	6.7		2.3	2.2		1.8	1.8	
Switzerland	3.7	3.6	3.5	4.2	4.0	4.0	2.3	2.2	2.2	1.8	1.8	1.8
Turkey	3.4	3.1	3.4	3.6	3.4	3.8	2.7	2.3	2.2	2.0	1.9	1.8
Yugoslavia	5.8	5.7	5.5	6.2	6.1	5.9	2.5	2.5	2.4	2.0	2.0	1.9

1. Unless otherwise stated below, the average length of stay in all means of accommodation is obtained by dividing the number of nights recorded in particular means of accommodation by the number of arrivals of tourists at the same means of accommodation (see country tables).
2. Hôtellerie.
3. The data relate to the territory of the Federal Republic of Germany prior to 3rd October 1990.

	Tourists from all foreign countries			Tourists from Europe (OECD)			Tourists from North America (OECD)			Tourists from Pacific (OECD)		
	1988	1989	1990	1988	1989	1990	1988	1989	1990	1988	1989	1990
	Average length of stay in the country visited[1]											
France	9.1	7.4		8.4	6.9		13.9	8.7		6.8	7.1	
Greece[2]	13.0											
Ireland[3]	8.8	9.2	9.2	8.7	9.1	9.3	10.5	11.1	10.5	14.4	15.2	14.4
Portugal[2]	7.6	7.7	7.4	7.6	7.7	7.4	9.5	10.3	11.3	7.7	7.5	8.0
Turkey	9.4	9.7	8.3	10.5	11.5	10.7	9.6	9.4	8.0	9.8	12.0	9.8
United Kingdom	11.0	11.0	11.0	9.0	8.0	9.0	11.0	10.0	10.0	18.0	16.0	16.0
Canada	5.9	6.0		13.0	12.2		4.4	4.4		8.5	7.9	
Australia	28.0	30.0	32.0	46.0	43.0	50.0	25.0	25.0	30.0	21.0	17.0	18.0
Japan	15.6	13.8	13.2									
New Zealand[2]	21.0	21.0	21.0				15.0	16.0	17.0	16.0	15.0	15.0

1. Unless otherwise stated below, the average length of stay in the country visited is expressed in number of nights spent.
2. Greece, New Zealand and Portugal: number of days.
3. Ireland: visitors on overseas routes.

10. Nights spent by foreign and domestic tourists in all means of accommodation[1]

In thousands

	Nights spent by foreign tourists			Nights spent by domestic tourists			Total nights			Proportion spent by foreign tourists (%)	
	1989	1990	% 90/89	1989	1990	% 90/89	1989	1990	% 90/89	1989	1990
Austria	94 968.5	94 788.3	−0.2	28 815.6	28 841.2	0.1	123 784.2	123 629.5	−0.1	76.7	76.7
Belgium[3]	12 168.3	12 886.2	5.9	23 798.8	23 953.1	0.6	35 967.1	36 839.3	2.4	33.8	35.0
Denmark	8 574.4	9 338.0	8.9	12 677.5	13 333.6	5.2	21 251.9	22 671.7	6.7	40.3	41.2
Finland	2 846.0	2 829.8	−0.6	10 130.3	10 261.1	1.3	12 976.4	13 090.9	0.9	21.9	21.6
Germany[4]	38 028.2	39 146.5	2.9	222 833.6	234 579.0	5.3	260 861.8	273 725.5	4.9	14.6	14.3
Greece	34 157.7	36 298.6	6.3	11 985.8	11 831.9	−1.3	46 143.5	48 130.5	4.3	74.0	75.4
Italy											
Netherlands	14 171.9	16 387.0	15.6	36 787.1	39 270.3	6.8	50 959.0	55 657.3	9.2	27.8	29.4
Norway	5 538.6	5 840.4	5.4	11 122.7	11 578.7	4.1	16 661.3	17 419.1	4.5	33.2	33.5
Portugal	18 229.8	19 349.4	6.1	12 588.6	13 206.5	4.9	30 818.3	32 555.9	5.6	59.2	59.4
Sweden	7 584.0	6 574.7	−13.3	28 634.9	27 111.9	−5.3	36 218.9	33 686.6	−7.0	20.9	19.5
Switzerland	35 952.3	36 875.6	2.6	39 817.6	38 934.8	−2.2	75 769.9	75 810.4	0.1	47.4	48.6
Turkey[2]	11 864.7	13 270.6	11.8	5 565.6	6 878.4	23.6	17 430.3	20 149.0	15.6	68.1	65.9
Canada					253 673.0						
Australia	30 210.0	36 358.2	20.4	122 901.0	120 811.0	−1.7	153 111.0	157 169.2	2.7	19.7	23.1
Yugoslavia	49 175.9	43 370.5	−11.8	51 112.9	45 002.7	−12.0	100 288.8	88 373.1	−11.9	49.0	49.1

1. For the "Types of accommodation covered by the statistics" see Table C.
2. Turkey: figures based on a monthly sample survey carried out amoung establishments licenced by the Ministry of Tourism.
3. Belgium: preliminary data for 1990.
4. The data relate to the territory of the Federal Republic of Germany prior to 3rd October 1990; from the unification, tourists from the former German Democratic Republic are regarded as domestic tourists.

11. Nights spent by foreign and domestic tourists in hotels and similar establishments[1]

In thousands

	Nights spent by foreign tourists			Nights spent by domestic tourists			Total nights			Proportion spent by foreign tourists (%)	
	1989	1990	% 90/89	1989	1990	% 90/89	1989	1990	% 90/89	1989	1990
Austria	61 428.4	61 893.6	0.8	14 875.6	15 152.1	1.9	76 304.0	77 045.7	1.0	80.5	80.3
Belgium[5]	6 574.8	6 873.5	4.5	2 610.7	2 706.9	3.7	9 185.5	9 580.4	4.3	71.6	71.7
Denmark	4 887.1	5 429.4	11.1	4 949.8	5 205.2	5.2	9 836.9	10 634.6	8.1	49.7	51.1
Finland	2 517.3	2 468.1	−2.0	8 054.1	8 208.9	1.9	10 571.4	10 677.0	1.0	23.8	23.1
France[2]	51 704.8	55 934.2	8.2	87 685.1	89 869.3	2.5	139 389.8	145 803.5	4.6	37.1	38.4
Germany[6]	28 388.7	29 766.2	4.9	118 591.1	125 620.7	5.9	146 979.9	155 387.0	5.7	19.3	19.2
Greece	32 938.5	35 012.1	6.3	11 396.2	11 346.4	−0.4	44 334.7	46 358.5	4.6	74.3	75.5
Italy											
Netherlands	7 178.5	8 104.0	12.9	5 941.1	6 380.7	7.4	13 119.6	14 484.7	10.4	54.7	55.9
Norway	3 431.4	3 536.6	3.1	8 192.9	8 484.9	3.6	11 624.3	12 021.5	3.4	29.5	29.4
Portugal	15 467.5	16 710.3	8.0	6 585.5	7 103.2	7.9	22 053.0	23 813.5	8.0	70.1	70.2
Spain	78 301.4			53 123.1			131 424.5			59.6	
Sweden	3 366.9	3 193.0	−5.2	13 607.9	13 033.0	−4.2	16 974.8	16 226.0	−4.4	19.8	19.7
Switzerland	20 489.4	21 040.7	2.7	13 659.9	13 586.9	−0.5	34 149.3	34 627.6	1.4	60.0	60.8
Turkey[4]	9 673.3	10 255.1	6.0	4 975.2	6 091.0	22.4	14 648.5	16 346.2	11.6	66.0	62.7
Canada[3]					51 514.0						
Australia	11 400.0			40 614.0	43 370.0	6.8	52 014.0			21.9	
Yugoslavia	27 931.0	27 020.4	−3.3	20 705.5	19 267.6	−6.9	48 636.5	46 288.0	−4.8	57.4	58.4

1. For the "Types of accommodation covered by the statistics" see Table C.
2. France: data covering all France except 3 regions (Pays de la Loire, Champagne-Ardennes and Corse).
3. Canada: includes nights spent by canadians in the United States with final destination in Canada.
4. Turkey: does not include thermal hotels.
5. Belgium: preliminary data for 1990.
6. The data relate to the territory of the Federal Republic of Germany prior to 3rd October 1990; from the unification, tourists from the former German Democratic Republic are regarded as domestic tourists.

12. Nights spent by foreign and domestic tourists in supplementary means of accommodation[1]

In thousands

	Nights spent by foreign tourists			Nights spent by domestic tourists			Total nights			Proportion spent by foreign tourists (%)	
	1989	1990	% 90/89	1989	1990	% 90/89	1989	1990	% 90/89	1989	1990
Austria	33 540.1	32 894.7	–1.9	13 940.0	13 689.1	–1.8	47 480.1	46 583.8	–1.9	70.6	70.6
Belgium[3]	5 593.5	6 012.7	7.5	21 188.1	21 246.2	0.3	26 781.6	27 258.9	1.8	20.9	22.1
Denmark	3 687.3	3 908.6	6.0	7 727.7	8 128.4	5.2	11 415.0	12 037.1	5.4	32.3	32.5
Finland	328.7	361.6	10.0	2 076.2	2 052.2	–1.2	2 404.9	2 413.8	0.4	13.7	15.0
Germany[4]	9 639.5	9 380.2	–2.7	104 242.4	108 958.3	4.5	113 881.9	118 338.5	3.9	8.5	7.9
Greece	1 219.2	1 286.5	5.5	589.6	485.5	–17.7	1 808.8	1 772.0	–2.0	67.4	72.6
Italy											
Netherlands	6 993.4	8 283.0	18.4	30 846.0	32 889.6	6.6	37 839.4	41 172.6	8.8	18.5	20.1
Norway	2 107.3	2 303.8	9.3	2 929.8	3.093.7	5.6	5 037.1	5 397.5	7.2	41.8	42.7
Portugal	2 762.3	2 639.1	–4.5	6 003.0	6 103.3	1.7	8 765.3	8 742.3	–0.3	31.5	30.2
Sweden	4 217.1	3 381.7	–19.8	15 027.0	14 079.0	–6.3	19 244.1	17 460.6	–9.3	21.9	19.4
Switzerland	15 462.9	15 834.9	2.4	26 157.7	25 347.9	–3.1	41 620.6	41 182.8	–1.1	37.2	38.5
Turkey	2 191.4	3 015.5	37.6	590.3	787.3	33.4	2 781.8	3 802.8	36.7	78.8	79.3
Canada[2]					202 159.0						
Australia	18 810.0	23 137.0	23.0	82 287.0	77 477.0	–5.8	101 097.0	100 614.0	–0.5	18.6	23.0
Yugoslavia	21 245.0	16 350.1	–23.0	30 407.4	25 735.1	–15.4	51 652.4	42 085.2	–18.5	41.1	38.8
Of which: **on camping sites**											
Austria	5 472.9	5 377.6	–1.7	1 208.4	1 240.9	2.7	6 681.3	6 618.5	–0.9	81.9	81.3
Belgium[3]	2 397.0	2 766.6	15.4	9 407.1	9 313.4	–1.0	11 804.1	12 080.0	2.3	20.3	22.9
Denmark	3 237.8	3 438.7	6.2	7 227.7	7 610.5	5.3	10 465.5	11 049.2	5.6	30.9	31.1
Finland	328.7	361.6	10.0	2 076.2	2 052.2	–1.2	2 404.9	2 413.8	0.4	13.7	15.0
Germany[4]	4 450.6	4 304.9	–3.3	13 017.0	13 695.7	5.2	17 467.7	18 000.6	3.1	25.5	23.9
Greece	1 219.2	1 286.5	5.5	589.6	485.5	–17.7	1 808.8	1 772.0	–2.0	67.4	72.6
Italy											
Netherlands	3 191.8	3 479.4	9.0	13 376.3	14 132.9	5.7	16 568.1	17 612.3	6.3	19.3	19.8
Norway	1 908.7	2 110.7	10.6	2 798.0	2 961.1	5.8	4 706.7	5 071.8	7.8	40.6	41.6
Portugal	2 666.3	2 548.9	–4.4	5 127.3	5 021.9	–2.1	7 793.6	7 570.9	–2.9	34.2	33.7
Sweden	3 256.0	2 535.9	–22.1	11 147.6	10 449.0	–6.3	14 403.6	12 984.9	–9.8	22.6	19.5
Switzerland	2 374.5	2 573.7	8.4	5 457.2	5 375.4	–1.5	7 831.7	7 949.1	1.5	30.3	32.4
Turkey	280.3	241.8	–13.7	56.0	50.9	–9.0	336.3	292.8	–12.9	83.4	82.6
Canada[2]					26 908.0						
Australia	2 280.0	2 644.0	16.0	23 375.0	23 398.0	0.1	25 655.0	26 042.0	1.5	8.9	10.2
Yugoslavia	10 607.8	8 595.4	–19.0	6 343.2	5 485.4	–13.5	16 951.0	14 080.8	–16.9	62.6	61.0
Of which: **in youth hostels**											
Austria	742.8	797.2	7.3	543.8	543.1	–0.1	1 286.6	1 340.3	4.2	57.7	59.5
Denmark	449.5	469.9	4.6	500.0	517.9	3.6	949.5	987.9	4.0	47.3	47.6
Germany[4]	1 166.0	1 216.4	4.3	9 313.1	9'581.9	2.9	10 479.1	10 798.3	3.0	11.1	11.3
Italy											
Netherlands	630.0	783.6	24.4	317.2	336.7	6.1	947.2	1 120.3	18.3	66.5	69.9
Norway	198.6	193.1	–2.8	131.8	132.7	0.6	330.4	325.8	–1.4	60.1	59.3
Sweden	262.2	253.2	–3.4	858.7	831.7	–3.1	1 120.9	1 084.9	–3.2	23.4	23.3
Switzerland	532.2	559.0	5.0	371.6	358.5	–3.5	903.8	917.5	1.5	58.9	60.9
Australia	5 700.0	2 644.0	–53.6	2 364.0	2 268.0	–4.1	8 064.0	4 912.0	–39.1	70.7	53.8
Yugoslavia	450.3	354.7	–21.2	3 983.8	3 097.6	–22.2	4 434.1	3 452.3	–22.1	10.2	10.3
Of which: **in private rooms,rented apartments and houses**											
Austria	16 088.8	15 129.5	–6.0	4 357.7	4 049.8	–7.1	20 446.5	19 179.3	–6.2	78.7	78.9
Belgium[3]	730.2	621.2	–14.9	6 337.6	6 235.4	–1.6	7 067.7	6 856.6	–3.0	10.3	9.1
Germany[4]	1 770.7	1 737.8	–1.9	19 699.8	21 899.7	11.2	21 470.5	23 637.5	10.1	8.2	7.4
Italy											
Switzerland	10 250.0	10 400.0	1.5	13 810.0	13 400.0	–3.0	24 060.0	23 800.0	–1.1	42.6	43.7
Australia	7 410.0	11 238.0	51.7	15 778.0	13 928.0	–11.7	23 188.0	25 166.0	8.5	32.0	44.7
Yugoslavia	9 007.7	6 164.5	–31.6	7 543.9	5 761.1	–23.6	16 551.6	11 925.6	–27.9	54.4	51.7

1. For the "Types of accommodatiom covered by the statistics" see Table C.
2. Canada: person-nights: includes nights spent by Canadians in the United States with final destination in Canada.
3. Belgium: preliminary data for 1990.
4. The data relate to the territory of the Federal Republic of Germany prior to 3rd October 1990; from the unification, tourists from the former German Democratic Republic are regarded as domestic tourists.

13. Capacity in hotels and similar establishments [1]

In thousands

	Hotels			Motels			Boarding houses			Inns			Others			Total		
	1989	1990	% 90/89	1989	1990	% 90/89	1989	1990	% 90/89	1989	1990	% 90/89	1989	1990	% 90/89	1989	1990	% 90/89
Austria [2]																656.9	650.6	–1.0
Belgium	92.5	93.7	1.3													92.5	93.7	1.3
Denmark [3]																85.0	99.1	16.6
Finland [4]	77.3	82.0	6.1				14.8	15.4	3.9							92.1	97.4	5.8
France [5]																		
Germany [6]	564.8	575.3	1.9				137.0	135.8	–0.9	243.0	240.8	–0.9	246.2	249.3	1.2	1 191.0	1 201.2	0.9
Greece	356.6	366.4	2.8	3.3	3.5	7.4	18.5	20.7	11.8	5.1	13.1	158.5	35.0	34.6	–1.2	418.5	438.4	4.7
Netherlands																108.2	110.3	1.9
Norway [7]													105.3	112.7	7.0	105.3	112.7	7.0
Portugal [8]	81.2	88.3	8.8	1.2	1.4	21.2	44.8	45.9	2.4	4.0	4.1	1.6	37.3	39.6	6.2	168.4	179.3	6.5
Spain [9]	708.0	735.7	3.9	210.7	193.8	–8.0	80.2	78.5	–2.1				94.8	94.2	–0.7	1 093.6	1 102.2	0.8
Sweden [14]	110.0	113.6	3.3				46.3	46.9	1.2							156.2	160.4	2.7
Switzerland [10]	235.7	236.0	0.1	6.1	5.5	–10.0				29.5	28.3	–4.0				271.2	269.8	–0.5
Turkey [11]	105.8	125.8	18.9	3.2	3.2	1.6	4.4	5.1	16.9	2.4	2.4	0.0	2.5	3.7	46.8	118.2	140.2	18.6
Australia [12]	125.7	153.8	22.4	286.0	297.6	4.0										421.7	451.4	7.0
Japan	116.6						94.3			95.6								
New Zealand																		
Yugoslavia [13]	336.7	339.3	0.8	11.4	11.2	–2.4	5.9	6.5	9.8	2.1	1.9	–7.9	6.1	5.4	–11.1	362.3	364.3	0.6

Notice : this table contains data on available bed capacity unless otherwise stated in the following notes by country.
1. For the "Types of accommodatiom covered by the statistics" see Table C.
2. Austria : position at 31st August.
3. Denmark : position at 31st July.
4. Finland : position at 31st December.
5. France : position at 31st December.
6. Germany : position at April; the data relate to the territory of the Federal Republic of Germany prior to 3rd October 1990.
7. Norway : position at 31st December.
8. Portugal : position at 31st July.
9. Spain : position at 31st December.
10. Switzerland : position at 31st December.
11. Turkey : position at 31st December of accommodation establishments approved by Ministry of Culture and Tourism.
12. Australia : position at December.
13. Yugoslavia : position at 31st August.
14. Sweden : position at December.

14. Capacity in supplementary means of accommodation[1]

In thousands

	Youth hostels			Camping sites Places			Holiday villages			Rented rooms, houses and flats			Sanatoria and health establishments			Recreational camps			Others			Total		
	1989	1990	% 90/89	1989	1990	% 90/89	1989	1990	% 90/89	1989	1990	% 90/89	1989	1990	% 90/89	1989	1990	% 90/89	1989	1990	% 90/89	1989	1990	% 90/89
Austria	11.5	13.0	12.7				110.7	122.9	11.0	313.6	296.4	-5.5	17.8	17.1	-4.2	28.5	28.7	0.7	32.3	31.3	-3.3	514.6	509.3	-1.0
Belgium				378.4	373.2	-1.4							3.5	4.8	37.3	24.4	22.7	-7.0	71.4	69.2	-3.1	477.7	469.9	-1.6
Denmark	10.4	10.6	2.2																					
Germany[4]	93.5	92.8	-0.8				23.9	23.1	-3.3	204.5	211.7	3.5	126.7	128.6	1.5				161.5	159.8	-1.1	610.0	615.9	1.0
Greece				79.6						219.6									7.4			306.6		
Italy																								
Norway	5.8	6.1	4.5																			5.8	6.1	4.5
Portugal				257.0	261.1	1.6										12.0	10.6	-11.3				268.9	271.7	1.0
Spain				470.4	571.3	21.5				335.8	384.9	14.6							10 808.7	7 171.0	-33.7	11 614.9	8 127.2	-30.0
Sweden	15.3	15.0	-2.2	395.0	395.0	0.0	45.9	45.1	-1.7													456.2		
Switzerland	8.1	8.1	-0.6	270.0	266.5	-1.3				360.0	360.0	0.0	6.9	6.8	-1.8				228.1	229.0	0.4	873.1	870.3	-0.3
Turkey[2]				8.7	8.2	-6.2	19.1	24.8	29.7				0.0	0.0	100.0							27.9	33.1	18.5
Australia[3]				564.1	564.3	0.0				135.6	144.1	6.3										702.7	708.4	0.8
Japan	28.1																							
Yugoslavia	58.9	51.8	-11.9	372.2	365.6	-1.8	111.5	105.8	-5.1	455.0	410.7	-9.7	17.2	18.8	9.4				24.1	24.4	1.1	1 038.8	977.1	-5.9

Notice: this table contains data on available bed capacity, unless otherwise stated in the following notes by country.

1. For the "Types of accommodatiom covered by the statistics" see Table C.
2. Turkey: the total doesn't include licenced yacht bed capacity (9 358) and beds registered by local municipalities in social tourism establishments (223 576).
3. Australia: assuming 3 beds per place.
4. The data relate to the territory of the Federal Republic of Germany prior to 3rd October 1990.

15. Monthly hotel occupancy rates

		Belgium (B)	Finland[1] (R)	Germany[10] (B)	Italy (B)	Netherlands[11] (R)	Norway[2] (B)	Portugal[8] (B)	Spain (B)	Sweden[3] (B)	Switzerland[9] (B)	Turkey[4] (B)	United Kingdom[5] (B)	Australia[6] (B)	Japan[7] (R)	Yugoslavia (B)
1988	January	18.1	43.8	25.8	24.2	20.0	32.5	34.3	44.6	22.2	27.3	32.1	30.0	35.2		25.4
	February	21.8	53.2	31.9	31.3	24.2	43.0	41.3	50.0	32.1	39.7	33.7	33.0			26.6
	March	7.6	56.0	32.4	32.1	26.7	42.5	49.7	52.4	34.5	39.3	37.2	37.0			29.2
	April	14.4	54.1	34.1	35.9	37.7	37.6	54.0	51.8	34.1	30.0	43.0	42.0			36.9
	May	16.4	54.6	41.1	32.7	41.9	29.4	57.5	54.9	28.7	25.6	55.2	42.0	33.5		56.6
	June	14.6	57.7	47.5	42.8	39.8	44.0	56.8	59.2	34.8	34.5	60.1	50.0			67.7
	July	36.3	60.0	53.1	60.5	41.7	53.5	64.3	66.9	49.7	45.8	63.4	56.0			75.3
	August	33.1	58.8	52.9	71.0	41.4	45.3	76.9	76.5	37.7	49.1	67.2	58.0	38.5		81.1
	September	13.1	59.1	50.8	47.2	39.2	35.3	65.1	65.2	30.2	43.9	65.6	57.0			71.7
	October	12.3	53.3	43.6	35.6	34.6	31.0	56.2	55.7	28.2	30.3	52.4	51.0			43.1
	November	15.6	54.3	28.8	22.8	28.5	30.4	40.5	46.9	28.0	16.7	33.3	39.0	34.4		22.2
	December	20.2	38.7	25.3	26.2	22.9	24.8	34.0	40.2	22.0	20.4	29.9	33.0			19.3
1989	January	18.5	43.2	27.0		21.1	30.6	33.1	43.0	23.7	30.0	23.7	26.0		60.6	25.0
	February	22.8	52.8	33.0		25.2	39.7	41.1	48.5	32.8	40.0	27.9	33.0	35.2	73.4	25.0
	March	25.9	52.4	34.9		30.4	39.7	50.9	53.5	33.0	43.2	34.0	40.0		77.2	30.1
	April	28.3	54.1	34.5		36.9	33.6	51.0	48.2	33.7	27.5	39.2	40.0		74.4	35.6
	May	33.2	52.6	43.4		43.6	27.0	55.4	52.7	29.7	28.8	56.0	45.0	32.8	75.5	55.5
	June	30.9	54.8	46.0		40.7	43.2	55.0	53.6	35.9	37.3	54.0	53.0		73.0	64.6
	July	39.6	58.5	53.5		44.7	53.2	60.5	62.8	49.0	49.5	58.7	56.0		74.4	73.2
	August	41.4	56.5	54.0		49.4	44.9	73.7	74.8	39.0	53.0	66.4	60.0	35.3	82.9	80.4
	September	34.8	56.9	51.8		42.8	34.7	67.4	60.7	32.7	46.7	61.7	59.0		77.5	68.7
	October	32.3	52.9	44.2		35.8	29.7	53.0	51.8	28.8	32.6	51.3	51.0		82.9	42.1
	November	27.9	52.5	30.3		30.1	29.0	37.8	44.1	29.0	18.1	32.5	40.0	32.0	81.0	20.3
	December	23.7	37.4	27.2		27.6	25.2	31.0	38.4	22.5	22.2	28.5	36.0		63.9	18.6
1990	January	19.1	43.3	27.4		15.7	28.8	31.9		24.5	28.7	25.3	29.0		65.0	21.4
	February	23.0	49.9	33.0		18.6	38.9	36.5		32.2	38.7	29.6	36.0	33.4	78.0	21.3
	March	25.4	53.8	33.6		17.0	39.7	46.6		33.5	40.0	32.7	38.0		79.1	23.6
	April	32.7	48.6	38.9		17.0	30.5	57.5		29.5	32.7	46.4	47.0		77.7	36.4
	May	33.3	50.3	45.9		22.3	27.8	52.8		31.3	29.5	52.8	48.0	30.2	79.6	51.7
	June	33.9	53.7	50.6		27.1	43.4	55.2		34.8	39.8	57.2	53.0		78.5	63.3
	July	41.2	53.2	55.7		43.5	51.1	60.4		45.4	50.9	69.0	58.0		78.5	73.1
	August	42.1	54.3	56.1		45.5	43.6	76.3		36.4	54.5	67.8	61.0	32.6	84.7	81.3
	September	35.1	53.5	54.4		19.7	33.0	69.4		30.6	47.6	56.0	57.0		80.5	65.1
	October	32.1	51.1	47.0		21.3	28.7	57.8		27.2	33.0	44.2	49.0		83.3	38.6
	November	27.2	50.0	33.2		20.9	27.6	40.1		25.6	18.0	31.7	40.0	30.7	82.0	19.3
	December	23.1	34.2	30.0		20.5	23.9	31.9		17.5	23.4	28.3	34.0		64.6	18.3

B = Beds.
R = Rooms.
Occupancy rates registered in hotels only, unless otherwise stated.
1. Finland: room occupancy rates in hotels and similar establishments.
2. Norway: Bed occupancy rates covers registered accommodation with 20 beds or more.
3. Sweden: occupancy rates in hotels, motels, resort hotels, holiday villages and youth hostels.
4. Turkey: bed occupancy rates in hotels, motels, boarding houses, inns, holiday villages, thermal resorts and campings.
5. United Kingdom: figures apply to England only.
6. Australia: quarterly figures in bed-places in hotels and motels with facilities in most rooms.
7. Japan: rates concerning hotels which are members of the "Japan Hotel Association".
8. Portugal: bed occupancy rates in hotels, studio-hotels, motels and state-owned inns.
9. Switzerland: bed occupancy rates in hotels, motels and inns.
10. Germany: bed occupancy rates cover registered accommodation with 9 beds or more; the data relate to the territory of the Federal Republic of Germany prior to 3rd October 1990.
11. Netherlands: room occupancy rates in hotels and similar establishments with 20 beds or more.

16. International fare payments

Rail, air, sea and road transport

In million dollars

	Receipts			Expenditure		
	1988	1989	1990	1988	1989	1990
Austria[1]						
Germany[2]	3 665.5	3 929.9	5 087.2	4 120.5	4 029.9	5 259.2
Greece	28.8	15.8		113.5	113.9	
Finland[3]	439.5	482.7	562.5	499.7	520.3	631.3
Ireland[3]	283.1	335.9	435.0			
Italy[3]	1 344.4	1 421.6		1 051.7	1 189.8	
Spain	906.5	792.2	878.9	211.2	287.2	378.6
Sweden[4]	732.9	874.0	1 156.7	717.1	773.5	923.7
Switzerland	1 438.8	1 436.9	1 681.3	956.9	883.5	1 134.1
Turkey[5]	286.4	264.5	326.4	1.6	1.4	1.7
Canada	968.8	1 047.3		1 469.0	1 635.1	
Australia	1 269.8	1 128.2	1 314.6	1 304.9	1 658.8	1 882.5

1. Austria: rail, air, inland waterways and road transport.
2. Germany: air, sea and rail transport. The data relate to the territory of the Federal Republic of Germany prior to 3rd October 1990.
3. Finland, Ireland and Italy: air and sea transport.
4. Sweden: sea and rail transport.
5. Turkey: air, sea and rail transport for receipts; rail transport only for expenditure.

17. Nominal exchange rates of national currencies against the dollar

	Exchange rates (units per dollar)			Per cent changes[1]	
	1988	1989	1990	89/88	90/89
Austria	12.34	13.23	11.37	7.2	–14.0
Belgium-Luxembourg	36.77	39.40	33.42	7.1	–15.2
Denmark	6.73	7.31	6.19	8.6	–15.4
Finland	4.19	4.29	3.82	2.4	–10.9
France	5.96	6.38	5.45	7.1	–14.6
Germany	1.76	1.88	1.62	7.1	–14.0
Greece	141.64	162.08	158.23	14.4	–2.4
Iceland	43.03	57.11	58.36	32.7	2.2
Ireland	0.66	0.71	0.60	7.4	–14.3
Italy	1 301.68	1 371.69	1 198.37	5.4	–12.6
Netherlands	1.98	2.12	1.82	7.3	–14.2
Norway	6.52	6.90	6.26	5.9	–9.3
Portugal	143.94	157.10	142.31	9.1	–9.4
Spain	116.49	118.40	101.94	1.6	–13.9
Sweden	6.13	6.45	5.92	5.2	–8.2
Switzerland	1.46	1.64	1.39	11.8	–15.1
Turkey	1 419.40	2 119.96	2 606.48	49.4	22.9
United Kingdom	0.56	0.61	0.56	8.7	–7.9
Canada	1.23	1.18	1.17	–3.9	–1.4
United States	1.00	1.00	1.00	0.0	0.0
Australia	1.28	1.26	1.28	–1.3	1.3
New Zealand	1.53	1.67	1.68	9.5	0.2
Japan	128.16	137.97	144.80	7.7	4.9
Yugoslavia	0.28	3.24	11.26	1057.1	247.5

Source: OECD Balance of Payments Division, except for Yugoslavia.

1. Minus signs indicate an appreciation of national currencies against the dollar.

18. International tourist receipts (R) and expenditure (E) in dollars

Regional breakdown

In million

	R/E	Europe			North America			Australasia-Japan		
		1989	1990	% 90/89	1989	1990	% 90/89	1989	1990	% 90/89
Austria[1]	R	9 047.7	10 272.3	13.5	681.5	849.2	24.6	74.8	107.5	43.6
	E	3 769.6	4 486.1	19.0	720.0	849.7	18.0	30.7	36.0	17.2
Belgium-Luxembourg	R									
	E									
Denmark	R	1 815.5	2 657.3	46.4	337.8	410.9	21.7	24.2	13.6	–43.9
	E	2 313.5	2 846.3	23.0	419.8	525.8	25.2	5.9	6.5	9.9
Finland	R	695.7	803.7	15.5	137.8	89.7	–34.9	6.8	6.8	0.6
	E	1 420.9	2 029.0	42.8	274.0	365.5	33.4	9.6	13.1	36.8
France	R	10 721.6			3 254.8			689.8		
	E	5 696.3			2 143.2			150.5		
Germany[6]	R	6 468.8	8 116.6	25.5	969.2	1 037.2	7.0	466.5	530.4	13.7
	E	18 646.2	23 013.0	23.4	1 305.3	1 893.8	45.1	272.3	328.0	20.4
Greece	R	1 274.0			634.3			35.4		
	E	516.7			278.3			8.0		
Iceland	R	74.0	91.4	23.5	33.3	29.9	–10.1	0.2	0.6	242.5
	E	83.6	98.7	18.1	92.2	118.0	28.0	0.2	0.4	122.4
Ireland[2]	R	759.6	1 099.9	44.8	248.0	271.2	9.4			
	E	877.3	1 012.2	15.4	99.2	130.7	31.7			
Italy[7]	R									
	E									
Netherlands	R	2 401.3	2 966.3	23.5	555.4	533.8	–3.9	27.3	65.9	141.0
	E	5 255.3	5 883.7	12.0	816.6	986.4	20.8	30.6	20.9	–31.9
Norway	R	1 136.9	1 308.4	15.1	182.1	184.4	1.3	7.0	8.0	14.9
	E	2 483.8	2 940.6	18.4	313.9	415.0	32.2	7.5	9.4	25.2
Portugal	R	1 913.4	2 675.4	39.8	734.5	802.5	9.3	9.4	11.5	22.9
	E	386.3	593.2	53.6	179.8	246.5	37.1	4.0	4.0	0.5
Spain	R									
	E									
Sweden	R	1 898.2	2 142.0	12.8	278.9	304.3	9.1	16.4	16.6	0.7
	E	3 677.2	4 487.6	22.0	872.0	1 124.8	29.0	39.6	38.2	–3.5
Switzerland	R									
	E									
Turkey	R									
	E									
United Kingdom[3]	R	4 759.8	5 739.2	20.6	2 779.0	3 456.6	24.4	1 092.6	1 431.7	31.0
	E	9 823.8	10 941.9	11.4	2 167.2	2 612.9	20.6	510.3	698.1	36.8
Canada[4]	R	553.2			3 309.0			332.8		
	E	1 330.2			3 139.2			161.3		
United States	R									
	E									
Australia	R									
	E									
New Zealand[5]	R									
	E									
Japan	R									
	E									
Yugoslavia	R									
	E									

Important notice: the amounts, excluding those concerning Canada, United States, Ireland, Italy, United Kingdom and Switzerland, refer to receipts and expenditure registered in foreign currency grouped regionally according to the denomination of the currency.

1. Austria: including international fare payments.

18. International tourist receipts (R) and expenditure (E) in dollars (Continued)

Regional breakdown

In million

Total OECD countries			Non-Member countries			All countries			
1989	1990	% 90/89	1989	1990	% 90/89	1989	1990	% 90/89	
9 804.0	11 229.0	14.5	912.1	524.8	-42.5	10 716.2	11 753.8	9.7	Austria[1]
4 520.2	5 371.8	18.8	1 745.6	840.2	-51.9	6 265.8	6 212.0	-0.9	
						3 082.6	3 698.5	20.0	Belgium-Luxembourg
						4 338.1	5 445.1	25.5	
2 177.4	3 081.8	41.5	133.7	239.7	79.4	2 311.1	3 321.5	43.7	Denmark
2 739.3	3 378.6	23.3	189.2	295.2	56.0	2 928.4	3 673.8	25.5	
840.2	900.7	7.2	176.3	261.1	48.1	1 016.5	1 161.8	14.3	Finland
1 709.6	2 409.9	41.0	330.5	344.8	4.3	2 040.1	2 754.7	35.0	
14 666.2			1 579.0			16 245.1	20 184.8	24.3	France
7 990.0			2 052.9			10 030.7	12 423.3	23.9	
7 904.4	9 684.2	22.5	847.9	998.9	17.8	8 752.3	10 683.1	22.1	Germany[6]
20 223.9	25 234.8	24.8	3 450.1	4 601.4	33.4	23 673.9	29 836.2	26.0	
1 943.7			32.2			2 003.3	2 577.3	28.7	Greece
803.0			13.3			822.4	1 092.7	32.9	
107.5	122.0	13.4	0.0	0.0	-2.2	107.6	122.0	13.4	Iceland
176.0	217.1	23.4	0.0	0.3	780.6	176.0	217.4	23.5	
1 007.7	1 371.1	36.1	62.4	76.1	22.0	1 070.0	1 447.2	35.2	Ireland[2]
976.5	1 142.9	17.0	12.8	16.5	29.7	989.2	1 159.4	17.2	
						11 987.4	19 741.7	64.7	Italy[7]
						6 773.4	13 826.2	104.1	
2 989.7	3 566.0	19.3	30.2	45.6	51.1	3 019.9	3 611.6	19.6	Netherlands
6 179.4	6 891.0	11.5	270.6	439.9	62.5	6 450.0	7 330.9	13.7	
1 325.9	1 500.7	13.2	9.4	16.0	69.7	1 335.3	1 516.7	13.6	Norway
2 805.2	3 365.0	20.0	45.3	49.2	8.5	2 850.5	3 414.2	19.8	
2 660.3	3 492.3	31.3	43.5	38.4	-11.6	2 703.8	3 530.8	30.6	Portugal
570.3	844.4	48.1	17.4	18.8	8.3	587.6	863.2	46.9	
						16 252.0	18 426.1	13.4	Spain
						3 080.3	4 211.2	36.7	
2 193.7	2 463.5	12.3	350.4	432.6	23.4	2 544.1	2 896.1	13.8	Sweden
4 602.6	5 664.1	23.1	366.6	403.2	10.0	4 969.1	6 067.3	22.1	
						5 597.8	6 869.2	22.7	Switzerland
						4 952.7	6 015.9	21.5	
						2 603.3	3 348.8	28.6	Turkey
						569.1	522.2	-8.2	
8 641.2	10 638.1	23.1	2 718.5	3 271.9	20.4	11 359.6	13 910.0	22.5	United Kingdom[3]
12 519.3	14 261.7	13.9	2 780.6	3 351.8	20.5	15 299.9	17 613.6	15.1	
4 194.9			818.4			5 013.3	5 259.6	4.9	Canada[4]
4 630.7			2 745.7			7 369.6	8 434.3	14.4	
						34 432.0	39 253.0	14.0	United States
						34 229.0	38 376.0	12.1	
						3 154.7	3 654.2	15.8	Australia
						3 849.6	4 141.8	7.6	
						1 360.2	1 520.4	11.8	New Zealand[5]
						911.0	996.5	9.4	
						3 156.1	3 582.7	13.5	Japan
						22 552.3	24 354.0	8.0	
						2 228.4	2 773.9	24.5	Yugoslavia

2. Ireland: expenditure include international fare payments.
3. United Kingdom: including estimates for the Channel Islands receipts and expenditure, and cruise expenditure.
4. Canada: excluding crew spending.
5. New Zealand: includes international airfares payments.
6. Germany: the data relate to the territory of the Federal Republic of Germany prior to 3rd October 1990. From July 1990, data include all transactions of the former German Democratic Republic with foreign countries.
7. Italy : change of methodology in 1990.

19. Foreign tourism by purpose of visit

	1989						1990					
	Business journeys (%) [1]	Private journeys (%)				Total volume in thousands	Business journeys (%) [1]	Private journeys (%)				Total volume in thousands
		Holidays	VFR [2]	Others	Total			Holidays	VFR [2]	Others	Total	
Greece [3]	9.1	81.1	4.0	5.8	90.9	8 081.9	9.1	82.8	3.9	4.1	90.9	8 873.3
Ireland [4]	17.2	38.8	37.3	6.6	82.8	2 733.0	16.5	43.3	34.5	5.7	83.5	3 068.0
Portugal [5]	2.4	92.2	0.8	4.6	97.6	7 115.9	2.4	92.0	0.9	4.7	97.6	8 019.9
Spain [6]	7.0	84.0	3.0	6.0	93.0	35 350.0	7.9	83.2	4.0	4.9	92.1	34 666.0
Turkey [12]	10.4	78.1	2.3	9.2	89.6	4 459.2	8.0	79.4	3.2	9.4	92.0	5 389.3
United Kingdom [7]		56.1	26.9	16.9	100.0	12 976.0		58.3	25.4	16.4	100.0	12 589.0
Canada [8]	17.7	54.2	24.1	3.9	82.3	15 111.2						
Australia [9]	12.3	53.2	22.1	12.4	87.7	2 080.3	11.9	55.7	20.6	11.8	88.1	2 214.8
New zealand [10]	11.7	49.9	24.4	14.0	88.3	901.1	11.3	50.2	24.1	14.5	88.7	976.0
Japan [11]	29.2	52.9		18.0	70.8	2 835.1	27.7	58.1		14.2	72.3	3 235.9
Yugoslavia [13]	2.6	81.5		15.9	97.4	8.6						

1. Includes : business, congresses, seminars, on missions, etc.
2. VFR : visits to friends and relatives.
3. Greece : number of tourists. "Others" includes journeys combining visiting relatives and holiday or business and holiday.
4. Ireland : number of visits on overseas routes.
5. Portugal : number of tourists. "Others" includes visits for cultural purposes and journeys for educational reasons.
6. Spain : number of tourists. "Others" includes journeys for educational reasons.
7. United Kingdom : number of visits. "Others" includes visits for religion, sports, health and visits of more than one purpose where none predominates.
8. Canada : number of tourists.
9. Australia : short-term visitors (less than one year). "Others" includes journeys for educational reasons.
10. New Zealand : number of tourists. "Others" includes journeys for educational reasons.
11. Japan : number of visitors. "Others" includes journeys for educational reasons.
12. Turkey : "Others" includes journeys combining shopping and transit and journeys for study, health, religious and sports purposes.
13. Yugoslavia : number of tourists. "Others" includes visits to friends and relatives, tours(cruises) and visits for sports, health and religion purposes. Estimate on the basis of sample survey of foreign tourists in accommodation establishments.

20. Foreign tourism by mode of transport

	1989					1990				
	Breakdown of arrivals (%)				Total volume in thousands	Breakdown of arrivals (%)				Total volume in thousands
	Air	Sea	Rail	Road		Air	Sea	Rail	Road	
Belgium [1]										
Iceland	95.8	4.2			130.5	96.2	3.8			141.7
Ireland [8]	62.2	37.8			2 732.0	62.8	37.2			3 069.0
Italy [2]	11.2	2.4	8.7	77.7	55 131.1					
Portugal [2]	16.2	1.5	0.9	81.4	16 475.8	16.8	1.4	0.8		18 422.1
Spain [3]	31.3	3.3	4.9	60.5	54 256.4	32.2	3.4	4.9	59.5	52 044.1
Turkey [4]	52.6	16.7	1.7	29.0	4 459.2	47.5	14.1	2.7		5 389.3
United Kingdom [2]	68.2	31.8			17 338.0	71.0	29.0			18 015.0
Canada [5]	29.2	2.1	0.4	68.2	15 111.2					
Australia [6]	99.5	0.5			2 080.2	99.6	0.4			2 214.9
New Zealand [5]	98.9	1.1			901.1	98.8	1.2			976.0
Japan [7]	96.7	3.3			2 985.8	97.0	3.0			3 504.5
Yugoslavia [2]	4.3	2.1	4.2	89.4	34 118.1	4.0	1.9	4.6	89.4	39 572.9

1. Belgium: air and sea include both arrivals and departures of foreign and domestic visitors. Rail refers to international traffic only.
2. Italy, Portugal, United Kingdom and Yugoslavia : visitor arrivals.
3. Spain: visitor arrivals, including Spaniards living abroad.
4. Turkey: traveller arrivals.
5. Canada and New Zealand: tourist arrivals.
6. Australia: arrivals of short-term visitors (less than one year).
7. Japan: visitor arrivals, including those of returning residents and excluding crew members.
8. Ireland: visitors on overseas routes (average of arrivals and departure).

21. Staff employed in tourism

		1988			1989			1990		
		Total	Men %	Women %	Total	Men %	Women %	Total	Men %	Women %
Austria[1]										
	HR	119 587	37.6	62.4	123 047	38.0	62.0	126 034	38.7	61.3
Belgium[8]										
	H	12 135	47.5	52.5	13 032	47.7	52.3			
	R	57 276	48.7	51.3	59 891	47.9	52.1			
	HR	88 825	47.3	52.7	93 376	46.7	53.3			
	V	3 829	35.6	64.4	4 099	34.8	65.2			
	A	9 861	50.1	49.9	10 607	49.7	50.3			
	O	5 724	36.3	63.7	5 747	35.2	64.8			
Finland[2]										
	HR	66 000	19.7	80.3	73 000	20.5	78.1	75 000	24.0	76.0
Germany[9]										
	HR	683 000	42.2	57.7	692 700	43.2	56.8			
Netherlands[3]										
	H	22 100	55.2	44.8						
	R	49 300	55.2	44.8						
	HR	71 400	55.2	44.8						
	V	8 300	44.6	55.4						
	O	46 900	4.7	53.1						
Norway[4]										
	HR	56 000			58 000			57 000		
Sweden										
	HR	88 500	37.3	62.7	94 500	37.6	62.4	98 000	37.8	62.2
Turkey[5]										
	HR	128 796			134 034			140 363		
	V	2 408			9 910	63.6	36.4	3 249		
	A	9 594	65.0	34.7	1 635	66.2	33.8	2 368	70.7	29.3
	O	1 456			1 868			1 455		
United Kingdom[6]										
	H	265 300	37.1	62.9	288 200	37.5	62.5	300 700	38.9	61.1
	R	261 600	37.7	62.4	287 500	36.5	61.3	302 900	41.2	58.8
	HR	526 800	37.4	62.6	575 700	37.0	61.9	603 700	40.1	59.9
	O	799 200	47.4	60.1	828 500	40.9	60.4	844 400	39.5	60.5
Canada										
	H	152 000	40.8	59.2	168 000	39.3	60.1			
	R	521 000	43.2	56.8	573 000	43.1	56.9			
	HR	673 000	42.6	57.4	768 000	41.7	58.2			
	V	25 000	28.0	72.0	27 000	25.9	74.1			
Australia[7]										
	H	94 000	39.4	60.6						
	HR	94 000	39.4	60.6						
	O	336 000	70.8	29.2						
Yugoslavia										
	H	124 083			123 717					
	R	171 120			167 309					
	V	12 773			12 280					

H: staff employed in hotels.
R: staff employed in restaurants.
HR: staff employed in hotels and restaurants.
V: staff employed in travel agencies.
A: staff employed in national tourism administrations.
O: staff employed in other sectors of tourist industry.

1. Austria: weighted average of peak season (August) and low season (November).
2. Finland: weighted average of peak season (July) and low season (January).
3. Netherlands: data registered at September. Includes staff employed less than 15 hours a week. O = holiday centers, youth hostels, camping sites, cafés, libraries, museums and cultural sites.
4. Norway: average of 1st and 4th quarters.
5. Turkey: data registered at 31 December of each year, except for O registered at 31 March and V registered at 31 October. V = minimum number of persons which travel agencies (central and local offices) have to employ. A includes regional tourism administrations and staff working at the Ministry of Tourism. O = tourist guides whose licences have been renewed.
6. United Kingdom: data registered at September. O = ''pubs'', bars, night clubs, clubs, librairies, museums, art galleries, sports and other recreational services.
7. Australia: data registered at December of each year.
8. Belgium: A = tourist offices, libraries, public archives, museums, botanical gardens and zoos. O = sleeper trains and restaurant cars, youth hostels, camping sites, holiday centers and holiday homes, recreation homes for children and furnished appartments.
9. The data relate to the territory of the Federal Republic of Germany prior to 3rd October 1990.

22. Trends in tourism prices

		%85/84	%86/85	%87/86	%88/87	%89/88	%90/89
Austria							
	H	4.5	3.9	3.0	3.8	2.2	3.3
	R	3.3	4.3	4.0	2.8	2.2	3.3
	T	3.5	1.9	0.9	2.1	2.8	3.3
	C	3.2	1.7	1.4	1.9	2.6	3.3
Belgium[1]							
	H		6:0	9.3	6.3	3.8	5.4
	R		6.0	3.7	2.4	3.4	4.6
	T		6.1	4.0	2.6	3.4	3.6
	C	4.9	1.3	1.6	1.2	3.1	3.4
Finland[2]							
	H	11.0	7.0	5.0	6.0	6.0	7.0
	R	7.0	5.0	7.0	7.0	8.0	8.0
	T	4.0					
	C	5.9	2.9	4.1	5.1	6.6	6.1
France							
	H	7.1	5.4	9.2	7.8	6.3	6.6
	R	6.1	5.1	7.1	5.4	5.0	6.1
	T				5.1	5.7	5.7
	C	5.8	2.5	3.3	2.7	3.5	3.4
Germany							
	H	2.7	3.2	3.4	4.3	4.4	4.8
	R	1.5	1.8	1.7	1.5	1.9	2.8
	T	4.9	4.4	1.3	1.0	1.8	0.5
	C	2.2	-0.1	0.2	1.3	2.8	2.7
Greece							
	H	21.0	18.0	40.0	10.0		
	R						
	T						
	C	19.3	23.0	16.4	13.5	13.7	20.4
Italy[3]							
	H	9.8	8.8	9.0	7.3		
	R	11.2	9.7	5.8	7.2		
	T	11.2	9.6	6.4	7.1		
	C	8.6	6.2	4.6	5.0	6.6	6.1
Netherlands[4]							
	H	3.0	1.0	2.0	2.0	2.0	3.0
	R	2.0	2.0	2.0	1.0	2.0	3.0
	T						
	C	2.3	0.1	-0.7	0.7	1.1	2.5
Norway[5]							
	H	9.1	10.8	12.0	11.5	9.0	6.0
	R	4.9	8.2	8.6	5.7	3.9	3.0
	T						
	C	5.7	7.2	8.7	6.7	4.6	4.1
Portugal[6]							
	H	28.0	30,0	23.0	12.0	14.0	17.0
	R	24.0	13.0	14.0	17.0	17.0	11.0
	T						
	C	19.6	11.8	9.4	9.7	12.6	13.4
Spain[7]							
	H	16.5	11.6	13.1	10.9	10.6	13.6
	R	10.7	10.2	5.1	8.7	10.9	10.5
	T	9.7	9.6	4.8	6.9	8.6	9.7
	C	8.8	8.8	5.2	4.8	6.8	6.7
Sweden[8]							
	H	11.6	11.0	-1.4	5.8	6.0	14.4
	R	10.3	10.4	6.6	9.5	9.3	18.8
	T						
	C	7.4	4.2	4.2	5.8	6.4	10.5
Switzerland[9]							
	H	6.3	6.3	5.6	5.5	6.6	92.0
	R	5.0	3.4	2.2	3.0	4.3	51.0
	T						
	C	3.4	0.8	1.4	1.9	3.2	5.4
Turkey[10]							
	H	50.0					
	R	45.0	50.0				
	T						
	C	45.0	34.6	38.9	75.4	69.6	60.3
United Kingdom[11]							
	H	9.1	12.5	9.9	10.9	8.7	
	R	5.4	7.0	7.0	6.8	6.7	
	T	7.4	7.0	6.3	8.1	7.5	
	C	6.1	3.4	4.1	4.9	7.8	9.5
Canada[12]							
	H	5.7	13.5	3.0	7.2	5.3	2.8
	R	4.2	4.7	4.0	4.6	5.3	5.0
	T	4.9	5.6	4.2	1.4	5.7	7.0
	C	4.0	4.2	4.4	4.0	5.0	4.8
Australia[13]							
	H	-1.9	27.2	16.2	16.6		
	R	9.4	8.7	6.7	7.3		
	T	13.2	6.3	6.6	13.5		
	C	6.7	8.9	8.6	7.2	7.6	7.3
Yugoslavia[14]							
	H	92.0	132:0	155.0	196.0	1664.0	544.1
	R	83.0	114.0	120.0	186.0	1300.0	548.7
	T						
	C	73.8	88.1	121.0	193.9	1249.8	584.7

NOTES TO TABLE 22

H: average increase in hotel prices.
R: average increase in restaurant prices.
T: average increase in travel prices.
C: average increase in consumer prices (CPI). Source: OECD Balance of Payments Division.

1. Belgium : H = hotels and campings, R = cafés, restaurants and bars, T = hotels, campings, cafés, restaurants, bars and package tours.
2. Finland: H = hotels, R = food and alcoholic beverages, T = transports and communications.
3. Italy: T = hotels, restaurants and public establishments (bars, night club, sea-side resorts....).
4. Netherlands: H = price of a night spent in an hotel, R = price of a certain number of typical expenses made in bars and restaurants (cup of coffee, fruit drinks, beer, jenever, croquette, fried potatoes, several hot meals, ham roll, ice cream).
5. Norway: H = approved hotels and boarding houses, R = restaurants and cafés.
6. Portugal: H = hotels of from 1 to 5 stars, R concerns Lisbon only.
7. Spain: H takes into account the types of accommodation presented in the official guide, R = hotels, restaurants, cafeteria and bars.
8. Sweden: position at December of each year H = hotel room, R = meals not taken at home (lunch, dinner, coffee with bread, hot sausage with bread).
9. Switzerland: H = hotels and similar establishments. R is estimated.
10. Turkey: H = hotels, motels, inns, boarding houses, holiday villages, health resorts. R = 1st and 2nd class restaurants. In 1985 H and R = freely determined prices approved by the Ministry of Culture and Tourism. C concerns the city of Ankara only.
11. United Kingdom: H = all holiday accommodation. R = meals and snacks including take-away. T = accommodation, meals, food, alcohol, tobacco, durable household goods, clothes, footwear, motoring and cycling fares, entertainment and other services.
12. Canada: H = hotels and motels. R = food purchases for restaurants, T is calculated from domestic tourist spending patterns only.
13. Australia: position every fourth quarter of each year. H = change in the price of a room in hotels, motels, and similar establishments. R = change in the price of meals taken outside home and take-away food (one component of the CPI). C = weighted average of eight State capital cities. T = air, bus and rail fares, hotel, motel and caravan park charges, package tours.
14. Yugoslavia: H = all categories of hotel.

INTERNATIONAL TOURIST FLOWS FROM MAIN GENERATING COUNTRIES

Tables 23 to 49 gather data available for the period 1979 to 1990 concerning physical flows to OECD Member countries and Yugoslavia.

These tables contain data on arrivals at frontiers and arrivals and nights spent at/in accommodation:

-- from all the foreign countries;
-- from the eight main generators of tourism to the OECD area (Canada, France, Germany, Italy, Japan, the Netherlands, the United Kingdom and the United States).

Data used in the synthesis tables are derived from data broken down by country of origin; when these data are not available, the tables are derived from monthly or quarterly statistics.

Methodological notes

These notes present on a country-by-country basis, and where appropriate, the main methodological and statistical changes affecting the series available between 1979 and 1990. For more detailed information, refer to the book "National and International Tourism Statistics 1974-1985", published in 1989.

Canada. Arrivals of foreign visitors at frontiers: change of series in 1980.

Finland. Arrivals of foreign visitors at frontiers: series discontinued from 1979.

France. Arrivals and nights spent at/in hotels and similar establishments: change of series in 1986.

Germany. Arrivals and nights spent at/in hotels and similar establishments and in all means of accommodation: changes of series in 1981 and in 1984.

Ireland. Arrivals and nights spent at/in hotels and similar establishments: series available from 1985.

Japan. Arrivals and nights spent at/in hotels and similar establishments: series discontinued from 1986.

Netherlands. Arrivals and nights spent at/in hotels and similar establishments: change of series in 1986. Arrivals and nights spent at/in all means of accommodations: new series from 1988.

Norway. Arrivals of foreign visitors at frontiers: series discontinued from 1984.

Portugal. Arrivals and nights spent at/in hotels and similar establishments and in all means of accommodation: change of series in 1979.

Sweden. Nights spent in all means of accommodation: change of series in 1985.

Switzerland. Arrivals of foreign tourists/visitors at frontiers: annual estimates.

Turkey. Arrivals and nights spent at/in all means of accommodation: change of series in 1980.

United States. Arrivals of foreign tourists at frontiers: estimates in 1979 and in 1980. Change of series in 1984.

Conventional signs

/ Break of series

Table/Tableau 23

ARRIVALS OF FOREIGN TOURISTS/VISITORS AT FRONTIERS
ARRIVÉES DE TOURISTES/VISITEURS ÉTRANGERS AUX FRONTIÈRES

1985=100 *1985=100*

	T/V	Volume 1979	1980	1981	1982	1983	1984	Volume 1985	1986	1987	1988	1989	1990	Volume 1990	T/V	
Austria (R)														195 670		Autriche (R)
	V													000	V	
Finland (R)	V	328 336													V	Finlande (R)
France (R)	T	28 763 000	81.9	82.9	91.1	92.6	96.3	36 748 000	98.2	100.6	104.2	134.8	144.7	53 157 000	T	France (R)
	V														V	
Greece (N)	T	5 232 973	73.0	77.5	76.6	72.7	84.0	6 574 000	107.8	115.2	118.3	122.9	135.0	8 873 310	T	Grèce (N)
	V	5 798 360	74.9	79.2	77.6	74.7	85.6	7 039 428	104.3	113.7	116.9	114.8	126.1	8 873 310	V	
Iceland (N)	T	76 912	67.7	73.8	74.5	79.6	87.6	97 443	116.5	133.0	132.2	131.7	142.5	138 833	T	Islande (N)
Ireland (R)	V	1 731 000	87.9	87.3	92.0	92.8	98.1	1 910 000	94.9	106.8	122.8	143.0	160.6	3 068 000	V	Irlande (R)
Italy (N)	T	22 177 853	86.4	78.7	87.4	88.4	92.0	25 046 777		102.8	104.4	103.5	106.5	26 679 000	T	Italie (N)
	V	48 742 600	89.0	81.2	90.1	86.8	91.6	53 634 408	99.4	98.3	103.8	102.8	112.4	60 295 923	V	
Norway (N)	V	478 009													V	Norvège (N)
Portugal (N)	T	2 255 100	54.3	60.6	63.4	74.4	82.6	4 989 060	108.4	122.3	132.8	142.6	160.8	8 019 919	T	Portugal (N)
	V	5 287 352	59.7	62.2	62.4	75.9	83.9	11 691 714	111.7	138.3	137.5	140.9	157.6	18 422 078	V	
Spain (N)	V	38 902 476	88.4	93.3	97.7	96.0	99.3	43 004 764	110.2	117.5	126.0	125.7	121.0	52 044 056	V	Espagne (N)
Switzerland (R)[1]	T	9 150 000	89.5	94.5	96.6	96.6	99.6	11 900 000	96.6	98.3	98.3	105.9	110.9	13 200 000	T	Suisse (R)[1]
														129 200		
	V	81 250 000	86.0	88.4	87.8	92.9	101.0	101 500 000	109.9	1·1.6	110.5	121.1	127.3	000	V	
Turkey (N)	V	1 523 658	49.3	53.7	53.2	62.1	81.0	2 614 924	91.4	109.2	159.6	170.5	206.1	5 389 308	V	Turquie (N)
United Kingdom (R)	V	12 486 000	86.0	79.3	80.5	86.3	94.4	14 449 500	96.2	107.7	109.3	120.0	124.7	18 015 000	V	Royaume-Uni (R)
Canada (R)	T	12 584 800	97.1	97.3	92.5	94.8	98.5	13 170 700	118.6	114.0	117.9	114.7	115.8	15 257 800	T	Canada (R)
	V	33 202 200	113.2	116.8	95.8	95.4	97.0	35 925 400	112.6	110.2	109.3	105.7	105.7	37 990 400	V	
United States (R)	T	20 310 068	87.8	92.7	85.2	85.2	105.9	25 416 990	96.7	113.2	107.9	144.1	153.8	39 089 000	T	États-Unis (R)
Australia (R)	V	793 300	79.2	82.0	83.6	82.6	89.0	1 142 600	125.1	156.2	196.9	182.1	193.8	2 214 900	V	Australie (R)
Japan (N)	V	1 112 606	56.6	68.0	77.1	84.6	90.7	2 327 047	88.6	92.6	101.2	121.8	139.1	3 236 752	V	Japon (N)
New Zealand (R)	T	432 382	69.5	71.4	71.9	75.9	84.8	669 558	109.5	126.1	129.2	134.6	145.8	976 010	T	Nouvelle-Zélande (R)
Yugoslavia (N)	V	22 217 443	87.4	87.8	76.7	80.2	84.4	23 357 333	105.9	112.0	126.9	146.1	169.4	39 572 852	V	Yougoslavie (N)

V Visitors (travellers in Austria, Germany and Turkey)
T Tourists
(R) Tourist count by country of residence
(N) Tourist count by country of nationality
1. Estimates

V Visiteurs (voyageurs en Allemagne, en Autriche et en Turquie)
T Touristes
(R) Recensement des touristes par pays de résidence
(N) Recensement des touristes par pays de nationalité
1. Estimations

Table/Tableau 24

ARRIVALS AND NIGHTS OF FOREIGN TOURISTS AT/IN HOTELS
ARRIVÉES ET NUITÉES DE TOURISTES ÉTRANGERS DANS L'HÔTELLERIE

1985=100 *1985=100*

	AH/NH	Volume 1979	1980	1981	1982	1983	1984	Volume 1985	1986	1987	1988	1989	1990	Volume 1990	AH/NH	
Austria (R)	NH	52 079 101	101.8	104.1	102.5	100.7	101.7	54 587 869	99.9	101.5	103.2	112.5	113.4	61 893 612	NH	Autriche (R)
	AH	8 935 483	88.5	90.1	91.1	93.5	99.3	10 947 899	98.3	104.0	108.9	120.1	126.3	13 827 347	AH	
Belgium (R)	NH	4 267 686	79.1	78.9	85.5	89.0	94.9	5 536 157	96.1	96.0	98.0	118.8	124.2	6 873 528	NH	Belgique (R)
Denmark (N)	NH	4 257 100	94.7	97.5	96.9	98.0	100.4	4 590 700	94.5	97.6	95.4	106.5	118.3	5 429 400	NH	Danemark (N)
Finland (R)	NH	1 723 404	87.9	98.0	96.5	98.3	100.7	2 097 101	96.4	105.3	109.6	120.0	117.7	2 468 132	NH	Finlande (R)
	AH														AH	
France (R)[1]	NH	16 068 889	91.7	91.3	88.0	91.7	98.8	18 166 400	200.5	200.4	228.7	284.6	307.9	55 934 153	NH	France (R)[1]
	AH	5 919 091	84.4	87.8	87.9	88.3	94.2	6 927 894	246.4	247.8	281.6	350.8	372.0	25 774 208	AH	
Germany (R)	NH	17 135 841	79.5	81.4	79.2	80.1	93.1	23 895 263	98.2	102.1	105.6	118.8	124.6	29 766 331	NH	Allemagne (R)
	AH	8 271 080	77.2	77.9	78.1	80.6	93.9	11 805 756	95.6	99.8	102.2	114.1	122.2	14 421 034	AH	
Greece (N)	NH	27 307 578	81.1	79.6	77.7	74.1	85.2	34 044 606	99.0	99.2	97.9	96.8	102.8	35 012 083	NH	Grèce (N)
	AH	5 334 926	78.9	81.8	80.5	76.5	93.1	6 544 962	90.0	94.2	91.8				AH	
Iceland (N)	NH														NH	Islande (N)
Ireland (R)	NH							5 280 000	99.9	104.7	117.1	140.8	148.2	7 823 000	NH	Irlande (R)
	AH							1 091 000	96.8	102.6	113.2	137.9	151.4	1 652 000	AH	
Italy (N)	NH	66 284 522	103.5	92.2	101.0	99.1	98.6	63 978 223	101.8	110.5	110.0	106.5	103.2	66 012 130	NH	Italie (N)
	AH	14 332 716	90.6	82.5	92.1	92.9	98.2	16 090 344	94.2	105.8	108.4	109.9	111.4	17 924 420	AH	
Luxembourg (R)	NH			.	99.9	97.8	95.0	932 108	97.3	101.0	103.9	109.1	115.5	1 076 495	NH	Luxembourg (R)
	AH				100.4	90.7	91.7	447 581	100.6	103.6	108.4		117.8	527 300	AH	
Netherlands (R)	NH	6 005 566	89.9	90.4	93.2	89.1	96.9	6 746 954	105.3	104.4	100.2	106.4	120.1	8 103 800	NH	Pays-Bas (R)
	AH	2 749 156	82.8	84.5	89.1	87.0	96.7	3 328 941	100.8	100.7	99.8	104.7	117.2	3 902 800	AH	
Norway (N)	NH	2 361 370	65.5	67.0	61.7	63.0	93.2	3 712 633	88.8	104.1	90.4	92.4	95.3	3 536 631	NH	Norvège (N)
	AH	1 252 178	64.8	66.2	62.7	65.8	90.2	1 933 172	84.7	92.2	88.1	96.6	101.1	1 954 821	AH	
Portugal (N)	NH	8 969 000	74.1	72.3	73.9	76.5	85.2	12 936 590	110.4	112.3	116.0	119.6	129.2	16 710 332	NH	Portugal (N)
	AH	1 776 642	69.8	67.6	69.3	75.8	87.0	2 733 425	103.7	112.4	116.8	122.7	132.9	3 632 242	AH	
Spain (N)	NH	70 492 951	74.3	89.7	97.2	101.0	112.9	78 919 141	111.1	117.1	112.0	99.2			NH	Espagne (N)
	AH	10 369 746	74.2	85.1	90.0	92.7	104.6	12 438 160	109.2	113.5	109.6	106.0	93.3	11 600 645	AH	
Sweden (N)	NH	2 809 829	74.9	77.1	77.3	85.2	92.3	3 548 476	93.3	91.4	90.0	94.9	90.0	3 193 162	NH	Suède (N)
Switzerland (R)	NH	16 923 742	98.3	104.3	98.3	97.7	99.3	20 319 847	96.3	96.1	94.0	100.8	103.5	21 040 743	NH	Suisse (R)
	AH	5 797 844	90.9	94.6	92.9	93.9	99.3	7 329 692	93.9	96.4	95.6	104.7	108.6	7 963 159	AH	
Turkey (N)	NH	1 340 133	22.2	33.7	40.4	58.7	78.3	4 446 049	113.3	146.6	212.1	219.1	231.7	10 300 574	NH	Turquie (N)
	AH	534 720	23.4	36.8	43.9	63.4	79.6	1 679 314	114.0	142.9	184.6	206.5	208.1	3 495 344	AH	
Australia (R)	NH	5 443 500		88.6		83.6	87.0	7 070 700	125.4	156.3	214.5	161.2	190.5	13 467 000	NH	Australie (R)
Japan (N)	NH	3 698 489	51.8	60.1	67.0	35.8	79.3	8 097 065							NH	Japon (N)
	AH	1 711 566	52.8	61.6	72.6	37.6	85.1	3 577 786							AH	
Yugoslavia (N)	NH	19 734 156	75.0	79.7	74.9	74.5	87.3	27 369 817	100.6	103.6	103.2	102.1	98.7	27 020 381	NH	Yougoslavie (N)
	AH	3 909 406	78.4	79.3	74.1	74.4	89.8	5 103 374	99.1	105.0	106.9	107.6	105.2	5 369 475	AH	

AH Arrivals at hotels and similar establishments
NH Nights in hotels and similar establishments
(R) Tourist count by country of residence
(N) Tourist count by country of nationality
1. Ile de France only

AH Arrivées dans les hôtels et les établissements assimilés
NH Nuitées dans les hôtels et établissements assimilés
(R) Recensement des touristes par pays de résidence
(N) Recensement des touristes par pays de nationalité
1. Ile de France seulement

Table/Tableau 25

ARRIVALS AND NIGHTS OF FOREIGN TOURISTS AT/IN ALL MEANS OF ACCOMMODATION
ARRIVÉES ET NUITÉES DE TOURISTES ÉTRANGERS DANS L'ENSEMBLE DES MOYENS D'HÉBERGEMENT

1985=100 *1985=100*

	AAA/NAA	Volume 1979	1980	1981	1982	1983	1984	Volume 1985	1986	1987	1988	1989	1990	Volume 1990	AEH/NEH	
Austria (R)	NAA	84 825 400	106.0	108.8	105.7	102.8	101.9	85 075 850	100.4	100.7	102.9	111.6	111.4	94 788 290	NEH	Autriche (R)
	AAA	12 875 292	91.0	93.4	93.5	95.0	99.1	15 247 830	99.0	103.4	108.7	119.4	124.7	19 011 398	AEH	
Belgium (R)	NAA	6 828 509	72.9	73.2	87.0	90.9	95.0	9 834 967	100.2	102.3	107.5	123.5	131.0	12 886 249	NEH	Belgique (R)
Denmark (N)	NAA	8 299 177	91.7	99.5	102.8	106.2	101.6	8 971 548	94.9	91.4	90.5	95.6	104.1	9 338 035	NEH	Danemark (N)
France (R)	NAA	252 530 000	77.3	77.3	90.7	93.4	97.1	329 595 000	100.8	103.1	105.3	98.6	102.9	339 263 000	NEH	France (R)
	AAA	28 763 000	81.9	82.9	91.1	92.6	96.3	36 748 000	98.2	100.6	104.2	117.1			AEH	
Germany (R)	NAA	20 814 415	80.9	76.0	74.3	76.8	93.1	28 079 191	99.0	103.6	107.3	119.6	124.1	34 841 539	NEH	Allemagne (R)
	AAA	8 940 223	76.5	74.5	74.6	77.5	94.1	12 686 374	96.3	100.7	103.4	115.5	123.2	15 626 858	AEH	
Greece (N)	NAA	28 835 611	87.8	85.8	83.9	76.6	93.0	35 709 851	99.3	100.1	97.4	95.7	101.6	36 298 604	NEH	Grèce (N)
	AAA	6 427 689	89.5	87.1	86.1	81.2	97.3	7 053 616	91.0	94.9	92.2				AEH	
Ireland (R)	NAA	20 629 800	110.2	91.9	91.5	99.4	102.3	18 827 800	100.8	120.2	139.1	166.8	178.9	33 684 000	NEH	Irlande (R)
	AAA	1 793 900	89.0	86.4	88.4	88.2	94.5	1 944 100	96.6		124.7	144.2	159.3	3 096 000	AEH	
Italy (N)	NAA	101 955 865	107.0	95.7	104.4	100.7	98.6	96 524 499	102.9	96.3	95.6	90.0	87.4	84 398 000	NEH	Italie (N)
	AAA	17 699 393	91.6	83.8	93.3	93.4	97.4	19 783 976	96.5	102.0	104.2	104.0	105.3	20 832 000	AEH	
Luxembourg (R)	NAA	2 497 619			92.7	94.0	111.7	2 193 825	107.4	98.9	97.5		110.2	2 416 763	NEH	Luxembourg (R)
	AAA	744 160				85.1	99.9	688 597	103.3	103.2	105.8		118.6	816 340	AEH	
Netherlands (R)	NAA	11 255 510	81.4	84.7	91.7	88.8	99.9	13 916 448	100.3		90.9	101.8	117.7	16 377 900	NEH	Pays-Bas (R)
	AAA	4 102 711	83.5	86.3	90.8	89.3	98.8	4 993 380	96.7		97.7	103.1	108.7	5 426 000	AEH	
Norway (N)	NAA	5 398 000	83.2	83.7	68.3	93.5	98.1	5 254 466		103.9	102.5	105.4	111.2	5 840 416	NEH	Norvège (N)
Portugal (N)	NAA	10 349 056	76.9	78.9	79.4	79.9	85.4	14 937 306	111.7	114.5	119.1	122.0	129.5	19 349 386	NEH	Portugal (N)
	AAA	2 145 642	72.2	70.9	72.4	77.3	86.7	3 307 617	107.4	115.8	120.6	125.9	134.1	4 434 728	AEH	
Spain (N)	NAA	73 084 540	74.8	89.6	96.8	101.5	121.9	81 482 396							NEH	Espagne (N)
	AAA	13 428 392	74.6	85.3	90.1	94.6	104.4	12 587 197		112.1	108.3	104.7			AEH	
Sweden (N)	NAA	5 860 988	75.3	80.9	82.1	97.1	98.2	7 485 744	95.8	94.7	95.0	101.3	87.8	6 575 667	NEH	Suède (N)
Switzerland (R)	NAA	30 054 100	102.4	111.4	104.4	102.3	99.4	35 182 400	99.3	98.3	97.9	102.2	104.8	36 875 642	NEH	Suisse (R)
	AAA	7 607 900	93.1	98.5	96.4	96.6	99.5	9 528 400	96.1	97.9	98.1	105.9	110.4	10 523 964	AEH	
Turkey (N)	NAA	1 631 354	22.9	32.3	38.7	58.2	76.3	4 878 817	121.6	170.6	238.9	243.2	272.0	13 270 641	NEH	Turquie (N)
	AAA	597 830	23.8	36.2	43.3	63.1	78.9	1 733 250	116.0	153.6	196.9	218.3	223.2	3 869 166	AEH	
United Kingdom (R)	NAA	154 563 000	81.5	81.1	81.6	86.8	92.5	166 979 000	94.7	106.7	103.5	112.2	117.6	196 382 000	NEH	Royaume-Uni (R)
Canada (R)	NAA	75 794 500	96.6	99.5	94.0	91.2	99.7	77 125 700	118.6	110.0	119.2	116.7			NEH	Canada (R)
	AAA	12 584 800	97.1	97.3	92.5	94.8	98.5	13 170 700	118.6	113.7	117.6	114.7			AEH	
Australia (R)	NAA	11 754 300		87.7		96.9	104.0	14 555 300	124.2	155.1	434.2	428.7	486.9	70 877 000	NEH	Australie (R)
New Zealand (R)	NAA						85.7	14 730 000	109.6	123.3	125.7	128.0	140.2	20 653 599	NEH	Nouvelle-Zélande (R)
Yugoslavia (N)	NAA	33 481 946	72.8	78.1	70.0	69.6	83.2	50 815 833	101.1	102.9	103.0	96.8	85.3	43 370 462	NEH	Yougoslavie (N)
	AAA	5 966 411	76.0	78.4	70.6	70.5	85.6	8 435 727	100.3	105.6	106.9	102.5	93.4	7 879 531	AEH	

AAA Arrivals in all means of accommodation
NAA Nights in all means of accommodation
(R) Tourist count by country of residence
(N) Tourist count by country of nationality

AEH Arrivées dans l'ensemble des moyens d'hébergement
NEH Nuitées dans l'ensemble des moyens d'hébergement
(R) Recensement des touristes par pays de résidence
(N) Recensement des touristes par pays de nationalité

Table/Tableau 26

ARRIVALS OF FOREIGN TOURISTS/VISITORS AT FRONTIERS
ARRIVÉES DE TOURISTES/VISITEURS ÉTRANGERS AUX FRONTIÈRES

From Germany — *En provenance de l'Allemagne*

1985=100 — *1985=100*

	T/V	Volume 1979	1980	1981	1982	1983	1984	Volume 1985	1986	1987	1988	1989	1990	Volume 1990	T/V	
Finland (R)	V	99 624													V	Finlande (R)
France (R)	T	7 291 000	86.3	88.6	96.3	92.4	95.0	8 723 000	96.5	102.2	104.5	121.4	138.7	12 097 000	T	France (R)
	V														V	
Greece (N)	T	555 171	66.0	59.5	57.7	69.4	82.3	1 050 078	109.0	114.8	131.6	157.6	183.0	1 922 029	T	Grèce (N)
Iceland (N)	T	9 680	96.0	96.5	90.4	93.1	102.1	9 419	144.4	148.8	168.7	196.3	219.1	20 638	T	Islande (N)
Ireland (R)	V		114.1	87.0	85.1	96.9	94.8	96 000	101.0	105.2	116.7	157.3	179.2	172 000	V	Irlande (R)
Italy (N)	V	10 791 300	89.9	79.7	88.6	88.5	92.3	11 717 155	81.6	82.1	89.4	86.5	91.1	10 676 781	V	Italie (N)
Norway (N)	V	99 618													V	Norvège (N)
Portugal (N)	T	228 300	69.8	72.6	65.9	84.5	79.8	369 161	103.6	130.7	143.5	153.0	168.3	621 418	T	Portugal (N)
	V	286 667	72.7	74.2	70.1	86.0	83.3	412 998	104.2	127.4	137.7	148.0	164.9	680 971	V	
Spain (N)	V	4 662 193	83.1	80.8	84.7	88.1	93.0	5 644 095	105.2	116.9	122.3	120.2	121.9	6 880 240	V	Espagne (N)
Turkey (N)	V	198 430	51.9	51.8	56.5	58.4	80.7	299 509	129.6	174.8	256.4	299.5	325.2	973 914	V	Turquie (N)
United Kingdom (R)	V	1 547 000	102.3	98.9	97.1	92.6	100.0	1 484 000	107.8	110.8	123.3	136.6	126.6	1 879 000	V	Royaume-Uni (R)
Canada (R)	T	181 000	120.8	127.8	117.4	104.2	108.6	156 500	126.7	153.0	171.2	167.9	163.1	255 200	T	Canada (R)
	V	235 000	130.5	132.4	120.7	105.0	110.0	182 000	129.6	164.1	176.8	169.5	159.6	290 500	V	
United States (R)	T	557 106	123.4	137.4	130.8	110.6	107.1	509 131	131.6	187.0	226.5	211.4	236.3	1 203 000	T	États-Unis (R)
Australia (R)	V	28 800	94.8	104.7	104.3	92.8	91.7	37 300	112.3	142.9	176.7	182.6	198.9	74 200	V	Australie (R)
Japan (N)	V	38 216	81.6	84.1	85.0	89.3	100.8	48 609	101.1	110.2	117.1	126.7	134.2	65 218	V	Japon (N)
New Zealand (R)	T	5 920	73.2	81.9	84.2	89.4	89.3	10 656	113.0	154.3	188.7	223.0	281.5	29 992	T	Nouvelle-Zélande (R)

V Visitors (travellers in Turkey)
T Tourists
(R) Tourist count by country of residence
(N) Tourist count by country of nationality

V Visiteurs (voyageurs en Turquie)
T Touristes
(R) Recensement des touristes par pays de résidence
(N) Recensement des touristes par pays de nationalité

Table/Tableau 27

ARRIVALS AND NIGHTS OF FOREIGN TOURISTS AT/IN HOTELS
ARRIVÉES ET NUITÉES DE TOURISTES ÉTRANGERS DANS L'HÔTELLERIE

From Germany — *En provenance de l'Allemagne*

1985=100 — *1985=100*

	AH/NH	Volume 1979	1980	1981	1982	1983	1984	Volume 1985	1986	1987	1988	1989	1990	Volume 1990	AH/NH	
Austria (R)	NH	36 195 295	116.3	116.4	111.0	107.7	103.4	32 802 153	101.1	100.3	101.9	108.7	103.7	34 019 547	NH	Autriche (R)
	AH	5 165 199	103.1	103.8	101.8	103.0	101.2	5 305 944	103.3	107.0	112.1	119.9	117.7	6 244 499	AH	
Belgium (R)	NH	671 549	89.7	87.0	94.6	96.5	99.7	746 951	101.9	104.3	107.3	124.9	120.3	898 645	NH	Belgique (R)
Denmark (N)	NH	1 379 800	148.4	153.1	127.7	119.5	110.7	967 200	96.2	97.5	96.1	110.9	133.2	1 288 200	NH	Danemark (N)
Finland (R)	NH	293 825	114.0	121.5	98.7	93.3	101.6	273 417	91.5	102.8	117.6	129.3	123.7	338 261	NH	Finlande (R)
	AH														AH	
France (R)[1]	NH	2 526 539	122.9	116.9	99.2	106.2	99.0	1 970 279	295.5	313.3	340.3	385.3	403.7	7 953 923	NH	France (R)[1]
	AH	946 648	110.0	107.9	95.9	102.0	92.8	797 106	358.7	382.2	420.6	477.0	494.8	3 944 278	AH	
Greece (N)	NH	4 980 744	81.4	77.3	70.2	66.5	79.4	6 884 733	103.6	104.6	114.3				NH	Grèce (N)
	AH	912 880	91.3	84.9	81.6	76.2	86.7	1 023 434	99.2	100.9	103.7				AH	
Iceland (N)	NH														NH	Islande (N)
Ireland (R)	NH							320 000	107.2	110.0	160.6	176.2	248.4	795 000	NH	Irlande (R)
	AH							50 000	108.0	116.0	134.0	174.0	192.0	96 000	AH	
Italy (N)	NH	27 477 195	109.4	95.1	104.3	102.0	98.8	24 918 807	107.8	113.6	114.0	104.3	96.0	23 917 334	NH	Italie (N)
	AH	3 929 209	96.0	84.9	96.1	96.8	97.6	4 164 722	108.0	118.5	121.2	117.2	113.2	4 714 956	AH	
Luxembourg (R)	NH				91.0	90.6	95.5	108 907	102.5	113.6	113.7		109.7	119 456	NH	Luxembourg (R)
	AH				98.0	90.0	94.0	61 934	102.2	109.4	114.3		111.5	69 074	AH	
Netherlands (R)	NH	1 501 984	107.9	104.6	102.1	100.6	102.9	1 376 379	118.4	114.3	107.1	110.7	121.0	1 664 900	NH	Pays-Bas (R)
	AH	623 521	100.0	98.5	96.3	96.4	100.9	608 603	113.5	109.4	109.2	110.9	121.0	736 400	AH	
Norway (N)	NH	431 892	88.5	91.3	72.6	68.9	97.3	510 236	97.2	99.0	105.7	113.8	113.6	579 869	NH	Norvège (N)
Portugal (N)	NH	1 603 721	91.6	76.9	68.7	67.3	72.8	1 699 976	111.2	120.7	121.0	122.5	138.8	2 360 295	NH	Portugal (N)
	AH	218 762	76.8	66.6	65.0	70.0	74.2	288 465	106.3	128.3	130.2	130.5	145.3	419 054	AH	
Spain (N)	NH	22 002 050	76.8	88.9	91.8	94.8	98.1	23 613 107	99.9	110.4	104.3	92.3			NH	Espagne (N)
	AH	2 181 369	76.3	84.8	88.3	93.6	96.9	2 499 864	104.0	113.4	107.7	99.3	94.5	2 361 519	AH	
Sweden (N)	NH	450 166	105.2	101.5	91.4	90.7	98.3	420 573	107.7	100.8	113.1	121.4	110.4	464 483	NH	Suède (N)
Switzerland (R)	NH	6 015 613	125.7	127.5	110.6	107.6	100.8	5 998 347	103.3	103.1	103.8	108.2	107.0	6 415 768	NH	Suisse (R)
	AH	1 779 375	114.4	115.4	106.5	105.9	101.4	1 833 430	104.7	107.4	110.0	116.2	114.7	2 102 289	AH	
Turkey (N)	NH				31.4	46.1	64.8	1 057 967	152.1	215.3	332.7	348.8	368.5	3 898 518	NH	Turquie (N)
	AH				34.7	53.9	68.5	353 947	146.8	200.2	253.4	268.4	271.4	960 575	AH	
Australia (R)	NH	207 200		102.6		86.1	79.4	302 700	110.3	140.3	187.3	181.7	192.3	582 000	NH	Australie (R)
Japan (N)	NH	167 207	73.3	81.6	74.8	34.4	96.1	229 342							NH	Japon (N)
	AH	61 995													AH	
Yugoslavia (N)	NH							9 348 448	100.9	102.9	100.6	93.9	83.7	7 829 061	NH	Yougoslavie (N)
	AH							1 327 214	102.6	107.9	106.0	98.7	88.3	1 172 280	AH	

AH Arrivals at hotels and similar establishments
NH Nights in hotels and similar establishments
(R) Tourist count by country of residence
(N) Tourist count by country of nationality
1. Ile de France only

AH Arrivées dans les hôtels et les établissements assimilés
NH Nuitées dans les hôtels et établissements assimilés
(R) Recensement des touristes par pays de résidence
(N) Recensement des touristes par pays de nationalité
1. Ile de France seulement

Table/Tableau 28

ARRIVALS AND NIGHTS OF FOREIGN TOURISTS AT/IN ALL MEANS OF ACCOMMODATION

ARRIVÉES ET NUITÉES DE TOURISTES ÉTRANGERS DANS L'ENSEMBLE DES MOYENS D'HÉBERGEMENT

From Germany — *En provenance de l'Allemagne*

1985=100 — *1985=100*

	AAA/NAA	Volume 1979	1980	1981	1982	1983	1984	Volume 1985	1986	1987	1988	1989	1990	Volume 1990	AEH/NEH	
Austria (R)	NAA	62 317 608	118.3	119.0	113.2	109.1	103.6	55 431 560	101.1	99.1	101.1	108.1	102.5	56 819 027	NEH	Autriche (R)
	AAA	8 018 985	104.6	106.0	103.6	104.0	101.6	8 145 318	103.0	105.4	110.5	118.7	115.6	9 418 695	AEH	
Belgium (R)	NAA	1 121 698	78.2	76.8	87.3	87.4	92.7	1 516 985	99.7	102.9	111.5	129.2	128.0	1 940 991	NEH	Belgique (R)
Denmark (N)	NAA	3 573 312	106.0	117.9	115.3	118.3	105.7	3 478 210	94.2	84.0	81.0	86.5	96.4	3 353 577	NEH	Danemark (N)
France (R)	NAA	59 000 000	78.8	80.9	98.3	95.0	96.6	76 406 000	100.0	103.2	105.0	81.2	83.8	64 022 000	NEH	France (R)
	AAA	7 291 000	86.3	88.6	96.3	92.4	95.0	8 723 000	96.5	102.2	104.5	104.2			AEH	
Greece (N)	NAA	5 633 548	87.3	83.2	76.1	71.6	84.7	7 357 032	103.2	104.9	113.0				NEH	Grèce (N)
	AAA	1 123 855	100.0	92.5	89.6	81.9	92.1	1 163 451	100.1	102.6	104.0				AEH	
Ireland (R)	NAA	1 398 800	120.8	82.2	93.2	104.3	96.8	1 262 900	105.4	120.7	139.9	176.7	219.9	2 777 000	NEH	Irlande (R)
	AAA	102 100	97.0	91.9	87.8	94.0	90.9	97 900	102.1		115.4	157.3	181.8	178 000	AEH	
Italy (N)	NAA	44 795 207	108.7	95.2	104.9	102.3	99.0	41 754 200	107.3	94.0	94.6	76.9			NEH	Italie (N)
	AAA	5 456 208	94.2	84.6	96.5	97.2	97.2	5 949 547	108.0	106.9	109.0	102.9			AEH	
Luxembourg (R)	NAA	161 805			79.5	77.7	99.0	165 205	95.3	106.5	106.4		101.3	167 304	NEH	Luxembourg (R)
	AAA	86 153				80.3	97.4	80 855	99.3	105.5	109.7		106.2	85 841	AEH	
Netherlands (R)	NAA	5 053 162	77.2	83.1	93.8	93.0	102.5	6 556 929	105.7		86.0	97.3	113.7	7 457 200	NEH	Pays-Bas (R)
	AAA	1 328 966	84.6	90.6	93.4	96.1	100.9	1 609 735	104.9		95.1	102.5	113.9	1 833 700	AEH	
Portugal (N)	NAA	1 992 417	93.0	88.7	79.6	74.2	74.3	2 242 476	112.9	124.4	124.0	122.7	132.2	2 963 668	NEH	Portugal (N)
	AAA	312 234	78.6	75.2	71.6	74.1	77.3	429 354	112.6	132.3	133.5	130.9	140.1	601 528	AEH	
Spain (N)	NAA	23 084 278	77.4	88.8	92.2	97.8	97.8	24 699 651							NEH	Espagne (N)
	AAA	2 319 904	76.8	84.7	88.5	94.3	96.9	2 659 138							AEH	
Sweden (N)	NAA	1 504 747	104.3	108.4	97.2	109.3	100.2	1 336 901	96.2	89.3	103.0	113.3	104.9	1 402 342	NEH	Suède (N)
Switzerland (R)	NAA	13 054 300	112.9	121.1	110.4	108.6	99.4	14 486 200	101.9	99.7	102.1	103.2	102.5	14 841 330	NEH	Suisse (R)
	AAA	2 559 500	107.6	112.6	106.1	106.3	100.3	2 882 000	103.9	104.8	108.5	112.8	112.8	3 250 844	AEH	
Turkey (N)	NAA	299 399	13.7	24.5	29.0	46.9	62.2	1 181 708	173.4	274.5	388.7	398.5	459.2	5 426 311	NEH	Turquie (N)
	AAA	99 840	15.5	27.3	33.8	53.9	67.7	366 597	152.8	227.2	280.7	295.1	303.8	1 113 735	AEH	
United Kingdom (R)	NAA	16 564 000	110.2	104.7	106.4	96.4	98.1	14 586 000	112.4	107.3	118.1	121.5	119.3	17 394 000	NEH	Royaume-Uni (R)
Canada (R)	NAA	2 769 700	119.1	128.7	124.8	107.6	111.6	2 260 800	120.6	134.4	158.4	143.6			NEH	Canada (R)
	AAA	181 000	120.8	127.8	117.4	104.2	108.6	156 500	126.7	149.6	168.1	167.9			AEH	
Australia (R)	NAA	447 000		107.0		112.0	78.4	688 700	114.0		392.0	375.8	528.0	3 636 000	NEH	Australie (R)
New Zealand (R)	NAA						90.6	320 000	128.3	179.7	195.5	231.4	276.5	884 655	NEH	Nouvelle-Zélande (R)
Yugoslavia (N)	NAA	13 633 140	84.3	90.7	77.3	75.8	82.6	19 410 269	101.6	103.3	102.0	90.3	72.3	14 024 046	NEH	Yougoslavie (N)
	AAA	1 851 543	81.6	85.4	73.4	74.0	82.2	2 608 629	101.1	106.8	105.4	94.4	76.0	1 981 362	AEH	

AAA Arrivals in all means of accommodation
NAA Nights in all means of accommodation
(R) Tourist count by country of residence
(N) Tourist count by country of nationality

AEH Arrivées dans l'ensemble des moyens d'hébergement
NEH Nuitées dans l'ensemble des moyens d'hébergement
(R) Recensement des touristes par pays de résidence
(N) Recensement des touristes par pays de nationalité

Table/Tableau 29

ARRIVALS OF FOREIGN TOURISTS/VISITORS AT FRONTIERS
ARRIVÉES DE TOURISTES/VISITEURS ÉTRANGERS AUX FRONTIÈRES

From Canada — *En provenance du Canada*

1985=100 — *1985=100*

	T/V	Volume 1979	1980	1981	1982	1983	1984	Volume 1985	1986	1987	1988	1989	1990	Volume 1990	T/V	
Finland (R)	V	8 222													V	Finlande (R)
France (R)	T	310 000	67.1	74.8	52.4	59.3	79.0	477 000	80.9	73.2	72.1				T	France (R)
	V														V	
Greece (N)	T	83 662	70.6	64.1	63.3	70.7	80.2	102 552	72.8	88.7	104.3	77.0	72.4	74 218	T	Grèce (N)
Iceland (N)	T	1 043	62.7	69.3	78.0	80.7	77.8	1 286	92.9	100.0	99.3	100.5	88.6	1 140	T	Islande (N)
Ireland (R)	V			102.2	65.0	84.0	84.0	25 000	112.0	100.0	112.0	148.0	152.0	38 000	V	Irlande (R)
Italy (N)	V	395 900	101.1	88.6	88.4	95.1	96.5	348 567	97.0	110.3	101.6	121.3	136.3	475 191	V	Italie (N)
Norway (N)	V	8 621													V	Norvège (N)
Portugal (N)	T	39 300	54.8	60.2	55.1	60.2	76.0	68 894	104.8	105.4	110.3	120.6	120.8	83 238	T	Portugal (N)
	V	40 675	57.4	61.9	59.8	66.6	79.9	70 275	105.1	110.3	112.5	129.7	129.2	90 830	V	
Spain (N)	V	142 058	60.2	71.1	69.8	72.5	81.4	191 087	92.6	93.5	87.9	90.2	82.6	157 756	V	Espagne (N)
Turkey (N)	V	20 916	53.7	53.5	39.7	66.9	83.8	21 530	60.8	96.7	135.7	146.7	160.6	34 575	V	Turquie (N)
United Kingdom (R)	V	477 300	61.3	61.7	64.8	82.2	89.8	631 200	87.9	94.1	103.2	101.2	111.2	702 000	V	Royaume-Uni (R)
United States (R)	T	10 716 068	104.6	100.5	95.9	109.9	100.9	10 880 131	100.6	114.1	127.2	141.2	158.7	17 262 000	T	États-Unis (R)
Australia (R)	V	23 200	69.6	75.7	79.3	80.7	84.4	40 900	114.9	128.9	163.1	132.5	131.3	53 700	V	Australie (R)
Japan (N)	V	34 476	67.2	73.5	79.1	87.8	86.8	61 052	90.5	95.5	95.3	97.9	104.6	63 850	V	Japon (N)
New Zealand (R)	T	14 296	62.2	61.4	60.4	68.6	77.2	29 833	115.1	119.2	124.5	103.6	113.9	33 983	T	Nouvelle-Zélande (R)

V Visitors (travellers in Turkey)
T Tourists
(R) Tourist count by country of residence
(N) Tourist count by country of nationality

V Visiteurs (voyageurs en Turquie)
T Touristes
(R) Recensement des touristes par pays de résidence
(N) Recensement des touristes par pays de nationalité

Table/Tableau 30

ARRIVALS AND NIGHTS OF FOREIGN TOURISTS AT/IN HOTELS
ARRIVÉES ET NUITÉES DE TOURISTES ÉTRANGERS DANS L'HÔTELLERIE

From Canada — *En provenance du Canada*

1985=100 — *1985=100*

	AH/NH	Volume 1979	1980	1981	1982	1983	1984	Volume 1985	1986	1987	1988	1989	1990	Volume 1990	AH/NH	
Austria (R)	NH	105 483	50.7	58.9	64.1	67.8	81.9	200 122	82.5	90.8	84.1	86.8	97.0	194 198	NH	Autriche (R)
	AH	38 895	50.3	52.2	57.4	67.5	83.8	79 234	77.7	87.1	85.0	91.3	105.7	83 732	AH	
Belgium (R)	NH	45 474	55.1	51.9	53.2	61.4	80.7	92 732	78.4	82.1	85.6	100.8	106.6	98 828	NH	Belgique (R)
Finland (R)	NH	16 228	48.2	62.2	71.4	88.8	92.1	29 917	85.0	97.1	101.7	111.1	107.1	32 056	NH	Finlande (R)
France (R)[1]	NH	264 622	48.3	53.6	58.8	70.7	82.8	561 332	144.0	132.8	134.2	170.2	184.0	1 032 776	NH	France (R)[1]
	AH	95 394	46.8	51.8	56.3	63.2	78.0	209 825	181.8	157.3	158.9	205.4	225.3	472 754	AH	
Germany (R)	NH	185 994	60.4	60.4	63.5	70.7	92.0	340 220	87.9	85.2	90.8	104.7	111.3	378 723	NH	Allemagne (R)
	AH	99 603	59.3	57.3	61.5	69.5	93.6	184 518	83.2	80.3	80.7	92.7	101.3	187 001	AH	
Greece (N)	NH	281 795	57.8	57.5	52.0	57.6	71.0	364 167	53.9	63.1	65.0				NH	Grèce (N)
	AH	101 986	58.1	53.8	51.0	56.1	73.3	137 819	54.9	64.3	66.2				AH	
Ireland (R)	NH													108 000	NH	Irlande (R)
	AH													21 000	AH	
Italy (N)	NH	412 792	58.3	55.5	66.5	78.6	87.7	670 203	78.0	90.5	85.6	93.9	94.6	633 774	NH	Italie (N)
	AH	143 860	55.4	51.3	62.6	77.2	90.5	267 326	76.6	88.7	86.8	91.0	94.6	252 987	AH	
Luxembourg (R)	NH														NH	Luxembourg (R)
	AH														AH	
Netherlands (R)	NH	120 263	64.5	58.6	61.4	77.7	88.7	194 286	84.6	89.7	90.3	92.7	95.7	185 900	NH	Pays-Bas (R)
	AH	61 238	59.7	53.5	55.2	76.1	86.8	113 770	82.5	86.8	90.4	82.5	80.8	91 900	AH	
Portugal (N)	NH	171 848	48.0	52.0	44.8	55.5	66.7	388 180	93.7	89.3	80.4	87.7	96.8	375 915	NH	Portugal (N)
	AH	47 848	50.1	54.9	52.4	62.5	76.6	98 383	93.9	102.5	93.2	101.2	102.5	100 852	AH	
Spain (N)	NH		50.1	57.6	60.2	73.5	85.2	483 637	70.6	46.9	37.8	36.8			NH	Espagne (N)
	AH													64 991	AH	
Sweden (N)	NH	24 467	90.2	97.9	76.3	82.4	102.6	28 069	78.3	100.0	81.4	89.3	92.5	25 972	NH	Suède (N)
Switzerland (R)	NH	155 028	53.8	58.2	62.3	73.0	82.8	317 813	82.3	75.5	65.9	68.5	74.0	235 059	NH	Suisse (R)
	AH	66 716	53.2	54.0	58.8	73.1	88.4	142 342	79.9	73.6	65.6	70.3	76.2	108 491	AH	
Turkey (N)	NH				69.1	75.1	98.5	13 978	117.3	136.0	211.8	220.4	200.6	28 044	NH	Turquie (N)
	AH				50.7	79.4	90.7	5 553	126.1	138.5	189.9	284.6	235.0	13 050	AH	
Australia (R)	NH	214 400		72.3		106.2	74.0	355 500	118.0	132.3	167.5	112.2			NH	Australie (R)
Japan (N)	NH	81 499													NH	Japon (N)
	AH	40 743													AH	
Yugoslavia (N)	NH							79 305	87.6	113.8	116.7	93.8	104.1	82 545	NH	Yougoslavie (N)
	AH							32 535	87.5	111.2	121.8	108.0	104.1	33 858	AH	

AH Arrivals at hotels and similar establishments
NH Nights in hotels and similar establishments
(R) Tourist count by country of residence
(N) Tourist count by country of nationality
1. Ile de France only

AH Arrivées dans les hôtels et les établissements assimilés
NH Nuitées dans les hôtels et établissements assimilés
(R) Recensement des touristes par pays de résidence
(N) Recensement des touristes par pays de nationalité
1. Ile de France seulement

Table/Tableau 31

ARRIVALS AND NIGHTS OF FOREIGN TOURISTS AT/IN ALL MEANS OF ACCOMMODATION
ARRIVÉES ET NUITÉES DE TOURISTES ÉTRANGERS DANS L'ENSEMBLE DES MOYENS D'HÉBERGEMENT

From Canada — *En provenance du Canada*

1985=100 — *1985=100*

	AAA/NAA	Volume 1979	1980	1981	1982	1983	1984	Volume 1985	1986	1987	1988	1989	1990	Volume 1990	AEH/NEH	
Austria (R)	NAA	139 411	57.6	61.2	68.8	71.9	85.3	245 932	85.3	92.5	90.9	89.7	101.2	248 783	NEH	Autriche (R)
	AAA	49 350	53.1	53.4	59.6	67.9	85.2	94 762	80.8	89.2	89.3	94.9	109.6	103 847	AEH	
Belgium (R)	NAA	53 070	57.3	52.4	55.6	62.4	81.2	105 945	82.8	81.1	85.6	99.4	107.2	113 574	NEH	Belgique (R)
France (R)	NAA	3 070 000	48.1	53.7	53.5	64.2	80.8	6 650 000	88.5	85.5	85.5	78.5	82.9	5 513 000	NEH	France (R)
	AAA	310 000	67.1	74.8	52.4	59.3	79.0	477 000	80.9	73.2	72.1	104.0			AEH	
Germany (R)	NAA	197 066	58.4	55.2	58.1	64.9	92.1	380 297	89.3	86.1	92.2	106.5	112.7	428 709	NEH	Allemagne (R)
	AAA	101 805	56.4	51.9	55.7	63.0	94.3	205 038	85.7	81.9	82.9	95.3	104.4	214 145	AEH	
Greece (N)	NAA	298 165	64.1	61.6	55.9	61.0	103.4	372 522	54.4	63.2	64.7				NEH	Grèce (N)
	AAA	112 700	64.2	58.2	55.5	60.2	79.1	140 776	55.5	64.7	66.2				AEH	
Ireland (R)	AAA													41 000	AEH	Irlande (R)
Italy (N)	NAA	600 266	70.9	65.8	76.2	83.3	90.6	809 504	81.3	87.0	83.4	90.8			NEH	Italie (N)
	AAA	166 614	58.8	54.2	64.6	78.5	91.5	292 060	79.1	89.4	88.7	92.4			AEH	
Luxembourg (R)	NAA														NEH	Luxembourg (R)
	AAA														AEH	
Netherlands (R)	NAA	157 882	73.4	64.0	66.4	79.9	90.5	222 785	81.0		91.7	94.7	99.5	221 700	NEH	Pays-Bas (R)
	AAA	80 639	65.9	59.0	60.5	78.3	89.1	131 052	79.1		93.7	82.9	83.0	108 800 .	AEH	
Portugal (N)	NAA	184 629	50.6	53.4	46.0	56.5	67.6	401 156	93.3	89.2	80.6	87.7	96.8	388 130	NEH	Portugal (N)
	AAA	52 467	53.2	56.4	53.5	63.4	77.2	102 744	93.6	102.2	93.4	101.4	103.4	106 216	AEH	
Sweden (N)	NAA	27 270	91.9	96.5	77.2	84.4	102.3	31 214	80.6	98.6	82.7	90.0	93.4	29 159	NEH	Suède (N)
Switzerland (R)	NAA	196 200	56.3	61.0	65.1	74.4	83.9	376 000	83.6	77.6	68.0	71.4	75.8	284 875	NEH	Suisse (R)
	AAA	87 100	56.4	57.2	61.7	74.4	88.0	169 400	81.0	74.1	67.4	72.2	77.4	131 118	AEH	
Turkey (N)	NAA	8 364	38.1	39.8	67.9	74.4	98.3	14 308	117.4	139.6	217.2	221.1	204.5	29 266	NEH	Turquie (N)
	AAA	3 584	36.3	44.3	49.7	78.2	89.4	5 691	124.5	140.9	196.1	283.5	236.4	13 454	AEH	
United Kingdom (R)	NAA	8 128 000	64.4	72.2	78.1	88.5	92.5	9 113 000	93.9	90.4	97.2	94.1	102.6	9 352 000	NEH	Royaume-Uni (R)
Australia (R)	NAA	461 200		89.2		171.8	103.1	771 900	111.7	125.3	158.6	135.4			NEH	Australie (R)
Yugoslavia (N)	NAA	78 695	53.9	58.2	56.7	63.1	94.2	112 269	86.8	111.7	112.5	90.7	91.7	102 919	NEH	Yougoslavie (N)
	AAA	28 122	57.0	56.5	53.4	60.3	84.5	39 501	87.2	109.6	119.9	104.7	100.0	39 507	AEH	

AAA Arrivals in all means of accommodation
NAA Nights in all means of accommodation
(R) Tourist count by country of residence
(N) Tourist count by country of nationality

AEH Arrivées dans l'ensemble des moyens d'hébergement
NEH Nuitées dans l'ensemble des moyens d'hébergement
(R) Recensement des touristes par pays de résidence
(N) Recensement des touristes par pays de nationalité

Table/Tableau 32

ARRIVALS OF FOREIGN TOURISTS/VISITORS AT FRONTIERS
ARRIVÉES DE TOURISTES/VISITEURS ÉTRANGERS AUX FRONTIÈRES

From the United States — *En provenance des États-Unis*

1985=100 — *1985=100*

	T/V	Volume 1979	1980	1981	1982	1983	1984	Volume 1985	1986	1987	1988	1989	1990	Volume 1990	T/V	
Finland (R)	V	40 272													V	Finlande (R)
France (R)	T	1 132 000	42.8	49.3	48.8	73.8	91.4	2 778 000	60.0	64.9	70.2	78.0	74.6	2 072 000	T	France (R)
	V														V	
Greece (N)	T	601 456	61.9	68.9	71.5	87.3	101.9	466 155	43.9	55.8	63.3	59.9	58.7	273 849	T	Grèce (N)
Iceland (N)	T	22 525	48.2	56.6	65.8	78.8	86.3	31 633	103.4	112.8	90.8	72.6	71.5	22 616	T	Islande (N)
Ireland (R)	V		63.8	64.3	79.9	70.9	80.2	378 000	78.8	94.7	98.7	100.5	104.8	396 000	V	Irlande (R)
Italy (N)	V	1 767 200	94.0	78.7	87.4	93.6	96.8	1 834 420	86.8	80.8	73.7	74.0	77.5	1 420 888	V	Italie (N)
Norway (N)	V	86 668													V	Norvège (N)
Portugal (N)	T	132 400	70.0	66.1	77.3	69.7	100.3	164 929	69.4	91.9	117.8	113.2	111.5	183 886	T	Portugal (N)
	V	153 807	59.0	61.7	67.2	81.4	91.2	229 496	65.3	85.0	97.3	102.6	109.8	252 057	V	
Spain (N)	V	890 398	81.9	77.4	76.0	81.3	93.8	997 774	77.2	86.8	86.1	95.6	83.8	836 292	V	Espagne (N)
Turkey (N)	V	160 767	60.5	52.8	53.3	96.2	108.7	196 261	40.6	66.5	84.3	104.2	104.9	205 831	V	Turquie (N)
United Kingdom (R)	V	1 718 700	53.5	54.2	54.5	73.2	87.3	3 166 100	72.3	88.4	82.8	89.8	96.3	3 049 000	V	Royaume-Uni (R)
Canada (R)	T	10 908 800	94.9	94.9	90.5	94.4	97.7	11 557 500	117.7	110.1	110.4	105.4	106.1	12 267 000	T	Canada (R)
	V	31 191 600	112.8	116.7	95.1	95.2	96.7	34 117 400	112.0	108.3	105.9	101.7	101.8	34 734 100	V	
Australia (R)	V	97 000	56.4	58.0	63.8	71.1	81.6	196 500	124.9	157.3	164.0	132.7	127.6	250 700	V	Australie (R)
Japan (N)	V	301 926	57.2	63.3	73.6	82.7	91.6	558 029	99.0	98.6	92.5	95.3	99.4	554 753	V	Japon (N)
New Zealand (R)	T	60 216	63.3	62.5	62.1	70.5	82.2	122 960	125.2	146.7	136.2	111.8	113.6	139 664	T	Nouvelle-Zélande (R)

V Visitors (travellers in Turkey)
T Tourists
(R) Tourist count by country of residence
(N) Tourist count by country of nationality

V Visiteurs (voyageurs en Turquie)
T Touristes
(R) Recensement des touristes par pays de résidence
(N) Recensement des touristes par pays de nationalité

Table/Tableau 33

ARRIVALS AND NIGHTS OF FOREIGN TOURISTS AT/IN HOTELS
ARRIVÉES ET NUITÉES DE TOURISTES ÉTRANGERS DANS L'HÔTELLERIE

From the United States — *En provenance des États-Unis*

1985=100 — *1985=100*

	AH/NH	Volume 1979	1980	1981	1982	1983	1984	Volume 1985	1986	1987	1988	1989	1990	Volume 1990	AH/NH	
Austria (R)	NH	943 002	54.4	47.0	59.4	72.6	92.8	2 182 863	57.5	71.1	65.4	70.2	89.8	1 959 781	NH	Autriche (R)
	AH	367 589	55.4	43.3	53.3	69.1	94.8	925 603	49.5	66.1	60.8	66.3	88.1	815 640	AH	
Belgium (R)	NH	492 454	60.2	60.2	70.5	75.3	89.2	771 965	77.8	69.8	60.1	71.8	75.9	586 137	NH	Belgique (R)
Denmark (N)	NH	384 200	63.2	58.9	72.2	87.6	92.6	573 000	72.3	77.5	66.0	72.4	69.7	399 500	NH	Danemark (N)
Finland (R)	NH	95 682	46.0	52.9	62.1	81.2	85.2	184 798	86.3	108.0	110.0	109.6	106.8	197 318	NH	Finlande (R)
	AH														AH	
France (R)[1]	NH	1 713 425	48.2	52.2	54.0	67.2	88.2	3 853 024	84.8	93.3	102.7	135.9	147.2	5 672 261	NH	France (R)[1]
	AH	657 233	47.2	50.7	56.9	66.8	90.2	1 423 997	99.0	107.3	123.7	162.2	173.4	2 468 889	AH	
Germany (R)	NH	2 174 355	55.6	50.3	57.6	71.2	92.3	4 846 727	74.0	83.3	75.4	82.2	91.7	4 444 619	NH	Allemagne (R)
	AH	1 113 214	57.0	49.5	56.9	71.5	94.6	2 537 543	69.7	77.9	70.3	77.4	91.0	2 308 179	AH	
Greece (N)	NH	1 572 298	77.0	74.5	77.5	97.7	117.0	1 670 809	30.5	47.3	49.6				NH	Grèce (N)
	AH	612 943	69.1	67.5	70.2	90.9	114.1	720 645	25.8	44.9	49.6				AH	
Iceland (N)	NH														NH	Islande (N)
Ireland (R)	NH							2 140 000	75.4	94.0	99.7	91.0	95.3	2 040 000	NH	Irlande (R)
	AH							403 000	77.4	94.5	94.3	93.8	92.8	374 000	AH	
Italy (N)	NH	3 905 473	55.5	52.3	63.3	79.4	93.6	6 577 523	51.5	72.4	69.8	73.7	75.9	4 990 826	NH	Italie (N)
	AH	1 498 326	52.5	48.6	59.7	77.3	94.2	2 820 366	45.4	66.8	66.1	68.8	72.5	2 044 360	AH	
Luxembourg (R)	NH				51.3	70.7	86.5	99 725	74.8	77.4	63.5		59.8	59 660	NH	Luxembourg (R)
	AH				52.2	69.3	84.2	57 590	74.5	77.6	57.8		57.5	33 101	AH	
Netherlands (R)	NH	682 136	60.8	62.0	76.2	81.3	99.5	1 076 412	77.4	77.7	70.2	76.1	85.4	918 900	NH	Pays-Bas (R)
	AH	316 938	56.2	55.0	71.1	78.9	99.7	576 357	73.0	74.1	66.1	71.6	79.4	457 600	AH	
Norway (N)	NH	347 276	51.3	52.1	58.3	69.7	87.3	642 959	64.0	71.1	54.1	54.0	56.7	364 544	NH	Norvège (N)
Portugal (N)	NH	597 723	58.1	58.3	59.1	76.0	90.0	788 833	62.9	79.5	82.4	85.9	85.2	672 205	NH	Portugal (N)
	AH	196 681	54.8	57.4	58.1	77.8	92.4	291 874	59.0	79.4	82.1	87.0	86.4	252 185	AH	
Spain (N)	NH	2 095 234	54.1	62.1	64.9	81.9	97.2	2 539 092	58.5	75.1	69.2	72.3			NH	Espagne (N)
	AH	816 618	44.4	50.5	52.6	78.2	93.5	1 241 087	57.2	64.9	62.5	66.6	63.8	791 753	AH	
Sweden (N)	NH	289 779	51.7	56.6	61.0	81.9	86.1	482 557	67.5	72.2	67.5	68.7	67.7	326 900	NH	Suède (N)
Switzerland (R)	NH	1 436 322	53.0	53.9	63.5	73.1	93.9	3 262 773	63.7	71.5	62.5	68.2	76.9	2 510 625	NH	Suisse (R)
	AH	631 264	53.3	51.2	61.5	73.0	95.7	1 519 517	58.8	68.3	61.1	68.0	79.2	1 204 047	AH	
Turkey (N)	NH				55.8	71.5	95.0	267 889	81.7	99.9	117.5	142.1	130.2	348 767	NH	Turquie (N)
	AH				56.5	80.9	89.6	88 370	86.2	105.0	133.6	189.6	179.3	158 428	AH	
Australia (R)	NH	824 400		55.5		74.9	65.2	1 660 500	129.9	163.6	190.2	126.8	136.3	2 264 000	NH	Australie (R)
Japan (N)	NH	1 044 435	47.2	55.6	62.5	35.6	80.3	2 367 929							NH	Japon (N)
	AH	479 532													AH	
Yugoslavia (N)	NH							510 398	60.1	91.6	101.3	90.8	87.6	447 013	NH	Yougoslavie (N)
	AH							220 054	59.7	94.3	113.9	100.7	97.0	213 401	AH	

AH Arrivals at hotels and similar establishments
NH Nights in hotels and similar establishments
(R) Tourist count by country of residence
(N) Tourist count by country of nationality
1. Ile de France only

AH Arrivées dans les hôtels et les établissements assimilés
NH Nuitées dans les hôtels et établissements assimilés
(R) Recensement des touristes par pays de résidence
(N) Recensement des touristes par pays de nationalité
1. Ile de France seulement

Table/Tableau 34

ARRIVALS AND NIGHTS OF FOREIGN TOURISTS AT/IN ALL MEANS OF ACCOMMODATION
ARRIVÉES ET NUITÉES DE TOURISTES ÉTRANGERS DANS L'ENSEMBLE DES MOYENS D'HÉBERGEMENT

From the United States — *En provenance des États-Unis*

1985=100 — *1985=100*

	AAA/NAA	Volume 1979	1980	1981	1982	1983	1984	Volume 1985	1986	1987	1988	1989	1990	Volume 1990	AEH/NEH	
Austria (R)	NAA	1 090 836	56.1	49.2	60.5	73.2	92.7	2 376 876	59.3	72.4	67.0	71.4	90.0	2 139 202	NEH	Autriche (R)
	AAA	409 815	56.1	44.6	54.2	69.6	94.3	987 722	51.6	68.0	62.8	68.4	89.6	885 337	AEH	
Belgium (R)	NAA	515 964	54.6	55.0	63.4	67.8	83.0	892 542	89.7	82.1	64.2	66.2	71.1	634 543	NEH	Belgique (R)
Denmark (N)	NAA	406 581	65.5	60.9	73.9	88.1	92.9	595 803	73.2	78.4	66.9	73.2	70.7	421 281	NEH	Danemark (N)
France (R)	NAA	9 570 000	30.8	35.4	48.7	73.6	88.3	30 938 000	75.0	82.3	85.0	57.5	60.4	18 689 000	NEH	France (R)
	AAA	1 132 000	42.8	49.3	48.8	73.8	91.4	2 778 000	60.0	64.9	70.2	78.0			AEH	
Germany (R)	NAA	2 270 982	56.1	48.5	55.6	69.3	92.3	5 091 998	74.5	83.9	76.1	83.1	92.6	4 714 849	NEH	Allemagne (R)
	AAA	1 131 714	57.1	47.9	55.1	69.5	95.0	2 630 553	70.4	78.8	71.4	78.6	92.3	2 428 067	AEH	
Greece (N)	NAA	1 701 665	84.0	79.4	81.7	102.3	123.5	1 683 109	31.0	47.5	49.7				NEH	Grèce (N)
	AAA	640 637	72.3	70.1	73.0	93.8	118.5	725 660	26.2	45.2	49.6				AEH	
Ireland (R)	NAA	3 581 500	72.8	63.7	75.3	87.3	82.0	4 093 000	80.4	97.8	100.4	111.0	108.3	4 434 000	NEH	Irlande (R)
	AAA	265 300	59.7	63.5	74.0	72.9	81.1	392 100	87.5		98.2	98.2	102.5	402 000	AEH	
Italy (N)	NAA	4 630 496	60.1	56.9	67.3	82.1	94.3	7 348 677	54.9	69.5	67.0	70.4			NEH	Italie (N)
	AAA	1 576 405	53.7	49.6	60.5	77.8	94.2	2 907 222	46.6	67.3	68.5	69.3			AEH	
Luxembourg (R)	NAA	67 772			49.9	67.9	87.6	106 051	75.9	80.1	66.2		62.7	66 547	NEH	Luxembourg (R)
	AAA	51 945				65.1	85.4	62 339	75.8	80.3	61.6		59.7	37 227	AEH	
Netherlands (R)	NAA	788 822	64.3	64.8	78.3	82.3	99.4	1 166 242	72.7		71.2	78.0	88.2	1 028 600	NEH	Pays-Bas (R)
	AAA	372 636	60.0	58.2	73.7	80.4	99.8	628 339	68.4		68.9	72.3	79.6	500 400	AEH	
Portugal (N)	NAA	614 818	59.4	59.4	60.2	76.5	89.8	806 857	63.3	80.8	82.7	85.8	85.2	687 311	NEH	Portugal (N)
	AAA	202 967	56.2	58.2	58.7	78.0	92.2	297 637	59.6	80.0	82.6	87.4	87.0	258 920	AEH	
Spain (N)	NAA	2 135 472	54.1	62.0	64.6	80.8	95.4	3 044 040							NEH	Espagne (N)
	AAA	825 415	52.6	59.7	62.1	78.3	93.6	1 247 221							AEH	
Sweden (N)	NAA	303 077	52.5	57.1	61.5	81.7	86.4	499 840	68.2	72.9	68.0	69.6	68.5	342 216	NEH	Suède (N)
Switzerland (R)	NAA	1 677 900	54.1	55.7	65.0	73.6	93.5	3 552 000	65.5	72.4	64.2	69.8	77.9	2 767 518	NEH	Suisse (R)
	AAA	710 600	54.9	53.1	63.2	74.0	95.4	1 611 400	60.0	69.3	62.4	69.1	80.0	1 288 588	AEH	
Turkey (N)	NAA	109 572	24.1	38.2	55.6	71.3	95.3	271 143	82.2	101.0	118.7	143.4	131.8	357 293	NEH	Turquie (N)
	AAA	43 058	26.4	40.5	56.3	80.4	89.7	89 572	86.1	106.1	134.9	189.7	179.8	161 058	AEH	
United Kingdom (R)	NAA	19 233 000	59.0	57.9	61.5	74.1	85.5	31 204 000	78.9	92.7	81.8	88.5	91.7	28 621 000	NEH	Royaume-Uni (R)
Canada (R)	NAA	52 530 800	93.7	95.7	87.9	89.8	98.5	53 822 600	117.6	102.9	104.4	99.6			NEH	Canada (R)
	AAA	10 908 800	94.9	94.9	90.5	94.4	97.7	11 557 500	117.7	110.1	110.4	105.4			AEH	
Australia (R)	NAA	1 486 500		57.6		75.6	72.1	2 943 100	113.8		275.2	195.6	213.7	6 290 000	NEH	Australie (R)
New Zealand (R)	NAA						79.2	1 970 000	116.0	124.3	114.6	102.5	108.0	2 127 440	NEH	Nouvelle-Zélande (R)
Yugoslavia (N)	NAA	452 872	56.1	57.4	61.1	75.1	101.6	594 562	63.5	97.6	121.1	106.5	94.1	559 565	NEH	Yougoslavie (N)
	AAA	181 142	59.5	59.2	56.8	70.3	95.1	238 405	61.7	97.2	123.9	108.2	100.6	239 948	AEH	

AAA Arrivals in all means of accommodation
NAA Nights in all means of accommodation
(R) Tourist count by country of residence
(N) Tourist count by country of nationality

AEH Arrivées dans l'ensemble des moyens d'hébergement
NEH Nuitées dans l'ensemble des moyens d'hébergement
(R) Recensement des touristes par pays de résidence
(N) Recensement des touristes par pays de nationalité

Table/Tableau 35

ARRIVALS OF FOREIGN TOURISTS/VISITORS AT FRONTIERS
ARRIVÉES DE TOURISTES/VISITEURS ÉTRANGERS AUX FRONTIÈRES

From France — *En provenance de la France*

1985=100 — *1985=100*

	T/V	Volume 1979	1980	1981	1982	1983	1984	Volume 1985	1986	1987	1988	1989	1990	Volume 1990	T/V	
Finland (R)	V	16 405													V	Finlande (R)
Greece (N)	T	319 483	68.0	67.2	76.0	67.9	92.0	441 148	106.2	115.6	106.3	108.4	128.2	565 407	T	Grèce (N)
Iceland (N)	T	3 829	79.9	94.8	98.8	87.5	108.1	4 483	125.3	118.5	137.0	182.6	223.5	10 021	T	Islande (N)
Ireland (R)	V		78.2	92.9	100.9	87.1	87.1	93 000	92.5	119.4	115.1	146.2	210.8	196 000	V	Irlande (R)
Italy (N)	V	6 929 400	85.0	85.7	97.3	90.6	97.2	8 708 159	98.4	103.8	103.1	107.8	105.9	9 219 317	V	Italie (N)
Norway (N)	V	25 770													V	Norvège (N)
Portugal (N)	T	168 300	69.7	71.4	87.3	98.6	97.7	320 188	106.4	129.2	176.6	190.8	193.0	617 873	T	Portugal (N)
	V	183 164	68.3	68.8	83.0	94.4	94.1	347 307	100.8	125.2	170.9	186.2	189.5	658 198	V	
Spain (N)	V	10 741 082	91.5	96.9	98.8	93.9	90.7	11 000 818	102.5	106.1	109.9	109.0	105.7	11 623 555	V	Espagne (N)
Turkey (N)	V	120 406	58.2	64.5	66.3	58.8	68.9	149 950	96.0	112.4	164.6	189.1	207.3	310 809	V	Turquie (N)
United Kingdom (R)	V	1 377 200	98.9	87.2	93.7	93.6	100.7	1 620 300	108.4	124.0	121.6	139.5	142.5	2 309 000	V	Royaume-Uni (R)
Canada (R)	T	105 800	106.2	110.7	110.1	84.5	103.3	107 300	130.8	176.9	215.1	226.4	241.9	259 600	T	Canada (R)
	V	128 600	114.8	117.0	113.1	85.3	104.0	117 200	133.0	179.9	212.8	223.4	235.2	275 700	V	
United States (R)	T	310 244	107.5	122.5	126.2	90.8	98.5	335 564	131.0	162.2	184.3	194.8	213.4	716 000	T	États-Unis (R)
Australia (R)	V	7 500	67.7	69.8	85.4	83.3	93.3	12 000	115.8	142.5	175.0	167.5	175.8	21 100	V	Australie (R)
Japan (N)	V	22 230	65.2	69.6	74.6	72.6	86.0	39 679	89.0	93.7	102.0	119.1	128.6	51 014	V	Japon (N)
New Zealand (R)	T	1 760	82.3	77.1	75.3	79.4	91.2	2 429	109.1	156.9	141.5	167.7	141.2	3 429	T	Nouvelle-Zélande (R)

V Visitors (travellers in Turkey)
T Tourists
(R) Tourist count by country of residence
(N) Tourist count by country of nationality

V Visiteurs (voyageurs en Turquie)
T Touristes
(R) Recensement des touristes par pays de résidence
(N) Recensement des touristes par pays de nationalité

Table/Tableau 36

ARRIVALS AND NIGHTS OF FOREIGN TOURISTS AT/IN HOTELS
ARRIVÉES ET NUITÉES DE TOURISTES ÉTRANGERS DANS L'HÔTELLERIE

From France — *En provenance de la France*

1985=100 — *1985=100*

	AH/NH	Volume 1979	1980	1981	1982	1983	1984	Volume 1985	1986	1987	1988	1989	1990	Volume 1990	AH/NH	
Austria (R)	NH	998 403	60.7	73.4	82.5	72.7	93.7	1 911 014	111.0	109.2	108.6	118.7	124.2	2 372 949	NH	Autriche (R)
	AH	318 449	69.7	82.1	86.5	74.7	94.8	525 910	109.3	105.4	106.5	117.9	124.7	655 594	AH	
Belgium (R)	NH	507 327	94.6	91.4	98.6	83.8	91.8	576 834	102.7	105.0	113.9	136.0	142.9	824 150	NH	Belgique (R)
Denmark (N)	NH	84 600	101.5	102.0	106.8	85.7	96.1	84 200	91.0	91.1	90.0	93.8	98.0	82 500	NH	Danemark (N)
Finland (R)	NH	43 599	81.0	81.1	87.7	80.3	101.7	57 854	94.0	107.0	114.8	123.2	144.7	83 691	NH	Finlande (R)
	AH														AH	
Germany (R)	NH	1 075 911	99.7	102.8	96.0	83.5	94.3	1 114 651	104.3	106.5	109.7	125.0	131.6	1 467 218	NH	Allemagne (R)
	AH	570 554	99.7	102.0	96.6	84.2	94.8	594 722	103.1	104.7	107.6	122.0	127.9	760 774	AH	
Greece (N)	NH	2 016 020	73.5	71.2	77.1	64.5	88.0	2 636 400	91.6	96.8	92.7				NH	Grèce (N)
	AH	667 182	79.6	77.7	84.9	68.9	94.4	804 666	94.8	96.7	89.7				AH	
Iceland (N)	NH														NH	Islande (N)
Ireland (R)	NH							360 000		98.1	124.2	130.6	261.9	943 000	NH	Irlande (R)
	AH							56 000		123.2	119.6	137.5	232.1	130 000	AH	
Italy (N)	NH	5 461 576	105.4	98.1	111.9	90.7	96.1	5 261 270	106.3	109.2	105.1	97.6	95.4	5 021 561	NH	Italie (N)
	AH	1 683 863	104.7	94.3	108.5	88.7	98.4	1 651 989	104.9	109.1	108.7	106.5	104.5	1 727 012	AH	
Luxembourg (R)	NH				103.0	82.5	89.5	66 384	103.5	114.4	128.1		162.8	108 078	NH	Luxembourg (R)
	AH				120.6	85.1	91.2	36 040	107.7	117.2	133.3		152.2	54 857	AH	
Netherlands (R)	NH	394 739	108.3	104.6	110.3	85.7	98.4	402 061	110.8	114.4	110.6	115.6	136.5	548 800	NH	Pays-Bas (R)
	AH	224 934	100.9	98.3	106.9	85.4	99.6	233 649	109.6	112.9	110.3	110.9	131.1	306 200	AH	
Norway (N)	NH	76 895	81.0	86.1	87.8	72.3	100.4	101 916	107.7	117.3	117.6	137.3	167.5	170 685	NH	Norvège (N)
Portugal (N)	NH	587 393	77.5	79.8	86.8	76.7	97.0	672 954	111.3	100.9	110.1	118.8	122.7	825 493	NH	Portugal (N)
	AH	160 654	75.3	76.1	85.3	76.7	96.5	220 299	113.7	115.1	127.1	134.9	140.7	309 988	AH	
Spain (N)	NH	6 177 430	92.2	101.7	103.7	100.5	106.2	5 991 113	103.5	113.7	118.8	117.7			NH	Espagne (N)
	AH	1 390 083	92.7	102.5	102.9	103.0	102.2	1 347 699	115.6	124.3	128.2	129.5	112.4	1 515 138	AH	
Sweden (N)	NH	94 856	104.7	100.2	99.8	86.5	98.6	84 424	104.5	99.8	107.7	113.9	116.4	98 268	NH	Suède (N)
Switzerland (R)	NH	1 608 032	110.6	119.3	107.7	93.5	99.9	1 612 672	105.1	100.0	96.6	97.8	95.2	1 535 088	NH	Suisse (R)
	AH	523 690	110.1	119.2	109.9	91.4	100.2	530 479	106.3	102.7	101.8	105.8	106.0	562 131	AH	
Turkey (N)	NH				46.8	56.0	64.7	543 000	116.1	156.1	206.4	208.8	221.8	1 204 113	NH	Turquie (N)
	AH				43.7	54.7	64.6	297 543	116.2	152.9	182.3	220.4	212.4	631 868	AH	
Australia (R)	NH	68 200		82.5		85.4	108.3	83 600	101.7						NH	Australie (R)
Japan (N)	NH	108 153	65.4	66.4	72.3	30.1	78.8	199 251							NH	Japon (N)
	AH	43 794													AH	
Yugoslavia (N)	NH							1 087 348	92.2	86.4	74.2	74.3	65.4	711 038	NH	Yougoslavie (N)
	AH							298 815	89.0	86.3	77.2	70.0	65.1	194 531	AH	

AH Arrivals at hotels and similar establishments
NH Nights in hotels and similar establishments
(R) Tourist count by country of residence
(N) Tourist count by country of nationality

AH Arrivées dans les hôtels et les établissements assimilés
NH Nuitées dans les hôtels et établissements assimilés
(R) Recensement des touristes par pays de résidence
(N) Recensement des touristes par pays de nationalité

Table/Tableau 37

ARRIVALS AND NIGHTS OF FOREIGN TOURISTS AT/IN ALL MEANS OF ACCOMMODATION
ARRIVÉES ET NUITÉES DE TOURISTES ÉTRANGERS DANS L'ENSEMBLE DES MOYENS D'HÉBERGEMENT

From France — *En provenance de la France*

1985=100 — *1985=100*

	AAA/NAA	Volume 1979	1980	1981	1982	1983	1984	Volume 1985	1986	1987	1988	1989	1990	Volume 1990	AEH/NEH	
Austria (R)	NAA	1 410 062	64.9	77.4	86.8	74.0	95.3	2 478 962	109.0	107.6	107.0	116.9	124.1	3 076 393	NEH	Autriche (R)
	AAA	420 394	71.3	83.1	88.8	74.0	96.1	664 933	108.7	104.3	105.5	117.1	125.9	837 297	AEH	
Belgium (R)	NAA	689 299	92.4	93.4	106.3	94.7	101.2	945 197	102.9	102.9	106.9	128.0	133.6	1 262 842	NEH	Belgique (R)
Denmark (N)	NAA	147 381	99.7	102.4	107.1	79.1	103.8	143 870	91.4	95.2	96.5	99.5	103.1	148 374	NEH	Danemark (N)
Germany (R)	NAA	1 234 269	97.2	92.6	87.0	75.8	93.5	1 294 241	103.9	107.9	113.3	128.1	135.4	1 752 874	NEH	Allemagne (R)
	AAA	597 493	94.4	94.5	89.6	78.1	94.8	651 717	103.2	105.6	109.6	124.0	130.3	849 395	AEH	
Greece (N)	NAA	2 478 605	85.7	84.1	90.7	75.6	99.3	2 796 583	92.3	97.6	92.8				NEH	Grèce (N)
	AAA	800 891	87.8	84.8	93.0	75.9	101.2	876 735	95.9	97.1	90.4				AEH	
Ireland (R)	NAA	1 034 000	118.9	93.5	100.4	98.8	79.5	1 091 900	95.9	132.9	143.4	197.6	285.7	3 120 000	NEH	Irlande (R)
	AAA	94 000	87.7	96.8	97.9	85.3	91.6	95 000	94.7		116.8	145.3	208.4	198 000	AEH	
Italy (N)	NAA	8 100 546	111.2	103.3	116.3	93.1	96.9	7 234 473	104.9	99.0	94.5	87.2			NEH	Italie (N)
	AAA	2 029 789	104.5	94.5	108.5	88.7	98.1	1 983 682	103.9	106.1	105.1	102.5			AEH	
Luxembourg (R)	NAA	93 626			99.9	77.1	94.9	86 917	101.6	110.2	124.8		153.5	133 430	NEH	Luxembourg (R)
	AAA	51 066				79.2	95.0	42 490	105.8	113.3	130.5		150.7	64 039	AEH	
Netherlands (R)	NAA	559 851	109.1	106.7	108.9	86.7	102.9	566 554	103.0		109.2	118.8	140.8	797 900	NEH	Pays-Bas (R)
	AAA	307 169	104.4	102.0	107.6	86.5	102.3	319 297	103.8	.	113.8	109.5	14.6	46 500	AEH	
Portugal (N)	NAA	894 950	89.7	101.0	105.9	91.5	97.4	1 024 107	116.1	110.8	122.5	129.9	128.6	1 316 761	NEH	Portugal (N)
	AAA	246 429	81.1	84.5	94.7	83.8	97.7	337 132	122.5	124.9	135.7	143.2	146.0	492 144	AEH	
Spain (N)	NAA	6 964 144	92.9	102.4	105.4	101.7	104.9	6 750 899							NEH	Espagne (N)
	AAA	1 506 914	92.8	102.5	103.4	103.4	101.5	1 477 958							AEH	
Sweden (N)	NAA	154 318	99.5	100.8	101.8	83.2	105.6	142 773	109.8	102.8	106.0	116.7	127.8	182 423	NEH	Suède (N)
Switzerland (R)	NAA	2 392 500	110.7	121.2	115.7	97.2	99.6	2 507 600	106.2	104.0	99.4	98.6	97.0	2 432 993	NEH	Suisse (R)
	AAA	656 800	107.2	117.4	111.3	92.0	100.4	697 700	107.1	104.0	103.1	106.0	107.5	750 306	AEH	
Turkey (N)	NAA	303 627	25.4	34.2	44.2	57.1	65.5	654 137	126.4	166.9	233.7	225.8	242.5	1 586 354	NEH	Turquie (N)
	AAA	111 650	20.7	34.5	42.5	54.3	63.7	316 448	117.8	155.3	187.9	224.3	219.5	694 566	AEH	
United Kingdom (R)	NAA	12 175 000	93.6	81.6	87.3	88.1	102.0	12 793 000	95.5	130.6	109.8	126.8	132.8	16 993 000	NEH	Royaume-Uni (R)
Canada (R)	NAA	1 228 500	99.0	116.8	110.1	88.1	103.3	1 372 000	131.8	169.3	207.1	213.0			NEH	Canada (R)
	AAA	105 800	106.2	110.7	110.1	84.5	103.3	107 300	130.8	174.8	214.1	226.4			AEH	
Australia (R)	NAA	131 500		94.9		84.4	128.6	175 300	109.9						NEH	Australie (R)
Yugoslavia (N)	NAA	1 298 953	77.6	87.3	87.3	67.9	97.2	1 543 527	93.3	88.3	79.2	72.7	63.4	978 545	NEH	Yougoslavie (N)
	AAA	367 460	79.1	84.8	79.1	58.3	94.7	456 240	90.4	89.2	81.4	69.1	64.3	293 268	AEH	

AAA Arrivals in all means of accommodation
NAA Nights in all means of accommodation
(R) Tourist count by country of residence
(N) Tourist count by country of nationality

AEH Arrivées dans l'ensemble des moyens d'hébergement
NEH Nuitées dans l'ensemble des moyens d'hébergement
(R) Recensement des touristes par pays de résidence
(N) Recensement des touristes par pays de nationalité

Table/Tableau 38

ARRIVALS OF FOREIGN TOURISTS/VISITORS AT FRONTIERS
ARRIVÉES DE TOURISTES/VISITEURS ÉTRANGERS AUX FRONTIÈRES

From Italy — *En provenance de l'Italie*

1985=100 — *1985=100*

	T/V	Volume 1979	1980	1981	1982	1983	1984	Volume 1985	1986	1987	1988	1989	1990	Volume 1990	T/V	
Finland (R)	V	6 451													V	Finlande (R)
France (R)	T	1 421 000	59.0	52.5	75.6	82.9	96.1	2 646 000	105.7	119.3	130.0	198.1	213.8	5 656 000	T	France (R)
	V														V	
Greece (N)	T	264 646	54.1	61.9	61.5	90.0	90.2	364 177	120.8	127.7	149.4	156.2	170.5	620 766	T	Grèce (N)
Iceland (N)	T	811	79.9	70.2	77.2	90.0	88.6	1 170	181.1	230.7	241.2	254.8	308.9	3 614	T	Islande (N)
Norway (N)	V	7 440													V	Norvège (N)
Portugal (N)	T	45 200	54.6	56.8	65.9	65.2	71.8	82 757	109.5	145.4	167.7	202.0	228.9	189 390	T	Portugal (N)
	V	70 145	77.8	73.1	77.6	70.7	76.8	93 411	116.2	143.9	165.6	198.2	236.7	221 113	V	
Spain (N)	V	442 337	47.2	54.7	64.4	65.5	79.7	1 022 050	106.6	116.7	130.4	147.9	162.1	1 656 906	V	Espagne (N)
Turkey (N)	V	80 957	84.5	90.5	59.6	77.0	88.0	74 803	117.1	136.8	192.9	206.0	209.0	156 342	V	Turquie (N)
United Kingdom (R)	V	407 600	82.6	82.8	80.5	92.7	96.1	494 300	99.9	138.1	133.7	143.3	144.4	714 000	V	Royaume-Uni (R)
Canada (R)	T	45 600	89.9	92.4	85.3	82.8	96.4	55 200	118.1	139.7	156.3	163.9	164.7	90 900	T	Canada (R)
	V	61 400	100.9	100.9	95.4	88.3	100.6	65 200	123.5	158.7	165.0	164.7	155.1	101 100	V	
United States (R)	T	178 418	92.5	104.0	105.5	90.1	99.1	220 346	121.7	144.7	161.8	161.1	179.7	396 000	T	États-Unis (R)
Australia (R)	V	10 600	84.8	83.8	83.4	82.8	92.4	14 500	119.3	133.1	173.8	141.4	168.3	24 400	V	Australie (R)
Japan (N)	V	10 652	57.6	67.9	63.4	66.0	72.8	21 578	87.2	96.8	108.7	128.2	138.1	29 798	V	Japon (N)
New Zealand (R)	T	940	88.9	79.7	72.7	68.6	75.9	1 260	135.9	207.2	223.4	208.6	250.2	3 152	T	Nouvelle-Zélande (R)

V Visitors (travellers in Turkey)
T Tourists
(R) Tourist count by country of residence
(N) Tourist count by country of nationality

V Visiteurs (voyageurs en Turquie)
T Touristes
(R) Recensement des touristes par pays de résidence
(N) Recensement des touristes par pays de nationalité

Table/Tableau 39

ARRIVALS AND NIGHTS OF FOREIGN TOURISTS AT/IN HOTELS
ARRIVÉES ET NUITÉES DE TOURISTES ÉTRANGERS DANS L'HÔTELLERIE

From Italy — *En provenance de l'Italie*

1985=100

	AH/NH	Volume 1979	1980	1981	1982	1983	1984	Volume 1985	1986	1987	1988	1989	1990	Volume 1990	AH/NH	
Austria (R)	NH	481 297	54.3	64.3	72.4	78.3	93.9	1 084 824	121.7	134.8	170.0	224.9	247.9	2 689 615	NH	Autriche (R)
	AH	230 376	59.5	68.0	74.2	79.5	95.5	472 412	121.4	134.2	166.0	210.4	225.7	1 066 073	AH	
Belgium (R)	NH	174 110	84.7	84.1	84.2	90.7	95.0	219 867	99.1	109.0	121.1	146.4	156.7	344 602	NH	Belgique (R)
Denmark (N)	NH	66 000	98.1	110.8	107.1	104.5	103.3	78 600	99.7	112.7	132.2	138.4	161.7	127 100	NH	Danemark (N)
Finland (R)	NH	24 005	64.5	65.6	80.4	84.5	95.6	47 021	107.6	143.1	174.0	184.8	168.6	79 275	NH	Finlande (R)
France (R)[1]	NH	1 028 758	91.3	97.8	93.4	96.1	102.1	1 337 332	270.7	295.9	393.4	509.5	524.0	7 007 067	NH	France (R)[1]
	AH	377 057	85.6	97.6	91.9	91.1	97.8	487 690	331.0	361.9	451.4	606.5	638.3	3 112 773	AH	
Germany (R)	NH	712 834	75.3	78.8	82.9	86.9	95.1	1 005 754	109.4	117.0	132.3	156.6	167.9	1 689 032	NH	Allemagne (R)
	AH	366 600	74.7	77.5	82.6	86.2	94.9	524 549	108.0	116.4	132.6	156.0	167.3	877 688	AH	
Greece (N)	NH	793 905	61.5	62.3	65.7	71.4	81.4	1 382 124	97.4	100.3	119.4				NH	Grèce (N)
	AH	260 779	62.3	63.9	68.9	78.9	87.8	442 272	98.3	113.0	112.5				AH	
Ireland (R)	NH													299 000	NH	Irlande (R)
	AH													49 000	AH	
Luxembourg (R)	NH														NH	Luxembourg (R)
	AH														AH	
Netherlands (R)	NH	172 959	88.4	92.7	94.8	86.2	95.3	222 726	120.7	139.7	162.4	184.6	272.4	606 800	NH	Pays-Bas (R)
	AH	78 207	76.7	83.6	86.8	82.3	92.5	108 933	115.2	131.0	151.4	191.8	273.7	298 200	AH	
Norway (N)	NH													103 215	NH	Norvège (N)
Portugal (N)	NH	145 328	67.3	60.7	69.7	71.2	79.5	212 433	116.0	143.0	165.1	178.4	216.4	459 771	NH	Portugal (N)
	AH	44 246	58.8	55.7	64.7	70.9	79.4	81 018	116.9	146.4	166.4	181.8	216.4	175 326	AH	
Spain (N)	NH	1 013 694	26.6	35.1	44.5	58.0	87.6	4 093 160	95.1	105.4	113.6	112.1			NH	Espagne (N)
	AH	342 825	33.8	42.8	53.1	64.2	89.4	1 065 347	103.8	101.9	105.7	112.5	99.2	1 056 418	AH	
Sweden (N)	NH	53 521	76.5	79.6	86.3	82.4	92.2	76 070	103.8	125.9	126.1	154.9	162.3	123 467	NH	Suède (N)
Switzerland (R)	NH	684 499	86.1	96.2	94.9	92.2	97.7	912 714	107.1	113.6	120.2	139.0	149.5	1 364 828	NH	Suisse (R)
	AH	335 750	85.3	93.9	92.4	92.0	97.6	453 373	107.3	112.7	118.0	135.5	140.6	637 318	AH	
Turkey (N)	NH				48.8	82.1	87.6	217 034	110.4	144.8	180.3	174.4	184.7	400 878	NH	Turquie (N)
	AH				47.1	77.1	84.3	106 117	107.8	143.7	176.5	186.1	195.4	207 337	AH	
Australia (R)	NH	68 500		79.7		51.0	76.9	93 400	139.6	155.8	203.3				NH	Australie (R)
Japan (N)	NH	55 219													NH	Japon (N)
	AH	21 995													AH	
Yugoslavia (N)	NH							1 735 755	97.6	110.1	120.5	151.4	179.2	3 109 623	NH	Yougoslavie (N)
	AH							618 332	99.5	111.7	116.2	141.5	153.5	949 407	AH	

AH Arrivals at hotels and similar establishments
NH Nights in hotels and similar establishments
(R) Tourist count by country of residence
(N) Tourist count by country of nationality

AH Arrivées dans les hôtels et les établissements assimilés
NH Nuitées dans les hôtels et établissements assimilés
(R) Recensement des touristes par pays de résidence
(N) Recensement des touristes par pays de nationalité

Table/Tableau 40

ARRIVALS AND NIGHTS OF FOREIGN TOURISTS AT/IN ALL MEANS OF ACCOMMODATION
ARRIVÉES ET NUITÉES DE TOURISTES ÉTRANGERS DANS L'ENSEMBLE DES MOYENS D'HÉBERGEMENT

From Italy — *En provenance de l'Italie*

1985=100 — *1985=100*

	AAA/NAA	Volume 1979	1980	1981	1982	1983	1984	Volume 1985	1986	1987	1988	1989	1990	Volume 1990	AEH/NEH	
Austria (R)	NAA	592 030	55.6	65.7	73.5	83.2	98.5	1 264 367	120.1	133.7	165.4	220.4	244.5	3 090 858	NEH	Autriche (R)
	AAA	264 755	59.3	67.5	74.4	81.2	101.0	534 756	119.9	132.3	162.0	206.0	221.6	1 184 841	AEH	
Belgium (R)	NAA	199 829	84.3	85.7	85.2	91.2	95.9	250 002	99.1	107.8	121.7	144.5	155.0	387 409	NEH	Belgique (R)
Denmark (N)	NAA	89 230	86.1	97.4	98.2	100.1	99.3	120 841	97.4	114.0	127.0	137.9	155.3	187 630	NEH	Danemark (N)
France (R)	NAA	8 280 000	45.2	40.2	81.5	87.3	97.7	20 724 000	111.7	128.6	136.1	142.6	147.2	30 504 000	NEH	France (R)
	AAA	1 421 000	59.0	52.5	75.6	82.9	96.1	2 646 000	105.7	119.3	130.0	167.9			AEH	
Germany (R)	NAA	757 606	75.0	76.4	80.4	84.0	94.3	1 058 306	110.1	117.8	133.6	157.3	168.4	1 782 457	NEH	Allemagne (R)
	AAA	374 031	73.5	75.4	80.4	83.8	94.6	542 130	108.6	117.3	133.6	156.8	168.2	911 931	AEH	
Greece (N)	NAA	989 685	70.2	70.2	73.5	77.5	93.5	1 572 733	96.5	111.7	114.0				NEH	Grèce (N)
	AAA	330 768	70.3	69.5	75.4	85.2	94.2	508 301	97.5	70.5	107.8				AEH	
Ireland (R)	AAA													73 000	AEH	Irlande (R)
Luxembourg (R)	NAA														NEH	Luxembourg (R)
	AAA														AEH	
Netherlands (R)	NAA	226 790	85.8	88.9	92.9	90.1	100.2	297 669	112.4		155.3	179.3	257.0	765 100	NEH	Pays-Bas (R)
	AAA	101 406	75.4	81.3	86.1	84.5	96.3	145 715	107.8		146.7	178.0	248.8	362 600	AEH	
Portugal (N)	NAA	176 420	72.6	72.5	80.1	73.7	75.2	268 808	119.7	138.4	158.7	172.5	199.2	535 542	NEH	Portugal (N)
	AAA	55 644	59.8	56.1	64.6	70.0	75.0	101 808	120.0	141.1	158.8	174.9	199.7	203 320	AEH	
Spain (N)	NAA	1 013 694	26.6	35.1	44.5	58.0	87.6	4 093 160							NEH	Espagne (N)
	AAA	342 825	33.8	42.8	53.1	64.2	89.4	1 065 347							AEH	
Sweden (N)	NAA	57 295	75.0	79.5	86.0	83.4	94.5	82 968	105.7	130.4	132.9	163.7	169.9	140 935	NEH	Suède (N)
Switzerland (R)	NAA	874 700	81.2	92.1	92.6	92.9	98.2	1 227 500	107.7	114.8	123.5	140.8	155.9	1 913 407	NEH	Suisse (R)
	AAA	374 800	82.2	91.2	90.9	91.5	97.5	530 100	107.5	112.3	118.2	134.3	141.2	748 470	AEH	
Turkey (N)	NAA	101 020	30.9	46.2	46.2	80.8	87.5	236 156	111.9	160.5	208.3	207.4	226.0	533 676	NEH	Turquie (N)
	AAA	40 062	27.8	41.8	46.4	76.6	84.7	108 609	107.8	158.6	196.5	207.5	216.5	235 140	AEH	
United Kingdom (R)	NAA	6 175 000	93.3	81.2	75.0	91.4	89.2	6 963 000	88.0	132.6	122.2	118.9	120.2	8 371 000	NEH	Royaume-Uni (R)
Canada (R)	NAA	671 600	78.2	89.2	97.2	71.8	96.8	755 400	110.7	132.4	141.7	133.3			NEH	Canada (R)
Australia (R)	NAA	112 400		100.5		92.5	92.3	143 400	210.6	234.9	306.8				NEH	Australie (R)
Yugoslavia (N)	NAA	2 341 399	54.3	57.8	60.0	65.1	83.8	4 965 718	93.5	100.3	108.1	123.7	129.7	6 440 330	NEH	Yougoslavie (N)
	AAA	587 171	60.1	61.6	60.1	64.8	86.5	1 108 838	96.8	106.9	111.7	128.4	134.8	1 494 320	AEH	

AAA Arrivals in all means of accommodation
NAA Nights in all means of accommodation
(R) Tourist count by country of residence
(N) Tourist count by country of nationality

AEH Arrivées dans l'ensemble des moyens d'hébergement
NEH Nuitées dans l'ensemble des moyens d'hébergement
(R) Recensement des touristes par pays de résidence
(N) Recensement des touristes par pays de nationalité

Table/Tableau 41

ARRIVALS OF FOREIGN TOURISTS/VISITORS AT FRONTIERS
ARRIVÉES DE TOURISTES/VISITEURS ÉTRANGERS AUX FRONTIÈRES

From Japan — *En provenance du Japon*

1985=100 — *1985=100*

	T/V	Volume 1979	1980	1981	1982	1983	1984	Volume 1985	1986	1987	1988	1989	1990	Volume 1990	T/V	
Finland (R)	V	5 872													V	Finlande (R)
France (R)	T	422 000	75.8	84.3			96.6	528 000	96.2	108.3	125.4	146.0	142.0	750 000	T	France (R)
Greece (N)	T	129 050	81.5	81.0	80.6	88.4	93.2	92 802	91.7	99.1	113.1	112.1	116.0	107 694	T	Grèce (N)
Iceland (N)	T	377	51.1	47.3	53.9	63.3	75.3	716	119.7	139.7	138.7	175.1	162.6	1 164	T	Islande (N)
Italy (N)	V	383 200	104.0	78.5	90.5	97.6	101.5	335 190	119.7	114.8	114.8	136.3	190.0	636 961	V	Italie (N)
Norway (N)	V	8 819													V	Norvège (N)
Portugal (N)	T	10 800	55.4	70.7	64.0	71.4	87.5	18 394	119.7	149.9	153.3	163.6	177.6	32 665	T	Portugal (N)
	V	12 794	64.4	74.0	69.2	71.8	97.6	19 986	116.3	143.1	148.4	160.7	177.3	35 433	V	
Spain (N)	V	70 995	69.5	68.5	63.4	75.0	85.7	126 639	95.6	103.0	134.5	171.0	192.5	243 775	V	Espagne (N)
Turkey (N)	V	7 392	40.8	41.3	37.3	46.3	77.7	16 811	99.6	125.3	166.6	192.1	210.3	35 358	V	Turquie (N)
United Kingdom (R)	V	139 500	77.1	77.7	75.7	80.8	95.2	210 700	97.5	141.1	184.2	239.6	271.5	572 000	V	Royaume-Uni (R)
Canada (R)	T	120 700	84.2	77.9	78.8	80.0	92.7	145 800	135.2	170.9	222.3	265.4	282.9	412 500	T	Canada (R)
	V	158 600	93.0	84.0	79.9	79.5	93.0	174 500	134.8	178.6	231.9	265.2	271.7	474 100	V	
United States (R)	T	1 042 232	80.1	90.5	96.0	85.7	94.6	1 496 202	112.4	142.3	169.4	205.9	215.9	3 231 000	T	États-Unis (R)
Australia (R)	V	41 600	45.4	49.9	56.1	66.7	81.7	107 600	135.3	200.4	327.4	324.8	446.0	479 900	V	Australie (R)
New Zealand (R)	T	15 724	38.2	51.2	54.4	64.6	83.3	50 264	124.7	151.5	186.6	193.6	214.5	107 840	T	Nouvelle-Zélande (R)

V Visitors (travellers in Austria, Germany and Turkey)
T Tourists
(R) Tourist count by country of residence
(N) Tourist count by country of nationality
1. Estimates

V Visiteurs (voyageurs en Allemagne, en Autriche et en Turquie)
T Touristes
(R) Recensement des touristes par pays de résidence
(N) Recensement des touristes par pays de nationalité
1. Estimations

Table/Tableau 42

ARRIVALS AND NIGHTS OF FOREIGN TOURISTS AT/IN HOTELS
ARRIVÉES ET NUITÉES DE TOURISTES ÉTRANGERS DANS L'HÔTELLERIE

From Japan — *En provenance du Japon*

1985=100

	AH/NH	Volume 1979	1980	1981	1982	1983	1984	Volume 1985	1986	1987	1988	1989	1990	Volume 1990	AH/NH	
Austria (R)	NH	129 721	54.4	66.6	71.0	77.6	84.4	234 070	98.4	131.7	136.9	158.3	200.3	468 795	NH	Autriche (R)
	AH	65 571	48.9	58.2	66.9	72.3	84.7	125 598	94.4	129.8	132.3	152.9	187.7	235 705	AH	
Belgium (R)	NH		72.0	86.5	84.0	76.8	90.3	94 191	101.2	113.0	128.0	177.8	164.7	155 174	NH	Belgique (R)
Denmark (N)	NH	85 800	105.1	102.2	95.3	105.3	101.9	78 000	89.9	106.3	138.1	150.5	138.5	108 000	NH	Danemark (N)
Finland (R)	NH	22 588	51.2	51.6	54.5	83.3	94.8	44 180	87.3	116.2	126.2	137.7	144.1	63 669	NH	Finlande (R)
France (R)[1]	NH	1 175 866	117.5	112.4	109.1	111.2	104.3	1 029 780	116.1	132.9	165.7	279.1	259.8	2 675 010	NH	France (R)[1]
	AH	445 449	92.0	94.6	99.8	97.2	95.2	470 298	115.6	130.1	164.6	267.2	269.0	1 264 895	AH	
Germany (R)	NH	533 351	64.0	72.8	76.3	77.3	84.3	825 788	101.6	113.9	122.3	147.3	160.1	1 321 676	NH	Allemagne (R)
	AH	299 258	60.6	68.8	73.3	74.6	83.9	474 345	100.9	120.0	126.2	155.1	169.8	805 462	AH	
Greece (N)	NH	232 425	80.8	79.1	83.7	85.3	92.2	257 192	80.6	92.7	101.6				NH	Grèce (N)
	AH	100 039	77.6	77.7	79.4	82.8	88.7	111 180	82.6	95.0	107.8				AH	
Italy (N)	NH	529 690	76.6	81.4	92.7	99.2	101.5	583 130	112.4	161.5	197.2	246.8	269.5	1 571 358	NH	Italie (N)
	AH	254 081	80.1	79.6	89.7	94.5	101.7	277 728	116.3	170.4	206.0	254.7	273.2	758 729	AH	
Luxembourg (R)	NH														NH	Luxembourg (R)
	AH														AH	
Netherlands (R)	NH	124 218	82.7	84.5	97.5	87.0	82.6	153 138	101.7	97.2	104.5	106.2	122.2	187 100	NH	Pays-Bas (R)
	AH	63 948	79.1	85.0	100.2	85.9	91.9	77 019	95.7	102.8	108.9	109.6	125.3	96 500	AH	
Norway (N)	NH	38 768	63.4	61.3	64.7	82.3	97.8	64 365	71.5	116.7	103.7	124.4	131.3	84 495	NH	Norvège (N)
Portugal (N)	NH	28 215	62.7	68.6	66.7	72.8	100.8	49 614	107.2	130.3	145.5	147.8	154.8	76 787	NH	Portugal (N)
	AH	11 127	50.4	57.7	59.5	68.8	99.5	23 102	106.3	131.7	139.9	143.6	148.0	34 199	AH	
Spain (N)	NH	276 804	65.4	79.5	78.9	80.2	86.7	390 805	107.9	151.1	163.6	219.3			NH	Espagne (N)
	AH	124 159	57.0	67.8	65.8	69.6	83.1	205 381	113.1	159.5	173.6	229.7	242.5	498 027	AH	
Sweden (N)	NH	53 339	96.3	87.5	96.4	90.2	101.2	57 781	92.5	107.6	128.6	141.2	163.3	94 350	NH	Suède (N)
Switzerland (R)	NH	410 353	78.1	81.7	87.2	94.3	96.3	515 961	104.1	121.0	126.6	151.6	158.7	818 604	NH	Suisse (R)
	AH	230 110	73.4	77.0	82.9	90.8	95.3	294 688	106.3	125.2	135.0	160.3	168.9	497 648	AH	
Turkey (N)	NH				45.6	65.6	62.4	71 683	124.4	137.2	163.3	188.0	187.3	134 267	NH	Turquie (N)
	AH				42.3	69.2	66.9	32 956	130.7	158.1	191.3	225.0	233.8	77 046	AH	
Australia (R)	NH	184 700		31.4		59.2	85.7	635 800	114.0	168.9	276.0	311.1	457.9	2 911 580	NH	Australie (R)
Yugoslavia (N)	NH							18 331	121.7	137.3	159.6	170.1	156.2	28 640	NH	Yougoslavie (N)
	AH							9 515	114.7	133.7	153.6	157.7	155.2	14 772	AH	

AH Arrivals at hotels and similar establishments
NH Nights in hotels and similar establishments
(R) Tourist count by country of residence
(N) Tourist count by country of nationality
1. Ile de France only

AH Arrivées dans les hôtels et les établissements assimilés
NH Nuitées dans les hôtels et établissements assimilés
(R) Recensement des touristes par pays de résidence
(N) Recensement des touristes par pays de nationalité
1. Ile de France seulement

Table/Tableau 43

ARRIVALS AND NIGHTS OF FOREIGN TOURISTS AT/IN ALL MEANS OF ACCOMMODATION
ARRIVÉES ET NUITÉES DE TOURISTES ÉTRANGERS DANS L'ENSEMBLE DES MOYENS D'HÉBERGEMENT

From Japan — *En provenance du Japon*

1985=100 — *1985=100*

	AAA/NAA	Volume 1979	1980	1981	1982	1983	1984	Volume 1985	1986	1987	1988	1989	1990	Volume 1990	AEH/NEH	
Austria (R)	NAA	129 721	54.4	66.6	71.0	77.6	84.4	234 070	98.4	131.7	136.9	158.3	200.3	468 795	NEH	Autriche (R)
	AAA	65 571	48.9	58.2	66.9	72.3	84.7	125 598	94.4	129.8	132.3	152.9	187.7	235 705	AEH	
Belgium (R)	NAA		73.2	85.6	82.4	76.2	90.3	98 203	100.7	112.2	127.7	176.3	165.2	162 249	NEH	Belgique (R)
Denmark (N)	NAA													108 000	NEH	Danemark (N)
France (R)	NAA	1 850 000	43.1	84.3			97.1	3 713 000	99.5	114.4	122.3				NEH	France (R)
	AAA	422 000	75.8	84.3			96.6	528 000	96.2	108.3	125.4				AEH	
Germany (R)	NAA	553 388	63.8	70.9	74.3	75.6	84.7	852 957	101.8	114.6	123.7	148.3	161.9	1 381 195	NEH	Allemagne (R)
	AAA	302 787	59.2	67.0	71.3	72.6	84.0	488 582	101.2	120.5	127.5	156.1	172.2	841 462	AEH	
Greece (N)	NAA	236 645	82.2	80.4	86.3	86.6	93.4	257 487	80.7	92.7	101.6				NEH	Grèce (N)
	AAA	101 637	78.9	78.9	81.3	83.7	89.9	111 325	82.7	94.9	107.7				AEH	
Italy (N)	NAA	573 962	78.5	82.7	93.5	98.4	101.1	628 546	113.1	155.5	189.3	235.2			NEH	Italie (N)
	AAA	259 860	80.0	79.3	89.2	94.0	101.2	285 320	116.4	169.2	204.4	252.0			AEH	
Luxembourg (R)	NAA														NEH	Luxembourg (R)
	AAA														AEH	
Netherlands (R)	NAA	129 955	83.7	85.3	97.2	88.4	83.9	158 079	94.2		104.4	106.0	123.2	194 800	NEH	Pays-Bas (R)
	AAA	67 834	80.5	85.9	100.0	86.3	92.8	80 345	88.8		109.0	108.4	125.2	100 600	AEH	
Portugal (N)	NAA	29 670	63.6	69.4	68.1	73.2	100.5	50 620	106.7	129.8	145.8	147.6	156.8	79 364	NEH	Portugal (N)
	AAA	11 753	51.6	58.7	60.4	69.3	99.5	23 498	106.1	131.4	141.2	143.9	150.8	35 438	AEH	
Spain (N)	NAA	276 804	65.4	79.5	78.9	80.2	86.7	390 805							NEH	Espagne (N)
	AAA	124 159	57.0	67.8	65.8	69.6	83.1	205 381							AEH	
Sweden (N)	NAA	54 955	94.8	86.7	95.1	90.7	100.4	59 928	91.3	107.3	127.8	139.9	162.1	97 126	NEH	Suède (N)
Switzerland (R)	NAA	430 400	78.9	82.2	86.9	93.7	96.0	538 000	104.4	121.1	126.3	151.1	157.9	849 689	NEH	Suisse (R)
	AAA	239 400	73.9	77.3	82.5	90.3	95.0	306 900	106.3	124.7	134.5	159.5	167.8	515 073	AEH	
Turkey (N)	NAA	14 690	24.6	29.4	45.5	65.5	62.6	71 970	124.3	139.4	163.3	188.0	187.7	135 101	NEH	Turquie (N)
	AAA	6 779	23.5	26.1	42.2	69.1	66.8	33 092	130.7	160.2	191.0	224.9	234.1	77 464	AEH	
United Kingdom (R)	NAA	1 697 000	47.1	50.8	45.8	41.1	63.9	2 398 000	73.1	97.2	122.8	137.2	164.9	3 954 000	NEH	Royaume-Uni (R)
Canada (R)	NAA	870 500	95.2	97.4	92.3	79.8	109.3	928 600	164.5	189.7	240.0	273.3			NEH	Canada (R)
Australia (R)	NAA	239 900		35.8		54.2	70.7	916 100	104.4	154.6	252.7	417.7	480.0	4 397 080	NEH	Australie (R)
Yugoslavia (N)	NAA	27 041	139.2	140.5	136.3	136.6	131.2	20 082	122.5	150.2	153.1	163.9	151.3	30 385	NEH	Yougoslavie (N)
	AAA	11 359	118.3	102.9	93.3	87.1	93.1	10 042	115.8	136.6	151.6	155.8	155.4	15 602	AEH	

AAA Arrivals in all means of accommodation
NAA Nights in all means of accommodation
(R) Tourist count by country of residence
(N) Tourist count by country of nationality

AEH Arrivées dans l'ensemble des moyens d'hébergement
NEH Nuitées dans l'ensemble des moyens d'hébergement
(R) Recensement des touristes par pays de résidence
(N) Recensement des touristes par pays de nationalité

Table/Tableau 44

ARRIVALS OF FOREIGN TOURISTS/VISITORS AT FRONTIERS
ARRIVÉES DE TOURISTES/VISITEURS ÉTRANGERS AUX FRONTIÈRES

From the Netherlands — *En provenance des Pays-Bas*

1985=100 — *1985=100*

	T/V	Volume 1979	1980	1981	1982	1983	1984	Volume 1985	1986	1987	1988	1989	1990	Volume 1990	T/V	
Finland (R)	V	18 868													V	Finlande (R)
France (R)	T	3 274 000	93.6	80.2	106.4	104.1	103.1	3 655 000	109.8	107.7	110.7	109.1	109.3	3 995 000	T	France (R)
	V														V	
Greece (N)	T	141 089	64.2	60.6	49.7	54.8	68.8	280 309	117.7	123.1	138.8	152.7	176.8	495 699	T	Grèce (N)
Iceland (N)	T	1 696	111.9	94.9	103.3	91.1	97.4	1 653	139.7	146.3	171.3	152.2	181.1	2 994	T	Islande (N)
Ireland (R)	V														V	Irlande (R)
Italy (N)	V	2 013 200	110.6	92.9	106.9	102.7	106.2	1 660 220	105.0	83.6	108.6	110.9	127.8	2 122 099	V	Italie (N)
Norway (N)	V	36 469													V	Norvège (N)
Portugal (N)	T	116 200	75.4	78.0	75.4	96.5	94.2	151 350	107.9	135.5	182.0	209.3	197.5	298 941	T	Portugal (N)
	V	129 844	78.0	78.6	76.2	95.4	92.7	163 794	104.8	130.8	174.1	203.2	201.3	329 797	V	
Spain (N)	V	1 380 372	96.6	97.5	95.6	92.8	97.7	1 417 274	109.8	118.9	141.4	143.6	137.9	1 953 887	V	Espagne (N)
Turkey (N)	V	24 888	61.0	73.8	71.3	84.2	86.8	31 217	126.4	159.9	259.6	341.8	481.6	150 337	V	Turquie (N)
United Kingdom (R)	V	976 100	119.4	97.7	92.0	96.4	97.2	762 200	100.9	112.2	115.6	123.4	130.0	991 000	V	Royaume-Uni (R)
Canada (R)	T	88 700	149.0	135.4	122.6	108.4	104.1	58 400	117.5	133.4	150.7	149.8	149.0	87 000	T	Canada (R)
	V	101 000	153.4	137.6	123.9	108.0	104.5	63 900	118.5	138.5	154.8	151.5	146.0	93 300	V	
United States (R)	T	159 826	135.9	150.3	144.5	110.4	102.1	131 398	123.9	153.5	188.6	198.5	216.1	284 000	T	États-Unis (R)
Australia (R)	V	16 300	118.6	116.9	108.8	96.8	91.6	15 400	103.2	112.3	145.5	130.5	137.0	21 100	V	Australie (R)
Japan (N)	V	9 751	70.8	78.7	74.4	83.2	91.9	15 407	94.0	103.2	102.9	106.7	114.1	17 573	V	Japon (N)
New Zealand (R)	T	4 008	91.9	95.7	95.1	89.1	95.4	5 413	106.9	116.8	130.5	131.6	143.7	7 780	T	Nouvelle-Zélande (R)

V Visitors (travellers in Turkey)
T Tourists
(R) Tourist count by country of residence
(N) Tourist count by country of nationality

V Visiteurs (voyageurs en Turquie)
T Touristes
(R) Recensement des touristes par pays de résidence
(N) Recensement des touristes par pays de nationalité

Table/Tableau 45

ARRIVALS AND NIGHTS OF FOREIGN TOURISTS AT/IN HOTELS
ARRIVÉES ET NUITÉES DE TOURISTES ÉTRANGERS DANS L'HÔTELLERIE

From the Netherlands — *En provenance des Pays-Bas*

1985=100 — *1985=100*

	AH/NH	Volume 1979	1980	1981	1982	1983	1984	Volume 1985	1986	1987	1988	1989	1990	Volume 1990	AH/NH	
Austria (R)	NH	5 491 071	113.5	116.5	109.3	101.8	104.5	5 079 537	99.1	100.6	98.4	103.5	98.3	4 992 080	NH	Autriche (R)
	AH	748 571	106.2	110.2	104.2	99.3	102.1	738 637	99.2	103.4	105.1	110.8	107.7	795 641	AH	
Belgium (R)	NH	499 226	74.0	69.3	79.1	92.7	100.5	658 740	102.7	108.3	112.5	140.1	143.6	945 765	NH	Belgique (R)
Denmark (N)	NH	121 700	123.6	121.9	117.2	123.0	110.5	98 000	95.7	102.6	104.2	110.1	116.1	113 800	NH	Danemark (N)
Finland (R)	NH	50 062	119.7	104.8	89.2	91.0	109.3	40 402	91.5	103.3	114.5	129.2	136.4	55 126	NH	Finlande (R)
France (R)[1]	NH	1 233 160	140.8	121.7	107.0	105.6	111.5	756 259	255.7	270.8	301.4	320.5	308.7	2 334 752	NH	France (R)[1]
	AH	453 207	142.5	122.0	109.0	106.6	105.4	297 233	348.2	372.1	426.0	426.3	421.9	1 254 164	AH	
Germany (R)	NH	3 203 469	103.6	107.8	102.4	94.9	99.1	3 152 571	105.2	109.2	109.0	114.9	112.0	3 531 524	NH	Allemagne (R)
	AH	1 410 778	100.9	104.9	99.5	95.0	99.5	1 443 282	101.3	106.6	107.9	111.3	110.8	1 598 614	AH	
Greece (N)	NH	1 139 708	56.2	56.3	52.1	48.1	67.6	1 886 048	103.4	87.4	87.9				NH	Grèce (N)
	AH	199 048	65.8	65.6	61.6	58.0	75.9	282 008	97.3	91.9	91.4				AH	
Ireland (R)	NH													218 000	NH	Irlande (R)
	AH													40 000	AH	
Italy (N)	NH	1 966 020	168.4	121.3	124.5	113.1	92.2	1 127 807	113.8	163.2	133.6	122.3	120.6	1 359 948	NH	Italie (N)
	AH	335 333	129.7	100.0	109.2	103.2	91.8	262 342	105.8	117.2	129.8	127.4	131.5	344 882	AH	
Luxembourg (R)	NH														NH	Luxembourg (R)
	AH														AH	
Norway (N)	NH	174 916	138.9	125.9	88.4	82.1	103.6	132 908	83.4	90.8	81.1	89.0	94.8	126 030	NH	Norvège (N)
Portugal (N)	NH	1 012 551	132.1	109.3	103.0	86.4	97.3	745 545	109.4	117.6	160.3	172.9	191.7	1 428 931	NH	Portugal (N)
	AH	109 507	98.1	88.6	89.1	89.1	96.5	106 486	103.3	121.6	159.3	172.5	194.7	207 358	AH	
Spain (N)	NH	3 472 405	84.7	105.1	105.6	99.6	114.4	3 426 664	113.7	99.0	97.0	82.0			NH	Espagne (N)
	AH	437 906	93.9	101.4	99.2	95.6	98.9	435 184		102.6	102.4	94.2	74.7	324 924	AH	
Sweden (N)	NH	142 311	164.4	164.5	134.1	156.3	108.8	77 063	95.1	90.9	89.9	98.7	101.1	77 938	NH	Suède (N)
Switzerland (R)	NH	1 056 944	157.0	157.3	129.8	117.8	102.8	800 700	105.8	103.2	100.1	107.4	107.6	861 937	NH	Suisse (R)
	AH	301 510	146.1	140.5	124.2	115.8	104.3	238 697	106.2	104.1	103.7	111.7	110.7	264 285	AH	
Australia (R)	NH	69 800		98.6		75.4	73.6	72 800	83.4	90.8	117.4				NH	Australie (R)
Japan (N)	NH	49 026													NH	Japon (N)
	AH	17 708													AH	
Yugoslavia (N)	NH							1 265 852	112.3	103.4	128.3	139.5	137.5	1 740 117	NH	Yougoslavie (N)
	AH							191 608	106.0	106.6	126.5	131.6	136.9	262 349	AH	

AH Arrivals at hotels and similar establishments
NH Nights in hotels and similar establishments
(R) Tourist count by country of residence
(N) Tourist count by country of nationality
1. Ile de France only

AH Arrivées dans les hôtels et les établissements assimilés
NH Nuitées dans les hôtels et établissements assimilés
(R) Recensement des touristes par pays de résidence
(N) Recensement des touristes par pays de nationalité
1. Ile de France seulement

Table/Tableau 46

ARRIVALS AND NIGHTS OF FOREIGN TOURISTS AT/IN ALL MEANS OF ACCOMMODATION
ARRIVÉES ET NUITÉES DE TOURISTES ÉTRANGERS DANS L'ENSEMBLE DES MOYENS D'HÉBERGEMENT

From the Netherlands — *En provenance des Pays-Bas*

1985=100 — *1985=100*

	AAA/NAA	Volume 1979	1980	1981	1982	1983	1984	Volume 1985	1986	1987	1988	1989	1990	Volume 1990	AEH/NEH	
Austria (R)	NAA	9 120 101	106.4	112.7	106.0	98.6	101.9	9 176 892	100.0	101.6	101.0	105.3	99.3	9 112 348	NEH	Autriche (R)
	AAA	1 178 016	100.6	107.8	101.6	96.5	100.3	1 247 378	99.7	104.2	106.7	112.5	107.8	1 345 130	AEH	
Belgium (R)	NAA	1 976 113	60.4	60.5	88.0	97.1	97.2	3 166 687	104.9	113.5	128.5	141.6	151.7	4 805 065	NEH	Belgique (R)
Denmark (N)	NAA	620 513	87.1	102.3	115.2	132.4	108.1	670 771	89.2	80.5	75.9	78.5	76.1	510 547	NEH	Danemark (N)
France (R)	NAA	24 800 000	76.5	65.5	107.1	105.1	107.2	31 293 000	110.5	105.2	106.8	104.0	107.4	33 605 000	NEH	France (R)
	AAA	3 274 000	93.6	80.2	106.4	104.1	103.1	3 655 000	109.8	107.7	110.7	100.9			AEH	
Germany (R)	NAA	5 126 841	106.8	91.4	87.5	88.5	98.6	5 053 815	105.6	111.6	112.6	118.0	114.0	5 760 363	NEH	Allemagne (R)
	AAA	1 662 662	101.2	96.9	92.2	91.4	99.6	1 706 906	102.5	108.8	110.1	114.5	112.2	1 915 925	AEH	
Greece (N)	NAA	1 326 447	61.5	63.0	58.7	53.6	77.1	2 003 661	102.9	87.7	87.4				NEH	Grèce (N)
	AAA	249 577	73.3	72.4	69.5	63.6	84.2	319 357	97.7	91.5	90.5				AEH	
Ireland (R)	AAA													72 000	AEH	Irlande (R)
Italy (N)	NAA	5 305 496	162.7	128.4	130.7	107.3	92.8	3 320 613	110.2	102.5	107.1	97.2			NEH	Italie (N)
	AAA	600 555	131.2	106.6	113.7	101.4	92.2	483 810	108.5	114.6	121.4	115.9			AEH	
Luxembourg (R)	NAA														NEH	Luxembourg (R)
	AAA														AEH	
Portugal (N)	NAA	1 208 777	120.8	109.5	104.0	86.9	93.9	1 012 434	111.8	120.6	163.0	172.2	182.7	1 849 867	NEH	Portugal (N)
	AAA	152 006	88.1	83.9	85.7	82.1	87.3	176 387	111.0	123.7	158.6	167.4	175.6	309 771	AEH	
Sweden (N)	NAA	487 671	89.6	117.7	100.4	152.2	110.5	471 118	80.3	79.6	73.0	84.8	80.7	380 364	NEH	Suède (N)
Switzerland (R)	NAA	3 270 700	144.3	156.9	132.7	120.6	106.6	2 777 400	110.1	107.2	107.4	113.8	118.2	3 283 748	NEH	Suisse (R)
	AAA	561 800	142.0	146.0	129.9	121.1	109.3	475 400	109.3	107.7	109.1	116.9	120.1	570 985	AEH	
United Kingdom (R)	NAA	7 254 000	118.2	99.3	82.2	88.2	84.9	5 374 000	81.4	96.1	103.6	96.6	102.7	5 517 000	NEH	Royaume-Uni (R)
Canada (R)	NAA	1 362 800	138.5	134.3	126.4	109.8	104.8	916 600	105.8	119.8	131.6	125.3			NEH	Canada (R)
Australia (R)	NAA	153 900		119.3		159.4	110.1	147 000	101.0	109.9	142.3				NEH	Australie (R)
Yugoslavia (N)	NAA	1 832 537	70.7	89.2	62.4	53.4	78.3	2 898 402	104.4	99.2	124.6	120.3	107.4	3 112 254	NEH	Yougoslavie (N)
	AAA	304 841	79.3	94.4	67.0	57.6	85.2	418 771	101.9	105.9	125.1	117.1	107.7	450 850	AEH	

AAA Arrivals in all means of accommodation
NAA Nights in all means of accommodation
(R) Tourist count by country of residence
(N) Tourist count by country of nationality

AEH Arrivées dans l'ensemble des moyens d'hébergement
NEH Nuitées dans l'ensemble des moyens d'hébergement
(R) Recensement des touristes par pays de résidence
(N) Recensement des touristes par pays de nationalité

Table/Tableau 47

ARRIVALS OF FOREIGN TOURISTS/VISITORS AT FRONTIERS
ARRIVÉES DE TOURISTES/VISITEURS ÉTRANGERS AUX FRONTIÈRES

From the United Kingdom — *En provenance du Royaume-Uni*

1985=100 — *1985=100*

	T/V	Volume 1979	1980	1981	1982	1983	1984	Volume 1985	1986	1987	1988	1989	1990	Volume 1990	T/V	
Finland (R)	V	29 873													V	Finlande (R)
France (R)	T	3 274 000	59.0	61.8	102.7	101.2	93.5	5 862 000	107.5	108.6	113.4	121.0	125.3	7 346 000	T	France (R)
	V														V	
Greece (N)	T	559 657	57.8	72.6	76.9	66.9	78.5	1 329 259	128.6	149.0	134.7	122.8	123.9	1 647 361	T	Grèce (N)
Iceland (N)	T	6 761	70.7	81.1	74.9	91.2	96.7	9 720	105.6	108.8	108.3	123.4	141.4	13 743	T	Islande (N)
Ireland (R)	V		95.8	93.0	97.5	102.3	107.6	1 104 000	98.2	109.5	132.7	151.1	161.8	1 786 000	V	Irlande (R)
Italy (N)	V	1 999 000	115.5	102.0	104.2	106.7	101.0	1 770 713	115.6	112.9	102.7	107.7	115.7	2 047 838	V	Italie (N)
Norway (N)	V	131 728													V	Norvège (N)
Portugal (N)	T	306 900	49.0	58.8	67.3	73.3	84.5	755 571	131.4	150.6	140.9	136.0	140.4	1 061 136	T	Portugal (N)
	V	399 771	55.0	62.3	64.8	71.5	80.6	880 388	121.4	136.8	129.5	129.2	136.6	1 202 874	V	
Spain (N)	V	3 427 455	71.3	80.7	96.3	103.0	119.7	5 035 050	127.7	150.0	151.8	145.9	124.9	6 286 433	V	Espagne (N)
Turkey (N)	V	70 032	49.9	48.4	47.8	67.7	72.0	124 677	123.7	214.1	373.1	325.6	281.9	351 458	V	Turquie (N)
Canada (R)	T	454 900	155.9	154.5	135.6	115.7	111.5	314 000	127.2	142.2	170.6	178.7	178.2	559 400	T	Canada (R)
	V	516 400	160.3	156.7	137.4	116.2	111.6	345 100	127.3	146.8	169.7	178.2	174.6	602 400	V	
United States (R)	T	1 029 697	151.3	182.9	150.3	118.1	107.8	860 837	131.7	158.3	211.2	258.1	260.7	2 244 000	T	États-Unis (R)
Australia (R)	V	114 500	83.1	92.7	112.9	96.3	94.9	153 400	114.7	129.7	169.7	177.9	181.2	277 900	V	Australie (R)
Japan (N)	V	72 100	49.7	66.5	83.5	95.5	91.4	182 804	77.7	81.1	84.6	97.0	117.3	214 413	V	Japon (N)
New Zealand (R)	T	32 364	78.2	87.3	87.0	89.6	92.2	43 612	113.9	140.0	166.7	170.5	200.1	87 255	T	Nouvelle-Zélande (R)

V Visitors (travellers in Turkey)
T Tourists
(R) Tourist count by country of residence
(N) Tourist count by country of nationality

V Visiteurs (voyageurs en Turquie)
T Touristes
(R) Recensement des touristes par pays de résidence
(N) Recensement des touristes par pays de nationalité

Table/Tableau 48

ARRIVALS AND NIGHTS OF FOREIGN TOURISTS AT/IN HOTELS
ARRIVÉES ET NUITÉES DE TOURISTES ÉTRANGERS DANS L'HÔTELLERIE

From the United Kingdom — *En provenance du Royaume-Uni*

1985=100 — *1985=100*

	AH/NH	Volume 1979	1980	1981	1982	1983	1984	Volume 1985	1986	1987	1988	1989	1990	Volume 1990	AH/NH	
Austria (R)	NH	1 351 399	52.9	62.9	84.7	96.5	104.4	3 744 144	102.2	100.8	99.4	111.6	117.2	4 388 522	NH	Autriche (R)
	AH	316 509	64.2	68.4	85.8	95.0	105.1	697 191	96.6	95.8	94.0	107.8	117.8	821 061	AH	
Belgium (R)	NH	801 682	81.8	85.4	91.7	101.0	100.0	1 050 809	92.9	86.2	81.5	100.4	114.1	1 199 470	NH	Belgique (R)
Denmark (N)	NH	292 400	94.7	101.0	109.0	102.3	90.2	333 300	93.5	91.3	87.0	91.6	100.1	333 500	NH	Danemark (N)
Finland (R)	NH	78 472	76.2	86.5	88.7	96.1	99.8	108 258	95.5	107.7	121.7	130.5	131.3	142 102	NH	Finlande (R)
	AH														AH	
France (R)[1]	NH	1 611 868	80.4	85.2	86.4	89.3	96.6	2 171 564	271.7	263.4	311.0	409.8	504.8	10 961 596	NH	France (R)[1]
	AH	657 951	80.3	88.6	88.9	89.8	92.2	880 303	352.4	349.7	397.8	524.8	553.5	4 872 717	AH	
Germany (R)	NH	1 709 505	89.4	83.7	82.8	83.8	95.8	2 277 775	104.4	100.5	101.9	118.6	132.4	3 015 443	NH	Allemagne (R)
	AH	788 036	84.1	82.0	85.6	86.5	97.2	1 110 364	101.1	99.0	100.6	114.9	130.1	1 444 579	AH	
Greece (N)	NH	4 330 726	74.5	90.6	82.6	68.6	82.6	7 543 832	114.0	111.7	95.7				NH	Grèce (N)
	AH	655 403	85.4	96.5	87.1	73.0	84.5	920 483	106.9	107.1	95.3				AH	
Iceland (N)	NH														NH	Islande (N)
Ireland (R)	NH							1 640 000	115.5	112.5	127.9	176.9	161.1	2 642 000	NH	Irlande (R)
	AH							409 000	108.6	104.6	129.3	165.8	174.3	713 000	AH	
Italy (N)	NH	5 218 692	127.6	107.6	118.6.	120.0	104.5	4 909 986	118.2	112.8	105.6	113.6	104.5	5 128 645	NH	Italie (N)
	AH	1 027 795	114.6	101.1	109.6	111.4	102.6	1 055 445	110.8	111.8	110.1	119.9	116.3	1 227 388	AH	
Luxembourg (R)	NH					97.2	93.2	45 722	118.0	112.6	121.8		138.6	63 358	NH	Luxembourg (R)
	AH					92.7	86.6	26 295	102.3	97.5	107.2		121.7	32 003	AH	
Netherlands (R)	NH	1 010 192	81.7	88.0	95.4	86.4	93.9	1 292 137	103.3	96.8	95.2	105.1	117.8	1 521 900	NH	Pays-Bas (R)
	AH	448 276	77.8	87.6	95.4	87.9	94.3	593 348	104.4	101.3	101.8	109.4	120.8	716 800	AH	
Norway (N)	NH	280 645	69.0	75.2	71.6	66.5	95.1	449 728	81.2	77.1	74.1	75.0	75.8	340 890	NH	Norvège (N)
Portugal (N)	NH	2 148 068	54.1	60.5	66.4	72.3	79.1	4 952 228	117.7	112.5	106.4	102.9	106.2	5 260 390	NH	Portugal (N)
	AH	264 407	50.6	56.3	60.8	69.7	79.3	643 421	109.9	107.4	101.7	100.7	108.1	695 680	AH	
Spain (N)	NH	21 054 211	72.4	95.1	111.9	119.9	140.5	25 024 453	135.2	134.9	125.0	100.9			NH	Espagne (N)
	AH	2 404 910	78.7	96.5	112.8	116.8	133.5	2 779 377	135.1	134.6	124.4	107.4	79.7	2 214 403	AH	
Sweden (N)	NH	232 797	91.3	95.2	94.8	98.3	98.7	259 063	95.1	87.1	92.4	102.6	104.5	270 767	NH	Suède (N)
Switzerland (R)	NH	1 048 880	69.9	90.8	101.9	104.4	101.1	1 933 088	104.3	94.2	91.8	99.5	104.7	2 023 310	NH	Suisse (R)
	AH	353 659	80.3	97.0	102.4	103.4	103.3	531 506	101.5	97.9	98.6	106.3	113.7	604 448	AH	
Turkey (N)	NH				34.0	59.4	65.2	253 759	129.3	200.4	351.1	305.1	250.3	635 154	NH	Turquie (N)
	AH				40.7	61.4	75.4	84 624	122.0	168.3	260.6	240.8	206.4	174 624	AH	
Australia (R)	NH	369 500		45.5		78.8	78.9	748 100	149.3	168.8	227.6	205.5	285.5	2 136 000	NH	Australie (R)
Japan (N)	NH	204 695	60.1	70.1	75.6	35.4	75.9	342 267							NH	Japon (N)
	AH	79 138													AH	
Yugoslavia (N)	NH							4 733 098	104.9	115.7	113.8	112.0	115.5	5 465 406	NH	Yougoslavie (N)
	AH							545 370	103.4	113.1	110.3	104.7	108.6	592 325	AH	

AH Arrivals at hotels and similar establishments
NH Nights in hotels and similar establishments
(R) Tourist count by country of residence
(N) Tourist count by country of nationality
1. Ile de France only

AH Arrivées dans les hôtels et les établissements assimilés
NH Nuitées dans les hôtels et établissements assimilés
(R) Recensement des touristes par pays de résidence
(N) Recensement des touristes par pays de nationalité
1. Ile de France seulement

Table/Tableau 49

ARRIVALS AND NIGHTS OF FOREIGN TOURISTS AT/IN ALL MEANS OF ACCOMMODATION
ARRIVÉES ET NUITÉES DE TOURISTES ÉTRANGERS DANS L'ENSEMBLE DES MOYENS D'HÉBERGEMENT

From the United Kingdom — *En provenance du Royaume-Uni*

1985=100 — *1985=100*

	AAA/NAA	Volume 1979	1980	1981	1982	1983	1984	Volume 1985	1986	1987	1988	1989	1990	Volume 1990	AEH/NEH	
Austria (R)	NAA	1 539 042	52.2	63.4	84.1	95.9	102.5	4 232 906	101.5	100.4	99.5	111.5	116.5	4 931 102	NEH	Autriche (R)
	AAA	366 512	63.7	69.4	85.4	94.9	103.3	795 973	97.1	96.1	94.6	108.5	117.5	935 476	AEH	
Belgium (R)	NAA	980 860	90.1	90.2	94.2	102.4	101.8	1 234 696	93.2	87.5	78.9	95.9	109.4	1 350 314	NEH	Belgique (R)
Denmark (N)	NAA	357 363	96.2	104.5	111.2	105.5	93.5	407 223	92.1	88.0	85.5	88.6	97.1	395 567	NEH	Danemark (N)
France (R)	NAA	28 300 000	58.7	61.4	97.2	98.0	94.3	53 053 000	110.5	114.1	118.2	92.7	99.9	52 981 000	NEH	France (R)
	AAA	3 274 000	59.0	61.8	102.7	101.2	93.5	5 862 000	107.5	108.6	113.4	105.0			AEH	
Germany (R)	NAA	1 836 435	89.1	78.8	78.2	79.5	95.2	2 479 414	104.0	102.7	103.2	119.5	131.6	3 263 549	NEH	Allemagne (R)
	AAA	812 003	83.6	77.8	81.3	82.2	96.9	1 179 126	100.5	99.6	100.6	115.0	129.4	1 526 140	AEH	
Greece (N)	NAA	4 594 151	78.1	95.3	86.4	72.1	89.2	7 629 747	113.9	111.5	95.5				NEH	Grèce (N)
	AAA	715 426	90.9	101.7	91.7	77.2	91.9	941 264	106.9	107.0	94.9				AEH	
Ireland (R)	NAA	11 199 700	116.6	98.6	98.4	105.0	113.1	9 574 900	101.8	125.8	144.2	168.5	162.7	15 583 000	NEH	Irlande (R)
	AAA	1 076 900	95.5	90.1	92.2	93.8	100.1	1 118 800	100.7		134.8	153.4	159.5	1 785 000	AEH	
Italy (N)	NAA	6 374 163	124.9	111.2	119.8	120.5	103.8	5 992 420	118.8	147.8	102.3	106.8			NEH	Italie (N)
	AAA	1 175 170	114.5	103.9	110.7	112.2	103.0	1 192 632	112.4	112.4	110.9	119.7			AEH	
Luxembourg (R)	NAA	67 146				96.0	104.6	67 710	106.9	107.7	114.4		132.6	89 769	NEH	Luxembourg (R)
	AAA	35 734				96.5	100.6	34 607	101.3	100.4	107.6		126.7	43 863	AEH	
Netherlands (R)	NAA	1 252 233	82.7	88.2	96.2	87.3	96.4	1 581 184	97.1		95.5	106.9	121.2	1 916 700	NEH	Pays-Bas (R)
	AAA	548 470	80.3	89.3	96.8	89.0	96.3	709 580	96.1		100.2	105.8	116.7	828 200	AEH	
Portugal (N)	NAA	2 225 371	54.7	62.1	67.9	73.3	79.6	5 087 016	117.8	112.9	106.4	103.0	106.6	5 423 920	NEH	Portugal (N)
	AAA	283 255	52.1	58.4	62.7	70.8	79.8	672 342	110.0	107.8	101.6	100.8	108.1	726 768	AEH	
Spain (N)	NAA	21 353 751	72.6	95.3	111.8	119.8	140.0	25 383 099							NEH	Espagne (N)
	AAA	2 455 211	79.0	96.7	112.7	116.8	132.9	2 832 192							AEH	
Sweden (N)	NAA	349 657	98.6	119.8	102.8	102.1	100.6	345 991	96.3	87.2	90.1	98.6	97.2	336 192	NEH	Suède (N)
Switzerland (R)	NAA	1 447 200	68.5	90.2	97.6	102.7	100.0	2 734 300	106.1	97.6	94.6	99.6	101.8	2 783 192	NEH	Suisse (R)
	AAA	455 700	82.8	100.8	103.6	104.8	103.5	675 600	102.7	98.9	98.1	105.9	110.9	749 277	AEH	
Turkey (N)	NAA	99 100	23.0	31.9	33.3	59.5	63.9	265 663	132.9	223.8	369.1	316.8	254.1	675 111	NEH	Turquie (N)
	AAA	34 408	23.7	38.3	40.3	61.5	75.1	86 177	124.0	176.4	269.0	248.4	211.1	181 942	AEH	
Canada (R)	NAA	6 461 000	146.1	146.1	134.2	116.5	112.6	4 608 800	124.5	123.7	147.8	148.2			NEH	Canada (R)
	AAA	454 900	155.9	154.5	135.6	115.7	111.5	314 000	127.2	139.9	167.9	178.5			AEH	
Australia (R)	NAA	704 300		66.1		175.3	109.4	1 366 600	195.7		863.5	*****	*****	16 433 000	NEH	Australie (R)
New Zealand (R)	NAA						92.1	1 890 000	113.2	135.9	153.9	151.3	168.9	3 192 891	NEH	Nouvelle-Zélande (R)
Yugoslavia (N)	NAA	2 498 298	43.5	53.6	53.8	55.5	71.9	4 963 210	107.3	122.0	118.1	118.5	119.7	5 941 799	NEH	Yougoslavie (N)
	AAA	339 897	52.1	58.6	57.3	59.5	74.8	595 119	105.0	117.5	113.2	109.2	111.0	660 768	AEH	

AAA Arrivals in all means of accommodation
NAA Nights in all means of accommodation
(R) Tourist count by country of residence
(N) Tourist count by country of nationality

AEH Arrivées dans l'ensemble des moyens d'hébergement
NEH Nuitées dans l'ensemble des moyens d'hébergement
(R) Recensement des touristes par pays de résidence
(N) Recensement des touristes par pays de nationalité

AUSTRALIA

ARRIVALS OF FOREIGN VISITORS AT FRONTIERS[1]

(by country of residence)

	1989	Relative share	1990	Relative share	% Variation over 1989
Austria	9 200	0.4	9 600	0.4	4.3
Belgium	3 700	0.2	4 200	0.2	13.5
Denmark	10 200	0.5	9 900	0.4	-2.9
Finland	5 200	0.2	5 800	0.3	11.5
France	20 100	1.0	21 100	1.0	5.0
Germany[2]	68 100	3.3	74 200	3.4	9.0
Greece	7 400	0.4	7 500	0.3	1.4
Iceland	100	0.0	200	0.0	100.0
Ireland	12 200	0.6	10 600	0.5	-13.1
Italy	20 500	1.0	24 400	1.1	19.0
Luxembourg	300	0.0	200	0.0	-33.3
Netherlands	20 100	1.0	21 100	1.0	5.0
Norway	3 700	0.2	4 400	0.2	18.9
Portugal	1 100	0.1	1 400	0.1	27.3
Spain	3 300	0.2	4 300	0.2	30.3
Sweden	24 100	1.2	22 000	1.0	-8.7
Switzerland	27 400	1.3	29 500	1.3	7.7
Turkey	1 300	0.1	1 500	0.1	15.4
United Kingdom	272 900	13.1	277 900	12.5	1.8
Other OECD-Europe	..	..	..	..	..
Total Europe	510 900	24.6	529 800	23.9	3.7
Canada	54 200	2.6	53 700	2.4	-0.9
United States	260 700	12.5	250 700	11.3	-3.8
Total North America	314 900	15.1	304 400	13.7	-3.3
Australia	..	..	..	..	..
New Zealand	449 300	21.6	418 400	18.9	-6.9
Japan	349 500	16.8	479 900	21.7	37.3
Total Australasia and Japan	798 800	38.4	898 300	40.6	12.5
Total OECD Countries	**1 624 600**	**78.1**	**1 732 500**	**78.2**	**6.6**
Yugoslavia	6 400	0.3	5 800	0.3	-9.4
Other European countries	14 700	0.7	14 200	0.6	-3.4
Bulgaria	400	0.0	400	0.0	0.0
Czechoslovakia	1 100	0.1	1 100	0.0	0.0
Germany (D. R.)	200	0.0	100	0.0	-50.0
Hungary	1 700	0.1	1 900	0.1	11.8
Poland	4 400	0.2	3 700	0.2	-15.9
Rumania	200	0.0	600	0.0	200.0
USSR	5 200	0.2	5 300	0.2	1.9
Latin America	11 700	0.6	12 600	0.6	7.7
Argentina	2 300	0.1	2 400	0.1	4.3
Brazil	2 500	0.1	2 900	0.1	16.0
Chile	1 700	0.1	1 600	0.1	-5.9
Colombia	400	0.0	400	0.0	0.0
Mexico	1 200	0.1	1 700	0.1	41.7
Venezuela	300	0.0	200	0.0	-33.3
Asia-Oceania	403 900	19.4	428 900	19.4	6.2
China	29 100	1.4	23 700	1.1	-18.6
Hong Kong	54 100	2.6	54 500	2.5	0.7
India	10 900	0.5	11 000	0.5	0.9
Iran	900	0.0	1 500	0.1	66.7
Israel	5 400	0.3	5 300	0.2	-1.9
Republic of Korea	10 400	0.5	14 100	0.6	35.6
Lebanon	1 700	0.1	1 700	0.1	0.0
Malaysia	44 300	2.1	46 600	2.1	5.2
Pakistan	2 100	0.1	1 900	0.1	-9.5
Philippines	11 000	0.5	13 600	0.6	23.6
Saudi Arabia	1 700	0.1	2 200	0.1	29.4
Singapore	65 200	3.1	75 900	3.4	16.4
Taiwan	21 500	1.0	25 300	1.1	17.7
Thailand	17 300	0.8	19 600	0.9	13.3
Africa	17 300	0.8	18 400	0.8	6.4
Algeria	200	0.0	100	0.0	-50.0
Egypt	1 100	0.1	1 100	0.0	0.0
Morocco	100	0.0	100	0.0	0.0
South Africa	8 000	0.4	9 100	0.4	13.8
Origin country undetermined	1 700	0.1	2 500	0.1	47.1
Total non-OECD Countries	**455 700**	**21.9**	**482 400**	**21.8**	**5.9**
TOTAL	**2 080 300**	**100.0**	**2 214 900**	**100.0**	**6.5**

1. Includes a small number of "in transit" passengers who leave the port or airport, but do not necessarily stay overnight in Australia.
2. Germany includes Federal and Democratic Republics.

AUSTRALIA

NIGHTS SPENT BY FOREIGN TOURISTS IN HOTELS

(by country of residence)

	1989	Relative share	1990	Relative share	% Variation over 1989
Austria	..	..	..	..	..
Belgium	..	..	..	..	..
Denmark	..	..	..	..	..
Finland	..	..	..	..	..
France	..	..	..	..	..
Germany	550 000	4.8	..	..	..
Greece	..	..	..	..	..
Iceland	..	..	..	..	..
Ireland	..	..	..	..	..
Italy	..	..	..	..	..
Luxembourg	..	..	..	..	..
Netherlands	..	..	..	..	..
Norway	..	..	..	..	..
Portugal	..	..	..	..	..
Spain	..	..	..	..	..
Sweden[1]	345 000	3.0	..	..	..
Switzerland	..	..	..	..	..
Turkey	..	..	..	..	..
United Kingdom[2]	1 430 000	12.5	2 345 850	17.7	64.0
Other OECD-Europe	923 000	8.1	1 870 950	14.2	102.7
Total Europe[3]	3 248 000	28.5	4 216 800	31.9	29.8
Canada	399 000	3.5	..	..	..
United States[4]	2 106 000	18.5	2 911 420	22.0	38.2
Total North America	2 505 000	22.0	2 911 420	22.0	16.2
Australia	..	..	..	..	..
New Zealand	1 530 000	13.4	1 493 110	11.3	-2.4
Japan	1 978 000	17.4	2 911 580	22.0	47.2
Total Australasia and Japan	3 508 000	30.8	4 404 690	33.3	25.6
Total OECD Countries	**9 261 000**	**81.2**	**11 532 910**	**87.2**	**24.5**
Yugoslavia	..	..	..	..	..
Hong Kong	224 000	2.0	..	..	..
Malaysia	182 000	1.6	..	..	..
Singapore	336 000	2.9	..	..	..
Origin country undetermined	2 139 000	18.8	1 688 090	12.8	-21.1
Total non-OECD Countries	**2 139 000**	**18.8**	**1 688 090**	**12.8**	**-21.1**
TOTAL	**11 400 000**	**100.0**	**13 221 000**	**100.0**	**16.0**

1. Sweden includes other scandinavian countries.
2. United Kingdom includes Ireland.
3. Total Europe includes other non OECD Europe.
4. For 1990, United States includes Canada.

AUSTRALIA

NIGHTS SPENT BY FOREIGN TOURISTS IN REGISTERED TOURIST ACCOMMODATION[1]

(by country of residence)

	1989	Relative share	1990	Relative share	% Variation over 1989
Austria	..	..	..	..	..
Belgium	..	..	..	..	..
Denmark	..	..	..	..	..
Finland	..	..	..	..	..
France	..	..	..	..	..
Germany	1 500 000	5.0	..	..	..
Greece	..	..	..	..	..
Iceland	..	..	..	..	..
Ireland	..	..	..	..	..
Italy	..	..	..	..	..
Luxembourg	..	..	..	..	..
Netherlands	..	..	..	..	..
Norway	..	..	..	..	..
Portugal	..	..	..	..	..
Spain	..	..	..	..	..
Sweden[2]	1 656 000	5.5	..	..	..
Switzerland	..	..	..	..	..
Turkey	..	..	..	..	..
United Kingdom[3]	6 110 000	20.2	9 070 620	24.9	48.5
Other OECD-Europe	2 197 000	7.3	7 109 610	19.6	223.6
Total Europe[4]	11 463 000	37.9	16 180 230	44.5	41.2
Canada	1 045 000	3.5	..	..	..
United States[5]	3 780 000	12.5	5 908 470	16.3	56.3
Total North America	4 825 000	16.0	5 908 470	16.3	22.5
Australia	..	..	..	..	..
New Zealand	4 320 000	14.3	3 688 860	10.1	–14.6
Japan	3 827 000	12.7	4 397 080	12.1	14.9
Total Australasia and Japan	8 147 000	27.0	8 085 940	22.2	–0.7
Total OECD Countries	**24 435 000**	**80.9**	**30 174 640**	**83.0**	**23.5**
Yugoslavia	..	..	..	..	..
Asia-Oceania	5 040 000	16.7	6 089 000	16.7	20.8
Hong Kong	812 000	2.7	..	..	..
Malaysia	546 000	1.8	..	..	..
Singapore	488 000	1.6	..	..	..
Origin country undetermined	735 000	2.4	94 660	0.3	–87.1
Total non-OECD Countries	**5 775 000**	**19.1**	**6 183 660**	**17.0**	**7.1**
TOTAL	**30 210 000**	**100.0**	**36 358 300**	**100.0**	**20.4**

1. Covers only commercial accommodation (ie excluding stays with friends/relatives).
2. Sweden includes other scandinavian countries.
3. United Kingdom includes Ireland.
4. Total Europe includes other non OECD Europe.
5. For 1990, United States includes Canada.

AUSTRIA

ARRIVALS OF FOREIGN TOURISTS AT HOTELS

(by country of residence)

	1989	Relative share	1990	Relative share	% Variation over 1989
Austria	..	..	..	..	..
Belgium [1]	299 497	2.3	320 314	2.3	7.0
Denmark	131 820	1.0	131 655	1.0	-0.1
Finland	59 347	0.5	66 128	0.5	11.4
France	620 227	4.7	655 594	4.7	5.7
Germany	6 362 138	48.4	6 244 499	45.2	-1.8
Greece	71 365	0.5	67 674	0.5	-5.2
Iceland [2]	..	..	..	..	..
Ireland	11 363	0.1	11 243	0.1	-1.1
Italy	994 132	7.6	1 066 073	7.7	7.2
Luxembourg [1]	..	..	..	..	..
Netherlands	818 385	6.2	795 641	5.8	-2.8
Norway	59 890	0.5	65 502	0.5	9.4
Portugal	11 612	0.1	23 306	0.2	100.7
Spain	226 304	1.7	262 856	1.9	16.2
Sweden	272 574	2.1	263 681	1.9	-3.3
Switzerland	641 679	4.9	673 853	4.9	5.0
Turkey	48 823	0.4	27 960	0.2	-42.7
United Kingdom	751 581	5.7	821 061	5.9	9.2
Other OECD-Europe	..	..	..	..	..
Total Europe	11 380 737	86.5	11 497 040	83.1	1.0
Canada	72 314	0.5	83 732	0.6	15.8
United States	613 624	4.7	815 640	5.9	32.9
Total North America	685 938	5.2	899 372	6.5	31.1
Australia [3]	101 996	0.8	114 728	0.8	12.5
New Zealand [3]	..	..	..	..	..
Japan	191 980	1.5	235 705	1.7	22.8
Total Australasia and Japan	293 976	2.2	350 433	2.5	19.2
Total OECD Countries	**12 360 651**	**94.0**	**12 746 845**	**92.2**	**3.1**
Yugoslavia	112 026	0.9	184 394	1.3	64.6
Other European countries [2]	314 089	2.4	328 679	2.4	4.6
Bulgaria	11 520	0.1	10 359	0.1	-10.1
Czechoslovakia	54 487	0.4	83 702	0.6	53.6
Hungary	159 303	1.2	145 899	1.1	-8.4
Poland	49 882	0.4	43 596	0.3	-12.6
Rumania	4 587	0.0	16 675	0.1	263.5
USSR	34 310	0.3	28 448	0.2	-17.1
Latin America	77 872	0.6	78 236	0.6	0.5
Asia-Oceania	168 178	1.3	167 038	1.2	-0.7
Africa	25 628	0.2	24 955	0.2	-2.6
Origin country undetermined	95 254	0.7	297 200	2.1	212.0
Total non-OECD Countries	**793 047**	**6.0**	**1 080 502**	**7.8**	**36.2**
TOTAL	**13 153 698**	**100.0**	**13 827 347**	**100.0**	**5.1**

1. Belgium includes Luxembourg.
2. "Other European countries" includes Iceland.
3. Australia includes New Zealand.

AUSTRIA

ARRIVALS OF FOREIGN TOURISTS AT REGISTERED TOURIST ACCOMMODATION

(by country of residence)

	1989	Relative share	1990	Relative share	% Variation over 1989
Austria	..	..	..	..	..
Belgium[1]	422 431	2.3	445 673	2.3	5.5
Denmark	203 524	1.1	201 144	1.1	-1.2
Finland	59 347	0.3	66 128	0.3	11.4
France	778 415	4.3	837 297	4.4	7.6
Germany	9 666 493	53.1	9 418 695	49.5	-2.6
Greece	76 802	0.4	72 194	0.4	-6.0
Iceland[2]	..	..	..	..	..
Ireland	11 363	0.1	11 243	0.1	-1.1
Italy	1 101 380	6.1	1 184 841	6.2	7.6
Luxembourg[1]	..	..	..	..	..
Netherlands	1 403 383	7.7	1 345 130	7.1	-4.2
Norway	59 890	0.3	65 502	0.3	9.4
Portugal	11 612	0.1	23 306	0.1	100.7
Spain	226 304	1.2	262 856	1.4	16.2
Sweden	350 512	1.9	340 459	1.8	-2.9
Switzerland	744 672	4.1	782 779	4.1	5.1
Turkey	48 823	0.3	27 960	0.1	-42.7
United Kingdom	863 534	4.7	935 476	4.9	8.3
Other OECD-Europe	..	..	..	..	..
Total Europe	16 028 485	88.1	16 020 683	84.3	-0.0
Canada	89 938	0.5	103 847	0.5	15.5
United States	676 085	3.7	885 337	4.7	31.0
Total North America	766 023	4.2	989 184	5.2	29.1
Australia[3]	101 996	0.6	114 728	0.6	12.5
New Zealand[3]	..	..	..	..	..
Japan	191 980	1.1	235 705	1.2	22.8
Total Australasia and Japan	293 976	1.6	350 433	1.8	19.2
Total OECD Countries	**17 088 484**	**93.9**	**17 360 300**	**91.3**	**1.6**
Yugoslavia	131 241	0.7	217 487	1.1	65.7
Other European countries[2]	443 689	2.4	475 021	2.5	7.1
Bulgaria	14 034	0.1	11 757	0.1	-16.2
Czechoslovakia	76 862	0.4	136 488	0.7	77.6
Hungary	229 795	1.3	199 109	1.0	-13.4
Poland	82 539	0.5	77 882	0.4	-5.6
Rumania	6 149	0.0	21 337	0.1	247.0
USSR	34 310	0.2	28 448	0.1	-17.1
Latin America	77 872	0.4	78 236	0.4	0.5
Asia-Oceania	174 915	1.0	174 774	0.9	-0.1
Africa	25 628	0.1	24 955	0.1	-2.6
Origin country undetermined	259 934	1.4	680 625	3.6	161.8
Total non-OECD Countries	**1 113 279**	**6.1**	**1 651 098**	**8.7**	**48.3**
TOTAL	**18 201 763**	**100.0**	**19 011 398**	**100.0**	**4.4**

1. Belgium includes Luxembourg.
2. "Other European countries" includes Iceland.
3. Australia includes New Zealand.

AUSTRIA

NIGHTS SPENT BY FOREIGN TOURISTS IN HOTELS

(by country of residence)

	1989	Relative share	1990	Relative share	% Variation over 1989
Austria	..	..	..	..	..
Belgium[1]	1 768 233	2.9	1 868 555	3.0	5.7
Denmark	670 669	1.1	663 815	1.1	-1.0
Finland	226 838	0.4	253 043	0.4	11.6
France	2 269 067	3.7	2 372 949	3.8	4.6
Germany	35 648 584	58.0	34 019 547	55.0	-4.6
Greece	170 843	0.3	167 710	0.3	-1.8
Iceland[2]	..	..	..	..	..
Ireland	58 004	0.1	61 078	0.1	5.3
Italy	2 440 075	4.0	2 689 615	4.3	10.2
Luxembourg[1]	..	..	..	..	..
Netherlands	5 254 985	8.6	4 992 080	8.1	-5.0
Norway	194 790	0.3	228 795	0.4	17.5
Portugal	24 185	0.0	44 440	0.1	83.8
Spain	456 040	0.7	534 001	0.9	17.1
Sweden	1 077 227	1.8	1 045 470	1.7	-2.9
Switzerland	2 394 604	3.9	2 580 244	4.2	7.8
Turkey	108 755	0.2	85 293	0.1	-21.6
United Kingdom	4 177 673	6.8	4 388 522	7.1	5.0
Other OECD-Europe	..	..	..	..	..
Total Europe	56 940 572	92.7	55 995 157	90.5	-1.7
Canada	173 757	0.3	194 198	0.3	11.8
United States	1 531 322	2.5	1 959 781	3.2	28.0
Total North America	1 705 079	2.8	2 153 979	3.5	26.3
Australia[3]	237 527	0.4	262 280	0.4	10.4
New Zealand[3]	..	..	..	..	..
Japan	370 537	0.6	468 795	0.8	26.5
Total Australasia and Japan	608 064	1.0	731 075	1.2	20.2
Total OECD Countries	**59 253 715**	**96.5**	**58 880 211**	**95.1**	**-0.6**
Yugoslavia	296 273	0.5	449 691	0.7	51.8
Other European countries[2]	936 486	1.5	932 892	1.5	-0.4
Bulgaria	30 126	0.0	33 212	0.1	10.2
Czechoslovakia	131 312	0.2	192 210	0.3	46.4
Hungary	360 425	0.6	331 550	0.5	-8.0
Poland	140 764	0.2	152 322	0.2	8.2
Rumania	18 209	0.0	66 461	0.1	265.0
USSR	255 650	0.4	157 137	0.3	-38.5
Latin America	162 815	0.3	158 433	0.3	-2.7
Asia-Oceania	430 319	0.7	424 800	0.7	-1.3
Africa	102 717	0.2	99 424	0.2	-3.2
Origin country undetermined	246 084	0.4	948 161	1.5	285.3
Total non-OECD Countries	**2 174 694**	**3.5**	**3 013 401**	**4.9**	**38.6**
TOTAL	**61 428 409**	**100.0**	**61 893 612**	**100.0**	**0.8**

1. Belgium includes Luxembourg.
2. "Other European countries" includes Iceland.
3. Australia includes New Zealand.

AUSTRIA

NIGHTS SPENT BY FOREIGN TOURISTS IN REGISTERED TOURIST ACCOMMODATION

(by country of residence)

	1989	Relative share	1990	Relative share	% Variation over 1989
Austria	..	..	..	..	..
Belgium[1]	2 656 856	2.8	2 762 052	2.9	4.0
Denmark	1 014 646	1.1	1 000 770	1.1	-1.4
Finland	226 838	0.2	253 043	0.3	11.6
France	2 897 071	3.1	3 076 393	3.2	6.2
Germany	59 921 841	63.1	56 819 027	59.9	-5.2
Greece	188 901	0.2	183 728	0.2	-2.7
Iceland[2]	..	..	..	..	..
Ireland	58 004	0.1	61 078	0.1	5.3
Italy	2 786 978	2.9	3 090 858	3.3	10.9
Luxembourg[1]	..	..	..	..	..
Netherlands	9 658 807	10.2	9 112 348	9.6	-5.7
Norway	194 790	0.2	228 795	0.2	17.5
Portugal	24 185	0.0	44 440	0.0	83.8
Spain	456 040	0.5	534 001	0.6	17.1
Sweden	1 416 555	1.5	1 382 316	1.5	-2.4
Switzerland	2 940 566	3.1	3 172 139	3.3	7.9
Turkey	108 755	0.1	85 293	0.1	-21.6
United Kingdom	4 720 360	5.0	4 931 102	5.2	4.5
Other OECD-Europe	..	..	..	..	..
Total Europe	89 271 193	94.0	86 737 383	91.5	-2.8
Canada	220 697	0.2	248 783	0.3	12.7
United States	1 697 928	1.8	2 139 202	2.3	26.0
Total North America	1 918 625	2.0	2 387 985	2.5	24.5
Australia[3]	237 527	0.3	262 280	0.3	10.4
New Zealand[3]	..	..	..	..	..
Japan	370 537	0.4	468 795	0.5	26.5
Total Australasia and Japan	608 064	0.6	731 075	0.8	20.2
Total OECD Countries	**91 797 882**	**96.7**	**89 856 443**	**94.8**	**-2.1**
Yugoslavia	408 548	0.4	620 565	0.7	51.9
Other European countries[2]	1 305 333	1.4	1 366 722	1.4	4.7
Bulgaria	42 859	0.0	42 289	0.0	-1.3
Czechoslovakia	182 672	0.2	307 862	0.3	68.5
Hungary	573 604	0.6	512 596	0.5	-10.6
Poland	227 449	0.2	241 482	0.3	6.2
Rumania	23 099	0.0	105 356	0.1	356.1
USSR	255 650	0.3	157 137	0.2	-38.5
Latin America	162 815	0.2	158 433	0.2	-2.7
Asia-Oceania	453 683	0.5	453 839	0.5	0.0
Africa	102 717	0.1	99 424	0.1	-3.2
Origin country undetermined	737 523	0.8	2 232 864	2.4	202.8
Total non-OECD Countries	**3 170 619**	**3.3**	**4 931 847**	**5.2**	**55.5**
TOTAL	**94 968 501**	**100.0**	**94 788 290**	**100.0**	**-0.2**

1. Belgium includes Luxembourg.
2. "Other European countries" includes Iceland.
3. Australia includes New Zealand.

BELGIUM

NIGHTS SPENT BY FOREIGN TOURISTS IN HOTELS

(by country of residence)

	1989	Relative share	1990	Relative share	% Variation over 1989
Austria	54 406	0.8	52 739	0.8	-3.1
Belgium	..	..	..	..	..
Denmark	79 270	1.2	85 638	1.2	8.0
Finland[1]	..	..	..	..	..
France	784 345	11.9	824 150	12.0	5.1
Germany	932 731	14.2	898 645	13.1	-3.7
Greece	79 823	1.2	77 631	1.1	-2.7
Iceland[1]	..	..	..	..	..
Ireland	41 576	0.6	48 324	0.7	16.2
Italy	321 965	4.9	344 602	5.0	7.0
Luxembourg	87 955	1.3	91 219	1.3	3.7
Netherlands	922 728	14.0	945 765	13.8	2.5
Norway	50 725	0.8	59 811	0.9	17.9
Portugal	72 881	1.1	80 494	1.2	10.4
Spain	238 159	3.6	251 056	3.7	5.4
Sweden	128 775	2.0	137 442	2.0	6.7
Switzerland	100 969	1.5	98 415	1.4	-2.5
Turkey	19 717	0.3	25 268	0.4	28.2
United Kingdom	1 055 331	16.1	1 199 470	17.5	13.7
Other OECD-Europe	..	..	..	..	..
Total Europe	4 971 356	75.6	5 220 669	76.0	5.0
Canada	93 477	1.4	98 828	1.4	5.7
United States	554 027	8.4	586 137	8.5	5.8
Total North America	647 504	9.8	684 965	10.0	5.8
Australia[2]	..	..	..	..	..
New Zealand[2]	..	..	..	..	..
Japan	167 454	2.5	155 174	2.3	-7.3
Total Australasia and Japan	167 454	2.5	155 174	2.3	-7.3
Total OECD Countries	**5 786 314**	**88.0**	**6 060 808**	**88.2**	**4.7**
Yugoslavia	..	..	..	..	..
Other European countries[1]	200 565	3.1	243 822	3.5	21.6
USSR	22 997	0.3	32 227	0.5	40.1
Latin America	57 145	0.9	54 294	0.8	-5.0
Mexico[3]	34 499	0.5	31 323	0.5	-9.2
Asia-Oceania[2]	226 107	3.4	217 906	3.2	-3.6
Africa	247 144	3.8	233 148	3.4	-5.7
Origin country undetermined	57 496	0.9	63 550	0.9	10.5
Total non-OECD Countries	**788 457**	**12.0**	**812 720**	**11.8**	**3.1**
TOTAL	**6 574 771**	**100.0**	**6 873 528**	**100.0**	**4.5**

1. "Other European countries" includes Finland and Iceland.
2. "Asia-Oceania" includes Australia and New Zealand.
3. Mexico includes Central America.

BELGIUM

NIGHTS SPENT BY FOREIGN TOURISTS IN REGISTERED TOURIST ACCOMMODATION
(by country of residence)

	1989	Relative share	1990	Relative share	% Variation over 1989
Austria	64 674	0.5	65 325	0.5	1.0
Belgium	..	..	..	..	..
Denmark	104 872	0.9	115 240	0.9	9.9
Finland[1]	..	..	..	..	..
France	1 210 213	9.9	1 262 842	9.8	4.3
Germany	1 959 329	16.1	1 940 991	15.1	-0.9
Greece	82 445	0.7	82 628	0.6	0.2
Iceland[1]	..	..	..	..	..
Ireland	49 913	0.4	55 914	0.4	12.0
Italy	361 299	3.0	387 409	3.0	7.2
Luxembourg	191 093	1.6	183 047	1.4	-4.2
Netherlands	4 484 153	36.9	4 805 065	37.3	7.2
Norway	60 789	0.5	67 765	0.5	11.5
Portugal	83 242	0.7	92 908	0.7	11.6
Spain	272 359	2.2	289 430	2.2	6.3
Sweden	143 998	1.2	149 758	1.2	4.0
Switzerland	108 888	0.9	107 516	0.8	-1.3
Turkey	22 115	0.2	28 068	0.2	26.9
United Kingdom	1 183 534	9.7	1 350 314	10.5	14.1
Other OECD-Europe	..	..	..	..	..
Total Europe	10 382 916	85.3	10 984 220	85.2	5.8
Canada	105 273	0.9	113 574	0.9	7.9
United States	590 724	4.9	634 543	4.9	7.4
Total North America	695 997	5.7	748 117	5.8	7.5
Australia[2]	..	..	..	..	..
New Zealand[2]	..	..	..	..	..
Japan	173 172	1.4	162 249	1.3	-6.3
Total Australasia and Japan	173 172	1.4	162 249	1.3	-6.3
Total OECD Countries	**11 252 085**	**92.5**	**11 894 586**	**92.3**	**5.7**
Yugoslavia	..	..	..	..	..
Other European countries[1]	244 104	2.0	306 563	2.4	25.6
USSR	25 346	0.2	38 311	0.3	51.2
Latin America	63 625	0.5	60 759	0.5	-4.5
Mexico[3]	38 615	0.3	44 293	0.3	14.7
Asia-Oceania[2]	252 385	2.1	251 164	1.9	-0.5
Africa	282 681	2.3	287 442	2.2	1.7
Origin country undetermined	73 423	0.6	85 735	0.7	16.8
Total non-OECD Countries	**916 218**	**7.5**	**991 663**	**7.7**	**8.2**
TOTAL	**12 168 303**	**100.0**	**12 886 249**	**100.0**	**5.9**

1. "Other European countries" includes Finland and Iceland.
2. "Asia-Oceania" includes Australia and New Zealand.
3. Mexico includes Central America.

CANADA

ARRIVALS OF FOREIGN TOURISTS AT FRONTIERS

(by country of residence)

	1989	Relative share	1990	Relative share	% Variation over 1989
Austria	21 100	0.1	22 100	0.1	4.7
Belgium[1]	29 200	0.2	30 900	0.2	5.8
Denmark	21 300	0.1	20 300	0.1	-4.7
Finland	17 400	0.1	17 800	0.1	2.3
France[2]	242 900	1.6	259 600	1.7	6.9
Germany	262 700	1.7	255 200	1.7	-2.9
Greece	17 800	0.1	18 200	0.1	2.2
Iceland	1 200	0.0	1 100	0.0	-8.3
Ireland	17 700	0.1	19 700	0.1	11.3
Italy	90 500	0.6	90 900	0.6	0.4
Luxembourg[1]	1 600	0.0	1 500	0.0	-6.3
Netherlands	87 500	0.6	87 000	0.6	-0.6
Norway	12 200	0.1	13 600	0.1	11.5
Portugal	18 800	0.1	15 500	0.1	-17.6
Spain	20 000	0.1	24 500	0.2	22.5
Sweden	30 900	0.2	29 600	0.2	-4.2
Switzerland	73 800	0.5	75 100	0.5	1.8
Turkey	2 900	0.0	3 600	0.0	24.1
United Kingdom	561 200	3.7	559 400	3.7	-0.3
Other OECD-Europe	..	..	..	..	..
Total Europe	1 530 700	10.1	1 545 600	10.2	1.0
Canada	..	..	..	..	..
United States	12 184 000	80.6	12 267 000	80.6	0.7
Total North America	12 184 000	80.6	12 267 000	80.6	0.7
Australia[4]	109 700	0.7	112 300	0.7	2.4
New Zealand	39 300	0.3	37 300	0.2	-5.1
Japan	387 000	2.6	412 500	2.7	6.6
Total Australasia and Japan	536 000	3.5	562 100	3.7	4.9
Total OECD Countries	**14 250 700**	**94.3**	**14 374 700**	**94.4**	**0.9**
Yugoslavia	15 300	0.1	13 000	0.1	-15.0
Other European countries	73 100	0.5	87 700	0.6	20.0
Bulgaria[1]	1 000	0.0	2 100	0.0	110.0
Czechoslovakia	8 300	0.1	10 500	0.1	26.5
Hungary	9 600	0.1	8 900	0.1	-7.3
Poland	33 600	0.2	31 400	0.2	-6.5
Rumania[1]	1 500	0.0	2 800	0.0	86.7
USSR	19 400	0.1	24 900	0.2	28.4
Latin America[3]	166 300	1.1	163 900	1.1	-1.4
Argentina	28 700	0.2	30 100	0.2	4.9
Brazil	32 200	0.2	33 600	0.2	4.3
Chile	6 700	0.0	6 400	0.0	-4.5
Colombia	7 000	0.0	5 500	0.0	-21.4
Mexico	63 200	0.4	63 900	0.4	1.1
Venezuela	8 700	0.1	11 100	0.1	27.6
Asia-Oceania	439 300	2.9	447 500	2.9	1.9
China[6]	27 900	0.2	25 600	0.2	-8.2
Hong Kong	117 900	0.8	125 100	0.8	6.1
India[1]	53 000	0.4	46 300	0.3	-12.6
Iran[1]	3 500	0.0	4 100	0.0	17.1
Israel	60 700	0.4	56 600	0.4	-6.8
Republic of Korea[1]	30 600	0.2	39 800	0.3	30.1
Lebanon	4 300	0.0	3 800	0.0	-11.6
Malaysia[1]	16 500	0.1	15 800	0.1	-4.2
Pakistan[1]	9 600	0.1	8 800	0.1	-8.3
Philippines[1]	20 100	0.1	20 800	0.1	3.5
Saudi Arabia[1]	8 100	0.1	7 800	0.1	-3.7
Singapore[1]	18 300	0.1	18 600	0.1	1.6
Taiwan	33 600	0.2	39 300	0.3	17.0
Thailand[1]	8 400	0.1	9 800	0.1	16.7
Africa	46 900	0.3	49 700	0.3	6.0
Algeria[1]	1 900	0.0	1 400	0.0	-26.3
Egypt[1]	5 600	0.0	5 400	0.0	-3.6
Morocco[1]	4 600	0.0	5 200	0.0	13.0
South Africa	10 700	0.1	11 300	0.1	5.6
Origin country undetermined[5]	119 400	0.8	84 000	0.6	-29.6
Total non-OECD Countries	**860 300**	**5.7**	**845 800**	**5.6**	**-1.7**
TOTAL[1]	15 111 000	100.0	15 220 500	100.0	0.7

1. Estimate.
2. France includes Andorra and Monaco.
3. Latin America includes South America, Central America and Mexico.
4. Australia includes Papua New Guinea, Solomon, Caroline and Christmas islands.
5. Origin country undetermined includes Bermuda, Caribbean, Greenland and St. Pierre and Miquelon.
6. China includes Mongolia and Tibet.

CANADA

ARRIVALS OF FOREIGN VISITORS AT FRONTIERS

(by country of residence)

	1989	Relative share	1990	Relative share	% Variation over 1989
Austria	24 800	0.1	23 500	0.1	-5.2
Belgium[1]	30 500	0.1	32 500	0.1	6.6
Denmark	24 600	0.1	21 900	0.1	-11.0
Finland	19 400	0.1	19 000	0.1	-2.1
France[2]	261 800	0.7	275 700	0.7	5.3
Germany	308 500	0.8	290 500	0.8	-5.8
Greece	19 300	0.1	19 500	0.1	1.0
Iceland	1 500	0.0	1 200	0.0	-20.0
Ireland	19 800	0.1	20 900	0.1	5.6
Italy	107 400	0.3	101 100	0.3	-5.9
Luxembourg[1]	1 700	0.0	1 500	0.0	-11.8
Netherlands	96 800	0.3	93 300	0.2	-3.6
Norway	13 600	0.0	14 500	0.0	6.6
Portugal	18 300	0.0	16 000	0.0	-12.6
Spain	24 400	0.1	27 000	0.1	10.7
Sweden	35 600	0.1	31 200	0.1	-12.4
Switzerland	81 700	0.2	79 700	0.2	-2.4
Turkey	3 200	0.0	3 900	0.0	21.9
United Kingdom	614 800	1.6	602 400	1.6	-2.0
Other OECD-Europe	..	..	..	..	..
Total Europe	1 707 700	4.5	1 675 300	4.4	-1.9
Canada	..	..	..	..	..
United States	34 705 100	91.4	34 734 100	91.4	0.1
Total North America	34 705 100	91.4	34 734 100	91.4	0.1
Australia[4]	120 300	0.3	122 300	0.3	1.7
New Zealand	42 600	0.1	39 500	0.1	-7.3
Japan	462 700	1.2	474 100	1.2	2.5
Total Australasia and Japan	625 600	1.6	635 900	1.7	1.6
Total OECD Countries	**37 038 400**	**97.5**	**37 045 300**	**97.5**	**0.0**
Yugoslavia	16 000	0.0	13 500	0.0	-15.6
Other European countries	81 100	0.2	89 800	0.2	10.7
Bulgaria[1]	1 000	0.0	2 100	0.0	110.0
Czechoslovakia	8 600	0.0	11 100	0.0	29.1
Hungary	9 900	0.0	9 100	0.0	-8.1
Poland	34 400	0.1	32 200	0.1	-6.4
Rumania[1]	1 600	0.0	3 000	0.0	87.5
USSR	19 600	0.1	25 100	0.1	28.1
Latin America[3]	189 800	0.5	190 700	0.5	0.5
Argentina	29 900	0.1	30 900	0.1	3.3
Brazil	34 000	0.1	35 500	0.1	4.4
Chile	7 100	0.0	6 800	0.0	-4.2
Colombia	8 000	0.0	6 300	0.0	-21.3
Mexico	72 800	0.2	71 000	0.2	-2.5
Venezuela	9 500	0.0	11 400	0.0	20.0
Asia-Oceania	485 800	1.3	488 000	1.3	0.5
China[6]	30 900	0.1	28 200	0.1	-8.7
Hong Kong	123 100	0.3	129 600	0.3	5.3
India[1]	63 100	0.2	54 600	0.1	-13.5
Iran[1]	3 600	0.0	4 200	0.0	16.7
Israel	69 500	0.2	63 700	0.2	-8.3
Republic of Korea[1]	35 600	0.1	41 700	0.1	17.1
Lebanon	4 900	0.0	4 400	0.0	-10.2
Malaysia[1]	19 100	0.1	19 600	0.1	2.6
Pakistan[1]	10 800	0.0	10 000	0.0	-7.4
Philippines[1]	22 200	0.1	23 000	0.1	3.6
Saudi Arabia[1]	8 600	0.0	8 100	0.0	-5.8
Singapore[1]	19 500	0.1	19 800	0.1	1.5
Taiwan	35 900	0.1	41 000	0.1	14.2
Thailand[1]	9 300	0.0	10 700	0.0	15.1
Africa	48 500	0.1	51 000	0.1	5.2
Algeria[1]	2 000	0.0	1 400	0.0	-30.0
Egypt[1]	5 900	0.0	5 600	0.0	-5.1
Morocco[1]	4 700	0.0	5 200	0.0	10.6
South Africa	11 100	0.0	11 700	0.0	5.4
Origin country undetermined[5]	122 400	0.3	111 500	0.3	-8.9
Total non-OECD Countries	**943 600**	**2.5**	**944 500**	**2.5**	**0.1**
TOTAL[1]	37 982 000	100.0	37 989 800	100.0	0.0

1. Estimate.
2. France includes Andorra and Monaco.
3. Latin America includes South America, Central America and Mexico.
4. Australia includes Papua New Guinea, Solomon, Caroline and Christmas islands.
5. Origin country undetermined includes Bermuda, Caribbean, Greenland and St. Pierre and Miquelon.
6. China includes Mongolia and Tibet.

CANADA

NIGHTS SPENT BY FOREIGN TOURISTS IN TOURIST ACCOMMODATION[1]

(by country of residence)

	1988	Relative share	1989	Relative share	% Variation over 1988
Austria	308 600	0.3	240 700	0.3	-22.0
Belgium	311 200	0.3	342 500	0.4	10.1
Denmark	233 100	0.3	268 100	0.3	15.0
Finland	141 300	0.2	163 400	0.2	15.6
France	2 841 800	3.1	2 922 100	3.2	2.8
Germany	3 580 900	3.9	3 247 300	3.6	-9.3
Greece	382 500	0.4	352 100	0.4	-7.9
Iceland	17 700	0.0	10 700	0.0	-39.5
Ireland	239 000	0.3	261 400	0.3	9.4
Italy	1 070 600	1.2	1 006 700	1.1	-6.0
Luxembourg	17 400	0.0	20 500	0.0	17.8
Netherlands	1 206 600	1.3	1 148 800	1.3	-4.8
Norway	143 500	0.2	119 400	0.1	-16.8
Portugal	356 700	0.4	329 700	0.4	-7.6
Spain	248 000	0.3	203 200	0.2	-18.1
Sweden	277 400	0.3	259 400	0.3	-6.5
Switzerland	929 600	1.0	923 300	1.0	-0.7
Turkey	64 500	0.1	67 600	0.1	4.8
United Kingdom	6 813 500	7.4	6 831 200	7.6	0.3
Other OECD-Europe	..	..	..	..	..
Total Europe	19 183 900	20.9	18 718 100	20.8	-2.4
Canada	..	..	..	..	..
United States	56 201 900	61.1	53 598 000	59.5	-4.6
Total North America	56 201 900	61.1	53 598 000	59.5	-4.6
Australia	1 154 000	1.3	1 269 600	1.4	10.0
New Zealand	427 600	0.5	420 100	0.5	-1.8
Japan	2 229 000	2.4	2 538 300	2.8	13.9
Total Australasia and Japan	3 810 600	4.1	4 228 000	4.7	11.0
Total OECD Countries	**79 196 400**	**86.2**	**76 544 100**	**85.0**	**-3.3**
Yugoslavia	458 300	0.5	349 200	0.4	-23.8
Other European countries	3 107 100	3.4	3 253 000	3.6	4.7
Bulgaria	18 200	0.0	25 800	0.0	41.8
Czechoslovakia	295 700	0.3	250 200	0.3	-15.4
Germany (D. R.)	49 900	0.1	31 200	0.0	-37.5
Hungary	234 100	0.3	198 800	0.2	-15.1
Poland	2 050 900	2.2	2 081 300	2.3	1.5
Rumania	38 800	0.0	17 100	0.0	-55.9
USSR	386 900	0.4	617 100	0.7	59.5
Latin America[2]	1 820 800	2.0	1 857 200	2.1	2.0
Mexico[2]	513 600	0.6	626 800	0.7	22.0
Asia-Oceania	4 760 300	5.2	5 620 600	6.2	18.1
China	564 900	0.6	913 800	1.0	61.8
Hong Kong	1 047 400	1.1	1 509 100	1.7	44.1
India	942 400	1.0	823 700	0.9	-12.6
Israel	508 000	0.6	593 200	0.7	16.8
Lebanon	61 300	0.1	65 300	0.1	6.5
Taiwan	205 800	0.2	260 600	0.3	26.6
Africa	785 600	0.9	795 500	0.9	1.3
South Africa	168 600	0.2	127 600	0.1	-24.3
Origin country undetermined	1 783 400	1.9	1 612 000	1.8	-9.6
Total non-OECD Countries	**12 715 500**	**13.8**	**13 487 500**	**15.0**	**6.1**
TOTAL	**91 911 900**	**100.0**	**90 031 600**	**100.0**	**-2.0**

1. Covers all forms of accommodation, including homes of friends or relatives.
2. Latin America includes Mexico.

DENMARK

NIGHTS SPENT BY FOREIGN TOURISTS IN HOTELS

(by country of nationality)

	1989	Relative share	1990	Relative share	% Variation over 1989
Austria[1]	..	..	..	..	..
Belgium[1]	..	..	..	..	..
Denmark	..	..	..	..	..
Finland	118 500	2.4	128 600	2.4	8.5
France	79 000	1.6	82 500	1.5	4.4
Germany	1 072 800	22.0	1 288 200	23.7	20.1
Greece[1]	..	..	..	..	..
Iceland[1]	..	..	..	..	..
Ireland[1]	..	..	..	..	..
Italy	108 800	2.2	127 100	2.3	16.8
Luxembourg[1]	..	..	..	..	..
Netherlands	107 900	2.2	113 800	2.1	5.5
Norway	679 300	13.9	709 800	13.1	4.5
Portugal[1]	..	..	..	..	..
Spain[1]	..	..	..	..	..
Sweden	1 268 100	25.9	1 477 500	27.2	16.5
Switzerland[1]	..	..	..	..	..
Turkey[1]	..	..	..	..	..
United Kingdom	305 400	6.2	333 500	6.1	9.2
Other OECD-Europe	263 500	5.4	277 900	5.1	5.5
Total Europe	4 003 300	81.9	4 538 900	83.6	13.4
Canada[2]	..	..	..	..	..
United States	414 800	8.5	399 500	7.4	-3.7
Total North America	414 800	8.5	399 500	7.4	-3.7
Australia[2]	..	..	..	..	..
New Zealand[2]	..	..	..	..	..
Japan	117 400	2.4	108 000	2.0	-8.0
Total Australasia and Japan	117 400	2.4	108 000	2.0	-8.0
Total OECD Countries	**4 535 500**	**92.8**	**5 046 400**	**92.9**	**11.3**
Yugoslavia	..	..	..	..	..
Origin country undetermined[2]	351 600	7.2	383 000	7.1	8.9
Total non-OECD Countries	**351 600**	**7.2**	**383 000**	**7.1**	**8.9**
TOTAL	**4 887 100**	**100.0**	**5 429 400**	**100.0**	**11.1**

1. Included in "Other European countries".
2. Included in "Origin country undetermined".

DENMARK

NIGHTS SPENT BY FOREIGN TOURISTS IN REGISTERED TOURIST ACCOMMODATION

(by country of nationality)

	1989	Relative share	1990	Relative share	% Variation over 1989
Austria	..	..	..	..	..
Belgium	..	..	..	..	..
Denmark	..	..	..	..	..
Finland	202 368	2.4	225 555	2.4	11.5
France	143 151	1.7	148 374	1.6	3.6
Germany	3 008 205	35.1	3 353 577	35.9	11.5
Greece	..	..	..	..	..
Iceland	..	..	..	..	..
Ireland	..	..	..	..	..
Italy	166 631	1.9	187 630	2.0	12.6
Luxembourg	..	..	..	..	..
Netherlands	526 481	6.1	510 547	5.5	-3.0
Norway	979 755	11.4	1 023 492	11.0	4.5
Portugal	..	..	..	..	..
Spain	..	..	..	..	..
Sweden	1 851 645	21.6	2 128 437	22.8	14.9
Switzerland	..	..	..	..	..
Turkey	..	..	..	..	..
United Kingdom	360 629	4.2	395 567	4.2	9.7
Other OECD-Europe	359 618	4.2	391 508	4.2	8.9
Total Europe	7 598 483	88.6	8 364 687	89.6	10.1
Canada[2]	..	..	..	..	..
United States	436 274	5.1	421 281	4.5	-3.4
Total North America	436 274	5.1	421 281	4.5	-3.4
Australia[2]	..	..	..	..	..
New Zealand[2]	..	..	..	..	..
Japan[3]	117 400	1.4	108 000	1.2	-8.0
Total Australasia and Japan	117 400	1.4	108 000	1.2	-8.0
Total OECD Countries	**8 152 157**	**95.1**	**8 893 968**	**95.2**	**9.1**
Yugoslavia	..	..	..	..	..
Origin country undetermined[2]	422 210	4.9	444 067	4.8	5.2
Total non-OECD Countries[1]	422 210	4.9	444 067	4.8	5.2
TOTAL	**8 574 367**	**100.0**	**9 338 035**	**100.0**	**8.9**

1. Includes nights spent by foreign tourists from Member countries.
2. Included in "Origin country undetermined".
3. Includes only nights spent in hotels.

FINLAND

NIGHTS SPENT BY FOREIGN TOURISTS IN HOTELS

(by country of residence)

	1989	Relative share	1990	Relative share	% Variation over 1989
Austria	26 239	1.0	24 272	1.0	-7.5
Belgium	17 080	0.7	15 168	0.6	-11.2
Denmark	77 147	3.1	75 211	3.0	-2.5
Finland	..	..	..	..	..
France	71 269	2.8	83 691	3.4	17.4
Germany	353 506	14.0	338 261	13.7	-4.3
Greece [1]	..	..	..	..	..
Iceland	6 325	0.3	7 036	0.3	11.2
Ireland [2]	..	..	..	..	..
Italy	86 910	3.5	79 275	3.2	-8.8
Luxembourg [1]	..	..	..	..	..
Netherlands	52 189	2.1	55 126	2.2	5.6
Norway	115 563	4.6	99 228	4.0	-14.1
Portugal [3]	..	..	..	..	..
Spain [3]	32 510	1.3	32 962	1.3	1.4
Sweden	584 866	23.2	518 101	21.0	-11.4
Switzerland	76 152	3.0	72 498	2.9	-4.8
Turkey [1]	..	..	..	..	..
United Kingdom [2]	141 265	5.6	142 102	5.8	0.6
Other OECD-Europe	..	..	..	..	..
Total Europe	1 641 021	65.2	1 542 931	62.5	-6.0
Canada	33 223	1.3	32 056	1.3	-3.5
United States	202 452	8.0	197 318	8.0	-2.5
Total North America	235 675	9.4	229 374	9.3	-2.7
Australia	..	..	..	..	..
New Zealand	..	..	..	..	..
Japan	60 855	2.4	63 669	2.6	4.6
Total Australasia and Japan	60 855	2.4	63 669	2.6	4.6
Total OECD Countries	**1 937 551**	**77.0**	**1 835 974**	**74.4**	**-5.2**
Yugoslavia	..	..	..	..	..
Other European countries [1]	438 185	17.4	425 246	17.2	-3.0
Bulgaria [4]	12 788	0.5	17 117	0.7	33.9
Czechoslovakia	15 224	0.6	13 893	0.6	-8.7
Germany (D. R.)	22 813	0.9	..	..	..
Hungary	20 450	0.8	16 816	0.7	-17.8
Poland	22 453	0.9	21 602	0.9	-3.8
USSR	313 549	12.5	355 818	14.4	13.5
Origin country undetermined [5]	141 564	5.6	206 912	8.4	46.2
Total non-OECD Countries	**579 749**	**23.0**	**632 158**	**25.6**	**9.0**
TOTAL	**2 517 300**	**100.0**	**2 468 132**	**100.0**	**-2.0**

1. "Other European countries" includes Greece, Luxembourg and Turkey.
2. United Kingdom includes Ireland.
3. Spain includes Portugal.
4. Bulgaria includes Rumania.
5. "Origin country undetermined" includes Latin America, Asia-Oceania and Africa.

FRANCE

ARRIVALS OF FOREIGN TOURISTS AT FRONTIERS[1]

(by country of residence)

	1989	Relative share	1990	Relative share	% Variation over 1989
Austria	..	..	..	..	..
Belgium[3]	..	..	..	..	..
Denmark	..	..	..	..	..
Finland[2]	..	..	..	..	..
France	..	..	..	..	..
Germany	10 593 000	21.4	12 097 000	22.8	14.2
Greece[5]	..	..	..	..	..
Iceland[2]	..	..	..	..	..
Ireland[4]	..	..	..	..	..
Italy	5 242 000	10.6	5 656 000	10.6	7.9
Luxembourg[3]	..	..	..	..	..
Netherlands	3 987 000	8.0	3 995 000	7.5	0.2
Norway[2]	..	..	..	..	..
Portugal[5]	..	..	..	..	..
Spain	3 014 000	6.1	3 207 000	6.0	6.4
Sweden[2]	..	..	..	..	..
Switzerland	..	..	..	..	..
Turkey[5]	..	..	..	..	..
United Kingdom[4]	7 091 000	14.3	7 346 000	13.8	3.6
Other OECD-Europe[5]	..	..	..	..	..
Total Europe	29 927 000	60.4	32 301 000	60.8	7.9
Canada	..	..	..	..	..
United States	2 167 000	4.4	2 072 000	3.9	-4.4
Total North America	2 167 000	4.4	2 072 000	3.9	-4.4
Australia[6]	..	..	..	..	..
New Zealand[6]	..	..	..	..	..
Japan	771 000	1.6	750 000	1.4	-2.7
Total Australasia and Japan	771 000	1.6	750 000	1.4	-2.7
Total OECD Countries	**32 865 000**	**66.3**	**35 123 000**	**66.1**	**6.9**
Yugoslavia[7]	..	..	..	..	..
Origin country undetermined	16 679 000	33.7	18 034 000	33.9	8.1
Total non-OECD Countries	**16 679 000**	**33.7**	**18 034 000**	**33.9**	**8.1**
TOTAL	**49 544 000**	**100.0**	**53 157 000**	**100.0**	**7.3**

1. Estimates of number of "trips", the same person coming perhaps several times in one year.
2. Sweden includes Iceland, Finland and Norway.
3. Belgium includes Luxembourg.
4. United Kingdom includes Ireland.
5. "Other OECD-Europe" includes Cyprus, Greece, Portugal and Turkey.
6. Australia includes New Zealand and Oceania.
7. "Other European countries" includes Yugoslavia.
8. Latin America includes Central America.
9. Asia only.

FRANCE[1]

ARRIVALS OF FOREIGN TOURISTS AT HOTELS

(by country of residence)

	1989	Relative share	1990	Relative share	% Variation over 1989
Austria[4]	..	..	..	..	..
Belgium[2]	1 610 110	6.6	1 655 391	6.4	2.8
Denmark[4]	..	..	..	..	..
Finland[4]	..	..	..	..	..
France	..	..	..	..	..
Germany	3 802 239	15.6	3 944 278	15.3	3.7
Greece[4]	..	..	..	..	..
Iceland[4]	..	..	..	..	..
Ireland[3]	..	..	..	..	..
Italy	2 957 751	12.2	3 112 773	12.1	5.2
Luxembourg[2]	..	..	..	..	..
Netherlands	1 267 183	5.2	1 254 164	4.9	–1.0
Norway[4]	..	..	..	..	..
Portugal[4]	..	..	..	..	..
Spain	1 300 930	5.4	1 391 514	5.4	7.0
Sweden[4]	..	..	..	..	..
Switzerland	1 089 470	4.5	1 107 120	4.3	1.6
Turkey[4]	..	..	..	..	..
United Kingdom[3]	4 619 462	19.0	4 872 717	18.9	5.5
Other OECD-Europe[4]	1 281 373	5.3	1 461 552	5.7	14.1
Total Europe	17 928 518	73.8	18 799 509	72.9	4.9
Canada	431 044	1.8	472 754	1.8	9.7
United States	2 310 428	9.5	2 468 889	9.6	6.9
Total North America	2 741 472	11.3	2 941 643	11.4	7.3
Australia[5]	173 651	0.7	180 759	0.7	4.1
New Zealand[5]	..	..	..	..	..
Japan	1 256 708	5.2	1 264 895	4.9	0.7
Total Australasia and Japan	1 430 359	5.9	1 445 654	5.6	1.1
Total OECD Countries	**22 100 349**	**90.9**	**23 186 806**	**90.0**	**4.9**
Yugoslavia	..	..	..	..	..
Latin America[6]	341 860	1.4	343 099	1.3	0.4
Asia-Oceania[7]	558 380	2.3	593 968	2.3	6.4
Africa	526 994	2.2	519 123	2.0	–1.5
Origin country undetermined	778 010	3.2	1 131 212	4.4	45.4
Total non-OECD Countries	**2 205 244**	**9.1**	**2 587 402**	**10.0**	**17.3**
TOTAL	**24 305 593**	**100.0**	**25 774 208**	**100.0**	**6.0**

1. Data covering all France except 3 regions(Pays de la Loire, Champagne-Ardennes and Corse).
2. Belgium includes Luxembourg.
3. United Kingdom includes Ireland.
4. "Other OECD-Europe" includes Austria, Denmark, Greece, Iceland, Finland, Norway, Portugal, Sweden , Turkey, USSR and Socialist countries of Eastern Europe.
5. Australia includes New Zealand and Oceania.
6. Latin America includes Central America.
7. Asia only.

FRANCE[1]

NIGHTS SPENT BY FOREIGN TOURISTS IN HOTELS

(by country of residence)

	1989	Relative share	1990	Relative share	% Variation over 1989
Austria[4]	..	..	..	..	..
Belgium[2]	3 417 824	6.6	3 498 661	6.3	2.4
Denmark[4]	..	..	..	..	..
Finland[4]	..	..	..	..	..
France	..	..	..	..	..
Germany	7 590 805	14.7	7 953 923	14.2	4.8
Greece[4]	..	..	..	..	..
Iceland[4]	..	..	..	..	..
Ireland[3]	..	..	..	..	..
Italy	6 813 470	13.2	7 007 067	12.5	2.8
Luxembourg[2]	..	..	..	..	..
Netherlands	2 423 976	4.7	2 334 752	4.2	-3.7
Norway[4]	..	..	..	..	..
Portugal[4]	..	..	..	..	..
Spain	2 430 695	4.7	2 764 800	4.9	13.7
Sweden[4]	..	..	..	..	..
Switzerland	2 294 221	4.4	2 346 506	4.2	2.3
Turkey[4]	..	..	..	..	..
United Kingdom[3]	8 899 962	17.2	10 961 596	19.6	23.2
Other OECD-Europe[4]	3 128 695	6.1	3 682 712	6.6	17.7
Total Europe	36 999 648	71.6	40 550 017	72.5	9.6
Canada	955 551	1.8	1 032 776	1.8	8.1
United States	5 235 825	10.1	5 672 261	10.1	8.3
Total North America	6 191 376	12.0	6 705 037	12.0	8.3
Australia[5]	382 198	0.7	408 044	0.7	6.8
New Zealand[5]	..	..	..	..	..
Japan	2 873 924	5.6	2 675 010	4.8	-6.9
Total Australasia and Japan	3 256 122	6.3	3 083 054	5.5	-5.3
Total OECD Countries	**46 447 146**	**89.8**	**50 338 108**	**90.0**	**8.4**
Yugoslavia	..	..	..	..	..
Latin America[6]	894 698	1.7	902 754	1.6	0.9
Asia-Oceania[7]	1 411 103	2.7	1 444 525	2.6	2.4
Africa	1 425 234	2.8	1 357 807	2.4	-4.7
Origin country undetermined	1 526 595	3.0	1 890 959	3.4	23.9
Total non-OECD Countries	**5 257 630**	**10.2**	**5 596 045**	**10.0**	**6.4**
TOTAL	**51 704 776**	**100.0**	**55 934 153**	**100.0**	**8.2**

1. Data covering all France except 3 regions(Pays de la Loire, Champagne-Ardennes and Corse).
2. Belgium includes Luxembourg.
3. United Kingdom includes Ireland.
4. "Other OECD-Europe" includes Austria, Denmark, Finland, Greece, Iceland, Norway, Portugal, Sweden , Turkey, USSR and Socialist countries of Eastern Europe.
5. Australia includes New Zealand and Oceania.
6. Latin America includes Central America.
7. Asia only.

FRANCE

NIGHTS SPENT BY FOREIGN TOURISTS IN TOURIST ACCOMMODATION[1]

(by country of residence)

	1989	Relative share	1990	Relative share	% Variation over 1989
Austria	3 153 000	1.0	3 146 000	0.9	-0.2
Belgium[3]	37 141 000	11.4	38 208 000	11.3	2.9
Denmark	3 963 000	1.2	4 102 000	1.2	3.5
Finland[2]	794 000	0.2	843 000	0.2	6.2
France	..	..	..	..	..
Germany	62 032 000	19.1	64 022 000	18.9	3.2
Greece[5]	1 205 000	0.4	1 305 000	0.4	8.3
Iceland[2]	..	..	..	..	..
Ireland[4]	..	..	..	..	..
Italy	29 561 000	9.1	30 504 000	9.0	3.2
Luxembourg[3]	..	..	..	..	..
Netherlands	32 543 000	10.0	33 605 000	9.9	3.3
Norway[2]	1 323 000	0.4	1 393 000	0.4	5.3
Portugal[5]	3 453 000	1.1	3 419 000	1.0	-1.0
Spain	9 929 000	3.1	10 113 000	3.0	1.9
Sweden[2]	4 016 000	1.2	4 171 000	1.2	3.9
Switzerland	22 361 000	6.9	22 797 000	6.7	1.9
Turkey[5]	..	..	..	..	..
United Kingdom[4]	49 158 000	15.1	52 981 000	15.6	7.8
Other OECD-Europe[5]	..	..	..	..	..
Total Europe	260 632 000	80.2	270 609 000	79.8	3.8
Canada	5 221 000	1.6	5 513 000	1.6	5.6
United States	17 787 000	5.5	18 689 000	5.5	5.1
Total North America	23 008 000	7.1	24 202 000	7.1	5.2
Australia[6]	..	..	..	..	..
New Zealand[6]	..	..	..	..	..
Japan	..	..	..	..	..
Total Australasia and Japan	..	..	..	..	..
Total OECD Countries	**283 640 000**	**87.3**	**294 811 000**	**86.9**	**3.9**
Yugoslavia[7]	..	..	..	..	..
Other European countries[7]	3 217 000	1.0	3 391 000	1.0	5.4
Latin America[8]	3 397 000	1.0	3 542 000	1.0	4.3
Asia-Oceania[9]	9 217 000	2.8	9 767 000	2.9	6.0
Africa	25 401 000	7.8	27 752 000	8.2	9.3
Algeria	13 284 000	4.1	14 605 000	4.3	9.9
Morocco	4 603 000	1.4	4 984 000	1.5	8.3
Total non-OECD Countries	**41 232 000**	**12.7**	**44 452 000**	**13.1**	**7.8**
TOTAL	**324 872 000**	**100.0**	**339 263 000**	**100.0**	**4.4**

1. The figures for 1988 are based on an update of the findings of the 1982 frontier survey while 1989 figures are based on the 1989 frontier survey; change of coverage between the two surveys.
2. Sweden includes Finland, Iceland and Norway.
3. Belgium includes Luxembourg.
4. United Kingdom includes Ireland.
5. "Other OECD-Europe" includes Cyprus, Greece, Portugal and Turkey.
6. Australia includes New Zealand and Oceania.
7. "Other European countries" includes Yugoslavia.
8. Latin America includes Central America.
9. Asia only.

GERMANY[1]

ARRIVALS OF FOREIGN TOURISTS AT HOTELS[2]

(by country of residence)

	1989	Relative share	1990	Relative share	% Variation over 1989
Austria	524 250	3.9	534 216	3.7	1.9
Belgium	449 240	3.3	461 318	3.2	2.7
Denmark	610 795	4.5	619 911	4.3	1.5
Finland	178 531	1.3	196 786	1.4	10.2
France	725 665	5.4	760 774	5.3	4.8
Germany	..		..		..
Greece	117 415	0.9	123 462	0.9	5.2
Iceland	23 633	0.2	22 002	0.2	-6.9
Ireland	31 977	0.2	34 748	0.2	8.7
Italy	818 386	6.1	877 688	6.1	7.2
Luxembourg	62 948	0.5	66 983	0.5	6.4
Netherlands	1 606 800	11.9	1 598 614	11.1	-0.5
Norway	298 117	2.2	296 761	2.1	-0.5
Portugal	43 409	0.3	45 869	0.3	5.7
Spain	282 019	2.1	301 900	2.1	7.0
Sweden	905 677	6.7	968 834	6.7	7.0
Switzerland	675 360	5.0	710 690	4.9	5.2
Turkey	82 704	0.6	91 779	0.6	11.0
United Kingdom	1 276 221	9.5	1 444 579	10.0	13.2
Other OECD-Europe	..	..	..	..	..
Total Europe	8 713 147	64.7	9 156 914	63.5	5.1
Canada	171 013	1.3	187 001	1.3	9.3
United States	1 963 587	14.6	2 308 179	16.0	17.5
Total North America	2 134 600	15.9	2 495 180	17.3	16.9
Australia	96 694	0.7	105 369	0.7	9.0
New Zealand	14 212	0.1	15 257	0.1	7.4
Japan	735 657	5.5	805 462	5.6	9.5
Total Australasia and Japan	846 563	6.3	926 088	6.4	9.4
Total OECD Countries	**11 694 310**	**86.8**	**12 578 182**	**87.2**	**7.6**
Yugoslavia	184 336	1.4	226 048	1.6	22.6
Other European countries	500 771	3.7	465 670	3.2	-7.0
Bulgaria	19 363	0.1	20 283	0.1	4.8
Czechoslovakia	68 525	0.5	93 007	0.6	35.7
Germany (D. R.)	117 001	0.9	..	..	..
Hungary	92 788	0.7	98 902	0.7	6.6
Poland	122 419	0.9	127 345	0.9	4.0
Rumania	12 238	0.1	25 934	0.2	111.9
USSR	68 437	0.5	100 199	0.7	46.4
Latin America	135 051	1.0	140 850	1.0	4.3
Argentina	23 927	0.2	26 301	0.2	9.9
Brazil	70 637	0.5	69 053	0.5	-2.2
Chile	8 607	0.1	8 655	0.1	0.6
Mexico	31 880	0.2	36 841	0.3	15.6
Asia-Oceania	119 061	0.9	117 635	0.8	-1.2
Israel	119 061	0.9	117 635	0.8	-1.2
Africa	43 994	0.3	43 080	0.3	-2.1
South Africa	43 994	0.3	43 080	0.3	-2.1
Origin country undetermined	789 261	5.9	849 569	5.9	7.6
Total non-OECD Countries	**1 772 474**	**13.2**	**1 842 852**	**12.8**	**4.0**
TOTAL	**13 466 784**	**100.0**	**14 421 034**	**100.0**	**7.1**

1. The data relate to the territory of the Federal Republic of Germany prior to 3rd October 1990; as of 1990, tourists from the former German Democratic Republic will be regarded as domestic tourists.
2. Arrivals at hotels (including "bed and breakfast"), boarding houses and inns.

GERMANY[1]

ARRIVALS OF FOREIGN TOURISTS AT REGISTERED TOURIST ACCOMMODATION[2]

(by country of residence)

	1989	Relative share	1990	Relative share	% Variation over 1989
Austria	545 392	3.7	555 146	3.6	1.8
Belgium	488 986	3.3	505 724	3.2	3.4
Denmark	680 758	4.6	690 983	4.4	1.5
Finland	192 145	1.3	211 811	1.4	10.2
France	808 102	5.5	849 395	5.4	5.1
Germany	..	..	..	..	..
Greece	121 274	0.8	127 189	0.8	4.9
Iceland	27 525	0.2	24 507	0.2	-11.0
Ireland	41 063	0.3	40 992	0.3	-0.2
Italy	850 151	5.8	911 931	5.8	7.3
Luxembourg	67 242	0.5	73 483	0.5	9.3
Netherlands	1 954 574	13.3	1 915 925	12.3	-2.0
Norway	311 482	2.1	314 131	2.0	0.9
Portugal	46 647	0.3	49 436	0.3	6.0
Spain	298 568	2.0	320 687	2.1	7.4
Sweden	942 251	6.4	1 007 987	6.5	7.0
Switzerland	706 668	4.8	743 299	4.8	5.2
Turkey	87 912	0.6	97 086	0.6	10.4
United Kingdom	1 355 507	9.3	1 526 140	9.8	12.6
Other OECD-Europe	..	..	..	..	..
Total Europe	9 526 247	65.0	9 965 852	63.8	4.6
Canada	195 312	1.3	214 145	1.4	9.6
United States	2 067 317	14.1	2 428 067	15.5	17.5
Total North America	2 262 629	15.4	2 642 212	16.9	16.8
Australia	132 574	0.9	143 503	0.9	8.2
New Zealand	21 614	0.1	21 436	0.1	-0.8
Japan	762 554	5.2	841 462	5.4	10.3
Total Australasia and Japan	916 742	6.3	1 006 401	6.4	9.8
Total OECD Countries	**12 705 618**	**86.7**	**13 614 465**	**87.1**	**7.2**
Yugoslavia	193 807	1.3	234 417	1.5	21.0
Other European countries	590 990	4.0	537 648	3.4	-9.0
Bulgaria	20 437	0.1	21 991	0.1	7.6
Czechoslovakia	78 141	0.5	107 751	0.7	37.9
Germany (D. R.)	150 675	1.0	..	..	..
Hungary	105 873	0.7	111 617	0.7	5.4
Poland	149 405	1.0	154 415	1.0	3.4
Rumania	12 597	0.1	28 261	0.2	124.3
USSR	73 862	0.5	113 613	0.7	53.8
Latin America	151 114	1.0	158 032	1.0	4.6
Argentina	27 076	0.2	29 543	0.2	9.1
Brazil	78 720	0.5	78 239	0.5	-0.6
Chile	10 697	0.1	10 196	0.1	-4.7
Mexico	34 621	0.2	40 054	0.3	15.7
Asia-Oceania	126 107	0.9	124 760	0.8	-1.1
Israel	126 107	0.9	124 760	0.8	-1.1
Africa	48 001	0.3	49 258	0.3	2.6
South Africa	48 001	0.3	49 258	0.3	2.6
Origin country undetermined	837 564	5.7	908 278	5.8	8.4
Total non-OECD Countries	**1 947 583**	**13.3**	**2 012 393**	**12.9**	**3.3**
TOTAL	**14 653 201**	**100.0**	**15 626 858**	**100.0**	**6.6**

1. The data relate to the territory of the Federal Republic of Germany prior to 3rd October 1990; as of 1990, tourists from the former German Democratic Republic will be regarded as domestic tourists.
2. Arrivals at hotels and similar establishments, holiday villages, sanatoria and recreation and holiday homes.

GERMANY[1]

NIGHTS SPENT BY FOREIGN TOURISTS IN HOTELS[2]

(by country of residence)

	1989	Relative share	1990	Relative share	% Variation over 1989
Austria	1 067 356	3.8	1 099 101	3.7	3.0
Belgium	1 014 032	3.6	1 049 860	3.5	3.5
Denmark	1 106 644	3.9	1 136 133	3.8	2.7
Finland	323 638	1.1	353 954	1.2	9.4
France	1 393 211	4.9	1 467 218	4.9	5.3
Germany	..	..	..	..	..
Greece	279 034	1.0	301 582	1.0	8.1
Iceland	52 988	0.2	49 133	0.2	-7.3
Ireland	78 038	0.3	84 489	0.3	8.3
Italy	1 575 388	5.5	1 689 032	5.7	7.2
Luxembourg	172 057	0.6	181 833	0.6	5.7
Netherlands	3 621 722	12.8	3 531 524	11.9	-2.5
Norway	502 629	1.8	488 571	1.6	-2.8
Portugal	104 335	0.4	114 959	0.4	10.2
Spain	569 378	2.0	612 458	2.1	7.6
Sweden	1 405 096	4.9	1 532 032	5.1	9.0
Switzerland	1 389 021	4.9	1 441 737	4.8	3.8
Turkey	221 728	0.8	242 253	0.8	9.3
United Kingdom	2 700 956	9.5	3 015 443	10.1	11.6
Other OECD-Europe	..	..	..	..	..
Total Europe	17 577 251	61.9	18 391 312	61.8	4.6
Canada	356 156	1.3	378 723	1.3	6.3
United States	3 982 998	14.0	4 444 619	14.9	11.6
Total North America	4 339 154	15.3	4 823 342	16.2	11.2
Australia	193 181	0.7	209 208	0.7	8.3
New Zealand	29 824	0.1	32 331	0.1	8.4
Japan	1 216 423	4.3	1 321 676	4.4	8.7
Total Australasia and Japan	1 439 428	5.1	1 563 215	5.3	8.6
Total OECD Countries	**23 355 833**	**82.3**	**24 777 869**	**83.2**	**6.1**
Yugoslavia	461 009	1.6	525 638	1.8	14.0
Other European countries	1 750 682	6.2	1 485 272	5.0	-15.2
Bulgaria	57 907	0.2	58 330	0.2	0.7
Czechoslovakia	172 654	0.6	236 193	0.8	36.8
Germany (D. R.)	376 971	1.3	..	..	..
Hungary	244 851	0.9	257 990	0.9	5.4
Poland	617 665	2.2	495 669	1.7	-19.8
Rumania	40 016	0.1	88 794	0.3	121.9
USSR	240 618	0.8	348 296	1.2	44.8
Latin America	325 352	1.1	336 544	1.1	3.4
Argentina	60 020	0.2	67 214	0.2	12.0
Brazil	169 503	0.6	165 972	0.6	-2.1
Chile	23 030	0.1	21 999	0.1	-4.5
Mexico	72 799	0.3	81 359	0.3	11.8
Asia-Oceania	338 622	1.2	323 528	1.1	-4.5
Israel	338 622	1.2	323 528	1.1	-4.5
Africa	105 914	0.4	109 385	0.4	3.3
South Africa	105 914	0.4	109 385	0.4	3.3
Origin country undetermined	2 051 321	7.2	2 207 995	7.4	7.6
Total non-OECD Countries	**5 032 900**	**17.7**	**4 988 362**	**16.8**	**-0.9**
TOTAL	**28 388 733**	**100.0**	**29 766 231**	**100.0**	**4.9**

1. The data relate to the territory of the Federal Republic of Germany prior to 3rd October 1990; as of 1990, tourists from the former German Democratic Republic will be regarded as domestic tourists.
2. Nights spent in hotels (including "bed and breakfast"), boarding houses and inns.

GERMANY[1]

NIGHTS SPENT BY FOREIGN TOURISTS IN REGISTERED TOURIST ACCOMMODATION[2]

(by country of residence)

	1989	Relative share	1990	Relative share	% Variation over 1989
Austria	1 138 589	3.4	1 174 296	3.4	3.1
Belgium	1 208 753	3.6	1 257 479	3.6	4.0
Denmark	1 404 417	4.2	1 433 058	4.1	2.0
Finland	354 274	1.1	382 995	1.1	8.1
France	1 657 966	4.9	1 752 874	5.0	5.7
Germany	..	..	..	..	..
Greece	291 574	0.9	316 083	0.9	8.4
Iceland	82 718	0.2	63 323	0.2	-23.4
Ireland	96 854	0.3	97 366	0.3	0.5
Italy	1 664 890	5.0	1 782 457	5.1	7.1
Luxembourg	196 940	0.6	223 486	0.6	13.5
Netherlands	5 963 364	17.8	5 760 363	16.5	-3.4
Norway	530 269	1.6	526 147	1.5	-0.8
Portugal	118 387	0.4	132 796	0.4	12.2
Spain	620 440	1.8	665 608	1.9	7.3
Sweden	1 499 421	4.5	1 626 785	4.7	8.5
Switzerland	1 513 276	4.5	1 575 520	4.5	4.1
Turkey	240 380	0.7	265 330	0.8	10.4
United Kingdom	2 963 561	8.8	3 263 549	9.4	10.1
Other OECD-Europe	..	..	..	..	..
Total Europe	21 546 073	64.2	22 299 515	64.0	3.5
Canada	404 892	1.2	428 709	1.2	5.9
United States	4 230 468	12.6	4 714 849	13.5	11.4
Total North America	4 635 360	13.8	5 143 558	14.8	11.0
Australia	249 411	0.7	271 047	0.8	8.7
New Zealand	40 971	0.1	41 748	0.1	1.9
Japan	1 265 140	3.8	1 381 195	4.0	9.2
Total Australasia and Japan	1 555 522	4.6	1 693 990	4.9	8.9
Total OECD Countries	**27 736 955**	**82.6**	**29 137 063**	**83.6**	**5.0**
Yugoslavia	496 349	1.5	562 697	1.6	13.4
Other European countries	2 274 906	6.8	1 892 265	5.4	-16.8
Bulgaria	61 017	0.2	63 835	0.2	4.6
Czechoslovakia	194 084	0.6	271 044	0.8	39.7
Germany (D. R.)	523 749	1.6	..	..	..
Hungary	276 507	0.8	295 330	0.8	6.8
Poland	911 084	2.7	755 832	2.2	-17.0
Rumania	43 378	0.1	96 911	0.3	123.4
USSR	265 087	0.8	409 313	1.2	54.4
Latin America	362 851	1.1	374 108	1.1	3.1
Argentina	67 050	0.2	73 928	0.2	10.3
Brazil	189 329	0.6	186 654	0.5	-1.4
Chile	28 211	0.1	25 450	0.1	-9.8
Mexico	78 261	0.2	88 076	0.3	12.5
Asia-Oceania	367 848	1.1	355 016	1.0	-3.5
Israel	367 848	1.1	355 016	1.0	-3.5
Africa	116 331	0.3	123 631	0.4	6.3
South Africa	116 331	0.3	123 631	0.4	6.3
Origin country undetermined	2 222 315	6.6	2 396 759	6.9	7.8
Total non-OECD Countries	**5 840 600**	**17.4**	**5 704 476**	**16.4**	**-2.3**
TOTAL	**33 577 555**	**100.0**	**34 841 539**	**100.0**	**3.8**

1. The data relate to the territory of the Federal Republic of Germany prior to 3rd October 1990; as of 1990, tourists from the former German Democratic Republic will be regarded as domestic tourists.
2. Nights spent in hotels and similar establishments, holiday villages, sanatoria, and recreation and holiday homes.

GREECE

ARRIVALS OF FOREIGN TOURISTS AT FRONTIERS[1]

(by country of nationality)

	1989	Relative share	1990	Relative share	% Variation over 1989
Austria	268 000	3.3	286 525	3.2	6.9
Belgium[2]	163 000	2.0	201 807	2.3	23.8
Denmark	316 000	3.9	281 598	3.2	-10.9
Finland	255 000	3.2	238 020	2.7	-6.7
France	478 000	5.9	565 407	6.4	18.3
Germany	1 655 000	20.5	1 922 029	21.7	16.1
Greece	..	..	..	..	..
Iceland[3]	..	..	..	..	..
Ireland	63 000	0.8	67 835	0.8	7.7
Italy	569 000	7.0	620 766	7.0	9.1
Luxembourg[2]	..	..	..	..	..
Netherlands	428 000	5.3	495 699	5.6	15.8
Norway	69 000	0.9	91 755	1.0	33.0
Portugal	36 000	0.4	27 408	0.3	-23.9
Spain	103 000	1.3	127 516	1.4	23.8
Sweden	261 000	3.2	259 669	2.9	-0.5
Switzerland	139 000	1.7	151 695	1.7	9.1
Turkey	43 000	0.5	43 406	0.5	0.9
United Kingdom	1 632 000	20.2	1 647 361	18.6	0.9
Other OECD-Europe	..	..	..	..	..
Total Europe	6 478 000	80.2	7 028 496	79.2	8.5
Canada	79 000	1.0	74 218	0.8	-6.1
United States	279 000	3.5	273 849	3.1	-1.8
Total North America	358 000	4.4	348 067	3.9	-2.8
Australia	114 000	1.4	101 142	1.1	-11.3
New Zealand[4]	14 000	0.2	12 948	0.1	-7.5
Japan	104 000	1.3	107 694	1.2	3.6
Total Australasia and Japan	232 000	2.9	221 784	2.5	-4.4
Total OECD Countries	**7 068 000**	**87.5**	**7 598 347**	**85.6**	**7.5**
Yugoslavia	369 000	4.6	580 733	6.5	57.4
Other European countries[3]	314 317	3.9	445 164	5.0	41.6
Bulgaria	73 622	0.9	133 767	1.5	81.7
Czechoslovakia	18 445	0.2	28 766	0.3	56.0
Hungary	54 167	0.7	60 692	0.7	12.0
Poland	67 770	0.8	61 073	0.7	-9.9
Rumania	6 853	0.1	11 258	0.1	64.3
USSR	23 996	0.3	40 956	0.5	70.7
Latin America	69 210	0.9	..	..	..
Argentina	6 105	0.1	4 506	0.1	-26.2
Brazil	15 348	0.2	11 313	0.1	-26.3
Mexico	8 482	0.1	6 264	0.1	-26.1
Asia-Oceania[4]	160 790	2.0	165 321	1.9	2.8
Iran	5 007	0.1	4 451	0.1	-11.1
Israel	36 338	0.4	32 772	0.4	-9.8
Lebanon	33 931	0.4	23 836	0.3	-29.8
Africa	100 534	1.2	83 745	0.9	-16.7
Egypt	30 419	0.4	23 056	0.3	-24.2
South Africa	20 274	0.3	19 982	0.2	-1.4
Total non-OECD Countries	**1 013 851**	**12.5**	**1 274 963**	**14.4**	**25.8**
TOTAL	**8 081 851**	**100.0**	**8 873 310**	**100.0**	**9.8**

1. Excluding Greek nationals residing abroad and cruise passengers.
2. Belgium includes Luxembourg.
3. "Other European countries" includes Iceland.
4. "Asia-Oceania" includes New Zealand.

IRELAND

ARRIVALS OF FOREIGN VISITORS AT FRONTIERS[1]

(by country of residence)

	1989	Relative share	1990	Relative share	% Variation over 1989
Austria[4]	..	..	..	..	..
Belgium[4]	..	..	..	..	..
Denmark[4]	..	..	..	..	..
Finland[4]	..	..	..	..	..
France	136 000	5.0	196 000	6.4	44.1
Germany	151 000	5.5	172 000	5.6	13.9
Greece[4]	..	..	..	..	..
Iceland[4]	..	..	..	..	..
Ireland	..	..	..	..	..
Italy[4]	..	..	..	..	..
Luxembourg[4]	..	..	..	..	..
Netherlands[4]	..	..	..	..	..
Norway[4]	..	..	..	..	..
Portugal[4]	..	..	..	..	..
Spain[4]	..	..	..	..	..
Sweden[4]	..	..	..	..	..
Switzerland[4]	..	..	..	..	..
Turkey[4]	..	..	..	..	..
United Kingdom	1 668 000	61.1	1 786 000	58.2	7.1
Other OECD-Europe[4]	251 000	9.2	362 000	11.8	44.2
Total Europe	2 206 000	80.7	2 516 000	82.0	14.1
Canada	37 000	1.4	38 000	1.2	2.7
United States	380 000	13.9	396 000	12.9	4.2
Total North America	417 000	15.3	434 000	14.1	4.1
Australia[2]	59 000	2.2	66 000	2.2	11.9
New Zealand[2]	..	..	..	..	..
Japan[3]	..	..	..	..	..
Total Australasia and Japan	59 000	2.2	66 000	2.2	11.9
Total OECD Countries	**2 682 000**	**98.2**	**3 016 000**	**98.3**	**12.5**
Yugoslavia	..	..	..	..	..
Origin country unspecified[3]	50 000	1.8	52 000	1.7	4.0
Total non-OECD Countries	**50 000**	**1.8**	**52 000**	**1.7**	**4.0**
TOTAL	**2 732 000**	**100.0**	**3 068 000**	**100.0**	**12.3**

1. Visitors arrivals on overseas routes only.
2. Australia includes New Zealand.
3. Origin country unspecified includes Japan.
4. Included in Other OECD-Europe.

IRELAND

ARRIVALS OF FOREIGN TOURISTS AT HOTELS

(by country of residence)

	1989	Relative share	1990	Relative share	% Variation over 1989
Austria	..	..	..	..	..
Belgium	..	..	20 000	1.2	..
Denmark	17 000	1.1	..	..	..
Finland	..	..	..	..	..
France	77 000	5.1	130 000	7.9	68.8
Germany	87 000	5.8	96 000	5.8	10.3
Greece	..	..	..	..	..
Iceland	..	..	..	..	..
Ireland	..	..	..	..	..
Italy	..	..	49 000	3.0	..
Luxembourg	..	..	..	..	..
Netherlands	33 000	2.2	40 000	2.4	21.2
Norway	..	..	..	..	..
Portugal	..	..	..	..	..
Spain	..	..	..	..	..
Sweden	..	..	..	..	..
Switzerland	..	..	32 000	1.9	..
Turkey	..	..	..	..	..
United Kingdom [1]	678 000	45.0	713 000	43.2	5.2
Other OECD-Europe	..	..	..	..	..
Total Europe	892 000	59.3	1 080 000	65.4	21.1
Canada	37 000	2.5	21 000	1.3	-43.2
United States	378 000	25.1	374 000	22.6	-1.1
Total North America	415 000	27.6	395 000	23.9	-4.8
Australia	..	..	..	..	..
New Zealand [2]	198 000	13.2	177 000	10.7	-10.6
Japan	..	..	..	..	..
Total Australasia and Japan	198 000	13.2	177 000	10.7	-10.6
Total OECD Countries	**1 505 000**	**100.0**	**1 652 000**	**100.0**	**9.8**
Yugoslavia	..	..	..	..	..
TOTAL	**1 505 000**	**100.0**	**1 652 000**	**100.0**	**9.8**

1. Excludes Northern Ireland.
2. New Zealand includes all others countries not specified.

IRELAND

NIGHTS SPENT BY FOREIGN TOURISTS IN HOTELS

(by country of residence)

	1989	Part relative	1990	Part relative	Variation en % par rapport à 1989
Autriche	..	..	..	..	..
Belgique	..	..	91 000	1.2	..
Danemark	86 000	1.2	..	..	..
Finlande	..	..	..	..	..
France	470 000	6.3	943 000	12.1	100.6
Allemagne	564 000	7.6	795 000	10.2	41.0
Grèce	..	..	..	..	..
Islande	..	..	..	..	..
Irlande	..	..	..	..	..
Italie	..	..	299 000	3.8	..
Luxembourg	..	..	..	..	..
Pays-Bas	200 000	2.7	218 000	2.8	9.0
Norvège	..	..	..	..	..
Portugal	..	..	..	..	..
Espagne	..	..	..	..	..
Suède	..	..	..	..	..
Suisse	..	..	187 000	2.4	..
Turquie	..	..	..	..	..
United Kingdom[1]	2 901 000	39.0	2 642 000	33.8	-8.9
Autres OCDE-Europe	..	..	..	..	..
Total Europe	4 221 000	56.8	5 175 000	66.2	22.6
Canada	254 000	3.4	108 000	1.4	-57.5
États-Unis	1 948 000	26.2	2 040 000	26.1	4.7
Total Amérique du Nord	2 202 000	29.6	2 148 000	27.5	-2.5
Australie	..	..	..	..	..
New Zealand[2]	1 011 000	13.6	500 000	6.4	-50.5
Japon	..	..	..	..	..
Total Australasie et Japon	1 011 000	13.6	500 000	6.4	-50.5
Total Pays OCDE	**7 434 000**	**100.0**	**7 823 000**	**100.0**	**5.2**
Yougoslavie	..	..	..	..	..
TOTAL	**7 434 000**	**100.0**	**7 823 000**	**100.0**	**5.2**

1. Excludes Northern Ireland.
2. New Zealand includes all other countries not specified.

ICELAND

ARRIVALS OF FOREIGN TOURISTS AT FRONTIERS[1]

(by country of nationality)

	1989	Relative share	1990	Relative share	% Variation over 1989
Austria	3 171	2.5	3 614	2.6	14.0
Belgium	1 017	0.8	941	0.7	-7.5
Denmark	16 159	12.6	15 176	10.9	-6.1
Finland	4 409	3.4	4 769	3.4	8.2
France	8 187	6.4	10 021	7.2	22.4
Germany	18 493	14.4	20 638	14.9	11.6
Greece	126	0.1	111	0.1	-11.9
Iceland	..	..	..	..	..
Ireland	574	0.4	570	0.4	-0.7
Italy	2 981	2.3	3 614	2.6	21.2
Luxembourg	378	0.3	314	0.2	-16.9
Netherlands	2 516	2.0	2 994	2.2	19.0
Norway	9 061	7.1	10 256	7.4	13.2
Portugal	141	0.1	204	0.1	44.7
Spain	844	0.7	1 103	0.8	30.7
Sweden	16 430	12.8	18 612	13.4	13.3
Switzerland	4 753	3.7	5 651	4.1	18.9
Turkey	214	0.2	90	0.1	-57.9
United Kingdom	11 990	9.3	13 743	9.9	14.6
Other OECD-Europe	..	..	..	..	..
Total Europe	101 444	79.1	112 421	81.0	10.8
Canada	1 292	1.0	1 140	0.8	-11.8
United States	22 952	17.9	22 616	16.3	-1.5
Total North America	24 244	18.9	23 756	17.1	-2.0
Australia	451	0.4	502	0.4	11.3
New Zealand	169	0.1	183	0.1	8.3
Japan	1 254	1.0	1 164	0.8	-7.2
Total Australasia and Japan	1 874	1.5	1 849	1.3	-1.3
Total OECD Countries	**127 562**	**99.4**	**138 026**	**99.4**	**8.2**
Yugoslavia	219	0.2	227	0.2	3.7
Other European countries	57	0.0	108	0.1	89.5
Bulgaria	56	0.0	87	0.1	55.4
Czechoslovakia	102	0.1	264	0.2	158.8
Hungary	237	0.2	267	0.2	12.7
Poland	328	0.3	441	0.3	34.5
Rumania	45	0.0	26	0.0	-42.2
USSR	321	0.3	452	0.3	40.8
Latin America	158	0.1	170	0.1	7.6
Argentina	21	0.0	30	0.0	42.9
Brazil	66	0.1	58	0.0	-12.1
Chile	35	0.0	53	0.0	51.4
Colombia	16	0.0	27	0.0	68.7
Mexico	52	0.0	28	0.0	-46.2
Venezuela	19	0.0	14	0.0	-26.3
Asia-Oceania	139	0.1	134	0.1	-3.6
China	87	0.1	122	0.1	40.2
Hong Kong	5	0.0	7	0.0	40.0
India	80	0.1	70	0.1	-12.5
Iran	28	0.0	32	0.0	14.3
Israel	124	0.1	177	0.1	42.7
Republic of Korea	52	0.0	42	0.0	-19.2
Lebanon	18	0.0	11	0.0	-38.9
Malaysia	22	0.0	22	0.0	0.0
Pakistan	19	0.0	14	0.0	-26.3
Philippines	84	0.1	154	0.1	83.3
Saudi Arabia	8	0.0	4	0.0	-50.0
Singapore	18	0.0	23	0.0	27.8
Taiwan	12	0.0	131	0.1	991.7
Thailand	94	0.1	104	0.1	10.6
Africa	173	0.1	168	0.1	-2.9
Algeria	29	0.0	26	0.0	-10.3
Egypt	19	0.0	20	0.0	5.3
Morocco	36	0.0	45	0.0	25.0
South Africa	136	0.1	108	0.1	-20.6
Total non-OECD Countries	**746**	**0.6**	**807**	**0.6**	**8.2**
TOTAL	**128 308**	**100.0**	**138 833**	**100.0**	**8.2**

1. Excluding shore excursionists.

ITALY

ARRIVALS OF FOREIGN VISITORS AT FRONTIERS[1]

(by country of nationality)

	1989	Relative share	1990	Relative share	% Variation over 1989
Austria	6 083 370	11.0	6 056 982	10.0	-0.4
Belgium	1 048 930	1.9	1 173 345	1.9	11.9
Denmark	646 335	1.2	623 414	1.0	-3.5
Finland	311 448	0.6	313 204	0.5	0.6
France	9 390 152	17.0	9 219 317	15.3	-1.8
Germany	10 134 213	18.4	10 676 781	17.7	5.4
Greece	508 838	0.9	519 016	0.9	2.0
Iceland[2]	..	..	..	..	..
Ireland	130 922	0.2	172 656	0.3	31.9
Italy	..	..	..	..	..
Luxembourg	193 983	0.4	129 728	0.2	-33.1
Netherlands	1 840 844	3.3	2 122 099	3.5	15.3
Norway	301 341	0.5	242 641	0.4	-19.5
Portugal	226 102	0.4	205 152	0.3	-9.3
Spain	700 609	1.3	679 487	1.1	-3.0
Sweden	597 104	1.1	517 249	0.9	-13.4
Switzerland	10 190 559	18.5	10 331 451	17.1	1.4
Turkey	193 036	0.4	195 146	0.3	1.1
United Kingdom	1 906 236	3.5	2 047 838	3.4	7.4
Other OECD-Europe	..	..	..	..	..
Total Europe	44 404 022	80.5	45 225 506	75.0	1.9
Canada	422 939	0.8	475 191	0.8	12.4
United States	1 356 662	2.5	1 420 888	2.4	4.7
Total North America	1 779 601	3.2	1 896 079	3.1	6.5
Australia	274 271	0.5	279 924	0.5	2.1
New Zealand	..	..	..	..	..
Japan	456 700	0.8	636 961	1.1	39.5
Total Australasia and Japan	730 971	1.3	916 885	1.5	25.4
Total OECD Countries	**46 914 594**	**85.1**	**48 038 470**	**79.7**	**2.4**
Yugoslavia	5 909 741	10.7	8 942 065	14.8	51.3
Other European countries[2]	806 804	1.5	1 767 130	2.9	119.0
USSR	93 092	0.2	83 709	0.1	-10.1
Latin America	493 425	0.9	616 785	1.0	25.0
Argentina	112 185	0.2	142 699	0.2	27.2
Brazil	121 368	0.2	154 373	0.3	27.2
Mexico	89 359	0.2	95 894	0.2	7.3
Venezuela	66 409	0.1	80 935	0.1	21.9
Asia-Oceania	166 460	0.3	169 644	0.3	1.9
Israel	91 084	0.2	79 952	0.1	-12.2
Africa	86 911	0.2	93 421	0.2	7.5
Egypt	39 807	0.1	44 967	0.1	13.0
South Africa	47 104	0.1	48 454	0.1	2.9
Origin country undetermined	753 163	1.4	668 408	1.1	-11.3
Total non-OECD Countries	**8 216 504**	**14.9**	**12 257 453**	**20.3**	**49.2**
TOTAL	**55 131 098**	**100.0**	**60 295 923**	**100.0**	**9.4**

1. Includes about 53% of excursionists.
2. "Other European countries" includes Iceland.

ITALY

ARRIVALS OF FOREIGN TOURISTS AT HOTELS

(by country of nationality)

	1989	Relative share	1990	Relative share	% Variation over 1989
Austria	832 178	4.7	850 627	4.7	2.2
Belgium	408 033	2.3	403 802	2.3	-1.0
Denmark	130 233	0.7	128 651	0.7	-1.2
Finland	116 398	0.7	107 534	0.6	-7.6
France	1 760 124	10.0	1 727 012	9.6	-1.9
Germany	4 879 953	27.6	4 714 956	26.3	-3.4
Greece	206 741	1.2	212 743	1.2	2.9
Iceland[1]	..	..	..	..	..
Ireland	52 630	0.3	64 188	0.4	22.0
Italy	..	..	..	..	..
Luxembourg	32 301	0.2	28 710	0.2	-11.1
Netherlands	334 176	1.9	344 882	1.9	3.2
Norway	68 517	0.4	74 408	0.4	8.6
Portugal	79 678	0.5	90 628	0.5	13.7
Spain	830 489	4.7	848 208	4.7	2.1
Sweden	240 141	1.4	228 805	1.3	-4.7
Switzerland	1 056 180	6.0	969 123	5.4	-8.2
Turkey	72 977	0.4	89 861	0.5	23.1
United Kingdom	1 264 964	7.2	1 227 388	6.8	-3.0
Other OECD-Europe	..	..	..	..	..
Total Europe	12 365 713	69.9	12 111 526	67.6	-2.1
Canada	243 361	1.4	252 987	1.4	4.0
United States	1 941 418	11.0	2 044 360	11.4	5.3
Total North America	2 184 779	12.4	2 297 347	12.8	5.2
Australia	248 932	1.4	260 889	1.5	4.8
New Zealand	..	..	..	..	..
Japan	707 377	4.0	758 729	4.2	7.3
Total Australasia and Japan	956 309	5.4	1 019 618	5.7	6.6
Total OECD Countries	**15 506 801**	**87.7**	**15 428 491**	**86.1**	**-0.5**
Yugoslavia	193 036	1.1	290 590	1.6	50.5
Other European countries[1]	377 072	2.1	502 999	2.8	33.4
USSR	94 908	0.5	94 731	0.5	-0.2
Latin America	526 467	3.0	583 713	3.3	10.9
Argentina	101 183	0.6	116 975	0.7	15.6
Brazil	198 185	1.1	220 140	1.2	11.1
Mexico	93 530	0.5	98 133	0.5	4.9
Venezuela	28 022	0.2	31 360	0.2	11.9
Asia-Oceania	218 355	1.2	204 195	1.1	-6.5
Israel	137 439	0.8	124 941	0.7	-9.1
Africa	61 411	0.3	67 371	0.4	9.7
Egypt	22 305	0.1	21 752	0.1	-2.5
South Africa	39 126	0.2	45 617	0.3	16.6
Origin country undetermined	799 449	4.5	847 061	4.7	6.0
Total non-OECD Countries	**2 175 790**	**12.3**	**2 495 929**	**13.9**	**14.7**
TOTAL	**17 682 591**	**100.0**	**17 924 420**	**100.0**	**1.4**

1. "Other European countries" includes Iceland.

ITALY

ARRIVALS OF FOREIGN TOURISTS AT REGISTERED TOURIST ACCOMMODATION

(by country of nationality)

	1988	Relative share	1989	Relative share	% Variation over 1988
Austria	1 119 539	5.4	988 551	4.8	-11.7
Belgium	476 000	2.3	478 324	2.3	0.5
Denmark	217 786	1.1	201 556	1.0	-7.5
Finland	128 299	0.6	132 516	0.6	3.3
France	2 085 589	10.1	2 033 431	9.9	-2.5
Germany	6 487 347	31.5	6 120 000	29.7	-5.7
Greece	182 854	0.9	213 171	1.0	16.6
Iceland[1]	..	..	..	..	..
Ireland	58 458	0.3	60 910	0.3	4.2
Italy	..	..	..	..	..
Luxembourg	40 316	0.2	35 887	0.2	-11.0
Netherlands	587 287	2.8	560 578	2.7	-4.5
Norway	94 405	0.5	83 198	0.4	-11.9
Portugal	83 479	0.4	92 546	0.4	10.9
Spain	877 663	4.3	898 275	4.4	2.3
Sweden	308 747	1.5	295 935	1.4	-4.1
Switzerland	1 225 998	5.9	1 198 913	5.8	-2.2
Turkey	71 833	0.3	79 236	0.4	10.3
United Kingdom	1 322 407	6.4	1 427 626	6.9	8.0
Other OECD-Europe	..	..	..	..	..
Total Europe	15 368 007	74.5	14 900 653	72.4	-3.0
Canada	259 056	1.3	269 871	1.3	4.2
United States	1 936 456	9.4	2 015 103	9.8	4.1
Total North America	2 195 512	10.6	2 284 974	11.1	4.1
Australia	249 520	1.2	297 191	1.4	19.1
New Zealand	..	..	..	..	..
Japan	583 158	2.8	718 881	3.5	23.3
Total Australasia and Japan	832 678	4.0	1 016 072	4.9	22.0
Total OECD Countries	**18 396 197**	**89.2**	**18 201 699**	**88.4**	**-1.1**
Yugoslavia	178 265	0.9	203 492	1.0	14.2
Other European countries[1]	403 876	2.0	474 834	2.3	17.6
USSR	47 953	0.2	96 595	0.5	101.4
Latin America	520 963	2.5	561 682	2.7	7.8
Argentina	106 110	0.5	110 357	0.5	4.0
Brazil	180 823	0.9	210 868	1.0	16.6
Mexico	90 975	0.4	98 896	0.5	8.7
Venezuela	35 248	0.2	29 738	0.1	-15.6
Asia-Oceania	225 385	1.1	228 982	1.1	1.6
Israel	147 236	0.7	144 877	0.7	-1.6
Africa	69 379	0.3	68 743	0.3	-0.9
Egypt	25 912	0.1	23 549	0.1	-9.1
South Africa	43 467	0.2	45 194	0.2	4.0
Origin country undetermined	826 125	4.0	845 130	4.1	2.3
Total non-OECD Countries	**2 223 993**	**10.8**	**2 382 863**	**11.6**	**7.1**
TOTAL	**20 620 190**	**100.0**	**20 584 562**	**100.0**	**-0.2**

1. "Other European countries" includes Iceland.

ITALY

NIGHTS SPENT BY FOREIGN TOURISTS IN HOTELS
(by country of nationality)

	1989	Relative share	1990	Relative share	% Variation over 1989
Austria	3 393 894	5.0	3 397 075	5.1	0.1
Belgium	1 919 674	2.8	1 802 579	2.7	-6.1
Denmark	588 382	0.9	557 274	0.8	-5.3
Finland	598 030	0.9	545 843	0.8	-8.7
France	5 133 599	7.5	5 021 561	7.6	-2.2
Germany	25 983 133	38.1	23 917 334	36.2	-8.0
Greece	463 657	0.7	479 734	0.7	3.5
Iceland[1]	..	..	..	..	..
Ireland	197 635	0.3	212 288	0.3	7.4
Italy	..	..	..	..	..
Luxembourg	216 456	0.3	180 353	0.3	-16.7
Netherlands	1 379 476	2.0	1 359 948	2.1	-1.4
Norway	254 640	0.4	286 121	0.4	12.4
Portugal	202 009	0.3	236 488	0.4	17.1
Spain	1 712 432	2.5	1 849 029	2.8	8.0
Sweden	965 097	1.4	888 336	1.3	-8.0
Switzerland	4 632 885	6.8	4 113 049	6.2	-11.2
Turkey	197 874	0.3	264 527	0.4	33.7
United Kingdom	5 577 226	8.2	5 128 645	7.8	-8.0
Other OECD-Europe	..	..	..	..	..
Total Europe	53 416 099	78.4	50 240 184	76.1	-5.9
Canada	629 007	0.9	633 774	1.0	0.8
United States	4 848 656	7.1	4 990 826	7.6	2.9
Total North America	5 477 663	8.0	5 624 600	8.5	2.7
Australia	563 393	0.8	592 012	0.9	5.1
New Zealand	..	..	..	..	..
Japan	1 439 456	2.1	1 571 358	2.4	9.2
Total Australasia and Japan	2 002 849	2.9	2 163 370	3.3	8.0
Total OECD Countries	**60 896 611**	**89.4**	**58 028 154**	**87.9**	**-4.7**
Yugoslavia	524 693	0.8	804 468	1.2	53.3
Other European countries[1]	1 941 772	2.8	1 973 870	3.0	1.7
USSR	771 261	1.1	498 451	0.8	-35.4
Latin America	1 471 890	2.2	1 737 936	2.6	18.1
Argentina	285 743	0.4	342 544	0.5	19.9
Brazil	561 256	0.8	666 024	1.0	18.7
Mexico	214 801	0.3	235 845	0.4	9.8
Venezuela	90 557	0.1	100 037	0.2	10.5
Asia-Oceania	580 031	0.9	561 399	0.9	-3.2
Israel	304 139	0.4	280 265	0.4	-7.8
Africa	209 706	0.3	233 782	0.4	11.5
Egypt	97 245	0.1	105 737	0.2	8.7
South Africa	112 461	0.2	128 945	0.2	14.7
Origin country undetermined	2 508 366	3.7	2 672 521	4.0	6.5
Total non-OECD Countries	**7 236 458**	**10.6**	**7 983 976**	**12.1**	**10.3**
TOTAL	**68 133 069**	**100.0**	**66 012 130**	**100.0**	**-3.1**

1. "Other European countries" includes Iceland.

ITALY

NIGHTS SPENT BY FOREIGN TOURISTS IN REGISTERED TOURIST ACCOMMODATION

(by country of nationality)

	1988	Relative share	1989	Relative share	% Variation over 1988
Austria	5 572 391	6.0	4 445 976	5.1	-20.2
Belgium	2 574 321	2.8	2 513 411	2.9	-2.4
Denmark	1 253 253	1.4	1 108 873	1.3	-11.5
Finland	697 599	0.8	694 126	0.8	-0.5
France	6 838 470	7.4	6 307 542	7.3	-7.8
Germany	39 498 355	42.7	35 104 255	40.4	-11.1
Greece	447 791	0.5	492 260	0.6	9.9
Iceland[1]	..	..	..	..	..
Ireland	246 039	0.3	227 181	0.3	-7.7
Italy	..	..	..	..	..
Luxembourg	281 222	0.3	246 666	0.3	-12.3
Netherlands	3 556 767	3.8	3 228 744	3.7	-9.2
Norway	413 120	0.4	348 424	0.4	-15.7
Portugal	210 734	0.2	235 945	0.3	12.0
Spain	1 896 142	2.1	1 913 070	2.2	0.9
Sweden	1 433 974	1.6	1 345 490	1.5	-6.2
Switzerland	6 296 880	6.8	5 706 003	6.6	-9.4
Turkey	201 021	0.2	230 652	0.3	14.7
United Kingdom	6 131 890	6.6	6 497 012	7.5	6.0
Other OECD-Europe	..	..	..	..	..
Total Europe	77 549 969	83.9	70 645 630	81.3	-8.9
Canada	675 189	0.7	735 273	0.8	8.9
United States	4 923 551	5.3	5 170 408	6.0	5.0
Total North America	5 598 740	6.1	5 905 681	6.8	5.5
Australia	574 932	0.6	679 640	0.8	18.2
New Zealand	..	..	..	..	..
Japan	1 189 552	1.3	1 478 535	1.7	24.3
Total Australasia and Japan	1 764 484	1.9	2 158 175	2.5	22.3
Total OECD Countries	**84 913 193**	**91.8**	**78 709 486**	**90.6**	**-7.3**
Yugoslavia	508 184	0.5	576 732	0.7	13.5
Other European countries[1]	1 866 138	2.0	2 382 840	2.7	27.7
USSR	168 931	0.2	780 728	0.9	362.2
Latin America	1 505 289	1.6	1 622 125	1.9	7.8
Argentina	331 396	0.4	329 218	0.4	-0.7
Brazil	506 109	0.5	617 128	0.7	21.9
Mexico	215 360	0.2	229 886	0.3	6.7
Venezuela	115 725	0.1	108 726	0.1	-6.0
Asia-Oceania	594 837	0.6	616 711	0.7	3.7
Israel	329 351	0.4	323 575	0.4	-1.8
Africa	220 061	0.2	255 718	0.3	16.2
Egypt	90 408	0.1	107 605	0.1	19.0
South Africa	129 653	0.1	148 113	0.2	14.2
Origin country undetermined	2 859 794	3.1	2 723 560	3.1	-4.8
Total non-OECD Countries	**7 554 303**	**8.2**	**8 177 686**	**9.4**	**8.3**
TOTAL	**92 467 496**	**100.0**	**86 887 172**	**100.0**	**-6.0**

1. "Other European countries" includes Iceland.

JAPAN

ARRIVALS OF FOREIGN VISITORS AT FRONTIERS

(by country of nationality)

	1989	Relative share	1990	Relative share	% Variation over 1989
Austria	8 684	0.3	8 144	0.3	-6.2
Belgium	7 606	0.3	8 818	0.3	15.9
Denmark	7 813	0.3	7 788	0.2	-0.3
Finland	9 271	0.3	8 941	0.3	-3.6
France	47 261	1.7	51 014	1.6	7.9
Germany	61 580	2.2	65 218	2.0	5.9
Greece	2 641	0.1	3 763	0.1	42.5
Iceland	546	0.0	419	0.0	-23.3
Ireland	4 034	0.1	4 650	0.1	15.3
Italy	27 665	1.0	29 798	0.9	7.7
Luxembourg	442	0.0	473	0.0	7.0
Netherlands	16 432	0.6	17 573	0.5	6.9
Norway	4 604	0.2	5 088	0.2	10.5
Portugal	4 448	0.2	5 787	0.2	30.1
Spain	12 877	0.5	16 150	0.5	25.4
Sweden	15 198	0.5	15 648	0.5	3.0
Switzerland	17 286	0.6	16 472	0.5	-4.7
Turkey	2 642	0.1	4 041	0.1	53.0
United Kingdom	177 259	6.3	214 413	6.6	21.0
Other OECD-Europe	..	..	..	..	..
Total Europe	428 289	15.1	484 198	15.0	13.1
Canada	59 754	2.1	63 850	2.0	6.9
United States	531 625	18.8	554 753	17.1	4.4
Total North America	591 379	20.9	618 603	19.1	4.6
Australia	55 586	2.0	56 238	1.7	1.2
New Zealand	15 564	0.5	16 197	0.5	4.1
Japan	..	..	..	..	..
Total Australasia and Japan	71 150	2.5	72 435	2.2	1.8
Total OECD Countries	**1 090 818**	**38.5**	**1 175 236**	**36.3**	**7.7**
Yugoslavia	1 360	0.0	1 550	0.0	14.0
Other European countries	28 221	1.0	35 310	1.1	25.1
Bulgaria	929	0.0	1 159	0.0	24.8
Hungary	1 880	0.1	2 050	0.1	9.0
Poland	3 176	0.1	3 588	0.1	13.0
Rumania	294	0.0	620	0.0	110.9
USSR	18 745	0.7	24 706	0.8	31.8
Latin America	62 414	2.2	92 807	2.9	48.7
Argentina	5 278	0.2	4 963	0.2	-6.0
Brazil	27 521	1.0	55 126	1.7	100.3
Chile	1 611	0.1	1 434	0.0	-11.0
Colombia	2 666	0.1	2 252	0.1	-15.5
Mexico	9 053	0.3	9 744	0.3	7.6
Venezuela	1 197	0.0	1 259	0.0	5.2
Asia-Oceania	1 637 612	57.8	1 916 952	59.2	17.1
China	98 255	3.5	105 993	3.3	7.9
Hong Kong	34 259	1.2	40 077	1.2	17.0
India	30 877	1.1	27 878	0.9	-9.7
Iran	16 798	0.6	31 832	1.0	89.5
Israel	6 784	0.2	7 644	0.2	12.7
Republic of Korea	609 984	21.5	740 441	22.9	21.4
Lebanon	388	0.0	435	0.0	12.1
Malaysia	54 397	1.9	57 752	1.8	6.2
Pakistan	7 115	0.3	6 412	0.2	-9.9
Philippines	96 624	3.4	108 108	3.3	11.9
Singapore	37 822	1.3	43 015	1.3	13.7
Taiwan	527 969	18.6	607 721	18.8	15.1
Thailand	53 288	1.9	74 678	2.3	40.1
Africa	11 883	0.4	12 135	0.4	2.1
Egypt	1 818	0.1	1 743	0.1	-4.1
South Africa	1 696	0.1	1 982	0.1	16.9
Origin country undetermined	2 756	0.1	2 762	0.1	0.2
Total non-OECD Countries	**1 744 246**	**61.5**	**2 061 516**	**63.7**	**18.2**
TOTAL	**2 835 064**	**100.0**	**3 236 752**	**100.0**	**14.2**

NETHERLANDS

ARRIVALS OF FOREIGN TOURISTS AT HOTELS

(by country of residence)

	1989	Relative share	1990	Relative share	% Variation over 1989
Austria[3]	..	..	..	..	..
Belgium	143 800	4.1	161 500	4.1	12.3
Denmark	72 100	2.1	70 100	1.8	-2.8
Finland	32 600	0.9	36 000	0.9	10.4
France	259 100	7.4	306 200	7.8	18.2
Germany	675 000	19.4	736 400	18.9	9.1
Greece[3]	..	..	..	..	..
Iceland[3]	..	..	..	..	..
Ireland	20 000	0.6	25 000	0.6	25.0
Italy	208 900	6.0	298 200	7.6	42.7
Luxembourg	11 500	0.3	13 000	0.3	13.0
Netherlands	..	..	..	..	..
Norway	53 900	1.5	46 400	1.2	-13.9
Portugal[1]	..	..	..	..	..
Spain[1]	127 600	3.7	151 200	3.9	18.5
Sweden	109 600	3.1	114 800	2.9	4.7
Switzerland	91 500	2.6	100 100	2.6	9.4
Turkey	..	..	..	..	..
United Kingdom	649 100	18.6	716 800	18.4	10.4
Other OECD-Europe[3]	127 600	3.7	157 200	4.0	23.2
Total Europe	2 582 300	74.1	2 932 900	75.1	13.6
Canada	93 900	2.7	91 900	2.4	-2.1
United States	412 400	11.8	457 600	11.7	11.0
Total North America	506 300	14.5	549 500	14.1	8.5
Australia[2]	50 200	1.4	59 500	1.5	18.5
New Zealand[2]	..	..	..	..	..
Japan	84 400	2.4	96 500	2.5	14.3
Total Australasia and Japan	134 600	3.9	156 000	4.0	15.9
Total OECD Countries	**3 223 200**	**92.4**	**3 638 400**	**93.2**	**12.9**
Yugoslavia	..	..	..	..	..
Latin America	64 300	1.8	64 900	1.7	0.9
Asia-Oceania	147 900	4.2	152 100	3.9	2.8
Africa	51 600	1.5	47 400	1.2	-8.1
Total non-OECD Countries	**263 800**	**7.6**	**264 400**	**6.8**	**0.2**
TOTAL	**3 487 000**	**100.0**	**3 902 800**	**100.0**	**11.9**

1. Spain includes Portugal.
2. Australia includes New Zealand.
3. Other OECD-Europe includes Austria, Greece, Iceland and all non-OECD European countries.

NETHERLANDS

ARRIVALS OF FOREIGN TOURISTS AT REGISTERED TOURIST ACCOMMODATION

(by country of residence)

	1989	Relative share	1990	Relative share	% Variation over 1989
Austria [3]	..	..	..	..	..
Belgium	298 000	5.8	330 200	6.1	10.8
Denmark	110 000	2.1	109 600	2.0	–0.4
Finland	40 700	0.8	44 900	0.8	10.3
France	349 500	6.8	46 500	0.9	–86.7
Germany	1 650 400	32.0	1 833 700	33.8	11.1
Greece [3]	..	..	..	..	..
Iceland [3]	..	..	..	..	..
Ireland	25 600	0.5	30 600	0.6	19.5
Italy	259 300	5.0	362 600	6.7	39.8
Luxembourg	12 700	0.2	14 200	0.3	11.8
Netherlands	..	..	..	..	..
Norway	64 100	1.2	59 400	1.1	–7.3
Portugal [1]	..	..	..	..	..
Spain [1]	163 400	3.2	196 600	3.6	20.3
Sweden	137 800	2.7	144 500	2.7	4.9
Switzerland	110 200	2.1	126 700	2.3	15.0
Turkey	..	..	..	..	..
United Kingdom	750 800	14.6	828 200	15.3	10.3
Other OECD-Europe [3]	152 800	3.0	198 200	3.7	29.7
Total Europe	4 125 300	80.1	4 325 900	79.7	4.9
Canada	108 700	2.1	108 800	2.0	0.1
United States	454 600	8.8	500 400	9.2	10.1
Total North America	563 300	10.9	609 200	11.2	8.1
Australia [2]	76 900	1.5	90 100	1.7	17.2
New Zealand [2]	..	..	..	..	..
Japan	87 100	1.7	100 600	1.9	15.5
Total Australasia and Japan	164 000	3.2	190 700	3.5	16.3
Total OECD Countries	**4 852 600**	**94.2**	**5 125 800**	**94.5**	**5.6**
Yugoslavia	..	..	..	..	..
Latin America	74 000	1.4	74 800	1.4	1.1
Asia-Oceania	164 100	3.2	167 500	3.1	2.1
Africa	59 400	1.2	57 900	1.1	–2.5
Total non-OECD Countries	**297 500**	**5.8**	**300 200**	**5.5**	**0.9**
TOTAL	**5 150 100**	**100.0**	**5 426 000**	**100.0**	**5.4**

1. Spain includes Portugal.
2. Australia includes New Zealand.
3. Other OECD-Europe includes Austria, Greece, Iceland and non-OECD European countries.

NETHERLANDS

NIGHTS SPENT BY FOREIGN TOURISTS IN HOTELS

(by country of residence)

	1989	Relative share	1990	Relative share	% Variation over 1989
Austria[3]	..	..	..	..	..
Belgium	264 400	3.7	295 700	3.6	11.8
Denmark	143 600	2.0	141 800	1.7	-1.3
Finland	65 700	0.9	73 100	0.9	11.3
France	464 700	6.5	548 800	6.8	18.1
Germany	1 523 100	21.2	1 664 900	20.5	9.3
Greece[3]	..	..	..	..	..
Iceland[3]	..	..	..	..	..
Ireland	44 400	0.6	55 700	0.7	25.5
Italy	411 200	5.7	606 800	7.5	47.6
Luxembourg	22 500	0.3	29 600	0.4	31.6
Netherlands	..	..	..	..	..
Norway	113 200	1.6	91 700	1.1	-19.0
Portugal[1]	..	..	..	..	..
Spain[1]	261 200	3.6	317 900	3.9	21.7
Sweden	214 400	3.0	217 800	2.7	1.6
Switzerland	185 800	2.6	205 800	2.5	10.8
Turkey	..	..	..	..	..
United Kingdom	1 358 600	18.9	1 521 900	18.8	12.0
Other OECD-Europe[3]	284 000	4.0	347 500	4.3	22.4
Total Europe	5 356 800	74.6	6 119 000	75.5	14.2
Canada	180 200	2.5	185 900	2.3	3.2
United States	819 400	11.4	918 900	11.3	12.1
Total North America	999 600	13.9	1 104 800	13.6	10.5
Australia[2]	102 500	1.4	112 700	1.4	10.0
New Zealand[2]	..	..	..	..	..
Japan	162 600	2.3	187 100	2.3	15.1
Total Australasia and Japan	265 100	3.7	299 800	3.7	13.1
Total OECD Countries	**6 621 500**	**92.2**	**7 523 600**	**92.8**	**13.6**
Yugoslavia	..	..	..	..	..
Latin America	132 000	1.8	142 000	1.8	7.6
Asia-Oceania	317 300	4.4	332 200	4.1	4.7
Africa	107 600	1.5	106 000	1.3	-1.5
Total non-OECD Countries	**556 900**	**7.8**	**580 200**	**7.2**	**4.2**
TOTAL	**7 178 400**	**100.0**	**8 103 800**	**100.0**	**12.9**

1. Spain includes Portugal.
2. Australia includes New Zealand.
3. Other OECD-Europe includes Austria, Greece, Iceland and all non-OECD European countries.

NETHERLANDS

NIGHTS SPENT BY FOREIGN TOURISTS IN REGISTERED TOURIST ACCOMMODATION

(by country of residence)

	1989	Relative share	1990	Relative share	% Variation over 1989
Austria [3]	..	..	..	..	..
Belgium	1 001 600	7.1	1 081 500	6.6	8.0
Denmark	274 000	1.9	269 400	1.6	-1.7
Finland	86 100	0.6	94 400	0.6	9.6
France	672 800	4.7	797 900	4.9	18.6
Germany	6 379 400	45.0	7 457 200	45.5	16.9
Greece [3]	..	..	..	..	..
Iceland [3]	..	..	..	..	..
Ireland	59 500	0.4	73 500	0.4	23.5
Italy	533 800	3.8	765 100	4.7	43.3
Luxembourg	27 100	0.2	34 400	0.2	26.9
Netherlands	..	..	..	..	..
Norway	140 400	1.0	118 200	0.7	-15.8
Portugal [1]	..	..	..	..	..
Spain [1]	351 400	2.5	433 800	2.6	23.4
Sweden	288 300	2.0	280 600	1.7	-2.7
Switzerland	241 900	1.7	289 200	1.8	19.6
Turkey	..	..	..	..	..
United Kingdom	1 690 300	11.9	1 916 700	11.7	13.4
Other OECD-Europe [3]	360 500	2.5	470 200	2.9	30.4
Total Europe	12 107 100	85.4	14 082 100	86.0	16.3
Canada	210 900	1.5	221 700	1.4	5.1
United States	909 400	6.4	1 028 600	6.3	13.1
Total North America	1 120 300	7.9	1 250 300	7.6	11.6
Australia [2]	161 000	1.1	182 100	1.1	13.1
New Zealand [2]	..	..	..	..	..
Japan	167 600	1.2	194 800	1.2	16.2
Total Australasia and Japan	328 600	2.3	376 900	2.3	14.7
Total OECD Countries	**13 556 000**	**95.7**	**15 709 300**	**95.9**	**15.9**
Yugoslavia	..	..	..	..	..
Latin America	147 900	1.0	162 300	1.0	9.7
Asia-Oceania	342 500	2.4	370 100	2.3	8.1
Africa	125 300	0.9	136 200	0.8	8.7
Total non-OECD Countries	**615 700**	**4.3**	**668 600**	**4.1**	**8.6**
TOTAL	**14 171 700**	**100.0**	**16 377 900**	**100.0**	**15.6**

1. Spain includes Portugal.
2. Australia includes New Zealand.
3. Other OECD-Europe includes Austria, Greece, Iceland and non-OECD European countries.

NEW ZEALAND

ARRIVALS OF FOREIGN TOURISTS AT FRONTIERS

(by country of residence)

	1989	Relative share	1990	Relative share	% Variation over 1989
Austria	2 083	0.2	2 565	0.3	23.1
Belgium	706	0.1	1 001	0.1	41.8
Denmark	3 195	0.4	3 401	0.3	6.4
Finland	1 197	0.1	1 499	0.2	25.2
France	4 074	0.5	3 429	0.4	-15.8
Germany	23 768	2.6	29 992	3.1	26.2
Greece	326	0.0	311	0.0	-4.6
Iceland	116	0.0	66	0.0	-43.1
Ireland	1 443	0.2	1 578	0.2	9.4
Italy	2 628	0.3	3 152	0.3	19.9
Luxembourg	100	0.0	130	0.0	30.0
Netherlands	7 126	0.8	7 780	0.8	9.2
Norway	1 275	0.1	1 614	0.2	26.6
Portugal	132	0.0	113	0.0	-14.4
Spain	837	0.1	1 155	0.1	38.0
Sweden	9 071	1.0	8 476	0.9	-6.6
Switzerland	9 638	1.1	10 642	1.1	10.4
Turkey	148	0.0	214	0.0	44.6
United Kingdom	74 337	8.2	87 255	8.9	17.4
Other OECD-Europe	..	..	..	..	..
Total Europe	142 200	15.8	164 373	16.8	15.6
Canada	30 919	3.4	33 983	3.5	9.9
United States	137 509	15.3	139 664	14.3	1.6
Total North America	168 428	18.7	173 647	17.8	3.1
Australia	312 217	34.6	341 713	35.0	9.4
New Zealand[1]	19 605	2.2	14 368	1.5	-26.7
Japan	97 322	10.8	107 840	11.0	10.8
Total Australasia and Japan	429 144	47.6	463 921	47.5	8.1
Total OECD Countries	**739 772**	**82.1**	**801 941**	**82.2**	**8.4**
Yugoslavia	208	0.0	267	0.0	28.4
Bulgaria	54	0.0	45	0.0	-16.7
Czechoslovakia	40	0.0	70	0.0	75.0
Germany (D. R.)	11	0.0	..	..	..
Hungary	116	0.0	139	0.0	19.8
Poland	160	0.0	123	0.0	-23.1
Rumania	20	0.0	64	0.0	220.0
USSR	1 933	0.2	4 519	0.5	133.8
Latin America	5 083	0.6	..	..	..
Argentina	1 472	0.2	1 458	0.1	-1.0
Brazil	1 073	0.1	924	0.1	-13.9
Chile	485	0.1	437	0.0	-9.9
Colombia	173	0.0	172	0.0	-0.6
Mexico	730	0.1	928	0.1	27.1
Venezuela	100	0.0	152	0.0	52.0
China	2 513	0.3	3 082	0.3	22.6
Hong Kong	15 474	1.7	15 460	1.6	-0.1
India	3 078	0.3	2 190	0.2	-28.8
Iran	186	0.0	392	0.0	110.8
Israel	937	0.1	1 089	0.1	16.2
Republic of Korea	2 845	0.3	4 184	0.4	47.1
Lebanon	79	0.0	42	0.0	-46.8
Malaysia	7 457	0.8	10 021	1.0	34.4
Pakistan	352	0.0	356	0.0	1.1
Philippines	2 462	0.3	2 880	0.3	17.0
Saudi Arabia	755	0.1	792	0.1	4.9
Singapore	14 808	1.6	15 207	1.6	2.7
Taiwan	13 828	1.5	12 845	1.3	-7.1
Thailand	3 827	0.4	5 568	0.6	45.5
Africa	3 050	0.3	..	..	..
Algeria	0	0.0	0	0.0	..
Egypt	168	0.0	114	0.0	-32.1
Morocco	9	0.0	22	0.0	144.4
South Africa	1 737	0.2	1 921	0.2	10.6
Origin country undetermined	152 965	17.0	173 802	17.8	13.6
Total non-OECD Countries	**161 306**	**17.9**	**174 069**	**17.8**	**7.9**
TOTAL	**901 078**	**100.0**	**976 010**	**100.0**	**8.3**

1. New Zealanders who have lived abroad for less than 12 months and who return for a short stay.

NORWAY

NIGHTS SPENT BY FOREIGN TOURISTS IN HOTELS

(by country of nationality)

	1989	Relative share	1990	Relative share	% Variation over 1989
Austria[1]	..	..	..	..	..
Belgium[1]	..	..	..	..	..
Denmark	648 444	18.9	623 812	17.6	-3.8
Finland	98 583	2.9	105 311	3.0	6.8
France	139 979	4.1	170 685	4.8	21.9
Germany	580 599	16.9	579 869	16.4	-0.1
Greece[1]	..	..	..	..	..
Iceland[1]	..	..	..	..	..
Ireland[1]	..	..	..	..	..
Italy[1]	..	..	103 215	2.9	..
Luxembourg[1]	..	..	..	..	..
Netherlands	118 262	3.4	126 030	3.6	6.6
Norway	..	..	..	..	..
Portugal[1]	..	..	..	..	..
Spain[1]	..	..	32 607	0.9	..
Sweden	518 707	15.1	566 595	16.0	9.2
Switzerland[1]	..	..	42 324	1.2	..
Turkey[1]	..	..	..	..	..
United Kingdom	337 364	9.8	340 890	9.6	1.0
Other OECD-Europe	265 117	7.7	142 244	4.0	-46.3
Total Europe	2 707 055	78.9	2 833 582	80.1	4.7
Canada[1]	..	..	..	..	..
United States	347 258	10.1	364 544	10.3	5.0
Total North America	347 258	10.1	364 544	10.3	5.0
Australia[1]	..	..	..	..	..
New Zealand[1]	..	..	..	..	..
Japan	80 093	2.3	84 495	2.4	5.5
Total Australasia and Japan	80 093	2.3	84 495	2.4	5.5
Total OECD Countries	**3 134 406**	**91.3**	**3 282 621**	**92.8**	**4.7**
Yugoslavia (S.F.R.)[1]	..	..	..	..	..
Origin country undetermined[1]	296 948	8.7	254 010	7.2	-14.5
Total non-OECD Countries	**296 948**	**8.7**	**254 010**	**7.2**	**-14.5**
TOTAL	**3 431 354**	**100.0**	**3 536 631**	**100.0**	**3.1**

1. Included in "Origin country undetermined".

PORTUGAL

ARRIVALS OF FOREIGN TOURISTS AT FRONTIERS

(by country of nationality)

	1989	Relative share	1990	Relative share	% Variation over 1989
Austria	32 730	0.5	37 082	0.5	13.3
Belgium	146 429	2.1	168 273	2.1	14.9
Denmark	83 949	1.2	100 739	1.3	20.0
Finland	64 092	0.9	87 231	1.1	36.1
France	610 896	8.6	617 873	7.7	1.1
Germany	564 726	7.9	621 418	7.7	10.0
Greece [1]	..	..	..	..	..
Iceland [1]	..	..	..	..	..
Ireland	59 982	0.8	69 204	0.9	15.4
Italy	167 179	2.3	189 390	2.4	13.3
Luxembourg	7 427	0.1	10 145	0.1	36.6
Netherlands	316 747	4.5	298 941	3.7	–5.6
Norway	21 042	0.3	27 746	0.3	31.9
Portugal	..	..	..	..	..
Spain	3 246 826	45.6	3 924 340	48.9	20.9
Sweden	81 771	1.1	88 168	1.1	7.8
Switzerland	68 135	1.0	69 311	0.9	1.7
Turkey [1]	..	..	..	..	..
United Kingdom	1 027 281	14.4	1 061 136	13.2	3.3
Other OECD-Europe	..	..	..	..	..
Total Europe	6 499 212	91.3	7 370 997	91.9	13.4
Canada	83 070	1.2	83 238	1.0	0.2
United States	186 736	2.6	183 886	2.3	–1.5
Total North America	269 806	3.8	267 124	3.3	–1.0
Australia [2]	20 044	0.3	21 481	0.3	7.2
New-Zealand [2]	..	..	..	..	..
Japan	30 101	0.4	32 665	0.4	8.5
Total Australasia and Japan	50 145	0.7	54 146	0.7	8.0
Total OECD Countries	**6 819 163**	**95.8**	**7 692 267**	**95.9**	**12.8**
Yugoslavia (S.F.R.) [1]	..	..	..	..	..
Other European countries [1]	42 674	0.6	52 474	0.7	23.0
Africa	93 118	1.3	102 030	1.3	9.6
Origin country undetermined	160 945	2.3	173 148	2.2	7.6
Total non-OECD Countries	**296 737**	**4.2**	**327 652**	**4.1**	**10.4**
TOTAL	**7 115 900**	**100.0**	**8 019 919**	**100.0**	**12.7**

1. "Other European countries" includes Greece, Iceland, Turkey and Yugoslavia.
2. Australia includes New Zealand.

PORTUGAL

ARRIVALS OF FOREIGN VISITORS AT FRONTIERS

(by country of nationality)

	1989	Relative share	1990	Relative share	% Variation over 1989
Austria	35 643	0.2	40 295	0.2	13.1
Belgium	150 731	0.9	173 062	0.9	14.8
Denmark	89 954	0.5	104 627	0.6	16.3
Finland	69 894	0.4	93 650	0.5	34.0
France	646 847	3.9	658 198	3.6	1.8
Germany	611 275	3.7	680 971	3.7	11.4
Greece	16 124	0.1	16 481	0.1	2.2
Iceland	3 098	0.0	2 448	0.0	–21.0
Ireland	60 797	0.4	71 784	0.4	18.1
Italy	185 154	1.1	221 113	1.2	19.4
Luxembourg	8 228	0.0	10 177	0.1	23.7
Netherlands	332 797	2.0	329 797	1.8	–0.9
Norway	25 481	0.2	31 314	0.2	22.9
Portugal	..	..	..	..	..
Spain	12 187 242	74.0	13 806 281	74.9	13.3
Sweden	94 752	0.6	97 577	0.5	3.0
Switzerland	77 763	0.5	78 029	0.4	0.3
Turkey	3 215	0.0	3 495	0.0	8.7
United Kingdom	1 137 481	6.9	1 202 874	6.5	5.7
Other OECD-Europe	..	..	..	..	..
Total Europe	15 736 476	95.5	17 622 173	95.7	12.0
Canada	91 126	0.6	90 830	0.5	–0.3
United States	235 503	1.4	252 057	1.4	7.0
Total North America	326 629	2.0	342 887	1.9	5.0
Australia	16 486	0.1	17 645	0.1	7.0
New Zealand	4 949	0.0	5 999	0.0	21.2
Japan	32 121	0.2	35 433	0.2	10.3
Total Australasia and Japan	53 556	0.3	59 077	0.3	10.3
Total OECD Countries	**16 116 661**	**97.8**	**18 024 137**	**97.8**	**11.8**
Yugoslavia	7 662	0.0	8 393	0.0	9.5
Other European countries	50 657	0.3	61 916	0.3	22.2
Bulgaria	2 177	0.0	2 173	0.0	–0.2
Czechoslovakia	2 984	0.0	3 003	0.0	0.6
Germany (D. R.)	3 737	0.0	4 298	0.0	15.0
Hungary	2 024	0.0	2 394	0.0	18.3
Poland	7 877	0.0	6 917	0.0	–12.2
Rumania	971	0.0	1 586	0.0	63.3
USSR	28 864	0.2	39 076	0.2	35.4
Latin America	155 131	0.9	169 544	0.9	9.3
Argentina	9 594	0.1	9 731	0.1	1.4
Brazil	102 990	0.6	118 926	0.6	15.5
Chile	2 990	0.0	3 233	0.0	8.1
Colombia	2 995	0.0	2 424	0.0	–19.1
Mexico	7 152	0.0	7 525	0.0	5.2
Venezuela	18 935	0.1	17 985	0.1	–5.0
Asia-Oceania	46 752	0.3	49 268	0.3	5.4
China	2 252	0.0	2 885	0.0	28.1
Hong Kong	786	0.0	1 097	0.0	39.6
India	8 144	0.0	7 179	0.0	–11.8
Iran	627	0.0	837	0.0	33.5
Israel	7 810	0.0	6 281	0.0	–19.6
Republic of Korea	4 703	0.0	6 552	0.0	39.3
Lebanon	579	0.0	632	0.0	9.2
Malaysia	837	0.0	935	0.0	11.7
Pakistan	1 372	0.0	1 410	0.0	2.8
Philippines	12 463	0.1	14 040	0.1	12.7
Saudi Arabia	568	0.0	405	0.0	–28.7
Singapore	949	0.0	1 155	0.0	21.7
Thailand	983	0.0	1 182	0.0	20.2
Africa	97 461	0.6	106 452	0.6	9.2
Algeria	1 533	0.0	1 993	0.0	30.0
Egypt	1 046	0.0	1 030	0.0	–1.5
Morocco	7 657	0.0	6 407	0.0	–16.3
South Africa	12 232	0.1	10 018	0.1	–18.1
Origin country undetermined	1 475	0.0	2 368	0.0	60.5
Total non-OECD Countries	**359 138**	**2.2**	**397 941**	**2.2**	**10.8**
TOTAL	**16 475 799**	**100.0**	**18 422 078**	**100.0**	**11.8**

PORTUGAL

ARRIVALS OF FOREIGN TOURISTS AT HOTELS[1]

(by country of residence)

	1989	Relative share	1990	Relative share	% Variation over 1989
Austria	30 948	0.9	34 711	1.0	12.2
Belgium	87 362	2.6	90 078	2.5	3.1
Denmark	57 947	1.7	60 180	1.7	3.9
Finland	62 852	1.9	78 333	2.2	24.6
France	297 166	8.9	309 988	8.5	4.3
Germany	376 477	11.2	419 054	11.5	11.3
Greece	8 728	0.3	9 114	0.3	4.4
Iceland	2 272	0.1	2 162	0.1	-4.8
Ireland	32 990	1.0	34 664	1.0	5.1
Italy	147 306	4.4	175 326	4.8	19.0
Luxembourg	3 870	0.1	4 570	0.1	18.1
Netherlands	183 682	5.5	207 358	5.7	12.9
Norway	25 413	0.8	25 465	0.7	0.2
Portugal	..	..	..	..	..
Spain	612 036	18.2	692 587	19.1	13.2
Sweden	91 861	2.7	92 784	2.6	1.0
Switzerland	96 843	2.9	95 336	2.6	-1.6
Turkey	1 103	0.0	1 458	0.0	32.2
United Kingdom	647 775	19.3	695 680	19.2	7.4
Other OECD-Europe	..	..	..	..	..
Total Europe	2 766 631	82.5	3 028 848	83.4	9.5
Canada	99 598	3.0	100 852	2.8	1.3
United States	254 047	7.6	252 185	6.9	-0.7
Total North America	353 645	10.5	353 037	9.7	-0.2
Australia	9 484	0.3	10 048	0.3	5.9
New Zealand	1 687	0.1	1 917	0.1	13.6
Japan	33 170	1.0	34 199	0.9	3.1
Total Australasia and Japan	44 341	1.3	46 164	1.3	4.1
Total OECD Countries	**3 164 617**	**94.3**	**3 428 049**	**94.4**	**8.3**
Yugoslavia	1 695	0.1	2 574	0.1	51.9
Other European countries	14 002	0.4	13 640	0.4	-2.6
Bulgaria	755	0.0	662	0.0	-12.3
Czechoslovakia	2 153	0.1	1 665	0.0	-22.7
Hungary	918	0.0	985	0.0	7.3
Poland	1 968	0.1	1 137	0.0	-42.2
Rumania	158	0.0	505	0.0	219.6
USSR	6 726	0.2	7 805	0.2	16.0
Latin America	103 221	3.1	111 793	3.1	8.3
Argentina	4 849	0.1	5 365	0.1	10.6
Brazil	82 885	2.5	92 712	2.6	11.9
Chile	1 000	0.0	954	0.0	-4.6
Colombia	1 293	0.0	914	0.0	-29.3
Mexico	3 294	0.1	3 989	0.1	21.1
Venezuela	6 306	0.2	4 643	0.1	-26.4
Asia-Oceania	21 515	0.6	18 069	0.5	-16.0
China	1 168	0.0	1 716	0.0	46.9
Iran	400	0.0	410	0.0	2.5
Israel	10 459	0.3	7 579	0.2	-27.5
Lebanon	351	0.0	255	0.0	-27.4
Philippines	989	0.0	1 187	0.0	20.0
Saudi Arabia	1 178	0.0	761	0.0	-35.4
Africa	49 551	1.5	58 117	1.6	17.3
Egypt	434	0.0	650	0.0	49.8
Morocco	4 500	0.1	4 130	0.1	-8.2
South Africa	15 358	0.5	17 972	0.5	17.0
Total non-OECD Countries	**189 984**	**5.7**	**204 193**	**5.6**	**7.5**
TOTAL	**3 354 601**	**100.0**	**3 632 242**	**100.0**	**8.3**

1. Includes arrivals at hotels, studio-hotels, holiday-flats, villages, motels, inns and boarding-houses.

PORTUGAL

ARRIVALS OF FOREIGN TOURISTS AT REGISTERED TOURIST ACCOMMODATION[1]

(by country of residence)

	1989	Relative share	1990	Relative share	% Variation over 1989
Austria	41 364	1.0	45 584	1.0	10.2
Belgium	121 429	2.9	122 430	2.8	0.8
Denmark	76 888	1.8	74 560	1.7	-3.0
Finland	64 603	1.6	80 601	1.8	24.8
France	482 700	11.6	492 144	11.1	2.0
Germany	561 958	13.5	601 528	13.6	7.0
Greece	9 065	0.2	9 519	0.2	5.0
Iceland	2 275	0.1	2 190	0.0	-3.7
Ireland	34 775	0.8	36 437	0.8	4.8
Italy	178 013	4.3	203 320	4.6	14.2
Luxembourg	4 597	0.1	5 393	0.1	17.3
Netherlands	295 265	7.1	309 771	7.0	4.9
Norway	26 531	0.6	26 539	0.6	0.0
Portugal	..	..	..	..	..
Spain	756 639	18.2	849 633	19.2	12.3
Sweden	95 008	2.3	96 369	2.2	1.4
Switzerland	108 546	2.6	105 600	2.4	-2.7
Turkey	1 267	0.0	1 567	0.0	23.7
United Kingdom	677 812	16.3	726 768	16.4	7.2
Other OECD-Europe	..	..	..	..	..
Total Europe	3 538 735	85.0	3 789 953	85.5	7.1
Canada	104 219	2.5	106 216	2.4	1.9
United States	260 107	6.2	258 920	5.8	-0.5
Total North America	364 326	8.8	365 136	8.2	0.2
Australia	16 905	0.4	18 173	0.4	7.5
New Zealand	6 328	0.2	6 619	0.1	4.6
Japan	33 822	0.8	35 438	0.8	4.8
Total Australasia and Japan	57 055	1.4	60 230	1.4	5.6
Total OECD Countries	**3 960 116**	**95.1**	**4 215 319**	**95.1**	**6.4**
Yugoslavia	2 591	0.1	3 459	0.1	33.5
Other European countries	16 752	0.4	16 207	0.4	-3.3
Bulgaria	787	0.0	788	0.0	0.1
Czechoslovakia	2 356	0.1	2 009	0.0	-14.7
Hungary	2 107	0.1	1 879	0.0	-10.8
Poland	3 189	0.1	1 998	0.0	-37.3
Rumania	172	0.0	526	0.0	205.8
USSR	6 769	0.2	7 874	0.2	16.3
Latin America	107 235	2.6	117 485	2.6	9.6
Argentina	5 279	0.1	5 762	0.1	9.1
Brazil	85 510	2.1	96 919	2.2	13.3
Chile	1 178	0.0	1 193	0.0	1.3
Colombia	1 375	0.0	968	0.0	-29.6
Mexico	3 451	0.1	4 223	0.1	22.4
Venezuela	6 450	0.2	4 892	0.1	-24.2
Asia-Oceania	22 244	0.5	18 968	0.4	-14.7
China	1 199	0.0	1 756	0.0	46.5
Iran	429	0.0	458	0.0	6.8
Israel	10 775	0.3	7 737	0.2	-28.2
Lebanon	359	0.0	267	0.0	-25.6
Philippines	997	0.0	1 192	0.0	19.6
Saudi Arabia	1 178	0.0	769	0.0	-34.7
Africa	53 909	1.3	63 290	1.4	17.4
Egypt	447	0.0	662	0.0	48.1
Morocco	6 046	0.1	6 077	0.1	0.5
South Africa	16 223	0.4	19 190	0.4	18.3
Total non-OECD Countries	**202 731**	**4.9**	**219 409**	**4.9**	**8.2**
TOTAL	**4 162 847**	**100.0**	**4 434 728**	**100.0**	**6.5**

1. Includes arrivals at hotels, studio-hotels, holiday-flats, villages, motels, inns, boarding-houses, recreation centres for children and camping-sites.

PORTUGAL

NIGHTS SPENT BY FOREIGN TOURISTS IN HOTELS[1]

(by country of residence)

	1989	Relative share	1990	Relative share	% Variation over 1989
Austria	132 738	0.9	142 782	0.9	7.6
Belgium	375 944	2.4	393 473	2.4	4.7
Denmark	362 462	2.3	404 479	2.4	11.6
Finland	448 780	2.9	532 914	3.2	18.7
France	799 573	5.2	825 493	4.9	3.2
Germany	2 081 997	13.5	2 360 295	14.1	13.4
Greece	25 118	0.2	26 356	0.2	4.9
Iceland	22 109	0.1	18 278	0.1	–17.3
Ireland	242 192	1.6	271 603	1.6	12.1
Italy	379 000	2.5	459 771	2.8	21.3
Luxembourg	14 673	0.1	24 770	0.1	68.8
Netherlands	1 289 410	8.3	1 428 931	8.6	10.8
Norway	139 886	0.9	167 464	1.0	19.7
Portugal	..	..	..	..	..
Spain	1 458 325	9.4	1 738 193	10.4	19.2
Sweden	560 968	3.6	549 742	3.3	–2.0
Switzerland	349 125	2.3	341 358	2.0	–2.2
Turkey	4 153	0.0	4 595	0.0	10.6
United Kingdom	5 096 614	33.0	5 260 390	31.5	3.2
Other OECD-Europe	..	..	..	..	..
Total Europe	13 783 067	89.1	14 950 887	89.5	8.5
Canada	340 529	2.2	375 915	2.2	10.4
United States	677 442	4.4	672 205	4.0	–0.8
Total North America	1 017 971	6.6	1 048 120	6.3	3.0
Australia	23 581	0.2	23 030	0.1	–2.3
New Zealand	4 185	0.0	4 971	0.0	18.8
Japan	73 312	0.5	76 787	0.5	4.7
Total Australasia and Japan	101 078	0.7	104 788	0.6	3.7
Total OECD Countries	**14 902 116**	**96.3**	**16 103 795**	**96.4**	**8.1**
Yugoslavia	5 172	0.0	8 343	0.0	61.3
Other European countries	40 823	0.3	41 577	0.2	1.8
Bulgaria	4 421	0.0	2 423	0.0	–45.2
Czechoslovakia	5 609	0.0	5 006	0.0	–10.8
Hungary	2 980	0.0	3 543	0.0	18.9
Poland	8 311	0.1	5 093	0.0	–38.7
Rumania	427	0.0	2 211	0.0	417.8
USSR	14 887	0.1	19 546	0.1	31.3
Latin America	272 897	1.8	288 089	1.7	5.6
Argentina	12 164	0.1	13 593	0.1	11.7
Brazil	220 424	1.4	238 759	1.4	8.3
Chile	3 007	0.0	2 996	0.0	–0.4
Colombia	3 138	0.0	2 208	0.0	–29.6
Mexico	7 105	0.0	8 740	0.1	23.0
Venezuela	17 767	0.1	13 374	0.1	–24.7
Asia-Oceania	60 874	0.4	49 104	0.3	–19.3
China	3 569	0.0	6 132	0.0	71.8
Iran	3 466	0.0	1 703	0.0	–50.9
Israel	22 219	0.1	16 968	0.1	–23.6
Lebanon	1 343	0.0	842	0.0	–37.3
Philippines	3 534	0.0	2 740	0.0	–22.5
Saudi Arabia	6 399	0.0	3 635	0.0	–43.2
Africa	185 606	1.2	219 424	1.3	18.2
Egypt	1 712	0.0	1 988	0.0	16.1
Morocco	14 603	0.1	12 263	0.1	–16.0
South Africa	47 464	0.3	56 185	0.3	18.4
Total non-OECD Countries	**565 372**	**3.7**	**606 537**	**3.6**	**7.3**
TOTAL	**15 467 488**	**100.0**	**16 710 332**	**100.0**	**8.0**

1. Includes nights spent at hotels, studio-hotels, holiday-flats, villages, motels, inns and boarding-houses.

PORTUGAL

NIGHTS SPENT BY FOREIGN TOURISTS IN REGISTERED TOURIST ACCOMMODATION[1]

(by country of residence)

	1989	Relative share	1990	Relative share	% Variation over 1989
Austria	162 388	0.9	170 710	0.9	5.1
Belgium	504 272	2.8	505 463	2.6	0.2
Denmark	435 519	2.4	459 741	2.4	5.6
Finland	455 568	2.5	543 694	2.8	19.3
France	1 329 929	7.3	1 316 761	6.8	–1.0
Germany	2 752 402	15.1	2 963 668	15.3	7.7
Greece	26 136	0.1	27 643	0.1	5.8
Iceland	22 116	0.1	18 359	0.1	–17.0
Ireland	248 838	1.4	278 212	1.4	11.8
Italy	463 722	2.5	535 542	2.8	15.5
Luxembourg	16 834	0.1	27 039	0.1	60.6
Netherlands	1 743 792	9.6	1 849 867	9.6	6.1
Norway	144 401	0.8	171 971	0.9	19.1
Portugal	..	..	..	..	..
Spain	1 931 155	10.6	2 245 750	11.6	16.3
Sweden	572 111	3.1	563 279	2.9	–1.5
Switzerland	383 391	2.1	370 429	1.9	–3.4
Turkey	4 670	0.0	4 919	0.0	5.3
United Kingdom	5 239 541	28.7	5 423 920	28.0	3.5
Other OECD-Europe	..	..	..	..	..
Total Europe	16 436 785	90.2	17 476 967	90.3	6.3
Canada	351 615	1.9	388 130	2.0	10.4
United States	692 615	3.8	687 311	3.6	–0.8
Total North America	1 044 230	5.7	1 075 441	5.6	3.0
Australia	41 232	0.2	40 909	0.2	–0.8
New Zealand	14 681	0.1	15 453	0.1	5.3
Japan	74 727	0.4	79 364	0.4	6.2
Total Australasia and Japan	130 640	0.7	135 726	0.7	3.9
Total OECD Countries	**17 611 655**	**96.6**	**18 688 134**	**96.6**	**6.1**
Yugoslavia	7 037	0.0	10 611	0.1	50.8
Other European countries	49 369	0.3	49 231	0.3	–0.3
Bulgaria	4 574	0.0	3 130	0.0	–31.6
Czechoslovakia	6 197	0.0	5 768	0.0	–6.9
Hungary	7 234	0.0	6 584	0.0	–9.0
Poland	11 050	0.1	7 045	0.0	–36.2
Rumania	801	0.0	2 785	0.0	247.7
USSR	15 150	0.1	19 640	0.1	29.6
Latin America	285 929	1.6	301 909	1.6	5.6
Argentina	13 370	0.1	14 439	0.1	8.0
Brazil	229 863	1.3	249 299	1.3	8.5
Chile	3 607	0.0	3 771	0.0	4.5
Colombia	3 315	0.0	2 294	0.0	–30.8
Mexico	7 421	0.0	9 105	0.0	22.7
Venezuela	18 189	0.1	13 892	0.1	–23.6
Asia-Oceania	63 105	0.3	50 831	0.3	–19.5
China	3 622	0.0	6 208	0.0	71.4
Iran	3 597	0.0	1 871	0.0	–48.0
Israel	22 931	0.1	17 214	0.1	–24.9
Lebanon	1 357	0.0	927	0.0	–31.7
Philippines	3 551	0.0	2 766	0.0	–22.1
Saudi Arabia	6 399	0.0	3 647	0.0	–43.0
Africa	212 690	1.2	248 670	1.3	16.9
Egypt	1 736	0.0	2 027	0.0	16.8
Morocco	21 118	0.1	19 729	0.1	–6.6
South Africa	49 593	0.3	59 207	0.3	19.4
Total non-OECD Countries	**618 130**	**3.4**	**661 252**	**3.4**	**7.0**
TOTAL	**18 229 785**	**100.0**	**19 349 386**	**100.0**	**6.1**

1. Includes nights spent at hotels, studio-hotels, holiday-flats, villages, motels, inns, boarding-houses, recreation centres for children and camping-sites.

SPAIN

ARRIVALS OF FOREIGN VISITORS AT FRONTIERS[1]

(by country of nationality)

	1989	Relative share	1990	Relative share	% Variation over 1989
Austria	306 073	0.6	279 034	0.5	-8.8
Belgium	1 374 776	2.5	1 261 204	2.4	-8.3
Denmark	537 332	1.0	482 583	0.9	-10.2
Finland	487 824	0.9	457 201	0.9	-6.3
France	11 994 421	22.2	11 623 555	22.3	-3.1
Germany	6 783 753	12.5	6 880 240	13.2	1.4
Greece	67 951	0.1	106 547	0.2	56.8
Iceland	23 044	0.0	18 700	0.0	-18.9
Ireland	232 617	0.4	178 058	0.3	-23.5
Italy	1 511 618	2.8	1 656 906	3.2	9.6
Luxembourg	88 262	0.2	80 292	0.2	-9.0
Netherlands	2 034 717	3.8	1 953 887	3.8	-4.0
Norway	346 083	0.6	350 690	0.7	1.3
Portugal	10 044 244	18.6	10 106 114	19.4	0.6
Spain[2]	3 144 905	5.8	3 299 309	6.3	4.9
Sweden	857 997	1.6	782 599	1.5	-8.8
Switzerland	1 138 923	2.1	1 086 079	2.1	-4.6
Turkey	16 659	0.0	19 193	0.0	15.2
United Kingdom	7 345 831	13.6	6 286 433	12.1	-14.4
Other OECD-Europe[3]	261 829	0.5	335 315	0.6	28.1
Total Europe	48 598 859	89.9	47 243 939	90.8	-2.8
Canada	172 357	0.3	157 756	0.3	-8.5
United States	953 782	1.8	836 292	1.6	-12.3
Total North America	1 126 139	2.1	994 048	1.9	-11.7
Australia	53 940	0.1	53 872	0.1	-0.1
New Zealand	16 971	0.0	16 985	0.0	0.1
Japan	216 535	0.4	243 775	0.5	12.6
Total Australasia and Japan	287 446	0.5	314 632	0.6	9.5
Total OECD Countries	**50 012 444**	**92.5**	**48 552 619**	**93.3**	**-2.9**
Yugoslavia	43 679	0.1	79 456	0.2	81.9
Other European countries	345 034	0.6	283 351	0.5	-17.9
Bulgaria	8 136	0.0	7 601	0.0	-6.6
Czechoslovakia	9 218	0.0	14 297	0.0	55.1
Germany (D. R.)	7 792	0.0	..	..	..
Hungary	11 797	0.0	14 031	0.0	18.9
Poland	36 529	0.1	33 002	0.1	-9.7
Rumania	17 344	0.0	10 485	0.0	-39.5
USSR	254 218	0.5	203 962	0.4	-19.8
Latin America	550 630	1.0	503 141	1.0	-8.6
Argentina	112 629	0.2	105 327	0.2	-6.5
Brazil	118 661	0.2	114 419	0.2	-3.6
Chile	28 722	0.1	24 685	0.0	-14.1
Colombia	39 145	0.1	27 230	0.1	-30.4
Mexico	80 283	0.1	65 876	0.1	-17.9
Venezuela	55 976	0.1	53 712	0.1	-4.0
Asia-Oceania	208 140	0.4	218 701	0.4	5.1
Africa	2 887 026	5.3	2 397 938	4.6	-16.9
Origin country undetermined	10 609	0.0	8 850	0.0	-16.6
Total non-OECD Countries	**4 045 118**	**7.5**	**3 491 437**	**6.7**	**-13.7**
TOTAL	**54 057 562**	**100.0**	**52 044 056**	**100.0**	**-3.7**

1. Includes about 34% of arrivals of excursionists.
2. Spanish nationals residing abroad.
3. "Other OECD-Europe" includes Andorra, Cyprus, Malta, Monaco, and the Vatican States.

SPAIN

ARRIVALS OF FOREIGN TOURISTS AT HOTELS[1]

(by country of nationality)

	1989	Relative share	1990	Relative share	% Variation over 1989
Austria	..	..	411 340	3.5	..
Belgium	468 090	3.6	..	..	..
Denmark	154 917	1.2	133 286	1.1	-14.0
Finland	..	..	..	..	..
France	1 745 352	13.2	1 515 138	13.1	-13.2
Germany	2 482 027	18.8	2 361 519	20.4	-4.9
Greece	43 737	0.3	39 550	0.3	-9.6
Iceland	..	..	..	..	..
Ireland	32 701	0.2	29 532	0.3	-9.7
Italy	1 198 243	9.1	1 056 418	9.1	-11.8
Luxembourg	28 750	0.2	20 214	0.2	-29.7
Netherlands	410 149	3.1	324 924	2.8	-20.8
Norway	61 639	0.5	57 955	0.5	-6.0
Portugal	340 523	2.6	323 356	2.8	-5.0
Spain	..	..	..	..	..
Sweden	205 291	1.6	198 126	1.7	-3.5
Switzerland	356 956	2.7	322 702	2.8	-9.6
Turkey	..	..	..	..	..
United Kingdom	2 984 820	22.6	2 214 403	19.1	-25.8
Other OECD-Europe	..	..	..	..	..
Total Europe	10 513 195	79.7	9 008 463	77.7	-14.3
Canada	75 274	0.6	64 991	0.6	-13.7
United States	826 781	6.3	791 753	6.8	-4.2
Total North America	902 055	6.8	856 744	7.4	-5.0
Australia	..	..	..	..	..
New Zealand	..	..	..	..	..
Japan	471 807	3.6	498 027	4.3	5.6
Total Australasia and Japan	471 807	3.6	498 027	4.3	5.6
Total OECD Countries	**11 887 057**	**90.2**	**10 363 234**	**89.3**	**-12.8**
Yugoslavia	..	..	..	..	..
Other European countries	343 333	2.6	319 476	2.8	-6.9
Latin America	499 165	3.8	442 397	3.8	-11.4
Origin country undetermined	454 857	3.4	475 538	4.1	4.5
Total non-OECD Countries	**1 297 355**	**9.8**	**1 237 411**	**10.7**	**-4.6**
TOTAL	**13 184 412**	**100.0**	**11 600 645**	**100.0**	**-12.0**

1. Arrivals recorded in hotels with "estrellas de oro" (golden stars) and "estrellas de plata" (silver stars).

SPAIN

NIGHTS SPENT BY FOREIGN TOURISTS IN HOTELS[1]

(by country of nationality)

	1988	Relative share	1989	Relative share	% Variation over 1988
Austria	..	..	..	..	..
Belgium	3 698 174	4.2	3 456 487	4.4	-6.5
Denmark	1 275 846	1.4	1 073 560	1.4	-15.9
Finland	..	..	..	..	..
France	7 115 042	8.1	7 049 426	9.0	-0.9
Germany	24 635 737	27.9	21 791 970	27.8	-11.5
Greece	84 078	0.1	99 195	0.1	18.0
Iceland	..	..	..	..	..
Ireland	196 135	0.2	150 897	0.2	-23.1
Italy	4 650 705	5.3	4 587 802	5.9	-1.4
Luxembourg	240 737	0.3	225 199	0.3	-6.5
Netherlands	3 324 088	3.8	2 810 356	3.6	-15.5
Norway	430 624	0.5	299 475	0.4	-30.5
Portugal	687 368	0.8	683 368	0.9	-0.6
Spain	..	..	..	..	..
Sweden	1 211 566	1.4	1 182 807	1.5	-2.4
Switzerland	2 400 842	2.7	2 171 330	2.8	-9.6
Turkey	..	..	..	..	..
United Kingdom	31 291 489	35.4	25 253 002	32.3	-19.3
Other OECD-Europe	..	..	..	..	..
Total Europe	81 242 431	92.0	70 834 874	90.5	-12.8
Canada	182 900	0.2	177 846	0.2	-2.8
United States	1 756 732	2.0	1 835 837	2.3	4.5
Total North America	1 939 632	2.2	2 013 683	2.6	3.8
Australia	..	..	..	..	..
New Zealand	..	..	..	..	..
Japan	639 230	0.7	857 065	1.1	34.1
Total Australasia and Japan	639 230	0.7	857 065	1.1	34.1
Total OECD Countries	**83 821 293**	**94.9**	**73 705 622**	**94.1**	**-12.1**
Yugoslavia	..	..	..	..	..
Other European countries	2 000 685	2.3	2 149 697	2.7	7.4
Latin America	1 190 002	1.3	1 164 819	1.5	-2.1
Origin country undetermined	1 339 017	1.5	1 281 268	1.6	-4.3
Total non-OECD Countries	**4 529 704**	**5.1**	**4 595 784**	**5.9**	**1.5**
TOTAL	**88 350 997**	**100.0**	**78 301 406**	**100.0**	**-11.4**

1. Nights recorded in hotels with "estrellas de oro" (golden stars) and "estrellas de plata" (silver stars).

SWEDEN

NIGHTS SPENT BY FOREIGN TOURISTS IN HOTELS

(by country of nationality)

	1989	Relative share	1990	Relative share	% Variation over 1989
Austria[1]	..	..	..	..	..
Belgium[1]	..	..	..	..	..
Denmark	218 040	6.5	198 396	6.2	-9.0
Finland	399 549	11.9	368 287	11.5	-7.8
France	96 153	2.9	98 268	3.1	2.2
Germany	510 670	15.2	464 483	14.5	-9.0
Greece[1]	..	..	..	..	..
Iceland[1]	..	..	..	..	..
Ireland[1]	..	..	..	..	..
Italy	117 855	3.5	123 467	3.9	4.8
Luxembourg[1]	..	..	..	..	..
Netherlands	76 064	2.3	77 938	2.4	2.5
Norway	588 033	17.5	464 483	14.5	-21.0
Portugal[1]	..	..	..	..	..
Spain[1]	..	..	..	..	..
Sweden	..	..	..	..	..
Switzerland	72 820	2.2	61 462	1.9	-15.6
Turkey[1]	..	..	..	..	..
United Kingdom	265 884	7.9	270 767	8.5	1.8
Other OECD-Europe	..	..	..	..	..
Total Europe	2 345 068	69.7	2 127 551	66.6	-9.3
Canada	25 075	0.7	25 972	0.8	3.6
United States	331 449	9.8	326 900	10.2	-1.4
Total North America	356 524	10.6	352 872	11.1	-1.0
Australia[2]	..	..	..	..	..
New Zealand[2]	..	..	..	..	..
Japan	81 581	2.4	94 350	3.0	15.7
Total Australasia and Japan	81 581	2.4	94 350	3.0	15.7
Total OECD Countries	**2 783 173**	**82.7**	**2 574 773**	**80.6**	**-7.5**
Yugoslavia	..	..	..	..	..
Other European countries[1]	251 372	7.5	285 941	9.0	13.8
Origin country undetermined[2]	332 354	9.9	332 448	10.4	0.0
Total non-OECD Countries	**583 726**	**17.3**	**618 389**	**19.4**	**5.9**
TOTAL	**3 366 899**	**100.0**	**3 193 162**	**100.0**	**-5.2**

1. Included in "Other European countries".
2. Included in "Origin country undetermined".

SWEDEN

NIGHTS SPENT BY FOREIGN TOURISTS IN REGISTERED TOURIST ACCOMMODATION

(by country of nationality)

	1989	Relative share	1990	Relative share	% Variation over 1989
Austria[1]	..	..	..	..	..
Belgium[1]	..	..	..	..	..
Denmark	656 744	8.7	586 946	8.9	–10.6
Finland	640 910	8.5	579 758	8.8	–9.5
France	166 622	2.2	182 423	2.8	9.5
Germany	1 514 151	20.0	1 402 342	21.3	–7.4
Greece[1]	..	..	..	..	..
Iceland[1]	..	..	..	..	..
Ireland[1]	..	..	..	..	..
Italy	135 843	1.8	140 935	2.1	3.7
Luxembourg[1]	..	..	..	..	..
Netherlands	399 479	5.3	380 364	5.8	–4.8
Norway	2 288 849	30.2	1 546 139	23.5	–32.4
Portugal[1]	..	..	..	..	..
Spain[1]	..	..	..	..	..
Sweden	..	..	..	..	..
Switzerland	88 266	1.2	77 931	1.2	–11.7
Turkey[1]	..	..	..	..	..
United Kingdom	341 204	4.5	336 192	5.1	–1.5
Other OECD-Europe	..	..	..	..	..
Total Europe	6 232 068	82.2	5 233 030	79.6	–16.0
Canada	28 101	0.4	29 159	0.4	3.8
United States	347 643	4.6	342 216	5.2	–1.6
Total North America	375 744	5.0	371 375	5.6	–1.2
Australia[2]	..	..	..	..	..
New Zealand[2]	..	..	..	..	..
Japan	83 817	1.1	97 126	1.5	15.9
Total Australasia and Japan	83 817	1.1	97 126	1.5	15.9
Total OECD Countries	**6 691 629**	**88.2**	**5 701 531**	**86.7**	**–14.8**
Yugoslavia	..	..	..	..	..
Other European countries[1]	424 704	5.6	431 156	6.6	1.5
Origin country undetermined[2]	467 688	6.2	442 980	6.7	–5.3
Total non-OECD Countries	**892 392**	**11.8**	**874 136**	**13.3**	**–2.0**
TOTAL	**7 584 021**	**100.0**	**6 575 667**	**100.0**	**–13.3**

1. Included in "Other European countries".
2. Included in "Origin country undetermined".

SWITZERLAND

ARRIVALS OF FOREIGN TOURISTS AT HOTELS

(by country of residence)

	1989	Relative share	1990	Relative share	% Variation over 1989
Austria	164 695	2.1	168 479	2.1	2.3
Belgium	219 331	2.9	215 508	2.7	-1.7
Denmark	44 620	0.6	41 627	0.5	-6.7
Finland	34 708	0.5	39 239	0.5	13.1
France	561 007	7.3	562 131	7.1	0.2
Germany	2 130 168	27.8	2 102 289	26.4	-1.3
Greece	55 013	0.7	58 435	0.7	6.2
Iceland [1]	..	..	..	..	..
Ireland	14 206	0.2	15 355	0.2	8.1
Italy	614 178	8.0	637 318	8.0	3.8
Luxembourg	26 401	0.3	26 381	0.3	-0.1
Netherlands	266 645	3.5	264 285	3.3	-0.9
Norway	34 102	0.4	33 641	0.4	-1.4
Portugal	38 083	0.5	42 052	0.5	10.4
Spain	249 237	3.2	262 749	3.3	5.4
Sweden	114 005	1.5	111 876	1.4	-1.9
Switzerland	..	..	..	..	..
Turkey	33 251	0.4	35 420	0.4	6.5
United Kingdom	565 255	7.4	604 448	7.6	6.9
Other OECD-Europe	..	..	..	..	..
Total Europe	5 164 905	67.3	5 221 233	65.6	1.1
Canada	100 031	1.3	108 491	1.4	8.5
United States	1 032 600	13.5	1 204 047	15.1	16.6
Total North America	1 132 631	14.8	1 312 538	16.5	15.9
Australia [2]	95 022	1.2	95 629	1.2	0.6
New Zealand [2]	..	..	..	..	..
Japan	472 268	6.2	497 648	6.2	5.4
Total Australasia and Japan	567 290	7.4	593 277	7.5	4.6
Total OECD Countries	**6 864 826**	**89.5**	**7 127 048**	**89.5**	**3.8**
Yugoslavia	46 094	0.6	52 384	0.7	13.6
Other European countries [1]	86 533	1.1	111 866	1.4	29.3
Germany (D. R.)	6 440	0.1	14 854	0.2	130.7
USSR	14 138	0.2	19 280	0.2	36.4
Latin America	146 413	1.9	142 508	1.8	-2.7
Argentina	19 708	0.3	19 651	0.2	-0.3
Brazil	55 604	0.7	57 154	0.7	2.8
Mexico	21 197	0.3	20 554	0.3	-3.0
Asia-Oceania	397 900	5.2	398 245	5.0	0.1
India	34 550	0.5	35 953	0.5	4.1
Iran	10 891	0.1	12 806	0.2	17.6
Israel	125 620	1.6	117 728	1.5	-6.3
Africa	131 359	1.7	131 108	1.6	-0.2
Egypt	22 767	0.3	19 297	0.2	-15.2
South Africa	29 683	0.4	31 449	0.4	5.9
Total non-OECD Countries	**808 299**	**10.5**	**836 111**	**10.5**	**3.4**
TOTAL	**7 673 125**	**100.0**	**7 963 159**	**100.0**	**3.8**

1. "Other European countries" includes Iceland.
2. Australia includes New Zealand.

SWITZERLAND

ARRIVALS OF FOREIGN TOURISTS AT REGISTERED TOURIST ACCOMMODATION

(by country of residence)

	1989	Relative share	1990	Relative share	% Variation over 1989
Austria	202 925	2.0	209 677	2.0	3.3
Belgium	342 237	3.4	353 697	3.4	3.3
Denmark	65 644	0.7	60 900	0.6	-7.2
Finland	44 461	0.4	49 513	0.5	11.4
France	739 647	7.3	750 306	7.1	1.4
Germany	3 251 271	32.2	3 250 844	30.9	-0.0
Greece	57 570	0.6	61 090	0.6	6.1
Iceland[1]	..	..	..	..	..
Ireland	19 076	0.2	20 295	0.2	6.4
Italy	711 687	7.1	748 470	7.1	5.2
Luxembourg	35 454	0.4	35 671	0.3	0.6
Netherlands	555 834	5.5	570 985	5.4	2.7
Norway	39 421	0.4	39 777	0.4	0.9
Portugal	45 410	0.4	49 238	0.5	8.4
Spain	314 676	3.1	341 770	3.2	8.6
Sweden	138 402	1.4	136 428	1.3	-1.4
Switzerland	..	..	..	..	..
Turkey	35 154	0.3	36 813	0.3	4.7
United Kingdom	715 429	7.1	749 277	7.1	4.7
Other OECD-Europe	..	..	..	..	..
Total Europe	7 314 298	72.5	7 464 751	70.9	2.1
Canada	122 360	1.2	131 118	1.2	7.2
United States	1 113 721	11.0	1 288 588	12.2	15.7
Total North America	1 236 081	12.2	1 419 706	13.5	14.9
Australia[2]	147 731	1.5	155 684	1.5	5.4
New Zealand[2]	..	..	..	..	..
Japan	489 542	4.9	515 073	4.9	5.2
Total Australasia and Japan	637 273	6.3	670 757	6.4	5.3
Total OECD Countries	**9 187 652**	**91.0**	**9 555 214**	**90.8**	**4.0**
Yugoslavia	52 602	0.5	60 100	0.6	14.3
Other European countries[1]	104 455	1.0	150 550	1.4	44.1
Latin America	162 019	1.6	160 393	1.5	-1.0
Argentina	22 192	0.2	22 193	0.2	0.0
Brazil	62 346	0.6	64 876	0.6	4.1
Mexico	23 600	0.2	23 325	0.2	-1.2
Asia-Oceania	434 975	4.3	442 635	4.2	1.8
India	36 660	0.4	38 297	0.4	4.5
Iran	11 632	0.1	13 704	0.1	17.8
Israel	139 049	1.4	130 702	1.2	-6.0
Africa	151 731	1.5	155 072	1.5	2.2
Egypt	24 220	0.2	20 049	0.2	-17.2
South Africa	35 545	0.4	38 948	0.4	9.6
Total non-OECD Countries	**905 782**	**9.0**	**968 750**	**9.2**	**7.0**
TOTAL	**10 093 434**	**100.0**	**10 523 964**	**100.0**	**4.3**

1. "Other European countries" includes Iceland.
2. Australia includes New Zealand.

SWITZERLAND

NIGHTS SPENT BY FOREIGN TOURISTS IN HOTELS

(by country of residence)

	1989	Relative share	1990	Relative share	% Variation over 1989
Austria	370 200	1.8	386 147	1.8	4.3
Belgium	858 430	4.2	863 649	4.1	0.6
Denmark	107 467	0.5	101 685	0.5	-5.4
Finland	80 599	0.4	91 757	0.4	13.8
France	1 576 870	7.7	1 535 088	7.3	-2.6
Germany	6 492 704	31.7	6 415 768	30.5	-1.2
Greece	133 050	0.6	139 765	0.7	5.0
Iceland [1]	..	..	..	..	..
Ireland	35 630	0.2	37 901	0.2	6.4
Italy	1 268 227	6.2	1 364 828	6.5	7.6
Luxembourg	97 245	0.5	99 427	0.5	2.2
Netherlands	859 552	4.2	861 937	4.1	0.3
Norway	73 996	0.4	73 991	0.4	-0.0
Portugal	85 948	0.4	89 556	0.4	4.2
Spain	454 118	2.2	470 186	2.2	3.5
Sweden	262 216	1.3	268 942	1.3	2.6
Switzerland	..	..	..	..	..
Turkey	159 690	0.8	141 378	0.7	-11.5
United Kingdom	1 923 820	9.4	2 023 310	9.6	5.2
Other OECD-Europe	..	..	..	..	..
Total Europe	14 839 762	72.4	14 965 315	71.1	0.8
Canada	217 828	1.1	235 059	1.1	7.9
United States	2 224 447	10.9	2 510 625	11.9	12.9
Total North America	2 442 275	11.9	2 745 684	13.0	12.4
Australia [2]	208 985	1.0	209 688	1.0	0.3
New Zealand [2]	..	..	..	..	..
Japan	782 234	3.8	818 604	3.9	4.6
Total Australasia and Japan	991 219	4.8	1 028 292	4.9	3.7
Total OECD Countries	**18 273 256**	**89.2**	**18 739 291**	**89.1**	**2.6**
Yugoslavia	110 571	0.5	139 924	0.7	26.5
Other European countries [1]	272 931	1.3	352 254	1.7	29.1
Germany (D. R.)	19 405	0.1	38 221	0.2	97.0
USSR	62 200	0.3	79 603	0.4	28.0
Latin America	346 958	1.7	342 309	1.6	-1.3
Argentina	51 169	0.2	49 925	0.2	-2.4
Brazil	134 777	0.7	134 575	0.6	-0.1
Mexico	43 374	0.2	44 672	0.2	3.0
Asia-Oceania	1 060 076	5.2	1 036 590	4.9	-2.2
India	91 541	0.4	94 192	0.4	2.9
Iran	38 919	0.2	44 368	0.2	14.0
Israel	335 419	1.6	303 112	1.4	-9.6
Africa	425 619	2.1	430 375	2.0	1.1
Egypt	75 013	0.4	69 296	0.3	-7.6
South Africa	80 758	0.4	82 511	0.4	2.2
Total non-OECD Countries	**2 216 155**	**10.8**	**2 301 452**	**10.9**	**3.8**
TOTAL	**20 489 411**	**100.0**	**21 040 743**	**100.0**	**2.7**

1. "Other European countries" includes Iceland.
2. Australia includes New Zealand.

SWITZERLAND

NIGHTS SPENT BY FOREIGN TOURISTS IN REGISTERED TOURIST ACCOMMODATION

(by country of residence)

	1989	Relative share	1990	Relative share	% Variation over 1989
Austria	519 278	1.4	543 010	1.5	4.6
Belgium	1 899 637	5.3	1 994 565	5.4	5.0
Denmark	206 792	0.6	191 860	0.5	-7.2
Finland	105 316	0.3	117 316	0.3	11.4
France	2 472 371	6.9	2 432 993	6.6	-1.6
Germany	14 942 990	41.6	14 841 330	40.2	-0.7
Greece	143 652	0.4	151 321	0.4	5.3
Iceland[1]	..	..	..	..	..
Ireland	48 987	0.1	50 500	0.1	3.1
Italy	1 728 169	4.8	1 913 407	5.2	10.7
Luxembourg	180 067	0.5	180 918	0.5	0.5
Netherlands	3 160 060	8.8	3 283 748	8.9	3.9
Norway	88 757	0.2	90 825	0.2	2.3
Portugal	105 524	0.3	109 583	0.3	3.8
Spain	639 787	1.8	700 777	1.9	9.5
Sweden	361 290	1.0	384 044	1.0	6.3
Switzerland	..	..	..	..	..
Turkey	187 304	0.5	151 392	0.4	-19.2
United Kingdom	2 723 658	7.6	2 783 192	7.5	2.2
Other OECD-Europe	..	..	..	..	..
Total Europe	29 513 639	82.1	29 920 781	81.1	1.4
Canada	268 632	0.7	284 875	0.8	6.0
United States	2 478 407	6.9	2 767 518	7.5	11.7
Total North America	2 747 039	7.6	3 052 393	8.3	11.1
Australia[2]	309 914	0.9	328 124	0.9	5.9
New Zealand[2]	..	..	..	..	..
Japan	813 156	2.3	849 689	2.3	4.5
Total Australasia and Japan	1 123 070	3.1	1 177 813	3.2	4.9
Total OECD Countries	**33 383 748**	**92.9**	**34 150 987**	**92.6**	**2.3**
Yugoslavia	133 887	0.4	168 052	0.5	25.5
Other European countries[1]	323 807	0.9	467 904	1.3	44.5
Latin America	392 040	1.1	389 149	1.1	-0.7
Argentina	57 817	0.2	55 333	0.2	-4.3
Brazil	153 689	0.4	153 482	0.4	-0.1
Mexico	48 380	0.1	49 930	0.1	3.2
Asia-Oceania	1 211 572	3.4	1 195 630	3.2	-1.3
India	97 027	0.3	101 159	0.3	4.3
Iran	42 874	0.1	47 895	0.1	11.7
Israel	414 584	1.2	378 634	1.0	-8.7
Africa	507 204	1.4	503 920	1.4	-0.6
Egypt	89 540	0.2	73 896	0.2	-17.5
South Africa	95 455	0.3	104 276	0.3	9.2
Total non-OECD Countries	**2 568 510**	**7.1**	**2 724 655**	**7.4**	**6.1**
TOTAL	**35 952 258**	**100.0**	**36 875 642**	**100.0**	**2.6**

1. "Other European countries" includes Iceland.
2. Australia includes New Zealand.

TURKEY

ARRIVALS OF FOREIGN TRAVELLERS AT FRONTIERS

(by country of nationality)

	1989	Relative share	1990	Relative share	% Variation over 1989
Austria	156 875	3.5	196 561	3.6	25.3
Belgium	47 533	1.1	56 258	1.0	18.4
Denmark	32 362	0.7	34 507	0.6	6.6
Finland	69 626	1.6	104 321	1.9	49.8
France	283 545	6.4	310 809	5.8	9.6
Germany	896 989	20.1	973 914	18.1	8.6
Greece	277 333	6.2	227 709	4.2	-17.9
Iceland[1]	..	..	..	..	..
Ireland[1]	..	..	..	..	..
Italy	154 083	3.5	156 342	2.9	1.5
Luxembourg[1]	..	..	..	..	..
Netherlands	106 709	2.4	150 337	2.8	40.9
Norway	25 735	0.6	39 889	0.7	55.0
Portugal[1]	..	..	..	..	..
Spain	56 176	1.3	62 220	1.2	10.8
Sweden	66 761	1.5	110 204	2.0	65.1
Switzerland	77 945	1.7	76 368	1.4	-2.0
Turkey	..	..	..	..	..
United Kingdom	405 943	9.1	351 458	6.5	-13.4
Other OECD-Europe[1]	32 215	0.7	35 359	0.7	9.8
Total Europe	2 689 830	60.3	2 886 256	53.6	7.3
Canada	31 587	0.7	34 575	0.6	9.5
United States	204 502	4.6	205 831	3.8	0.6
Total North America	236 089	5.3	240 406	4.5	1.8
Australia	33 628	0.8	37 045	0.7	10.2
New Zealand	9 584	0.2	12 937	0.2	35.0
Japan	32 298	0.7	35 358	0.7	9.5
Total Australasia and Japan	75 510	1.7	85 340	1.6	13.0
Total OECD Countries	**3 001 429**	**67.3**	**3 212 002**	**59.6**	**7.0**
Yugoslavia	217 266	4.9	325 703	6.0	49.9
Other European countries	481 178	10.8	1 134 160	21.0	135.7
Bulgaria	15 626	0.4	72 741	1.3	365.5
Czechoslovakia	11 942	0.3	66 224	1.2	454.5
Germany (D. R.)	2 719	0.1	10 512	0.2	286.6
Hungary	194 391	4.4	172 357	3.2	-11.3
Poland	196 376	4.4	206 682	3.8	5.2
Rumania	13 223	0.3	377 275	7.0	2753.2
USSR	43 369	1.0	223 211	4.1	414.7
Latin America	27 158	0.6	30 470	0.6	12.2
Argentina	3 147	0.1	2 491	0.0	-20.8
Brazil	7 531	0.2	5 336	0.1	-29.1
Chile	1 236	0.0	878	0.0	-29.0
Mexico	7 048	0.2	6 162	0.1	-12.6
Asia-Oceania	591 049	13.3	590 824	11.0	-0.0
Iran	240 972	5.4	253 452	4.7	5.2
Israel	41 058	0.9	40 064	0.7	-2.4
Lebanon	16 766	0.4	14 655	0.3	-12.6
Pakistan	14 136	0.3	15 252	0.3	7.9
Saudi Arabia	27 338	0.6	16 417	0.3	-39.9
Africa	133 912	3.0	89 924	1.7	-32.8
Algeria	17 575	0.4	9 737	0.2	-44.6
Egypt	15 452	0.3	11 102	0.2	-28.2
Morocco	6 074	0.1	5 695	0.1	-6.2
Origin country undetermined[2]	7 159	0.2	6 225	0.1	-13.0
Total non-OECD Countries	**1 457 722**	**32.7**	**2 177 306**	**40.4**	**49.4**
TOTAL	**4 459 151**	**100.0**	**5 389 308**	**100.0**	**20.9**

1. "Other OECD-Europe" includes Iceland, Ireland, Luxembourg and Portugal.
2. "Origin country undetermined" includes Other North America and Stateless persons.

TURKEY

ARRIVALS OF FOREIGN TOURISTS AT HOTELS

(by country of nationality)

	1989	Relative share	1990	Relative share	% Variation over 1989
Austria	101 591	2.9	114 267	3.3	12.5
Belgium[1]	178 147	5.1	206 345	5.9	15.8
Denmark[2]	150 754	4.3	169 596	4.9	12.5
Finland[2]	..	..	..	..	..
France	655 816	18.9	631 868	18.1	-3.7
Germany	950 001	27.4	960 575	27.5	1.1
Greece	65 501	1.9	65 124	1.9	-0.6
Iceland	..	..	..	..	..
Ireland	..	..	..	..	..
Italy	197 465	5.7	207 337	5.9	5.0
Luxembourg[1]	..	..	..	..	..
Netherlands[1]	..	..	..	..	..
Norway[2]	..	..	..	..	..
Portugal	..	..	..	..	..
Spain	89 576	2.6	92 355	2.6	3.1
Sweden[2]	..	..	..	..	..
Switzerland	67 857	2.0	65 089	1.9	-4.1
Turkey	..	..	..	..	..
United Kingdom	203 779	5.9	174 624	5.0	-14.3
Other OECD-Europe	..	..	..	..	..
Total Europe	2 660 487	76.7	2 687 180	76.9	1.0
Canada	15 802	0.5	13 050	0.4	-17.4
United States	167 555	4.8	158 428	4.5	-5.4
Total North America	183 357	5.3	171 478	4.9	-6.5
Australia	14 905	0.4	17 612	0.5	18.2
New Zealand	..	..	..	..	..
Japan	74 163	2.1	77 046	2.2	3.9
Total Australasia and Japan	89 068	2.6	94 658	2.7	6.3
Total OECD Countries	**2 932 912**	**84.6**	**2 953 316**	**84.5**	**0.7**
Yugoslavia	22 523	0.6	48 721	1.4	116.3
Other European countries	113 298	3.3	144 781	4.1	27.8
Bulgaria	5 611	0.2	10 825	0.3	92.9
Hungary	55 719	1.6	41 868	1.2	-24.9
Poland	32 628	0.9	37 109	1.1	13.7
Rumania	5 101	0.1	27 959	0.8	448.1
USSR	14 239	0.4	27 020	0.8	89.8
Asia-Oceania[3]	157 162	4.5	115 702	3.3	-26.4
Iran	54 966	1.6	45 111	1.3	-17.9
Lebanon	8 307	0.2	6 440	0.2	-22.5
Pakistan	10 297	0.3	7 836	0.2	-23.9
Saudi Arabia	32 899	0.9	21 334	0.6	-35.2
Africa	18 753	0.5	14 190	0.4	-24.3
Egypt	8 671	0.3	5 279	0.2	-39.1
Origin country undetermined	223 177	6.4	218 634	6.3	-2.0
Total non-OECD Countries	**534 913**	**15.4**	**542 028**	**15.5**	**1.3**
TOTAL	**3 467 825**	**100.0**	**3 495 344**	**100.0**	**0.8**

1. Belgium includes Luxembourg and Netherlands.
2. Denmark includes Finland, Norway and Sweden.
3. Asia-Oceania includes Iraq, Kuwait, Lebanon, Syria, Saudi Arabia, Jordan, Iran and Pakistan.

TURKEY

ARRIVALS OF FOREIGN TOURISTS AT REGISTERED TOURIST ACCOMMODATION

(by country of nationality)

	1989	Relative share	1990	Relative share	% Variation over 1989
Austria	128 908	3.4	167 894	4.3	30.2
Belgium[1]	193 948	5.1	223 308	5.8	15.1
Denmark[2]	163 183	4.3	176 140	4.6	7.9
Finland[2]	..	..	..	..	..
France	709 696	18.8	694 566	18.0	-2.1
Germany	1 081 801	28.6	1 113 735	28.8	3.0
Greece	66 457	1.8	66 293	1.7	-0.2
Iceland	..	..	..	..	..
Ireland	..	..	..	..	..
Italy	225 353	6.0	235 140	6.1	4.3
Luxembourg[1]	..	..	..	..	..
Netherlands[1]	..	..	..	..	..
Norway[2]	..	..	..	..	..
Portugal	..	..	..	..	..
Spain	90 951	2.4	93 659	2.4	3.0
Sweden[2]	..	..	..	..	..
Switzerland	80 235	2.1	84 103	2.2	4.8
Turkey	..	..	..	..	..
United Kingdom	214 096	5.7	181 942	4.7	-15.0
Other OECD-Europe	..	..	..	..	..
Total Europe	2 954 628	78.1	3 036 780	78.5	2.8
Canada	16 132	0.4	13 454	0.3	-16.6
United States	169 919	4.5	161 058	4.2	-5.2
Total North America	186 051	4.9	174 512	4.5	-6.2
Australia	15 370	0.4	18 912	0.5	23.0
New Zealand	..	..	..	..	..
Japan	74 421	2.0	77 464	2.0	4.1
Total Australasia and Japan	89 791	2.4	96 376	2.5	7.3
Total OECD Countries	**3 230 470**	**85.4**	**3 307 668**	**85.5**	**2.4**
Yugoslavia	22 933	0.6	49 286	1.3	114.9
Other European countries	116 808	3.1	151 801	3.9	30.0
Bulgaria	5 612	0.1	11 091	0.3	97.6
Hungary	56 456	1.5	43 625	1.1	-22.7
Poland	34 157	0.9	40 468	1.0	18.5
Rumania	6 067	0.2	29 037	0.8	378.6
USSR	14 516	0.4	27 580	0.7	90.0
Asia-Oceania[3]	164 731	4.4	120 694	3.1	-26.7
Iran	56 062	1.5	46 313	1.2	-17.4
Lebanon	8 699	0.2	6 667	0.2	-23.4
Pakistan	10 626	0.3	7 958	0.2	-25.1
Saudi Arabia	37 191	1.0	23 712	0.6	-36.2
Africa	19 144	0.5	14 451	0.4	-24.5
Egypt	8 880	0.2	5 501	0.1	-38.1
Origin country undetermined	229 855	6.1	225 266	5.8	-2.0
Total non-OECD Countries	**553 471**	**14.6**	**561 498**	**14.5**	**1.5**
TOTAL	**3 783 941**	**100.0**	**3 869 166**	**100.0**	**2.3**

1. Belgium includes Luxembourg and Netherlands.
2. Denmark includes Finland, Norway and Sweden.
3. Asia-Oceania includes Iraq, Kuwait, Lebanon, Syria, Saudi Arabia, Jordan, Iran and Pakistan.

TURKEY

NIGHTS SPENT BY FOREIGN TOURISTS IN HOTELS

(by country of nationality)

	1989	Relative share	1990	Relative share	% Variation over 1989
Austria	380 915	3.9	486 455	4.7	27.7
Belgium [1]	459 583	4.7	640 452	6.2	39.4
Denmark [2]	660 992	6.8	751 576	7.3	13.7
Finland [2]	..	..	..	..	..
France	1 133 899	11.6	1 204 113	11.7	6.2
Germany	3 689 697	37.9	3 898 518	37.8	5.7
Greece	124 253	1.3	129 816	1.3	4.5
Iceland	..	..	..	..	..
Ireland	..	..	..	..	..
Italy	378 578	3.9	400 878	3.9	5.9
Luxembourg [1]	..	..	..	..	..
Netherlands [1]	..	..	..	..	..
Norway [2]	..	..	..	..	..
Portugal	..	..	..	..	..
Spain	169 652	1.7	185 758	1.8	9.5
Sweden [2]	..	..	..	..	..
Switzerland	225 407	2.3	249 466	2.4	10.7
Turkey	..	..	..	..	..
United Kingdom	774 132	7.9	635 154	6.2	-18.0
Other OECD-Europe	..	..	..	..	..
Total Europe	7 997 108	82.1	8 582 186	83.3	7.3
Canada	30 801	0.3	28 044	0.3	-9.0
United States	380 779	3.9	348 767	3.4	-8.4
Total North America	411 580	4.2	376 811	3.7	-8.4
Australia	28 925	0.3	32 576	0.3	12.6
New Zealand	..	..	..	..	..
Japan	134 742	1.4	134 267	1.3	-0.4
Total Australasia and Japan	163 667	1.7	166 843	1.6	1.9
Total OECD Countries	**8 572 355**	**88.0**	**9 125 840**	**88.6**	**6.5**
Yugoslavia	39 147	0.4	81 503	0.8	108.2
Other European countries	289 634	3.0	337 269	3.3	16.4
Bulgaria	7 635	0.1	15 422	0.1	102.0
Hungary	139 683	1.4	96 717	0.9	-30.8
Poland	95 463	1.0	98 717	1.0	3.4
Rumania	14 217	0.1	65 556	0.6	361.1
USSR	32 636	0.3	60 857	0.6	86.5
Asia-Oceania [3]	331 859	3.4	262 305	2.5	-21.0
Iran	119 271	1.2	113 151	1.1	-5.1
Lebanon	17 643	0.2	12 980	0.1	-26.4
Pakistan	16 745	0.2	14 292	0.1	-14.6
Saudi Arabia	75 676	0.8	46 509	0.5	-38.5
Africa	46 514	0.5	36 225	0.4	-22.1
Egypt	21 168	0.2	13 967	0.1	-34.0
Origin country undetermined	462 803	4.8	457 432	4.4	-1.2
Total non-OECD Countries	**1 169 957**	**12.0**	**1 174 734**	**11.4**	**0.4**
TOTAL	**9 742 312**	**100.0**	**10 300 574**	**100.0**	**5.7**

1. Belgium includes Luxembourg and Netherlands.
2. Denmark includes Finland, Norway and Sweden.
3. Asia-Oceania includes Iraq, Kuwait, Lebanon, Syria, Saudi Arabia, Jordan, Iran and Pakistan.

TURKEY

NIGHTS SPENT BY FOREIGN TOURISTS IN REGISTERED TOURIST ACCOMMODATION

(by country of nationality)

	1989	Relative share	1990	Relative share	% Variation over 1989
Austria	594 535	5.0	1 004 432	7.6	68.9
Belgium[1]	569 652	4.8	737 729	5.6	29.5
Denmark[2]	744 163	6.3	802 997	6.1	7.9
Finland[2]	..	..	..	..	..
France	1 476 849	12.4	1 586 354	12.0	7.4
Germany	4 709 013	39.7	5 426 311	40.9	15.2
Greece	127 697	1.1	132 419	1.0	3.7
Iceland	..	..	..	..	..
Ireland	..	..	..	..	..
Italy	489 819	4.1	533 676	4.0	9.0
Luxembourg[1]	..	..	..	..	..
Netherlands[1]	..	..	..	..	..
Norway[2]	..	..	..	..	..
Portugal	..	..	..	..	..
Spain	173 057	1.5	191 621	1.4	10.7
Sweden[2]	..	..	..	..	..
Switzerland	343 405	2.9	394 564	3.0	14.9
Turkey	..	..	..	..	..
United Kingdom	841 727	7.1	675 111	5.1	-19.8
Other OECD-Europe	..	..	..	..	..
Total Europe	10 069 917	84.9	11 485 214	86.5	14.1
Canada	31 631	0.3	29 266	0.2	-7.5
United States	388 945	3.3	357 293	2.7	-8.1
Total North America	420 576	3.5	386 559	2.9	-8.1
Australia	30 819	0.3	36 207	0.3	17.5
New Zealand	..	..	..	..	..
Japan	135 295	1.1	135 101	1.0	-0.1
Total Australasia and Japan	166 114	1.4	171 308	1.3	3.1
Total OECD Countries	**10 656 607**	**89.8**	**12 043 081**	**90.7**	**13.0**
Yugoslavia	39 956	0.3	82 633	0.6	106.8
Other European countries	296 660	2.5	353 297	2.7	19.1
Bulgaria	7 651	0.1	15 823	0.1	106.8
Hungary	141 550	1.2	101 001	0.8	-28.6
Poland	98 388	0.8	106 780	0.8	8.5
Rumania	15 549	0.1	67 617	0.5	334.9
USSR	33 522	0.3	62 076	0.5	85.2
Asia-Oceania[3]	347 236	2.9	274 000	2.1	-21.1
Iran	121 363	1.0	115 569	0.9	-4.8
Lebanon	18 454	0.2	13 480	0.1	-27.0
Pakistan	17 303	0.1	14 439	0.1	-16.6
Saudi Arabia	84 779	0.7	51 728	0.4	-39.0
Africa	47 218	0.4	36 803	0.3	-22.1
Egypt	21 575	0.2	14 465	0.1	-33.0
Libyan Arab Jamahiriya	25 643	0.2	22 338	0.2	-12.9
Origin country undetermined	477 069	4.0	480 827	3.6	0.8
Total non-OECD Countries	**1 208 139**	**10.2**	**1 227 560**	**9.3**	**1.6**
TOTAL	**11 864 746**	**100.0**	**13 270 641**	**100.0**	**11.8**

1. Belgium includes Luxembourg and Netherlands.
2. Denmark includes Finland, Norway and Sweden.
3. Asia-Oceania includes Iraq, Kuwait, Lebanon, Syria, Saudi Arabia, Jordan, Iran and Pakistan.

UNITED KINGDOM

ARRIVALS OF FOREIGN VISITORS AT FRONTIERS

(by country of residence)

	1989	Relative share	1990	Relative share	% Variation over 1989
Austria	147 700	0.9	154 000	0.9	4.3
Belgium	591 300	3.4	546 000	3.0	-7.7
Denmark	259 200	1.5	228 000	1.3	-12.0
Finland	165 700	1.0	134 000	0.7	-19.1
France	2 260 500	13.0	2 309 000	12.8	2.1
Germany	2 026 900	11.7	1 879 000	10.4	-7.3
Greece	128 100	0.7	134 000	0.7	4.6
Iceland	30 300	0.2	50 000	0.3	65.0
Ireland	1 301 800	7.5	1 317 000	7.3	1.2
Italy	708 100	4.1	714 000	4.0	0.8
Luxembourg	26 700	0.2	26 000	0.1	-2.6
Netherlands	940 500	5.4	991 000	5.5	5.4
Norway	286 700	1.7	272 000	1.5	-5.1
Portugal	95 200	0.5	105 000	0.6	10.3
Spain	622 000	3.6	605 000	3.4	-2.7
Sweden	481 100	2.8	470 000	2.6	-2.3
Switzerland	424 200	2.4	446 000	2.5	5.1
Turkey	50 200	0.3	65 000	0.4	29.5
United Kingdom	..	..	..	..	..
Other OECD-Europe	..	..	..	..	..
Total Europe	10 546 200	60.8	10 445 000	58.0	-1.0
Canada	638 600	3.7	702 000	3.9	9.9
United States	2 842 200	16.4	3 049 000	16.9	7.3
Total North America	3 480 800	20.1	3 751 000	20.8	7.8
Australia	535 400	3.1	629 000	3.5	17.5
New Zealand	122 600	0.7	126 000	0.7	2.8
Japan	504 800	2.9	572 000	3.2	13.3
Total Australasia and Japan	1 162 800	6.7	1 327 000	7.4	14.1
Total OECD Countries	**15 189 800**	**87.6**	**15 523 000**	**86.2**	**2.2**
Yugoslavia	30 900	0.2	64 000	0.4	107.1
Other European countries	275 800	1.6	438 000	2.4	58.8
Latin America	178 900	1.0	187 000	1.0	4.5
Asia-Oceania	1 039 215	6.0	1 167 000	6.5	12.3
Africa	547 900	3.2	562 000	3.1	2.6
Origin country undetermined	74 800	0.4	74 000	0.4	-1.1
Total non-OECD Countries	**2 147 515**	**12.4**	**2 492 000**	**13.8**	**16.0**
TOTAL	**17 337 315**	**100.0**	**18 015 000**	**100.0**	**3.9**

UNITED KINGDOM

NIGHTS SPENT BY FOREIGN TOURISTS IN TOURIST ACCOMMODATION[1]

(by country of residence)

	1989	Relative share	1990	Relative share	% Variation over 1989
Austria	2 028 000	1.1	1 702 000	0.9	-16.1
Belgium	2 624 000	1.4	2 280 000	1.2	-13.1
Denmark	1 921 000	1.0	2 184 000	1.1	13.7
Finland	1 405 000	0.7	983 000	0.5	-30.0
France	16 222 000	8.7	16 993 000	8.7	4.8
Germany	17 717 000	9.5	17 394 000	8.9	-1.8
Greece	1 898 000	1.0	1 946 000	1.0	2.5
Iceland	242 000	0.1	315 000	0.2	30.2
Ireland	11 117 000	5.9	11 433 000	5.8	2.8
Italy	8 279 000	4.4	8 371 000	4.3	1.1
Luxembourg	140 000	0.1	172 000	0.1	22.9
Netherlands	5 189 000	2.8	5 517 000	2.8	6.3
Norway	2 139 000	1.1	1 698 000	0.9	-20.6
Portugal	1 015 000	0.5	1 269 000	0.6	25.0
Spain[2]	8 384 000	4.5	8 626 000	4.4	2.9
Sweden	3 314 000	1.8	3 167 000	1.6	-4.4
Switzerland	3 864 000	2.1	4 257 000	2.2	10.2
Turkey	1 192 000	0.6	1 594 000	0.8	33.7
United Kingdom	..	..	..	..	..
Other OECD-Europe	..	..	..	..	..
Total Europe	88 690 000	47.3	89 901 000	45.8	1.4
Canada	8 579 000	4.6	9 352 000	4.8	9.0
United States	27 623 000	14.7	28 621 000	14.6	3.6
Total North America	36 202 000	19.3	37 973 000	19.3	4.9
Australia	11 822 000	6.3	14 257 000	7.3	20.6
New Zealand	3 093 000	1.7	3 222 000	1.6	4.2
Japan	3 290 000	1.8	3 954 000	2.0	20.2
Total Australasia and Japan	18 205 000	9.7	21 433 000	10.9	17.7
Total OECD Countries	**143 097 000**	**76.4**	**149 307 000**	**76.0**	**4.3**
Yugoslavia	501 000	0.3	1 678 000	0.9	234.9
Other European countries	6 055 000	3.2	7 033 000	3.6	16.2
Latin America	2 542 000	1.4	2 237 000	1.1	-12.0
Asia-Oceania	20 695 000	11.0	21 436 000	10.9	3.6
Africa	11 281 000	6.0	12 462 000	6.3	10.5
Origin country undetermined	3 176 000	1.7	2 229 000	1.1	-29.8
Total non-OECD Countries	**44 250 000**	**23.6**	**47 075 000**	**24.0**	**6.4**
TOTAL	**187 347 000**	**100.0**	**196 382 000**	**100.0**	**4.8**

1. Estimates of total number of nights spent in all forms of accommodation, including stays with friends and relatives. Excluding: visitors in transit, visits of merchant seamen, airline personnel and military on duty.
2. Spain includes Canary Islands.

UNITED STATES

ARRIVALS OF FOREIGN TOURISTS AT FRONTIERS

(by country of residence)

	1989	Relative share	1990	Relative share	% Variation over 1989
Austria	95 760	0.3	107 000	0.3	11.7
Belgium	115 439	0.3	138 000	0.4	19.5
Denmark	107 062	0.3	97 000	0.2	-9.4
Finland	92 992	0.3	..	..	..
France	653 685	1.8	716 000	1.8	9.5
Germany	1 076 385	2.9	1 203 000	3.1	11.8
Greece	53 184	0.1	..	..	..
Iceland	13 531	0.0	..	..	..
Ireland	105 429	0.3	99 000	0.3	-6.1
Italy	354 920	1.0	396 000	1.0	11.6
Luxembourg	8 752	0.0	..	..	..
Netherlands	260 840	0.7	284 000	0.7	8.9
Norway	105 147	0.3	104 000	0.3	-1.1
Portugal	35 468	0.1	..	..	..
Spain	201 947	0.6	243 000	0.6	20.3
Sweden	281 261	0.8	282 000	0.7	0.3
Switzerland	274 885	0.8	294 000	0.8	7.0
Turkey	23 449	0.1	..	..	..
United Kingdom	2 221 871	6.1	2 244 000	5.7	1.0
Other OECD-Europe	..	..	253 000	0.6	..
Total Europe	6 082 007	16.6	6 460 000	16.5	6.2
Canada	15 365 937	42.0	17 262 000	44.2	12.3
United States	..	..	..	..	..
Total North America	15 365 937	42.0	17 262 000	44.2	12.3
Australia	406 392	1.1	466 000	1.2	14.7
New Zealand	166 774	0.5	174 000	0.4	4.3
Japan	3 080 396	8.4	3 231 000	8.3	4.9
Total Australasia and Japan	3 653 562	10.0	3 871 000	9.9	6.0
Total OECD Countries	**25 101 506**	**68.5**	**27 593 000**	**70.6**	**9.9**
Yugoslavia	28 092	0.1	..	..	..
Other European countries	156 570	0.4	199 000	0.5	27.1
Czechoslovakia	8 984	0.0	..	..	..
Hungary	18 924	0.1	..	..	..
Poland	63 202	0.2	61 000	0.2	-3.5
Rumania	4 776	0.0	..	..	..
USSR	56 818	0.2	81 000	0.2	42.6
Latin America [1]	9 889 113	27.0	9 645 000	24.7	-2.5
Argentina	132 432	0.4	185 000	0.5	39.7
Brazil	333 489	0.9	398 000	1.0	19.3
Chile	70 018	0.2	69 000	0.2	-1.5
Colombia	152 319	0.4	155 000	0.4	1.8
Cuba	26 069	0.1	..	..	..
Mexico	7 261 802	19.8	6 768 000	17.3	-6.8
Venezuela	219 345	0.6	264 000	0.7	20.4
Asia-Oceania	945 458	2.6	1 129 000	2.9	19.4
China	239 955	0.7	..	..	..
Hong Kong	142 911	0.4	163 000	0.4	14.1
India	106 908	0.3	110 000	0.3	2.9
Iran	15 625	0.0	..	..	..
Iraq	2 712	0.0	..	..	..
Israel	156 289	0.4	162 000	0.4	3.7
Jordan	17 209	0.0	..	..	..
Republic of Korea	149 323	0.4	211 000	0.5	41.3
Kuwait	19 843	0.1	..	..	..
Lebanon	14 767	0.0	..	..	..
Malaysia	40 472	0.1	..	..	..
Oman	2 047	0.0	..	..	..
Pakistan	31 364	0.1	..	..	..
Philippines	89 155	0.2	98 000	0.3	9.9
Saudi Arabia	48 526	0.1	..	..	..
Singapore	48 567	0.1	..	..	..
Syrian Arab Republic	7 768	0.0	..	..	..
Taiwan	239 968	0.7	305 000	0.8	27.1
Thailand	36 173	0.1	..	..	..
Africa	136 863	0.4	137 000	0.4	0.1
Egypt	21 605	0.1	..	..	..
Kenya	7 151	0.0	..	..	..
Morocco	726	0.0	..	..	..
Nigeria	1 582	0.0	..	..	..
South Africa	3 300	0.0	..	..	..
Origin country undetermined [2]	370 677	1.0	386 000	1.0	4.1
Total non-OECD Countries	**11 526 773**	**31.5**	**11 496 000**	**29.4**	**-0.3**
TOTAL	**36 628 279**	**100.0**	**39 089 000**	**100.0**	**6.7**

1. Latin America includes Central America, Carribean, South America and Mexico.
2. Origin country undetermined includes Middle East only.

YUGOSLAVIA

ARRIVALS OF FOREIGN TOURISTS AT HOTELS

(by country of nationality)

	1989	Relative share	1990	Relative share	% Variation over 1989
Austria	471 277	8.6	399 845	7.4	-15.2
Belgium	106 026	1.9	113 616	2.1	7.2
Denmark	34 851	0.6	30 023	0.6	-13.9
Finland	19 948	0.4	17 163	0.3	-14.0
France	209 226	3.8	194 531	3.6	-7.0
Germany	1 309 745	23.8	1 172 280	21.8	-10.5
Greece	148 532	2.7	125 488	2.3	-15.5
Iceland	1 171	0.0	2 086	0.0	78.1
Ireland	6 072	0.1	11 461	0.2	88.8
Italy	875 132	15.9	949 407	17.7	8.5
Luxembourg	..	..	..	..	..
Netherlands	252 120	4.6	262 349	4.9	4.1
Norway	23 977	0.4	16 544	0.3	-31.0
Portugal	3 913	0.1	5 793	0.1	48.0
Spain	55 133	1.0	68 467	1.3	24.2
Sweden	72 817	1.3	63 862	1.2	-12.3
Switzerland	62 594	1.1	59 690	1.1	-4.6
Turkey	72 297	1.3	76 719	1.4	6.1
United Kingdom	571 042	10.4	592 325	11.0	3.7
Other OECD-Europe	..	..	..	..	..
Total Europe	4 295 873	78.2	4 161 649	77.5	-3.1
Canada	35 123	0.6	33 858	0.6	-3.6
United States	221 624	4.0	213 401	4.0	-3.7
Total North America	256 747	4.7	247 259	4.6	-3.7
Australia	24 541	0.4	28 399	0.5	15.7
New Zealand	4 232	0.1	3 832	0.1	-9.5
Japan	15 005	0.3	14 772	0.3	-1.6
Total Australasia and Japan	43 778	0.8	47 003	0.9	7.4
Total OECD Countries	**4 596 398**	**83.7**	**4 455 911**	**83.0**	**-3.1**
Yugoslavia	..	..	..	..	..
Other European countries	725 627	13.2	749 566	14.0	3.3
Bulgaria	21 722	0.4	78 455	1.5	261.2
Czechoslovakia	134 636	2.5	122 743	2.3	-8.8
Germany (D. R.)	35 034	0.6	52 257	1.0	49.2
Hungary	95 004	1.7	64 098	1.2	-32.5
Poland	42 786	0.8	38 888	0.7	-9.1
Rumania	6 651	0.1	29 863	0.6	349.0
USSR	362 198	6.6	328 846	6.1	-9.2
Origin country undetermined	170 653	3.1	163 998	3.1	-3.9
Total non-OECD Countries	**896 280**	**16.3**	**913 564**	**17.0**	**1.9**
TOTAL	**5 492 678**	**100.0**	**5 369 475**	**100.0**	**-2.2**

YUGOSLAVIA

ARRIVALS OF FOREIGN TOURISTS AT REGISTERED TOURIST ACCOMMODATION

(by country of nationality)

	1989	Relative share	1990	Relative share	% Variation over 1989
Austria	745 691	8.6	583 754	7.4	-21.7
Belgium	169 590	2.0	165 213	2.1	-2.6
Denmark	74 933	0.9	62 182	0.8	-17.0
Finland	26 974	0.3	22 525	0.3	-16.5
France	315 177	3.6	293 268	3.7	-7.0
Germany	2 462 455	28.5	1 981 362	25.1	-19.5
Greece	164 292	1.9	137 997	1.8	-16.0
Iceland	1 587	0.0	5 538	0.1	249.0
Ireland	16 159	0.2	21 645	0.3	34.0
Italy	1 424 021	16.5	1 494 320	19.0	4.9
Luxembourg	..	..	..	..	..
Netherlands	490 541	5.7	450 850	5.7	-8.1
Norway	38 077	0.4	29 627	0.4	-22.2
Portugal	5 973	0.1	8 168	0.1	36.7
Spain	80 186	0.9	89 726	1.1	11.9
Sweden	120 735	1.4	99 557	1.3	-17.5
Switzerland	121 143	1.4	108 298	1.4	-10.6
Turkey	79 629	0.9	85 371	1.1	7.2
United Kingdom	649 875	7.5	660 768	8.4	1.7
Other OECD-Europe	..	..	..	..	..
Total Europe	6 987 038	80.8	6 300 169	80.0	-9.8
Canada	41 364	0.5	39 507	0.5	-4.5
United States	257 978	3.0	239 948	3.0	-7.0
Total North America	299 342	3.5	279 455	3.5	-6.6
Australia	32 273	0.4	34 479	0.4	6.8
New Zealand	8 725	0.1	7 753	0.1	-11.1
Japan	15 641	0.2	15 602	0.2	-0.2
Total Australasia and Japan	56 639	0.7	57 834	0.7	2.1
Total OECD Countries	**7 343 019**	**84.9**	**6 637 458**	**84.2**	**-9.6**
Yugoslavia	..	..	..	..	..
Other European countries	1 108 076	12.8	1 055 435	13.4	-4.8
Bulgaria	24 166	0.3	90 395	1.1	274.1
Czechoslovakia	245 229	2.8	224 799	2.9	-8.3
Germany (D. R.)	54 800	0.6	80 694	1.0	47.3
Hungary	201 680	2.3	119 887	1.5	-40.6
Poland	113 176	1.3	90 360	1.1	-20.2
Rumania	7 865	0.1	33 912	0.4	331.2
USSR	407 926	4.7	368 519	4.7	-9.7
Origin country undetermined	192 985	2.2	186 638	2.4	-3.3
Total non-OECD Countries	**1 301 061**	**15.1**	**1 242 073**	**15.8**	**-4.5**
TOTAL	**8 644 080**	**100.0**	**7 879 531**	**100.0**	**-8.8**

YUGOSLAVIA

NIGHTS SPENT BY FOREIGN TOURISTS IN HOTELS

(by country of nationality)

	1989	Relative share	1990	Relative share	% Variation over 1989
Austria	2 510 472	9.0	2 171 683	8.0	-13.5
Belgium	653 376	2.3	686 630	2.5	5.1
Denmark	215 115	0.8	169 987	0.6	-21.0
Finland	126 862	0.5	115 552	0.4	-8.9
France	808 225	2.9	711 038	2.6	-12.0
Germany	8 781 176	31.4	7 829 061	29.0	-10.8
Greece	214 158	0.8	185 702	0.7	-13.3
Iceland	3 079	0.0	7 411	0.0	140.7
Ireland	39 374	0.1	74 086	0.3	88.2
Italy	2 628 237	9.4	3 109 623	11.5	18.3
Luxembourg	..	..	..	..	..
Netherlands	1 766 036	6.3	1 740 117	6.4	-1.5
Norway	117 445	0.4	92 584	0.3	-21.2
Portugal	7 325	0.0	10 673	0.0	45.7
Spain	100 303	0.4	130 918	0.5	30.5
Sweden	393 509	1.4	340 788	1.3	-13.4
Switzerland	289 026	1.0	282 652	1.0	-2.2
Turkey	90 812	0.3	99 429	0.4	9.5
United Kingdom	5 300 494	19.0	5 465 406	20.2	3.1
Other OECD-Europe	..	..	..	..	..
Total Europe	24 045 024	86.1	23 223 340	85.9	-3.4
Canada	74 387	0.3	82 545	0.3	11.0
United States	463 586	1.7	447 013	1.7	-3.6
Total North America	537 973	1.9	529 558	2.0	-1.6
Australia	42 063	0.2	49 794	0.2	18.4
New Zealand	7 124	0.0	6 702	0.0	-5.9
Japan	31 175	0.1	28 640	0.1	-8.1
Total Australasia and Japan	80 362	0.3	85 136	0.3	5.9
Total OECD Countries	**24 663 359**	**88.3**	**23 838 034**	**88.2**	**-3.3**
Yugoslavia	..	..	..	..	..
Other European countries	2 889 905	10.3	2 830 998	10.5	-2.0
Bulgaria	49 936	0.2	145 080	0.5	190.5
Czechoslovakia	1 231 620	4.4	1 080 571	4.0	-12.3
Germany (D. R.)	161 665	0.6	207 242	0.8	28.2
Hungary	296 402	1.1	246 832	0.9	-16.7
Poland	191 955	0.7	151 707	0.6	-21.0
Rumania	35 732	0.1	71 025	0.3	98.8
USSR	832 999	3.0	792 652	2.9	-4.8
Origin country undetermined	377 703	1.4	351 349	1.3	-7.0
Total non-OECD Countries	**3 267 608**	**11.7**	**3 182 347**	**11.8**	**-2.6**
TOTAL	**27 930 967**	**100.0**	**27 020 381**	**100.0**	**-3.3**

YUGOSLAVIA

NIGHTS SPENT BY FOREIGN TOURISTS IN REGISTERED TOURIST ACCOMMODATION

(by country of nationality)

	1989	Relative share	1990	Relative share	% Variation over 1989
Austria	4 515 219	9.2	3 466 548	8.0	-23.2
Belgium	1 082 666	2.2	1 022 836	2.4	-5.5
Denmark	505 461	1.0	398 967	0.9	-21.1
Finland	160 671	0.3	140 066	0.3	-12.8
France	1 122 647	2.3	978 545	2.3	-12.8
Germany	17 530 275	35.6	14 024 046	32.3	-20.0
Greece	235 603	0.5	205 474	0.5	-12.8
Iceland	4 662	0.0	29 680	0.1	536.6
Ireland	95 354	0.2	132 680	0.3	39.1
Italy	6 144 277	12.5	6 440 330	14.8	4.8
Luxembourg	..	..	..	..	..
Netherlands	3 485 615	7.1	3 112 254	7.2	-10.7
Norway	248 578	0.5	211 926	0.5	-14.7
Portugal	12 613	0.0	14 859	0.0	17.8
Spain	156 001	0.3	176 646	0.4	13.2
Sweden	710 499	1.4	563 043	1.3	-20.8
Switzerland	485 003	1.0	427 891	1.0	-11.8
Turkey	103 378	0.2	112 292	0.3	8.6
United Kingdom	5 879 335	12.0	5 941 799	13.7	1.1
Other OECD-Europe	..	..	..	..	..
Total Europe	42 477 857	86.4	37 399 882	86.2	-12.0
Canada	101 857	0.2	102 919	0.2	1.0
United States	633 199	1.3	559 565	1.3	-11.6
Total North America	735 056	1.5	662 484	1.5	-9.9
Australia	65 010	0.1	64 319	0.1	-1.1
New Zealand	15 239	0.0	14 223	0.0	-6.7
Japan	32 917	0.1	30 385	0.1	-7.7
Total Australasia and Japan	113 166	0.2	108 927	0.3	-3.7
Total OECD Countries	**43 326 079**	**88.1**	**38 171 293**	**88.0**	**-11.9**
Yugoslavia	..	..	..	..	..
Other European countries	5 381 224	10.9	4 770 682	11.0	-11.3
Bulgaria	57 424	0.1	163 512	0.4	184.7
Czechoslovakia	2 239 148	4.6	1 905 791	4.4	-14.9
Germany (D. R.)	347 424	0.7	425 387	1.0	22.4
Hungary	931 175	1.9	617 973	1.4	-33.6
Poland	540 503	1.1	387 815	0.9	-28.2
Rumania	40 679	0.1	83 306	0.2	104.8
USSR	1 043 925	2.1	1 003 722	2.3	-3.9
Origin country undetermined	468 624	1.0	428 487	1.0	-8.6
Total non-OECD Countries	**5 849 848**	**11.9**	**5 199 169**	**12.0**	**-11.1**
TOTAL	**49 175 927**	**100.0**	**43 370 462**	**100.0**	**-11.8**

MAIN SALES OUTLETS OF OECD PUBLICATIONS
PRINCIPAUX POINTS DE VENTE DES PUBLICATIONS DE L'OCDE

ARGENTINA – ARGENTINE
Carlos Hirsch S.R.L.
Galería Güemes, Florida 165, 4° Piso
1333 Buenos Aires Tel. (1) 331.1787 y 331.2391
Telefax: (1) 331.1787

AUSTRALIA – AUSTRALIE
D.A. Book (Aust.) Pty. Ltd.
648 Whitehorse Road, P.O.B 163
Mitcham, Victoria 3132 Tel. (03) 873.4411
Telefax: (03) 873.5679

AUSTRIA – AUTRICHE
Gerold & Co.
Graben 31
Wien I Tel. (0222) 533.50.14

BELGIUM – BELGIQUE
Jean De Lannoy
Avenue du Roi 202
B-1060 Bruxelles Tel. (02) 538.51.69/538.08.41
Telefax: (02) 538.08.41

CANADA
Renouf Publishing Company Ltd.
1294 Algoma Road
Ottawa, ON K1B 3W8 Tel. (613) 741.4333
Telefax: (613) 741.5439
Stores:
61 Sparks Street
Ottawa, ON K1P 5R1 Tel. (613) 238.8985
211 Yonge Street
Toronto, ON M5B 1M4 Tel. (416) 363.3171

Les Éditions La Liberté Inc.
3020 Chemin Sainte-Foy
Sainte-Foy, PQ G1X 3V6 Tel. (418) 658.3763
Telefax: (418) 658.3763

Federal Publications
165 University Avenue
Toronto, ON M5H 3B8 Tel. (416) 581.1552
Telefax: (416) 581.1743

CHINA – CHINE
China National Publications Import
Export Corporation (CNPIEC)
P.O. Box 88
Beijing Tel. 403.5533
Telefax: 401.5664

DENMARK – DANEMARK
Munksgaard Export and Subscription Service
35, Nørre Søgade, P.O. Box 2148
DK-1016 København K Tel. (33) 12.85.70
Telefax: (33) 12.93.87

FINLAND – FINLANDE
Akateeminen Kirjakauppa
Keskuskatu 1, P.O. Box 128
00100 Helsinki Tel. (358 0) 12141
Telefax: (358 0) 121.4441

FRANCE
OECD/OCDE
Mail Orders/Commandes par correspondance:
2, rue André-Pascal
75775 Paris Cedex 16 Tel. (33-1) 45.24.82.00
Telefax: (33-1) 45.24.85.00 or (33-1) 45.24.81.76
Telex: 620 160 OCDE

OECD Bookshop/Librairie de l'OCDE :
33, rue Octave-Feuillet
75016 Paris Tel. (33-1) 45.24.81.67
(33-1) 45.24.81.81

Documentation Française
29, quai Voltaire
75007 Paris Tel. 40.15.70.00

Gibert Jeune (Droit-Économie)
6, place Saint-Michel
75006 Paris Tel. 43.25.91.19

Librairie du Commerce International
10, avenue d'Iéna
75016 Paris Tel. 40.73.34.60

Librairie Dunod
Université Paris-Dauphine
Place du Maréchal de Lattre de Tassigny
75016 Paris Tel. 47.27.18.56

Librairie Lavoisier
11, rue Lavoisier
75008 Paris Tel. 42.65.39.95

Librairie L.G.D.J. - Montchrestien
20, rue Soufflot
75005 Paris Tel. 46.33.89.85

Librairie des Sciences Politiques
30, rue Saint-Guillaume
75007 Paris Tel. 45.48.36.02

P.U.F.
49, boulevard Saint-Michel
75005 Paris Tel. 43.25.83.40

Librairie de l'Université
12a, rue Nazareth
13100 Aix-en-Provence Tel. (16) 42.26.18.08

Documentation Française
165, rue Garibaldi
69003 Lyon Tel. (16) 78.63.32.23

GERMANY – ALLEMAGNE
OECD Publications and Information Centre
Schedestrasse 7
D-W 5300 Bonn 1 Tel. (0228) 21.60.45
Telefax: (0228) 26.11.04

GREECE – GRÈCE
Librairie Kauffmann
Mavrokordatou 9
106 78 Athens Tel. 322.21.60
Telefax: 363.39.67

HONG-KONG
Swindon Book Co. Ltd.
13–15 Lock Road
Kowloon, Hong Kong Tel. 366.80.31
Telefax: 739.49.75

ICELAND – ISLANDE
Mál Mog Menning
Laugavegi 18, Pósthólf 392
121 Reykjavik Tel. 162.35.23

INDIA – INDE
Oxford Book and Stationery Co.
Scindia House
New Delhi 110001 Tel.(11) 331.5896/5308
Telefax: (11) 332.5993

17 Park Street
Calcutta 700016 Tel. 240832

INDONESIA – INDONÉSIE
Pdii-Lipi
P.O. Box 4298
Jakarta 12042 Tel. 583467
Telex: 62 875

IRELAND – IRLANDE
TDC Publishers – Library Suppliers
12 North Frederick Street
Dublin 1 Tel. 74.48.35/74.96.77
Telefax: 74.84.16

ISRAEL
Electronic Publications only
Publications électroniques seulement
Sophist Systems Ltd.
71 Allenby Street
Tel-Aviv 65134 Tel. 3-29.00.21
Telefax: 3-29.92.39

ITALY – ITALIE
Libreria Commissionaria Sansoni
Via Duca di Calabria 1/1
50125 Firenze Tel. (055) 64.54.15
Telefax: (055) 64.12.57

Via Bartolini 29
20155 Milano Tel. (02) 36.50.83

Editrice e Libreria Herder
Piazza Montecitorio 120
00186 Roma Tel. 679.46.28
Telefax: 678.47.51

Libreria Hoepli
Via Hoepli 5
20121 Milano Tel. (02) 86.54.46
Telefax: (02) 805.28.86

Libreria Scientifica
Dott. Lucio de Biasio 'Aeiou'
Via Coronelli, 6
20146 Milano Tel. (02) 48.95.45.52
Telefax: (02) 48.95.45.48

JAPAN – JAPON
OECD Publications and Information Centre
Landic Akasaka Building
2-3-4 Akasaka, Minato-ku
Tokyo 107 Tel. (81.3) 3586.2016
Telefax: (81.3) 3584.7929

KOREA – CORÉE
Kyobo Book Centre Co. Ltd.
P.O. Box 1658, Kwang Hwa Moon
Seoul Tel. 730.78.91
Telefax: 735.00.30

MALAYSIA – MALAISIE
Co-operative Bookshop Ltd.
University of Malaya
P.O. Box 1127, Jalan Pantai Baru
59700 Kuala Lumpur
Malaysia Tel. 756.5000/756.5425
Telefax: 755.4424

NETHERLANDS – PAYS-BAS
SDU Uitgeverij
Christoffel Plantijnstraat 2
Postbus 20014
2500 EA's-Gravenhage Tel. (070 3) 78.99.11
Voor bestellingen: Tel. (070 3) 78.98.80
Telefax: (070 3) 47.63.51

NEW ZEALAND
NOUVELLE-ZÉLANDE
Legislation Services
P.O. Box 12418
Thorndon, Wellington Tel. (04) 496.5652
Telefax: (04) 496.5698

NORWAY – NORVÈGE
Narvesen Info Center – NIC
Bertrand Narvesens vei 2
P.O. Box 6125 Etterstad
0602 Oslo 6 Tel. (02) 57.33.00
Telefax: (02) 68.19.01

PAKISTAN
Mirza Book Agency
65 Shahrah Quaid-E-Azam
Lahore 3 Tel. 66.839
Telex: 44886 UBL PK. Attn: MIRZA BK

PORTUGAL
Livraria Portugal
Rua do Carmo 70-74
Apart. 2681
1117 Lisboa Codex Tel.: (01) 347.49.82/3/4/5
Telefax: (01) 347.02.64

SINGAPORE – SINGAPOUR

Information Publications Pte
Golden Wheel Bldg.
41, Kallang Pudding, #04-03
Singapore 1334 Tel. 741.5166
Telefax: 742.9356

SPAIN – ESPAGNE

Mundi-Prensa Libros S.A.
Castelló 37, Apartado 1223
Madrid 28001 Tel. (91) 431.33.99
Telefax: (91) 575.39.98

Libreria Internacional AEDOS
Consejo de Ciento 391
08009 – Barcelona Tel. (93) 488.34.92
Telefax: (93) 487.76.59

Llibreria de la Generalitat
Palau Moja
Rambla dels Estudis, 118
08002 – Barcelona
(Subscripcions) Tel. (93) 318.80.12
(Publicacions) Tel. (93) 302.67.23
Telefax: (93) 412.18.54

SRI LANKA

Centre for Policy Research
c/o Colombo Agencies Ltd.
No. 300-304, Galle Road
Colombo 3 Tel. (1) 574240, 573551-2
Telefax: (1) 575394, 510711

SWEDEN – SUÈDE

Fritzes Fackboksföretaget
Box 16356
Regeringsgatan 12
103 27 Stockholm Tel. (08) 23.89.00
Telefax: (08) 20.50.21

Subscription Agency-Agence d'abonnements
Wennergren-Williams AB
Nordenflychtsvägen 74
Box 30004
104 25 Stockholm Tel. (08) 13.67.00
Telefax: (08) 618.62.32

SWITZERLAND – SUISSE

Maditec S.A. (Books and Periodicals - Livres et périodiques)
Chemin des Palettes 4
1020 Renens/Lausanne Tel. (021) 635.08.65
Telefax: (021) 635.07.80

Mail orders only - Commandes par correspondance seulement
Librairie Payot
C.P. 3212
1002 Lausanne Telefax: (021) 311.13.92

Librairie Unilivres
6, rue de Candolle
1205 Genève Tel. (022) 320.26.23
Telefax: (022) 329.73.18

Subscription Agency - Agence d'abonnement
Naville S.A.
38 avenue Vibert
1227 Carouge Tél.: (022) 308.05.56/57
Telefax: (022) 308.05.88

See also – Voir aussi :
OECD Publications and Information Centre
Schedestrasse 7
D-W 5300 Bonn 1 (Germany)
Tel. (49.228) 21.60.45
Telefax: (49.228) 26.11.04

TAIWAN – FORMOSE

Good Faith Worldwide Int'l. Co. Ltd.
9th Floor, No. 118, Sec. 2
Chung Hsiao E. Road
Taipei Tel. (02) 391.7396/391.7397
Telefax: (02) 394.9176

THAILAND – THAÏLANDE

Suksit Siam Co. Ltd.
113, 115 Fuang Nakhon Rd.
Opp. Wat Rajbopith
Bangkok 10200 Tel. (662) 251.1630
Telefax: (662) 236.7783

TURKEY – TURQUIE

Kültur Yayinlari Is-Türk Ltd. Sti.
Atatürk Bulvari No. 191/Kat. 13
Kavaklidere/Ankara Tel. 428.11.40 Ext. 2458
Dolmabahce Cad. No. 29
Besiktas/Istanbul Tel. 160.71.88
Telex: 43482B

UNITED KINGDOM – ROYAUME-UNI

HMSO
Gen. enquiries Tel. (071) 873 0011
Postal orders only:
P.O. Box 276, London SW8 5DT
Personal Callers HMSO Bookshop
49 High Holborn, London WC1V 6HB
Telefax: (071) 873 8200
Branches at: Belfast, Birmingham, Bristol, Edinburgh, Manchester

UNITED STATES – ÉTATS-UNIS

OECD Publications and Information Centre
2001 L Street N.W., Suite 700
Washington, D.C. 20036-4910 Tel. (202) 785.6323
Telefax: (202) 785.0350

VENEZUELA

Libreria del Este
Avda F. Miranda 52, Aptdo. 60337
Edificio Galipán
Caracas 106 Tel. 951.1705/951.2307/951.1297
Telegram: Libreste Caracas

YUGOSLAVIA – YOUGOSLAVIE

Jugoslovenska Knjiga
Knez Mihajlova 2, P.O. Box 36
Beograd Tel. (011) 621.992
Telefax: (011) 625.970

Orders and inquiries from countries where Distributors have not yet been appointed should be sent to: OECD Publications Service, 2 rue André-Pascal, 75775 Paris Cedex 16, France.

Les commandes provenant de pays où l'OCDE n'a pas encore désigné de distributeur devraient être adressées à : OCDE, Service des Publications, 2, rue André-Pascal, 75775 Paris Cedex 16, France.

Subscription to OECD periodicals may also be placed through main subscription agencies.

Les abonnements aux publications périodiques de l'OCDE peuvent être souscrits auprès des principales agences d'abonnement.

OECD PUBLICATIONS, 2 rue André Pascal, 75775 PARIS CEDEX 16
PRINTED IN FRANCE
(78 92 01 1) ISBN 92-64-13734-3 - No. 45741 1992
ISSN 0256-7598